The Me

THE
HOLY
QUR'AN

Translation by
by
Abdullah Yusuf Ali
with a Brief Index of Subjects

Revised Modern English Edition

Revised by: Dr. S. M. Bleher

IDCI
Islamic Dawah Centre Interntional

Copyrigh © (revised edition) 2014 IDCI. All rights reserved.

1st Revised Edition printed 2004
2nd Revised Edition printed 2007
3rd Revised Edition with Brief Index of Subjects printed 2010, 2013
4th Revised Edition with Brief Index of Subjects printed 2014, 2017, 2019, 2022

A catalogue record for this book is available from the British Library

ISBN 978-1-910432-01-3

Revised by Dr. Sahib Mustaqim Bleher

Although initially produced in the early parts of the last century, Yusuf Ali's translation remains a favourite with many English readers of the Qur'an. To improve the readability of the text, the translation has been carefully adapted by Dr S.M. Bleher, replacing some of the more archaic terms with those in current usage without generally altering the flow and register of the original work.

Utmost care has been taken to produce this present print without any typographical errors. However, we do request readers to please inform us if any errors are found so that future reprints can be corrected.

Published by IDCI
Islamic Dawah Centre International
Tel: 0121 327 2277 | Web: www.idci.co.uk
Registered Charity No. 1092139

Typeset and cover design by Abdul-Majid Zameer
Printed by Avea Basim - Mega Print, Istanbul, Turkey

Table of Contents

Editor's Introduction	5	32. *As-Sajdah*	237
1. *Al-Fatihah*	7	33. *Al-Ahzab*	239
2. *Al-Baqarah*	7	34. *Saba*	244
3. *Al-`Imran*	31	35. *Fatir*	248
4. *An-Nisa*	45	36. *Ya Sin*	251
5. *Al-Ma'idah*	60	37. *As-Saffat*	255
6. *Al-An'am*	71	38. *Sad*	260
7. *Al-A'raf*	83	39. *Az-Zumar*	264
8. *Al-Anfal*	98	40. *Ghafir or Al-Mu'min*	269
9. *At-Taubah*	103	41. *Fussilat*	275
10. *Yunus*	114	42. *Ash-Shura*	278
11. *Hud*	121	43. *Az-Zukhruf*	282
12. *Yusuf*	129	44. *Ad-Dukhan*	286
13. *Ar-Ra'd*	137	45. *Al-Jathiyah*	288
14. *Ibrahim*	141	46. *Al-Ahqaf*	290
15. *Al-Hijr*	145	47. *Muhammad*	293
16. *An-Nahl*	148	48. *Al-Fath*	296
17. *Bani Israel*	157	49. *Al-Hujurat*	298
18. *Al-Kahf*	164	50. *Qaf*	300
19. *Maryam*	171	51. *Adh-Dhariyat*	302
20. *Ta-Ha*	176	52. *At-Tur*	304
21. *Al-Anbiya*	182	53. *An-Najm*	305
22. *Al-Hajj*	188	54. *Al-Qamar*	307
23. *Al-Mu'minun*	193	55. *Ar-Rahman*	309
24. *An-Nur*	198	56. *Al-Waqi'ah*	312
25. *Al-Furqan*	204	57. *Al-Hadid*	314
26. *Ash-Shu'ara*	208	58. *Al-Mujadilah*	317
27. *An-Naml*	215	59. *Al-Hashr*	319
28. *Al-Qasas*	220	60. *Al-Mumtahanah*	321
29. *Al-'Ankabut*	227	61. *As-Saff*	322
30. *Ar-Rum*	231	62. *Al-Jummu'ah*	323
31. *Luqman*	234	63. *Al-Munafiqun*	324

63. *At-Taghabun*	325	
65. *At-Talaq*	326	
66. *At-Tahrim*	328	
67. *Al-Mulk*	329	
68. *Al-Qalam*	330	
69. *Al-Haqqah*	332	
70. *Al-Ma'arij*	334	
71. *Nuh*	335	
72. *Al-Jinn*	336	
73. *Al-Muzzammil*	338	
74. *Al-Muddaththir*	339	
75. *Al-Qiyamah*	340	
76. *Ad-Dahr or Al-Insan*	342	
77. *Al-Mursalat*	343	
78. *An-Naba*	344	
79. *An-Nazi'at*	345	
80. *Abasa*	347	
81. *At-Takwir*	348	
82. *Al-Infitar*	349	
83. *Al-Muttaffifin*	349	
84. *Al-Inshiqaq*	350	
85. *Al-Buruj*	351	
86. *At-Tariq*	352	
87. *Al-A'la*	352	
88. *Al-Ghashiyah*	353	
89. *Al-Fajr*	354	
90. *Al-Balad*	355	
91. *Ash-Shams*	355	
92. *Al-Lail*	356	
93. *Ad-Duha*	356	
94. *Ash-Sharh*	357	
95. *At-Tin*	357	

96. *Al-'Alaq*	357
97. *Al-Qadr*	358
98. *Al-Bayyinah*	358
99. *Al-Zalzalah*	358
100. *Al-'Adiyat*	359
101. *Al-Qari'ah*	359
102. *At-Takathur*	359
103. *Al-'Asr*	360
104. *Al-Humazah*	360
105. *Al-Fil*	360
106. *Quraysh*	360
107. *Al-Maun*	361
108. *Al-Kauthar*	361
109. *Al-Kafirun*	361
110. *An-Nasr*	361
111. *Al-Lahab*	361
112. *Al-Ikhlas*	362
113. *Al-Falaq*	362
114. *An-Nas*	362
Brief Index of Subjects	363

Editor's Introduction

The Qur'an is no ordinary book. To Muslims it is the eternal word of God (Allah), dictated to the prophet Muhammad - peace be with him - via the angel Gabriel (*Jibreel*). Originally revealed in Arabic, its style is unrivalled, its language eloquent, its meaning deep. It is beyond any translation to render all this richness of expression in another language. Yet, the Qur'an is primarily a book of guidance and must, therefore, be accessible to those who seek the truth contained in it. Whilst a translation cannot be an authoritative replacement of the original, it can make the meaning of its verses available to a non-Arabic speaking readership.

The verses (*Ayahs*) of the Qur'an were revealed throughout the 23 years of Prophet Muhammad's prophethood, often in connection with events of the time. They were then memorised, recorded in writing, collected and arranged into chapters (Surahs). Within those verses we find narratives describing the creation of the world from earliest times or recounting the missions of earlier prophets, we come across general exhortation to belief and righteous conduct, we are given the tools and principles for reflection and sound judgement in a multitude of life's situations, and we receive detailed rulings on important aspects of criminal and civil law. Thus the Qur'an is not only a text of inspiration but also the foundation of the legal and social structure of Islamic society.

The text of the Qur'an has not changed since the days the prophet Muhammad - peace be with him - received this revelation, yet its content retains its relevance, validity and dynamics and continues to inspire believers of every generation as well as challenge the status quo of human society. The convincing observations of the Qur'an which, after all, are a communication from our Maker, are a powerful call to action and a rebuttal of complacency. They appeal to both the mind and the heart of the reader or listener; they call for justice and compassion; they decry and defy falsehood, pretence and oppression. They represent an uncomfortable truth for those who would like to banish the courage of one's conviction and do not want us to use our intellect and power of reflection to guide us along our path in life.

Although produced nearly a century ago, Yusuf Ali's translation of the meaning of the Holy Qur'an has not lost its power of conveyance. In spite of the difficulties of finding suitable equivalents between the expressions of a Semitic language like Arabic and a Roman language like English, the translator has taken every care to produce a fluent and rich representation of the message of the Qur'an whilst retaining as much of its poetry and eloquence as possible. His first translation was published side by side with the Arabic text and with an extensive commentary. In this edition only the English translation is published to reduce the size of this volume and make it more accessible as a paperback for general use. This edition is based on the revised text produced by the Young Muslims (YM) in which some of the more archaic terms have been replaced by modern equivalents. This text was then checked and carefully revised once more by Dr Sahib Mustaqim Bleher on behalf of IDCI. Anyone wishing to reproduce this present edition is kindly requested to get in contact with us first.

Surah 1: **Al-Fatihah**
(The Opening)

1. *In the name of Allah,*
Most Gracious, Most Merciful.

2. Praise be to Allah the Cherisher and Sustainer of the Worlds;

3. Most Gracious, Most Merciful;

4. Master of the Day of Judgement.

5. You do we worship, and Your aid we seek.

6. Show us the straight way,

7. The way of those on whom You have bestowed Your Grace, those whose (portion) is not wrath, and who go not astray.

Surah 2: **Al-Baqarah**
(The Heifer)

In the name of Allah,
Most Gracious, Most Merciful.

1. *Alif Lam Mim.*

2. This is the book; in it is guidance sure, without doubt, to those who fear Allah;

3. Who believe in the unseen, are steadfast in prayer, and spend out of what We have provided for them;

4. And who believe in the revelation sent to you, and sent before your time, and (in their hearts) have the assurance of the Hereafter.

5. They are on (true) guidance from their Lord, and it is these who will prosper.

6. As to those who reject faith, it is the same to them whether you warn them or do not warn them; they will not believe.

7. Allah has set a seal on their hearts and on their hearing, and on their eyes is a veil; great is the penalty they (incur).

8. Of the people there are some who say: "We believe in Allah and the last day"; but they do not (really) believe.

9. They would like to deceive Allah and those who believe, but they only deceive themselves and realise (it) not!

10. In their hearts is a disease; and Allah has increased their disease; and grievous is the penalty they (incur), because they are false (to themselves).

11. When it is said to them: "Make not mischief on the earth," they say: "Why, we only want to make peace!"

12. Certainly, they are the ones who make mischief, but they realise (it) not.

13. When it is said to them: "Believe as the others believe:" they say: "Shall we believe as the fools believe?" - Nay, certainly they are the fools, but they do not know.

14. When they meet those who believe, they say: "We believe"; but when they are alone with their evil ones, they say: "We are really with you, we (were) only jesting."

15. Allah will throw back their mockery on them, and give them rope in their trespasses; so they will wander like blind ones (to and fro).

16. These are they who have bartered guidance for error: but their traffic is profitless, and they have lost true direction.

17. Their similitude is that of a man who kindled a fire; when it lighted all round him, Allah took away their light and left them in utter darkness, so they could not see.

18. Deaf, dumb and blind, they will not return (to the path).

19. Or (another similitude) is that of a rain-laden cloud from the sky: in it are zones of darkness, and thunder and lightning, they press their fingers in their ears to keep out the stunning thunderclap, the while they are in terror of death. But Allah is ever round the rejecters of faith!

20. The lightning all but snatches away their sight; every time the light (helps) them, they walk in it, and when the darkness grows on them, they stand still. And if Allah willed, He could take away their faculty of hearing and seeing; for Allah has power over all things.

21. O you people! Adore your Guardian-Lord, Who created you and those who came before you, that you may become righteous,

22. Who has made the earth your couch, and the heaven your canopy; and sent down rain from the heaven; and brought out with it fruits for your sustenance; then set not up rivals to Allah when you know (the truth).

23. And if you are in doubt as to what We have revealed from time to time to Our servant, then produce a Surah like it; and call your witnesses or helpers (if there are any) besides Allah, if your (doubts) are true.

24. But if you cannot - and certainly you cannot - then fear the fire whose fuel is men and stones - which is prepared for those who reject faith.

25. But give glad tidings to those who believe and work righteousness, that their portion is gardens, beneath which rivers flow. Every time they are fed with fruits from it, they say: "Why, this is what we were fed with before," for they are given things in similitude; and they have in it companions pure (and holy); and they remain in it (forever).

26. Allah disdains not to use the similitude of things, lowest as well as highest. Those who believe know that it is truth from their Lord; but those who reject faith say: "What means Allah by this similitude?" By it He causes many to stray, and many He leads into the right path; but He causes not to stray, except those who forsake (the path) -

27. Those who break Allah's covenant after it is ratified, and who break what Allah has ordered to be joined, and do mischief on earth: these cause loss (only) to themselves.

28. How can you reject the faith in Allah? - Seeing that you were without life, and He gave you life; then will He cause you to die, and will again bring you to life; and again to Him will you return.

29. It is He who has created for you all things that are on earth; then He turned to the heaven and made them into seven firmaments. And of all things He has perfect knowledge.

30. Behold, your Lord said to the angels: "I will create a vicegerent on earth." They said: "Will You place in it one who will make mischief in it and shed blood? - Whilst we do celebrate Your praises and glorify Your holy (name)?" He said: "I know what you know not."

31. And He taught Adam the names of all things; then He placed them before the angels, and said: "Tell Me the names of these if you are right."

32. They said: "Glory to You: of knowledge we have none, save what You have taught us: in truth it is You who are perfect in knowledge and wisdom."

33. He said: "O Adam! Tell them their names." When he had told them their names, Allah said: "Did I not tell you that I know the secrets of heaven and earth, and I know what you reveal and what you conceal?"

34. And behold, We said to the angels: "Bow down to Adam," and they bowed down: not so Iblis, he refused and was haughty, he was of those who reject faith.

35. And We said: "O Adam! Dwell you and your wife in the garden; and eat of the bountiful things in it as (where and when) you will; but approach not this tree, or you shall run into harm and transgression."

36. Then did Satan make them slip from the (garden), and get them out of the state (of felicity) in which they had been. And We said: "Get you down, all (you people), with enmity between yourselves. On earth will be your dwelling place and your means of livelihood - for a time."

37. Then learnt Adam from his Lord words of inspiration, and his Lord turned toward him; for He is Oft-Returning, Most Merciful.

38. We said: "Get you down all from here: and if, as is sure, there comes to you guidance from Me, whosoever follows My guidance, on them shall be no fear, nor shall they grieve.

39. "But those who reject faith and belie Our signs, they shall be companions of the fire; they shall remain in it."

40. O Children of Israel call to mind the (special) favour which I bestowed upon you, and fulfil your covenant with Me as I fulfil My covenant with you, and fear none but Me.

41. And believe in what I reveal, confirming the revelation which is with you, and be not the first to reject faith in it, nor sell My signs for a small price; and fear Me, and Me alone.

42. And cover not truth with falsehood, nor conceal the truth when you know (what it is).

43. And be steadfast in prayer; practice regular charity; and bow down your heads with those who bow down (in worship).

44. Do you enjoin right conduct on the people, and forget (to practice it) yourselves? And yet you study the scripture? Will you not understand?

45. Nay, seek (Allah's) help with patient perseverance and prayer: it is indeed hard, except to those who bring a humble spirit -

46. Who bear in mind the certainty that they are to meet their Lord, and that they are to return to Him.

47. O Children of Israel! Call to mind the (special) favour which I bestowed upon You, and that I preferred you to all others (for My message).

48. Then guard yourselves against a day when one soul shall not benefit another nor shall intercession be accepted for her, nor shall compensation be taken from her, nor shall anyone be helped (from outside).

49. And remember, We delivered you from the people of Pharaoh: they set you hard tasks and punishments, slaughtered your sons and let your womenfolk live; in it was a tremendous trial from your Lord.

50. And remember We divided the sea for you and saved you and drowned Pharaoh's people within your very sight.

51. And remember We appointed forty nights for Moses, and in his absence you took the calf (for worship), and you did grievous wrong.

52. Even then We did forgive you, there was a chance for you to be grateful.

53. And remember We gave Moses the scripture and the criterion (between right and wrong), there was a chance for you to be guided aright.

54. And remember Moses said to his people: "O my people! You have indeed wronged yourselves by your worship of the calf: so turn (in repentance) to your Maker, and slay yourselves (the wrong-doers); that will be better for you in the sight of your Maker." Then He turned towards you (in forgiveness): for He is Oft-Returning, Most Merciful.

55. And remember you said: "O Moses! We shall never believe in you until we see Allah manifestly," but you were dazed by thunder and lightning even as you looked on.

56. Then We raised you up after your death; you had the chance to be grateful.

57. And We gave you the shade of clouds and sent down to you manna and quails, saying: "Eat of the good things We have provided for you:" (but they rebelled); to Us they did no harm, but they harmed their own souls.

58. And remember We said: "Enter this town, and eat of the plenty in it as you wish; but enter the gate with humility, in posture and in words, and We shall forgive you your faults and increase (the portion of) those who do good"

59. But the transgressors changed the word from that which had been given them; so We sent on the transgressors a plague from heaven, for that they infringed (Our command) repeatedly.

60. And remember Moses prayed for water for his people; We said: "Strike the rock with your staff." Then gushed out from it twelve springs. Each group knew its own place for water. So eat and drink of the sustenance provided by Allah. And do no evil nor mischief on the (face of the) earth.

61. And remember you said: "O Moses! We cannot endure one kind of food (always); so ask your Lord for us to produce for us of what the earth grows - its pot-herbs, and cucumbers, its garlic, lentils, and onions." He said: "Will you exchange the better for the worse? Go you down to any town, and you shall find what you want!"

They were covered with humiliation and misery; they drew on themselves the wrath of Allah. This because they went on rejecting the signs of Allah and slaying His prophets without just cause. This because they rebelled and went on transgressing.

62. Those who believe (in the Qur'an), and those who follow the Jewish (scriptures), and the Christians and the Sabians - any who believe in Allah and the last day, and work righteousness, shall have their reward with their Lord; on them shall be no fear, nor shall they grieve.

63. And remember We took your covenant and We raised above you (the towering height) of mount (Sinai) (saying): "Hold firmly to what We have given you and bring (ever) to remembrance what is in it: perhaps you may fear Allah."

64. But you turned back after that; had it not been for the grace and mercy of Allah to you, you had surely been among the lost.

65. And well you knew those amongst you who transgressed in the matter of the Sabbath; We said to them: "Be you apes, despised and rejected."

66. So We made it an example to their own time and to their posterity, and a lesson to those who fear Allah.

67. And remember Moses said to his people: "Allah commands that you sacrifice a heifer." They said: "Do you make a laughing-stock of us?" He said: "Allah save me from being an ignorant (fool)!"

68. They said: "Ask on our behalf your Lord to make plain to us what (heifer) it is!" He said: "He says: the heifer should be neither too old nor too young, but of medium age: now do what you are commanded!"

69. They said: "Ask on our behalf your Lord to make plain to us her colour." He said: "He says: a fawn-coloured heifer, pure and rich in tone, the admiration of onlookers!"

70. They said "Ask on our behalf your Lord to make plain to us what she is: to us are all heifers alike: we wish indeed for guidance if Allah wills."

71. He said: "He says: a heifer not trained to till the soil or water the fields; sound and without blemish." They said: "Now have you brought the truth." Then they offered her in sacrifice but not with goodwill.

72. Remember you slew a man and fell into a dispute among yourselves as to the crime: but Allah was to bring out what you did hide.

73. So We said: "Strike the (body) with a piece of the (heifer)." Thus Allah brings the dead to life and shows you His signs: perhaps you may understand.

74. From then on were your hearts hardened: they became like a rock and even worse in hardness. For among rocks there are some from which rivers gush out; others there are which when split apart send out water; and others which sink for fear of Allah. And Allah is not unmindful of what you do.

75. Can you (O you men of faith) entertain the hope that they will believe in you? - Seeing that a party of them heard the word of Allah, and perverted it knowingly after they understood it.

76. See! When they meet the men of faith, they say: "We believe": but when they meet each other in private, they say: "Shall you tell them what Allah has revealed to you, that they may engage you in argument about it before your Lord?" - Do you not understand (their aim)?

77. Do they not know that Allah knows what they conceal and what they reveal?

78. And there are among them illiterates, who know not the Book, but (see in it their own) desires, and they do nothing but conjecture.

79. Then woe to those who write the Book with their own hands, and then say: "This is from Allah," to trade with it for a miserable price! - Woe to them for what their hands do write, and for the gain they make by it.

80. And they say: "The fire shall not touch us but for a few numbered days;" Say: "Have you taken a promise from Allah, for He never breaks His promise? Or is it that you say of Allah what you do not know?"

81. Nay, those who seek gain in evil, and are surrounded by their sins - they are companions of the fire: in it shall they remain (forever).

82. But those who have faith and work righteousness, they are companions of the garden: in it shall they remain (forever).

83. And remember We took a covenant from the children of Israel (to this effect): worship none but Allah; treat with kindness your parents and relations, and orphans and those in need; speak fair to the people; be steadfast in prayer; and practice regular charity. Then did you turn back except a few among you, and you backslide (even now).

84. And remember We took your covenant (to this effect): shed no blood amongst you, nor turn out your own people from your homes: and this you solemnly ratified, and to this you can bear witness.

85. After this it is you, the same people, who slay among yourselves, and banish a party of you from their homes; assist (their enemies) against them, in guilt and transgression; and if they come to you as captives, you ransom them, though it was not lawful for you to banish them. Then is it only a part of the book that you believe in, and do you reject the rest? But what is the reward for those among you who behave like this but disgrace in this life? - and on the day of judgement they shall be consigned to the most grievous penalty. For Allah is not unmindful of what you do.

86. These are the people who buy the life of this world at the price of the hereafter: their penalty shall not be lightened nor shall they be helped.

87. We gave Moses the book and followed him up with a succession of messengers; We gave Jesus, the son of Mary, clear (signs) and strengthened him with the Holy Spirit. Is it that whenever there comes to you a messenger with what you yourselves desire not, you are puffed up with pride? - Some you called imposters, and others you slay!

88. They say, "Our hearts are the wrappings (which preserve Allah's Word: we need no more)." Nay, Allah's curse is on them for their blasphemy: little is it they believe.

89. And when there comes to them a Book from Allah, confirming what is with them - although from of old they had prayed for victory against those without faith - when there comes to them that which they (should) have recognised. They refused to believe in it but the curse of Allah is on those without faith.

90. Miserable is the price for which they have sold their souls, in that they deny (the revelation) which Allah has sent down, in insolent envy that Allah of His grace should send it to any of His servants He pleases: thus have they drawn on themselves wrath upon wrath, and humiliating is the punishment of those who reject faith.

91. When it is said to them, "Believe in what Allah has sent down," they say, "We believe in what was sent down to us;" yet they reject all besides, even if it be the truth confirming what is with them. Say: "Why then have you slain the prophets of Allah in times gone by, if you did indeed believe?"

92. There came to you Moses with clear (signs); yet you worshipped the calf (even) after that, and you did behave wrongfully.

93. And remember We took your covenant and We raised above you (the towering height) of Mount (Sinai): (saying): "Hold firmly to what We have given you, and listen (to the Law)": they said: "We hear and we disobey", and they had to drink into their hearts (of the taint) of the calf because of their faithlessness. Say: "Vile indeed are the behests of your faith if you have any faith!"

94. Say: "If the last home, with Allah, be for you specially, and not for anyone else, then seek you for death, if you are sincere."

95. But they will never seek for death, on account of the (sins) which their hands have sent on before them. And Allah is well acquainted with the wrongdoers.

96. You will indeed find them, of all people, most greedy of life - even more than the idolaters: each one of them wishes he could be given a life of a thousand years: but the grant of such life will not save him from (due) punishment. For Allah sees well all that they do.

97. Say: Whoever is an enemy to Gabriel - for he brings down the (revelation) to your heart by Allah's Will, a confirmation of what went before. And guidance and glad tidings for those who believe -

98. Whoever is an enemy to Allah and His angels and messengers, to Gabriel and Michael - Allah is an enemy to those who reject faith.

99. We have sent down to you manifest signs (*ayat*); and none reject them but those who are perverse.

100. Is it not (the case) that every time they make a covenant, some party among them throw it aside? - Nay, most of them are faithless.

101. And when came to them a messenger from Allah, confirming what was with them, a party of the People of the Book threw away the book of Allah behind their backs. As if (it had been something) they did not know!

102. They followed what the evil ones gave out (falsely) against the power of Solomon: the blasphemers were not Solomon, but the evil ones, teaching men magic, and such things as came down at Babylon to the angels Harut and Marut. But neither of these taught anyone (such things) without saying: "We are only for trial; so do not blaspheme." They learned from them the means to sow discord between man and wife. But they could not thus harm anyone except by Allah's permission. And they learned what harmed them, not what profited them. And they knew that the buyers of (magic) would have no share in the happiness of the hereafter. And vile was the price for which they did sell their souls, if they but knew!

103. If they had kept their faith and guarded themselves from evil, far better had been the reward from their Lord, if they but knew!

104. O you of faith! Say not (to the prophet) words of ambiguous import, but words of respect; and listen (to

him): to those without faith is a grievous punishment.

105. It is never the wish of those without faith among the People of the Book, nor of the pagans, that anything good should come down to you from your Lord. But Allah will choose for His special mercy whom He will - for Allah is Lord of grace abounding.

106. None of Our revelations do We abrogate or cause to be forgotten, but We substitute something better or similar: do you not know that Allah has power over all things?

107. Do you not know that to Allah belongs the dominion of the heavens and the earth? And besides Him you have neither patron nor helper.

108. Would you question your messenger as Moses was questioned of old? But whoever changes from faith to unbelief, has strayed without doubt from the even way.

109. Quite a number of the People of the Book wish they could turn you (people) back to infidelity after you have believed. From selfish envy, after the truth has become manifest to them: but forgive and overlook, till Allah accomplishes His purpose: for Allah has power over all things.

110. And be steadfast in prayer and regular in charity: and whatever good you send for your souls before you, you shall find it with Allah: for Allah sees well all that you do.

111. And they say: "None shall enter paradise unless he be a Jew or a Christian." Those are their (vain) desires. Say: "Produce your proof if you are truthful."

112. Nay - whoever submits his whole self to Allah and is a doer of good - he will get his reward with his Lord; on such shall be no fear, nor shall they grieve.

113. The Jews say: "The Christians have nothing (to stand) upon"; and the Christians say: "The Jews have nothing (to stand) upon." Yet they (profess to) study the (same) book. Similar to their word is what those say who know not; but Allah will judge between them in their quarrel on the day of judgement.

114. And who is more unjust than he who forbids that in places for the worship of Allah His name should be celebrated? - Whose zeal is (in fact) to ruin them? It was not fitting that such should themselves enter them except in fear. For them there is nothing but disgrace in this world, and in the world to come, an exceeding torment.

115. To Allah belong the east and the west: whichever way you turn, there is Allah's countenance. For Allah is All-Embracing, All-Knowing.

116. They say: "Allah has begotten a son": Glory be to Him - Nay, to Him belongs all that is in the heavens and on earth: everything renders worship to Him.

117. To Him is due the primal origin of the heavens and the earth: when He decrees a matter, He says to it: "Be," and it is.

118. Say those without knowledge: "Why speaks not Allah to us? Or why comes not to us a sign?" So said the people before them words of similar import. Their hearts are alike. We have indeed made clear the signs to any people who hold firmly to faith (in their hearts).

119. Verily, We have sent you in truth as a bearer of glad tidings and a warner: But of you no question shall be asked of the companions of the blazing fire.

120. Never will the Jews or the Christians be satisfied with you unless you follow their form of religion. Say: "The guidance of Allah - that is the (only) guidance." Were you to follow their desires after the knowledge which has reached you, then would you find neither protector nor helper against Allah.

121. Those to whom We have sent the book study it as it should be studied: they are the ones that believe in it: those who reject faith in it - the loss is their own.

122. O Children of Israel! Call to mind the special favour which I bestowed upon you, and that I preferred you to all others (for My message).

123. Then guard yourselves against a day when one soul shall not benefit another. Nor shall compensation be accepted from her nor shall intercession profit her nor shall anyone be helped (from outside).

124. And remember that Abraham was tried by his Lord with certain commands, which he fulfilled: He said: "I will make you an Imam to the nations." He pleaded: "And also (Imams) from my offspring!" He answered: "But My promise is not within the reach of evildoers."

125. Remember We made the House a place of assembly for men and a place of safety; and take you the station of Abraham as a place of prayer; and We covenanted with Abraham and Ishmael, that they should sanctify My House for those who go around it, or use it as a retreat, or bow, or prostrate themselves (in it in prayer).

126. And remember Abraham said: "My Lord, make this a city of peace, and feed its people with fruits - such of them as believe in Allah and the last day." He said: "(Yea), and such as reject faith - for a while will I grant them their pleasure, but will soon drive them to the torment of fire - an evil destination (indeed)!"

127. And remember Abraham and Ishmael raised the foundations of the House (with this prayer): "Our Lord! Accept (this service) from us: for You are the All-Hearing, the All-Knowing.

128. "Our Lord! Make of us Muslims, bowing to Your (will), and of our progeny a people Muslim, bowing to Your (will); and show us our places for the celebration of (due) rites; and turn to us (in mercy); for You are the Oft-Returning, Most Merciful.

129. "Our Lord! Send amongst them a messenger of their own, who shall rehearse Your signs to them and instruct them in scripture and wisdom, and sanctify them: for You are the Exalted in Might, the Wise."

130. And who turns away from the religion of Abraham but such as debase their souls with folly? Him We chose and rendered pure in this world:

and he will be in the hereafter in the ranks of the righteous.

131. See! His Lord said to him: "Bow (your will) to Me": He said: "I bow (my will) to the Lord and Cherisher of the Universe."

132. And this was the legacy that Abraham left to his sons, and so did Jacob; "O my sons! Allah has chosen the faith for you; then die not except in the state of submission (to Allah).

133. Were you witnesses when Death appeared before Jacob? See, he said to his sons: "What will you worship after me?" They said: "We shall worship your God and the God of your fathers, - of Abraham, Ishmael, and Isaac - the One (True) God: to Him we bow (in Islam)."

134. That was a people that has passed away. They shall reap the fruit of what they did, and you of what you do! Of their merits there is no question in your case!

135. They say: "Become Jews or Christians if you would be guided (to salvation)." Say you: "Nay! (I would rather) the religion of Abraham, the true, and he joined not gods with Allah."

136. Say you: "We believe in Allah, and the revelation given to us, and to Abraham, Ishmael, Isaac, Jacob, and the tribes, and that given to Moses and Jesus, and that given to (all) prophets from their Lord: We make no difference between one and another of them: and we bow to Allah (in Islam)."

137. So if they believe as you believe, they are indeed on the right path; but if they turn back, it is they who are in schism; but Allah will suffice you as against them, and He is the All-Hearing, the All- Knowing.

138. (Our religion is) the baptism of Allah: and who can baptize better than Allah? And it is He Whom we worship.

139. Say: Will you dispute with us about Allah, seeing that He is our Lord and your Lord; that we are responsible for our doings and you for yours; and that we are sincere (in our faith) in Him?

140. Or do you say that Abraham, Ishmael, Isaac, Jacob and the tribes were Jews or Christians? Say: Do you know better than Allah? Ah! Who is more unjust than those who conceal the testimony they have from Allah? But Allah is not unmindful of what you do!

141. That was a people that have passed away. They shall reap the fruit of what they did and you of what you do! Of their merits there is no question in your case.

142. The fools among the people will say: "What has turned them from the Qiblah to which they were used?" Say: To Allah belong east and west: He guides whom He will to a way that is straight.

143. Thus have We made of you an Ummah justly balanced, that you might be witnesses over the nations, and the messenger a witness over yourselves; and We appointed the Qiblah to which you were used, only to test those who followed the messenger from those who would turn on their heels (from the faith). Indeed it was (a change) momentous, except to those guided by Allah. And never would

Allah make your faith of no effect. For Allah is to all people most surely full of kindness, Most Merciful.

144. We see the turning of your face (for guidance) to the heavens: now shall We turn you to a Qiblah that shall please you. Turn then your face in the direction of the Sacred Mosque: wherever you are, turn your faces in that direction. The People of the Book know well that that is the truth from their Lord, nor is Allah unmindful of what they do.

145. Even if you were to bring to the People of the Book all the signs (together), they would not follow your Qiblah; nor are you going to follow their Qiblah; nor indeed will they follow each other's Qiblah. If you, after the knowledge has reached you, were to follow their (vain) desires - then would you indeed be (clearly) in the wrong.

146. The People of the Book know this as they know their own sons; but some of them conceal the truth which they themselves know.

147. The truth is from your Lord so be not at all in doubt.

148. To each is a goal to which Allah turns him; then strive together (as in a race) towards all that is good. Wheresoever you are, Allah will bring you together. For Allah has power over all things.

149. From wheresoever you start out turn your face in the direction of the Sacred Mosque; that is indeed the truth from your Lord. And Allah is not unmindful of what you do.

150. So from wheresoever you start out, turn your face in the direction of the Sacred Mosque; And wheresoever you are, turn your face there: that there be no ground of dispute against you among the people, except those of them that are bent on wickedness; so fear them not, but fear Me; and that I may complete My favours on you, and you may (consent to) be guided;

151. A similar (favour have you already received) in that We have sent among you a messenger of your own, rehearsing to you Our Signs, and purifying you, and instructing you in scripture and wisdom, and in new knowledge.

152. Then do you remember Me; I will remember you. Be grateful to Me, and reject not faith.

153. O you who believe! Seek help with patient perseverance and prayer: for Allah is with those who patiently persevere.

154. And say not of those who are slain in the way of Allah: "They are dead." Nay, they are living, though you perceive (it) not.

155. Be sure We shall test you with something of fear and hunger, some loss in goods or lives or the fruits (of your toil), but give glad tidings to those who patiently persevere -

156. Who say, when afflicted with calamity: " To Allah we belong, and to Him is our return" -

157. They are those on whom (descend) blessings from their Lord, and mercy, and they are the ones that receive guidance.

158. Behold! as-Safa and al-Marwah are among the symbols of Allah. So if those who visit the House in the season or at other times, should go around them, it is no sin in them. And if anyone obeys his own impulse to good - be sure that Allah is He Who recognises and knows.

159. Those who conceal the clear (signs) We have sent down, and the guidance, after We have made it clear for the people in the Book - on them shall be Allah's curse, and the curse of those entitled to curse -

160. Except those who repent and make amends and openly declare (the truth): to them I turn; for I am Oft-Returning, Most Merciful.

161. Those who reject faith, and die rejecting - on them is Allah's curse, and the curse of angels, and of all mankind;

162. They will remain in it: Their penalty will not be lightened, nor will respite be their (lot).

163. And your God is One God: there is no god but He, Most Gracious, Most Merciful.

164. See! In the creation of the heavens and the earth; in the alternation of the night and the day; in the sailing of the ships through the ocean for the profit of mankind; in the rain which Allah sends down from the skies, and the life which He gives with it to an earth that is dead; in the beasts of all kinds that He scatters through the earth; in the change of the winds, and the clouds which they trail like their slaves between the sky and the earth - (here) indeed are signs for a people that are wise.

165. Yet there are men who take (for worship) others besides Allah, as equal (with Allah): they love them as they should love Allah. But those of faith are overflowing in their love for Allah. If only the unrighteous could see, they would see the punishment: that to Allah belongs all power, and Allah will strongly enforce the punishment.

166. Then would those who are followed clear themselves of those who follow (them): they would see the penalty, and all relations between them would be cut off.

167. And those who followed would say: "If only we had one more chance, we would clear ourselves of them, as they have cleared themselves of us." Thus will Allah show them (the fruits of) their deeds as (nothing but) regrets. Nor will there be a way for them out of the fire.

168. O you people! Eat of what is on earth, lawful and good; and do not follow the footsteps of the evil one, for he is to you an avowed enemy.

169. For he commands you what is evil and shameful, and that you should say of Allah that of which you have no knowledge.

170. When it is said to them: "Follow what Allah has revealed:" they say: "Nay! We shall follow the ways of our fathers:" What! Even though their fathers were void of wisdom and guidance?

171. The parable of those who reject faith is as if one were to shout like a goat-herd, to things that listen to nothing but calls and cries: deaf, dumb and blind, they are void of wisdom.

172. O you who believe! Eat of the good things that We have provided for you and be grateful to Allah, if it is Him you worship.

173. He has only forbidden you dead meat, and blood, and the flesh of swine, and that on which any other name has been invoked besides that of Allah. But if one is forced by necessity, without wilful disobedience, nor transgressing due limits - then is he guiltless. For Allah is Oft-Forgiving, Most Merciful.

174. Those who conceal Allah's revelations in the Book, and purchase for them a miserable profit - they swallow into themselves nothing but fire; Allah will not address them on the day of resurrection, nor purify them; grievous will be their penalty.

175. They are the ones who buy error in place of guidance and torment in place of forgiveness. Ah! What boldness (they show) for the fire!

176. (Their doom is) because Allah sent down the book in truth but those who seek causes of dispute in the book are in a schism far (from the purpose).

177. It is not righteousness that you turn your faces toward east or west; but it is righteousness to believe in Allah and the last day, and the angels, and the book, and the prophets; to spend of your substance, out of love for Him, for your relatives, for orphans, for the needy, for the wayfarer, for those who ask, and for the ransom of slaves; to be steadfast in prayer, and practice regular charity, to fulfil the contracts which you have made; and to be firm and patient, in pain (or suffering) and adversity, and throughout all periods of panic. Such are the people of truth, the God-fearing.

178. O you who believe! The law of equality is prescribed to you in cases of murder: the free for the free, the slave for the slave, the woman for the woman. But if any remission is made by the brother of the slain, then grant any reasonable demand, and compensate him with handsome gratitude. This is a concession and a mercy from your Lord. After this, whoever exceeds the limits shall be in grave penalty.

179. In the law of equality there is (saving of) life to you, O you men of understanding; that you may restrain yourselves.

180. It is prescribed, when death approaches any of you, if he leave any goods, that he make a bequest to parents and near relatives, according to reasonable usage; this is due from the God-fearing.

181. If anyone changes the bequest after hearing it, the guilt shall be on those who make the change. For Allah hears and knows (all things).

182. But if anyone fears partiality or wrongdoing on the part of the testator, and makes peace between (the parties concerned), there is no wrong in him: for Allah is Oft-Forgiving, Most Merciful.

183. O you who believe! Fasting is prescribed to you as it was prescribed to those before you, that you may (learn) self-restraint -

184. (Fasting) for a fixed number of days; but if any of you is ill, or on a journey, the prescribed number (should be made up) from days later. For those who can do it (with hardship), is a ransom, the feeding of one that is needy. But he that will give more, of his own free will - it is better for him. And it is better for you that you fast, if you only knew.

185. Ramadan is the (month) in which was sent down the Qur'an, as a guide to mankind, also clear (signs) for guidance and judgement (between right and wrong). So every one of you who is present (at his home) during that month should spend it in fasting, but if any one is ill, or on a journey, the prescribed period (should be made up) by days later. Allah intends every facility for you; He does not want to put you to difficulties. (He wants you) to complete the prescribed period, and to glorify Him in that He has guided you; and perhaps you shall be grateful.

186. When my servants ask you concerning Me, I am indeed close (to them): I listen to the prayer of every supplicant when he calls on Me: let them also, with a will, listen to My call, and believe in Me: that they may walk in the right way.

187. Permitted to you, on the night of the fasts, is the approach to your wives. They are your garments and you are their garments. Allah knows what you used to do secretly among yourselves; but He turned to you and forgave you; so now associate with them, and seek what Allah has ordained for you, and eat and drink, until the white thread of dawn appear to you distinct from its black thread; then complete your fast till the night appears; but do not associate with your wives while you are in retreat in the mosques. Those are limits (set by) Allah: come not near to it. Thus does Allah make clear His signs to men: that they may learn self-restraint.

188. And do not eat up your property among yourselves for vanities, nor use it as bait for the judges, with intent that you may eat up wrongfully and knowingly a little of (other) people's property.

189. They ask you concerning the new moons. Say: they are but signs to mark fixed periods of time in (the affairs of) men, and for pilgrimage. It is no virtue if you enter your houses from the back: it is virtue if you fear Allah. Enter houses through the proper doors: and fear Allah: that you may prosper.

190. Fight in the cause of Allah those who fight you, but do not transgress limits; for Allah loves not transgressors.

191. And slay them wherever you catch them, and turn them out from where they have turned you out; for tumult and oppression are worse than slaughter; but fight them not at the Sacred Mosque, unless they (first) fight you there; but if they fight you, slay them. Such is the reward of those who suppress faith.

192. But if they cease, Allah is Oft-Forgiving, Most Merciful.

193. And fight them on until there is no more tumult or oppression, and there prevail justice and faith in Allah; but if they cease, let there be no hostility except to those who practice oppression.

194. The prohibited month - for the prohibited month, and so for all things prohibited - there is the law of equality. If then anyone transgresses the prohibition against you, transgress you likewise against him. But fear Allah, and know that Allah is with those who restrain themselves.

195. And spend of your substance in the cause of Allah, and make not your own hands contribute to (your) destruction; but do good; for Allah loves those who do good.

196. And complete the Hajj or Umrah in the service of Allah, but if you are prevented (from completing it), send an offering for sacrifice, such as you may find, and do not shave your heads until the offering reaches the place of sacrifice. And if any of you is ill, or has an ailment in his scalp, (necessitating shaving), (he should) in compensation either fast, or feed the poor, or offer sacrifice; and when you are in peaceful conditions (again), if anyone wishes to continue the Umrah on to the Hajj, he must make an offering such as he can afford, but if he cannot afford it, he should fast three days during the Hajj and seven days on his return, making ten days in all. This is for those whose household is not in (the precincts of) the Sacred Mosque, and fear Allah, and know that Allah is strict in punishment.

197. For Hajj are the months well-known. If anyone undertakes that duty in them, let there be no obscenity, nor wickedness, nor wrangling in the Hajj and whatever good you do, (be sure) Allah knows it. And take a provision (with you) for the journey, but the best of provisions is right conduct. So fear Me, O you that are wise.

198. It is no crime in you if you seek of the bounty of your Lord (during pilgrimage). Then when you pour down from (mount) Arafat, celebrate the praises of Allah at the Sacred Monument, and celebrate His praises as He has directed you, even though, before this, you went astray.

199. Then pass on at a quick pace from the place from where it is usual for the multitude to do so, and ask for Allah's forgiveness. For Allah is Oft-Forgiving, Most Merciful.

200. So when you have accomplished your holy rites, celebrate the praises of Allah, as you used to celebrate the praises of your fathers - yea, with far more heart and soul. There are men who say: "Our Lord! Give us (Your bounties) in this world!" But they will have no portion in the hereafter.

201. And there are men who say: "Our Lord! Give us good in this world and good in the hereafter, and defend us from the torment of the fire!"

202. To these will be allotted what they have earned; and Allah is quick in account.

203. Celebrate the praises of Allah during the appointed days. But if anyone hastens to leave in two days,

there is no blame on him, and if anyone stays on, there is no blame on him, if his aim is to do right. Then fear Allah, and know that you will surely be gathered to Him.

204. There is the type of man whose speech about this world's life may dazzle you, and he calls Allah to witness about what is in his heart; yet is he the most contentious of enemies.

205. When he turns his back, his aim everywhere is to spread mischief through the earth and destroy crops and cattle. But Allah loves not mischief.

206. When it is said to him, "Fear Allah," he is led by arrogance to (more) crime. Enough for him is hell - an evil bed indeed (to lie on)!

207. And there is the type of man who gives his life to earn the pleasure of Allah; and Allah is full of kindness to (His) devotees.

208. O you who believe! Enter into Islam wholeheartedly; and follow not the footsteps of the evil one; for he is to you an avowed enemy.

209. If you backslide after the clear (signs) have come to you, then know that Allah is Exalted in Power, Wise.

210. Will they wait until Allah comes to them in canopies of clouds, with angels (in His train) and the question is (thus) settled? But to Allah do all questions go back (for decision).

211. Ask the Children of Israel how many clear (signs) We have sent them. But if anyone, after Allah's favour has come to him, substitutes (something else), Allah is strict in punishment.

212. The life of this world is alluring to those who reject faith, and they mock those who believe. But the righteous will be above them on the day of resurrection; for Allah bestows His abundance without measure on whom He will.

213. Mankind was one single nation, and Allah sent prophets with glad tidings and warnings; and with them He sent the book in truth, to judge between people in matters in which they differed; but the People of the Book, after the clear signs came to them, did not differ among themselves, except through selfish rebellion. Allah by His grace guided the believers to the truth, in which they differed. For Allah guides whom He will to a path that is straight.

214. Or do you think that you shall enter the garden (of bliss) without such (trials) as came to those who passed away before you? They encountered suffering and adversity, and were so shaken in spirit that even the messenger and those of faith who were with him cried: "When (will come) the help of Allah?" Ah! Verily, the help of Allah is (always) near!

215. They ask you what they should spend (in charity). Say: Whatever you spend that is good, is for parents and relations and orphans and those in want and for wayfarers. And whatever you do that is good - Allah knows it well.

216. Fighting is prescribed for you, and you dislike it. But it is possible that you dislike a thing which is good for you, and that you love a thing which is bad for you. But Allah knows, and you know not.

217. They ask you concerning fighting in the prohibited month. Say: "Fighting in it is a grave (offence); but graver is it in the sight of Allah to prevent access to the path of Allah, to deny Him, to prevent access to the Sacred Mosque, and drive out its members." Tumult and oppression are worse than slaughter. Nor will they cease fighting you until they turn you back from your faith if they can. And if any of you turn back from their faith and die in unbelief, their works will bear no fruit in this life and in the hereafter; they will be companions of the fire and will remain in it.

218. Those who believed and those who suffered exile and fought (and strove and struggled) in the path of Allah - they have the hope of the mercy of Allah: and Allah is Oft-Forgiving, Most Merciful.

219. They ask you concerning wine and gambling. Say: "In them is great sin, and some profit for men; but the sin is greater than the profit." They ask you how much they are to spend; say: "What is beyond your needs." Thus does Allah make clear to you His signs: in order that you may consider -

220. (Their bearings) on this life and the hereafter. They ask you concerning orphans. Say: "The best thing to do is what is for their good; if you mix their affairs with yours, they are your brothers; but Allah knows the man who means mischief from the man who means good. And if Allah had wished, He could have put you into difficulties: He is indeed Exalted in Power, Wise."

221. Do not marry unbelieving women until they believe: a slave woman who believes is better than an unbelieving woman, even though she allure you. Nor marry (your girls) to unbelievers until they believe: a man slave who believes is better than an unbeliever even though he allure you. Unbelievers do (but) invite you to the fire. But Allah invites by His grace to the garden (of bliss) and forgiveness, and makes His signs clear to mankind: that they may receive admonition.

222. They ask you concerning women's courses. Say: They are a hurt and a pollution: so keep away from women in their courses, and do not approach them until they are clean. But when they have purified themselves, you may approach them in any manner, time, or place ordained for you by Allah. For Allah loves those who turn to Him constantly and He loves those who keep themselves pure and clean.

223. Your wives are as a tilth to you so approach your tilth when or how you will; but do some good act for your souls beforehand; and fear Allah, and know that you are to meet Him (in the hereafter), and give (these) good tidings to those who believe.

224. And make not Allah's (name) an excuse in your oaths against doing good, or acting rightly, or making peace between persons; for Allah is One who hears and knows all things.

225. Allah will not call you to account for thoughtlessness in your oaths, but for the intention in your hearts, and He is Oft-Forgiving, Most Forbearing.

226. For those who take an oath for abstention from their wives, a waiting for four months is ordained; if then they return, Allah is Oft-Forgiving, Most Merciful.

227. But if their intention is firm for divorce, Allah hears and knows all things.

228. Divorced women shall wait concerning themselves for three monthly periods. Nor is it lawful for them to hide what Allah has created in their wombs, if they have faith in Allah and the last day. And their husbands have the better right to take them back in that period, if they wish for reconciliation. And women shall have rights similar to the rights against them, according to what is equitable; but men have a degree (of advantage) over them. And Allah is Exalted in Power, Wise.

229. A divorce is only permissible twice: after that, the parties should either hold together on equitable terms, or separate with kindness. It is not lawful for you, (men), to take back any of your gifts (from your wives), except when both parties fear that they would be unable to keep the limits ordained by Allah. If you (judges) do indeed fear that they would be unable to keep the limits ordained by Allah, there is no blame on either of them if she gives something for her freedom. These are the limits ordained by Allah; so do not transgress them. If any do transgress the limits ordained by Allah, such persons wrong (themselves as well as others).

230. So if a husband divorces his wife (irrevocably), he cannot, after that, remarry her until after she has married another husband and he has divorced her. In that case there is no blame on either of them if they reunite, provided they feel that they can keep the limits ordained by Allah. Such are the limits ordained by Allah, which He makes plain to those who understand.

231. When you divorce women, and they fulfil the term of their (Iddah), either take them back on equitable terms or set them free on equitable terms; but do not take them back to injure them, (or) to take undue advantage; if anyone does that, he wrongs his own soul. Do not treat Allah's signs as a jest, but solemnly rehearse Allah's favours on you, and the fact that He sent down to you the book and wisdom, for your instruction. And fear Allah, and know that Allah is well-acquainted with all things.

232. When you divorce women, and they fulfil the term of their (Iddah), do not prevent them from marrying their (former) husbands, if they mutually agree on equitable terms. This instruction is for all amongst you, who believe in Allah and the last day. That is (the course making for) most virtue and purity amongst you. And Allah knows, and you know not.

233. The mothers shall give suck to their offspring for two whole years, if the father desires to complete the term. But he shall bear the cost of their food and clothing on equitable terms. No soul shall have a burden laid on it greater than it can bear. No mother shall be treated unfairly on account of her child, nor a father on account of his

child, and the heir shall be chargeable in the same way. If they both decide on weaning, by mutual consent, and after due consultation, there is no blame on them. If you decide on a foster-mother for your offspring there is no blame on you, provided you pay (the mother) what you offered on equitable terms. But fear Allah and know that Allah sees well what you do.

234. If any of you die and leave widows behind, they shall wait concerning themselves four months and ten days: when they have fulfilled their term, there is no blame on you if they dispose of themselves in a just and reasonable manner. And Allah is well acquainted with what you do.

235. There is no blame on you if you make an offer of betrothal or hold it in your hearts. Allah knows that you cherish them in your hearts: but do not make a secret contract with them except in terms honourable, nor resolve on the tie of marriage till the term prescribed is fulfilled. And know that Allah knows what is in your hearts, and take heed of Him; and know that Allah is Oft-Forgiving, Most Forbearing.

236. There is no blame on you if you divorce women before consummation or the fixation of their dower; but bestow on them (a suitable gift), the wealthy according to his means, and the poor according to his means - a gift of a reasonable amount is due from those who wish to do the right thing.

237. And if you divorce them before consummation, but after the fixation of a dower for them, then the half of the dower (is due to them), unless they remit it or (the man's half) is remitted by him in whose hands is the marriage tie; and the remission (of the man's half) is the nearest to righteousness and do not forget liberality between yourselves. For Allah sees well all that you do.

238. Guard strictly your (habit) of prayers, especially the middle prayer; and stand before Allah in a devout (frame of mind).

239. If you fear (an enemy), pray on foot, or riding, (as may be most convenient), but when you are in security, celebrate Allah's praises in the manner He has taught you, which you knew not (before).

240. Those of you who die and leave widows should bequeath for their widows a year's maintenance and residence; but if they leave (the residence), there is no blame on you for what they do with themselves, provided it is reasonable. And Allah is Exalted in Power, Wise.

241. For divorced women maintenance (should be provided) on a reasonable (scale). This is a duty on the righteous.

242. Thus does Allah make clear His signs to you: in order that you may understand.

243. Did you not turn your vision to those who abandoned their homes, though they were thousands (in number), for fear of death? Allah said to them: "Die": Then He restored them to life. For Allah is full of bounty to mankind, but most of them are ungrateful.

244. Then fight in the cause of Allah, and know that Allah hears and knows all things.

245. Who is he that will loan to Allah a beautiful loan, which Allah will double to his credit and multiply many times? It is Allah that gives (you) want or plenty, and to Him shall be your return.

246. Have you not turned your vision to the chiefs of the Children of Israel after (the time of) Moses? They said to a prophet (that was) among them: "Appoint for us a king, that we may fight in the cause of Allah." He said: "Is it not possible, if you were commanded to fight, that you will not fight?" They said: "How could we refuse to fight in the cause of Allah, seeing that we were turned out of our homes and our families?" But when they were commanded to fight, they turned back, except a small band among them. But Allah has full knowledge of those who do wrong.

247. Their Prophet said to them: "Allah has appointed Saul (Talut) as king over you." They said: "How can he exercise authority over us when we are better fitted than he to exercise authority, and he is not even gifted with wealth in abundance?" He said: "Allah has chosen him above you, and has gifted him abundantly with knowledge and bodily prowess: Allah grants His authority to whom He pleases. Allah is All-Embracing, and He knows all things."

248. And (further) their Prophet said to them: "A sign of his authority is that there shall come to you the ark of the covenant, with (an assurance) in it of security from your Lord, and the relics left by the family of Moses and the family of Aaron, carried by angels. In this is a symbol for you if you indeed have faith."

249. When Saul (Talut) set out with the armies, he said: "Allah will test you at the stream; if any drinks of its water, he goes not with my army; only those who taste not of it go with me; a mere sip out of the hand is excused." But they all drank of it, except a few. When they crossed the river - he and the faithful ones with him, they said: "This day we cannot cope with Goliath and his forces." But those who were convinced that they must meet Allah, said: "How often, by Allah's Will, has a small force conquered a big one? Allah is with those who steadfastly persevere."

250. When they advanced to meet Goliath and his forces, they prayed: "Our Lord! Pour out constancy on us and make our steps firm: help us against those that reject faith."

251. By Allah's Will, they routed them: and David slew Goliath: and Allah gave him power and wisdom and taught him whatever (else) He willed. And did not Allah check one set of people by means of another, the earth would indeed be full of mischief: but Allah is full of bounty to all the worlds.

252. These are the signs of Allah: We rehearse them to you in truth: verily you are one of the messengers.

253. Those messengers We endowed with gifts, some above others: to one of them Allah spoke; others He raised to degrees (of honour); to Jesus, the son of Mary, We gave clear (signs), and strengthened him with the Holy Spirit. If Allah had so willed, succeeding generations would not have fought among each other, after clear (signs) had come to them but they (chose) to wrangle, some believing and others rejecting. If Allah had so willed, they would not have fought each other; but Allah fulfils His plan.

254. O you who believe! Spend out of (the bounties) We have provided for you, before the day comes when no bargaining (will benefit), nor friendship nor intercession. Those who reject faith - they are the wrongdoers.

255. Allah! There is no god but He - the Living, the Self-subsisting, Eternal. No slumber can seize Him nor sleep. His are all things in the heavens and on earth. Who is there who can intercede in His presence except as He permits? He knows what (appears to his creatures as) before or after or behind them. Nor shall they encompass anything of His knowledge except as He wills. His Throne does extend over the heavens and the earth, and He feels no fatigue in guarding and preserving them. For He is the Most High, the Supreme (in glory).

256. Let there be no compulsion in religion: Truth stands out clear from error: whoever rejects evil and believes in Allah has grasped the most trustworthy handhold, that never breaks. And Allah hears and knows all things.

257. Allah is the Protector of those who have faith; from the depths of darkness He will lead them out into light. Of those who reject faith the patrons are the evil Ones; from light they will lead them out into the depths of darkness. They will be companions of the fire, to dwell in it (forever).

258. Have you not turned your vision to one who disputed with Abraham about his Lord, because Allah had granted him power? Abraham said: "My Lord is He Who gives life and death." He said: "I give life and death." Said Abraham: "But it is Allah that causes the sun to rise from the east: do you then cause it to rise from the west?" Thus was he confounded who (in arrogance) rejected faith. Nor does Allah give guidance to a people unjust.

259. Or (take) the similitude of one who passed by a hamlet, all in ruins to its roofs. He said: "Oh! How shall Allah bring it (ever) to life, after (this) its death?" But Allah caused him to die for a hundred years, then raised him up (again). He said: "How long did you stay (thus)?" He said: "(Perhaps) a day or part of a day." He said: "Nay, you have stayed thus a hundred years; but look at your food and your drink; they show no signs of age; and look at your donkey; and that We may make of you a sign to the people, look further at the bones, how We bring them together and clothe them with flesh. When this was shown clearly to him, he said: "I know that Allah has power over all things."

260. See! Abraham said: "My Lord! Show me how You give life to the dead." He said: "Do you not then believe?" He said: "Yea! But to satisfy my own

understanding." He said: "Take four birds; tame them to turn to you; put a portion of them on every hill, and call to them; they will come to you, (flying) with speed. Then know that Allah is Exalted in Power, Wise."

261. The parable of those who spend their substance in the way of Allah is that of a grain of corn: it grows seven ears, and each ear has a hundred grains. Allah gives manifold increase to whom He pleases: and Allah cares for all and He knows all things.

262. Those who spend their substance in the cause of Allah, and follow not up their gifts with reminders of their generosity or with injury - for them their reward is with their Lord; on them shall be no fear, nor shall they grieve.

263. Kind words and the covering of faults are better than charity followed by injury. Allah is free of all wants, and He is most forbearing.

264. O you who believe! Cancel not your charity by reminders of your generosity or by injury - like those who spend their substance to be seen of men, but believe neither in Allah nor in the last day. They are in parable like a hard barren rock, on which is a little soil; on it falls heavy rain, which leaves it (just) a bare stone. They will be able to do nothing with anything they have earned. And Allah guides not those who reject faith.

265. And the likeness of those who spend their substance, seeking to please Allah and to strengthen their souls, is as a garden, high and fertile; heavy rain falls on it but makes it yield a double increase of harvest, and if it receives not heavy rain, light moisture suffices it. Allah sees well whatever you do.

266. Do any of you wish that he should have a garden with date palms and vines and streams flowing underneath, and all kinds of fruit, while he is stricken with old age, and his children are not strong (enough to look after themselves) - that it should be caught in a whirlwind, with fire in it, and be burnt up? Thus does Allah make clear to you (His) signs: that you may consider.

267. O you who believe! Give of the good things which you have (honourably) earned, and of the fruits of the earth which We have produced for you, and do not even aim at getting anything which is bad, in order that out of it you may give away something, when you yourselves would not receive it except with closed eyes. And know that Allah is free of all wants, and worthy of all praise.

268. The evil one threatens you with poverty and bids you to conduct unseemly. Allah promises you His forgiveness and bounties, And Allah cares for all and He knows all things.

269. He grants wisdom to whom He pleases; and he to whom wisdom is granted receives indeed a benefit overflowing; but none will grasp the message but men of understanding.

270. And whatever you spend in charity or devotion, be sure Allah knows it all. But the wrongdoers have no helpers.

271. If you disclose (acts of) charity, even so it is well, but if you conceal them, and make them reach those (really) in need, that is best for you: it will remove from you some of your (stains of) evil. And Allah is well acquainted with what you do.

272. It is not required of you (O messenger), to set them on the right path, but Allah sets on the right path whom He pleases. Whatever of good you give benefits your own souls, and you shall only do so seeking the "Face" of Allah. Whatever good you give, shall be rendered back to you, and you shall not be dealt with unjustly.

273. (Charity is) for those in need, who in Allah's cause are restricted (from travel) and cannot move about in the land, seeking (for trade or work): The ignorant man thinks, because of their modesty, that they are free from want. You shall know them by their (unfailing) mark: they beg not importunately from all and sundry, and whatever of good you give, be assured Allah knows it well.

274. Those who (in charity) spend of their goods by night and by day, in secret and in public, have their reward with their Lord; on them shall be no fear, nor shall they grieve.

275. Those who devour usury will not stand except as one whom the evil one by his touch has driven to madness. That is because they say: "Trade is like usury," but Allah has permitted trade and forbidden usury. Those who after receiving direction from their Lord, desist, shall be pardoned for the past; their case is for Allah (to judge), but those who repeat (the offence) are companions of the fire: they will remain in it (forever).

276. Allah will deprive usury of all blessing, but will give increase for deeds of charity; for He loves not creatures ungrateful and wicked.

277. Those who believe, and do deeds of righteousness, and establish regular prayers and regular charity, will have their reward with their Lord: on them shall be no fear, nor shall they grieve.

278. O you who believe! Fear Allah, and give up what remains of your demand for usury, if you are indeed believers.

279. If you do it not, take notice of war from Allah and His messenger: but if you turn back, you shall have your capital sums; deal not unjustly, and you shall not be dealt with unjustly.

280. If the debtor is in a difficulty, grant him time till it is easy for him to repay. But if you remit it by way of charity, that is best for you if you only knew.

281. And fear the Day when you shall be brought back to Allah. Then shall every soul be paid what it earned, and none shall be dealt with unjustly.

282. O you who believe! When you deal with each other, in transactions involving future obligations in a fixed period of time, reduce them to writing. Let a scribe write down faithfully as between the parties; let not the scribe refuse to write: as Allah has taught him, so let him write. Let him who incurs the liability dictate, but let him fear his Lord Allah, and not diminish anything of what he owes. If the party liable is mentally deficient, or weak, or unable himself to dictate, let his guardian dictate faithfully. And get two witnesses, out

of your own men, and if there are not two men, then a man and two women, such as you choose, for witnesses, so that if one of them errs, the other can remind her. The witnesses should not refuse when they are called on (for evidence). Disdain not to reduce to writing (your contract) for a future period, whether it be small or big: it is more just in the sight of Allah, more suitable as evidence, and more convenient to prevent doubts among yourselves. But if it be a transaction which you carry out on the spot among yourselves there is no blame on you if you reduce it not to writing. But take witnesses whenever you make a commercial contract; and let neither scribe nor witness suffer harm. If you do (such harm), it would be wickedness in you. So fear Allah; for it is Allah that teaches you. And Allah is well acquainted with all things.

283. If you are on a journey, and cannot find a scribe, a pledge with possession (may serve the purpose). And if one of you deposits a thing on trust with another, let the trustee (faithfully) discharge his trust, and let him fear his Lord. Conceal not evidence; for whoever conceals it, his heart is tainted with sin. And Allah knows all that you do.

284. To Allah belongs all that is in the heavens and on earth. Whether you show what is in your minds or conceal it, Allah calls you to account for it. He forgives whom He pleases, and punishes whom He pleases. For Allah has power over all things.

285. The messenger believes in what has been revealed to him from his Lord, as do the men of faith. Each one (of them) believes in Allah, His angels, His books, and His messengers. "We make no distinction (they say) between one and another of His messengers." And they say: "We hear, and we obey: (We seek) Your forgiveness, Our Lord, and to You is the end of all journeys."

286. On no soul does Allah place a burden greater than it can bear. It gets every good that it earns, and it suffers every ill that it earns. (Pray): "Our Lord! Condemn us not if we forget or fall into error; our Lord! Lay not on us a burden like that which You did lay on those before us; Our Lord! Lay not on us a burden greater than we have strength to bear. Blot out our sins, and grant us forgiveness. Have mercy on us. You are our Protector; help us against those who stand against faith."

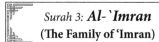

Surah 3: *Al-`Imran*
(The Family of 'Imran)

In the name of Allah, Most Gracious, Most Merciful.

1. *Alif Lam Mim.*

2. Allah! There is no god but He - the Living, the Self-Subsisting, Eternal.

3. It is He Who sent down to you (step by step), in truth, the book, confirming what went before it; and He sent down the Law (of Moses) and the Gospel (of Jesus).

4. Before this, as a guide to mankind, and He sent down the criterion (of judgement between right and wrong).

Then those who reject faith in the signs of Allah will suffer the severest penalty, and Allah is Exalted in Might, Lord of Retribution.

5. From Allah, verily nothing is hidden on earth or in the heavens.

6. He it is Who shapes you in the wombs as He pleases. There is no god but He, the Exalted in Might, the Wise.

7. He it is Who has sent down to you the book; in it are verses basic or fundamental (of established meaning); they are the foundation of the book: others are not of well-established meaning. But those in whose hearts is perversity follow the part of it that is not of well-established meaning. Seeking discord, and searching for its hidden meanings, but no one knows its true meanings except Allah. And those who are firmly grounded in knowledge say: "We believe in the book; the whole of it is from our Lord:" and none will grasp the message except men of understanding.

8. "Our Lord!" (they say), "let not our hearts deviate now after You have guided us, but grant us mercy from Your own Presence; for You are the Grantor of Bounties without measure.

9. "Our Lord! You are He that will gather mankind together against a day about which there is no doubt; for Allah never fails in His promise."

10. Those who reject faith, neither their possessions nor their (numerous) progeny will benefit them anything against Allah; they are themselves but fuel for the fire.

11. (Their plight will be) no better than that of the people of Pharaoh, and their predecessors: they denied Our signs, and Allah called them to account for their sins. For Allah is strict in punishment.

12. Say to those who reject faith: "Soon will you be vanquished and gathered together to hell - an evil bed indeed (to lie on)!"

13. "There has already been for you a sign in the two armies that met (in combat): one was fighting in the cause of Allah, the other resisting Allah; these saw with their own eyes twice their number. But Allah does support with His aid whom He pleases. In this is a warning for such as have eyes to see."

14. Fair in the eyes of men is the love of things they covet: women and sons; heaped-up hoards of gold and silver; horses branded (for blood and excellence); and (wealth of) cattle and well-tilled land. Such are the possessions of this world's life; but in nearness to Allah is the best of the goals (to return to).

15. Say: Shall I give you glad tidings of things far better than those? For the righteous are gardens in nearness to their Lord, with rivers flowing beneath; in it is their eternal home; with companions pure (and holy) and the good pleasure of Allah. For in Allah's sight are (all) His servants -

16. (Namely), those who say: "Our Lord! We have indeed believed: forgive us, then, our sins, and save us from the agony of the fire" -

17. Those who show patience, firmness and self-control; who are true (in word and deed); who worship devoutly; who spend (in the way of Allah); and who pray for forgiveness in the early hours of the morning.

18. There is no god but He: that is the witness of Allah, His angels, and those endued with knowledge, standing firm on justice. There is no god but He, the Exalted in Power, the Wise.

19. The religion before Allah is Islam (submission to His will): nor did the People of the Book dissent from it except through envy of each other, after knowledge had come to them. But if any deny the signs of Allah, Allah is swift in calling to account.

20. So if they dispute with you, say: "I have submitted my whole self to Allah and so have those who follow me." And say to the People of the Book and to those who are unlearned: "Do you (also) submit yourselves?" If they do, they are in right guidance, but if they turn back, your duty is to convey the Message; and in Allah's sight are (all) His servants.

21. As to those who deny the signs of Allah, and in defiance of right, slay the prophets, and slay those who teach just dealing with mankind, announce to them a grievous penalty.

22. They are those whose works will bear no fruit in this world and in the hereafter, nor will they have anyone to help.

23. Have you not turned your vision to those who have been given a portion of the book? They are invited to the book of Allah, to settle their dispute, but a party of them turn back and decline (the arbitration).

24. This because they say: "The fire shall not touch us but for a few numbered days"; for their forgeries deceive them as to their own religion.

25. But how (will they fare) when We gather them together against a day about which there is no doubt, and each soul will be paid out just what it has earned, without (favour or) injustice?

26. Say: "O Allah! Lord of power (and rule), You give power to whom You please, and You strip off power from whom You please: You endue with honour whom You please, and You bring low whom You please: in Your Hand is all good. Verily, over all things You have power.

27. "You cause the night to gain on the day, and You cause the day to gain on the night; You bring the living out of the dead, and You bring the dead out of the living; and You give sustenance to whom You please, without measure."

28. Let not the believers take for friends or helpers unbelievers rather than believers; if any do that, in nothing will there be help from Allah: except by way of precaution, that you may guard yourselves from them. But Allah cautions you (to remember) Himself; for the final goal is to Allah.

29. Say: "Whether you hide what is in your hearts or reveal it, Allah knows it all: He knows what is in the heavens, and what is on earth. And Allah has power over all things.

30. "On the day when every soul will be confronted with all the good it has done, and all the evil it has done, it will wish there were a great distance between it and its evil. But Allah cautions you (to remember) Himself. And Allah is full of kindness to those that serve Him.

31. Say: "If you do love Allah, follow me: Allah will love you and forgive you your sins; for Allah is Oft-Forgiving, Most Merciful."

32. Say: "Obey Allah and His messenger": but if they turn back, Allah loves not those who reject faith.

33. Allah did choose Adam and Noah, the family of Abraham, and the family of Imran above all people -

34. Offspring, one of the other; and Allah hears and knows all things.

35. See! A woman of Imran said: "O my Lord! I do dedicate to You what is in my womb for Your special service: so accept this of me: for You hear and know all things."

36. When she was delivered, she said: "O my Lord! See! I am delivered of a female child!" - And Allah knew best what she brought out - "and no wise is the male like the female. I have named her Mary, and I commend her and her offspring to Your protection from the evil one, the rejected."

37. Right graciously did her Lord accept her: He made her grow in purity and beauty; to the care of Zakariya was she assigned. Every time that he entered (her) chamber to see her, he found her supplied with sustenance. He said: "O Mary! From where (comes) this to you?" She said: "From Allah: for Allah provides sustenance to whom He pleases, without measure."

38. There did Zakariya pray to his Lord, saying: "O my Lord! Grant to me from You a progeny that is pure: for You are He that hears prayer!"

39. While he was standing in prayer in the chamber, the angels called to him: "Allah does give you glad tidings of Yahya, witnessing the truth of a Word from Allah, and (besides) noble, chaste, and a Prophet - of the (goodly) company of the righteous."

40. He said: "O my Lord! How shall I have a son, seeing I am very old, and my wife is barren?" "Thus," was the answer, "does Allah accomplish what He wills."

41. He said: "O my Lord! Give me a sign!" "Your sign," was the answer, "Shall be that you shall speak to no man for three days but with signals. Then celebrate the praises of your Lord again and again, and glorify Him in the evening and in the morning."

42. See! The angels said: "O Mary! Allah has chosen you and purified you - chosen you above the women of all nations."

43. "O Mary! Worship your Lord devoutly: prostrate yourself, and bow down (in prayer) with those who bow down."

44. This is part of the tidings of the things unseen, which We reveal to you (O prophet!) by inspiration: you were not with them when they cast lots with arrows, as to which of them should be charged with the care of Mary: nor were you with them when they disputed (the point).

45. See! The angels said: "O Mary! Allah gives you glad tidings of a word from Him: his name will be Messiah Jesus, the son of Mary, held in honour in this world and the hereafter and of (the company of) those nearest to Allah;"

46. "He shall speak to the people in childhood and in maturity. And he shall be (of the company) of the righteous."

47. She said: "O my Lord! How shall I have a son when no man has touched me?" He said: "Even so: Allah creates what He wills: when He has decreed a plan, He but says to it, 'Be,' and it is!"

48. "And Allah will teach him the book and wisdom, the Law and the Gospel,"

49. "And (appoint him) a messenger to the Children of Israel, (with this message): "I have come to you, with a sign from your Lord, in that I make for you out of clay, as it were, the figure of a bird, and breathe into it, and it becomes a bird by Allah's permission: and I heal those born blind, and the lepers, and I revive the dead, by Allah's permission; and I declare to you what you eat, and what you store in your houses. Surely in it is a sign for you if you did believe;"

50. "(I have come to you), to attest the Law which was before me. And to make lawful to you part of what was (before) forbidden to you; I have come to you with a sign from your Lord. So fear Allah and obey me."

51. "It is Allah who is my Lord and your Lord; then worship Him. This is a way that is straight."

52. When Jesus found unbelief on their part he said: "Who will be my helpers to (the work of) Allah?" Said the disciples: "We are Allah's helpers: we believe in Allah, and do you bear witness that we are Muslims."

53. "Our Lord! We believe in what you have revealed, and we follow the messenger; then write us down among those who bear witness."

54. And (the unbelievers) plotted and planned, and Allah too planned, and the best of planners is Allah.

55. See! Allah said: "O Jesus! I will take you and raise you to Myself and clear you (of the falsehoods) of those who blaspheme; I will make those who follow you superior to those who reject faith, to the day of resurrection: then shall you all return to Me, and I will judge between you of the matters in which you dispute."

56. "As to those who reject faith, I will punish them with terrible agony in this world and in the hereafter, nor will they have anyone to help."

57. "As to those who believe and work righteousness, Allah will pay them (in full) their reward: but Allah loves not those who do wrong."

58. "This is what We rehearse to you of the signs and the message of wisdom."

59. The similitude of Jesus before Allah is as that of Adam; He created him from dust, then said to him: "Be": and he was.

60. The truth (comes) from Allah alone; so be not of those who doubt.

61. If anyone disputes in this matter with you, now after (full) knowledge has come to you, say: "Come! Let us gather together - our sons and your sons, our women and your women, ourselves and yourselves: then let us earnestly pray, and invoke the curse of Allah on those who lie!"

62. This is the true account: there is no god except Allah; and Allah - He is indeed the Exalted in Power, the Wise.

63. But if they turn back, Allah has full knowledge of those who do mischief.

64. Say: "O People of the Book! Come to common terms as between us and you: that we worship none but Allah; that we associate no partners with Him; that we erect not, from among ourselves, lords and patrons other than Allah." If then they turn back, say you: "Bear witness that we (at least) are Muslims (bowing to Allah's Will)."

65. You People of the Book! Why dispute you about Abraham, when the Law and the Gospel were not revealed till after him? Have you no understanding?

66. Ah! You are those who fell to disputing (even) in matters of which you had some knowledge! But why dispute you in matters of which you have no knowledge? It is Allah Who knows, and you who know not!

67. Abraham was not a Jew nor yet a Christian; but he was true in faith, and bowed his will to Allah's, (which is Islam), and he joined not gods with Allah.

68. Without doubt, among men, the nearest relation to Abraham are those who follow him, as are also this prophet and those who believe; and Allah is the protector of those who have faith.

69. It is the wish of a section of the People of the Book to lead you astray. But they shall lead astray (not you), but themselves, and they do not perceive!

70. You People of the Book! Why reject you the signs of Allah, of which you are (yourselves) witnesses?

71. You People of the Book! Why do you clothe truth with falsehood, and conceal the truth, while you have knowledge?

72. A section of the People of the Book say: "Believe in the morning what is revealed to the believers, but reject it at the end of the day; perhaps they may (themselves) turn back;

73. "And believe no one unless he follows your religion." Say: "True guidance is the guidance of Allah; (fear you) lest a revelation be sent to someone (else) like that which was sent to you. Or that those (receiving such revelation) should engage you in argument before your Lord?" Say: "All bounties are in the Hand of Allah: He grants them to whom He pleases: and Allah cares for all, and He knows all things."

74. For His Mercy He specially chooses whom He pleases; for Allah is the Lord of bounties unbounded.

75. Among the People of the Book are some who, if entrusted with a hoard of gold, will (readily) pay it back; others who, if entrusted with a single silver coin, will not repay it unless

you constantly stood demanding, because they say, "There is no call on us (to keep faith) with these ignorant (pagans)." But they tell a lie against Allah and (well) they know it.

76. Nay - those that keep their promised faith and act aright - verily Allah loves those who act aright.

77. As for those who sell the faith they owe to Allah and their own promised word for a small price, they shall have no portion in the hereafter: nor will Allah (deign to) speak to them or look at them on the day of judgement, nor will He cleanse them (of sin): they shall have a grievous penalty.

78. There is among them a section who distort the book with their tongues: (as they read) you would think it is a part of the book, but it is no part of the book; and they say, "That is from Allah," but it is not from Allah: it is they who tell a lie against Allah, and (well) they know it!

79. It is not (possible) that a man, to whom is given the book and wisdom, and the prophetic office, should say to people: "Be you my worshippers rather than Allah's: on the contrary (he would say): "Be you worshippers of Him Who is truly the Cherisher of all: for you have taught the book and you have studied it earnestly."

80. Nor would he instruct you to take angels and prophets for Lords and patrons. What! Would he invite you to unbelief after you have bowed your will (to Allah in Islam)?

81. See! Allah took the covenant of the prophets, saying: "I give you a book and wisdom; then comes to you a messenger, confirming what is with you; do you believe in him and render him help?" Allah said: "Do you agree, and take this My covenant as binding on you?" They said: "We agree." He said: "Then bear witness, and I am with you among the witnesses."

82. If any turn back after this, they are perverted transgressors.

83. Do they seek for other than the religion of Allah? - While all creatures in the heavens and on earth have, willing or unwilling, bowed to His Will (accepted Islam), and to Him shall they all be brought back.

84. Say: "We believe in Allah, and in what has been revealed to us and what was revealed to Abraham, Ishmael; Isaac, Jacob, and the tribes, and in (the Books) given to Moses, Jesus, and the prophets, from their Lord: we make no distinction between one and another among them, and to Allah do we bow our will (in Islam)."

85. If anyone desires a religion other than Islam (submission to Allah), never will it be accepted of him; and in the hereafter he will be in the ranks of those who have lost (all spiritual good).

86. How shall Allah guide those who reject faith after they accepted it and bore witness that the messenger was true and that clear signs had come to them? But Allah guides not a people unjust.

87. Of such the reward is that on them (rests) the curse of Allah, of His angels, and of all mankind -

88. In that will they dwell; nor will their penalty be lightened, nor respite be their (lot);

89. Except for those that repent (even) after that, and make amends; for verily Allah is Oft-Forgiving, Most Merciful.

90. But those who reject faith after they accepted it, and then go on adding to their defiance of faith - never will their repentance be accepted; for they are those who have (of set purpose) gone astray.

91. As to those who reject faith, and die rejecting - never would be accepted from any such as much gold as the earth contains, though they should offer it for ransom. For such is (in store) a penalty grievous, and they will find no helpers.

92. By no means shall you attain righteousness unless you give (freely) of that which you love; and whatever you give, truly Allah knows it well.

93. All food was lawful to the Children of Israel, except what Israel made unlawful for itself, before the Law (of Moses) was revealed. Say: "Bring you the Law and study it, if you be men of truth."

94. If any, after this, invent a lie and attribute it to Allah, they are indeed unjust wrongdoers.

95. Say: "Allah speaks the truth: follow the religion of Abraham, the sane in faith; he was not of the pagans."

96. The first House (of worship) appointed for men was that at Bakkah; full of blessing and of guidance for all kinds of beings:

97. In it are signs manifest; (for example) the Station of Abraham; whoever enters it attains security; pilgrimage to it is a duty men owe to Allah - those who can afford the journey; but if any deny faith, Allah stands not in need of any of His creatures.

98. Say: "O People of the Book! Why reject you the signs of Allah, when Allah is Himself witness to all you do?"

99. Say: "O you People of the Book! Why obstruct you those who believe, from the path of Allah, seeking to make it crooked, while you were yourselves witnesses (to Allah's covenant)? But Allah is not unmindful of all that you do."

100. O you who believe! If you listen to a faction among the People of the Book, they would (indeed) render you apostates after you have believed!

101. And how would you deny faith while to you are rehearsed the signs of Allah, and among you lives the messenger? Whoever holds firmly to Allah will be shown a way that is straight.

102. O you who believe! Fear Allah as He should be feared, and die not except in a state of Islam.

103. And hold fast, all together by the rope which Allah (stretches out for you), and be not divided among yourselves; and remember with gratitude Allah's favour on you; for you were enemies and He joined your hearts in love, so that by His grace, you became brothers; and you were on the brink of the pit of fire, and He saved you from it. Thus

does Allah make His signs clear to you: that you may be guided.

104. Let there arise out of you a band of people inviting to all that is good, enjoining what is right, and forbidding what is wrong: they are the ones to attain felicity.

105. Be not like those who are divided amongst themselves and fall into disputations after receiving clear signs: for them is a dreadful penalty -

106. On the day when some faces will be (lit up with) white, and some faces will be (in the gloom of) black: to those whose faces will be black, (will be said): "Did you reject faith after accepting it? Taste then the penalty for rejecting faith."

107. But those whose faces will be (lit with) white - they will be in (the Light of) Allah's Mercy; in it to dwell (forever).

108. These are the signs of Allah: We rehearse them to you in truth; and Allah means no injustice to any of His creatures.

109. To Allah belongs all that is in the heavens and on earth; to Him do all questions go back (for decision).

110. You are the best of peoples, evolved for mankind, enjoining what is right, forbidding what is wrong, and believing in Allah. If only the People of the Book had faith, it were best for them: among them are some who have faith, but most of them are perverted transgressors.

111. They will do you no harm, barring a trifling annoyance; if they come out to fight you, they will show you their backs, and no help shall they get.

112. Shame is pitched over them (like a tent) wherever they are found, except when under a covenant (of protection) from Allah and from men; they draw on themselves wrath from Allah, and pitched over them is (the tent of) destitution. This because they rejected the signs of Allah, and slew the prophets in defiance of right; this because they rebelled and transgressed beyond bounds.

113. Not all of them are alike: of the People of the Book are a portion that stand (for the right); they rehearse the signs of Allah all night long, and they prostrate themselves in adoration.

114. They believe in Allah and the last day; they enjoin what is right, and forbid what is wrong; and they hasten (in emulation) in (all) good works: they are in the ranks of the righteous.

115. Of the good that they do, nothing will be rejected of them; for Allah knows well those that do right.

116. Those who reject faith - neither their possessions nor their (numerous) progeny will benefit them anything against Allah: they will be companions of the fire - dwelling in it (forever).

117. What they spend in the life of this (material) world may be likened to a wind which brings a nipping frost: it strikes and destroys the harvest of men who have wronged their own souls; it is not Allah that has wronged them, but they wrong themselves.

118. O you who believe! Take not into your intimacy those outside your ranks: they will not fail to corrupt you. They only desire your ruin: rank

hatred has already appeared from their mouths: what their hearts conceal is far worse. We have made plain to you the signs, if you have wisdom.

119. Ah! You are those who love them, but they love you not - though you believe in the whole of the book, when they meet you, they say, "We believe": but when they are alone, they bite off the very tips of their fingers at you in their rage. Say: "Perish in your rage; Allah knows well all the secrets of the heart."

120. If anything that is good befalls you, it grieves them; but if some misfortune overtakes you, they rejoice at it. But if you are constant and do right, not the least harm will their cunning do to you; for Allah encompasses round about all that they do.

121. Remember that morning you did leave the household (early) to post the faithful at their stations for battle; and Allah hears and knows all things:

122. Remember two of your parties meditated cowardice; but Allah was their protector, and in Allah should the faithful (ever) put their trust.

123. Allah had helped you at Badr, when you were a contemptible little force; then fear Allah; thus may you show your gratitude.

124. Remember you said to the faithful: "Is it not enough for you that Allah should help you with three thousand angels (specially) sent down?

125. "Yea - if you remain firm, and act aright, even if the enemy should rush here on you in hot haste, your Lord would help you with five thousand angels making a terrific onslaught."

126. Allah made it but a message of hope for you, and an assurance to your hearts: (in any case) there is no help except from Allah, the Exalted, the Wise.

127. That He might cut off a fringe of the unbelievers or expose them to infamy, and they should then be turned back, frustrated of their purpose.

128. Not for you (but for Allah), is the decision: whether He turn in mercy to them, or punish them; for they are indeed wrongdoers.

129. To Allah belongs all that is in the heavens and on earth. He forgives whom He pleases and punishes whom He pleases; but Allah is Oft-Forgiving, Most Merciful.

130. O you who believe! Devour not usury, doubled and multiplied; but fear Allah; that you may (really) prosper.

131. Fear the fire, which is prepared for those who reject faith;

132. And obey Allah and the messenger; that you may obtain mercy.

133. Be quick in the race for forgiveness from your Lord, and for a garden whose width is that (of the whole) of the heavens and of the earth, prepared for the righteous -

134. Those who spend (freely), whether in prosperity, or in adversity; who restrain anger, and pardon (all) men - for Allah loves those who do good -

135. And those who, having done something to be ashamed of, or wronged their own souls, earnestly bring Allah to mind, and ask for forgiveness for their sins - and who can forgive sins except Allah? - And are

never obstinate in persisting knowingly in (the wrong) they have done.

136. For such the reward is forgiveness from their Lord, and gardens with rivers flowing underneath - an eternal dwelling: how excellent a recompense for those who work (and strive)!

137. Many were the ways of life that have passed away before you: travel through the earth, and see what was the end of those who rejected truth.

138. Here is a plain statement to men, a guidance and instruction to those who fear Allah!

139. So lose not heart, nor fall into despair: for you must gain mastery if you are true in faith.

140. If a wound has touched you, be sure a similar wound has touched the others. Such days (of varying fortunes) We give to men and men by turns: that Allah may know those that believe, and that He may take to Himself from your ranks martyr-witnesses (to truth). And Allah loves not those that do wrong.

141. Allah's object also is to purge those that are true in faith and to deprive of blessing those that resist faith.

142. Did you think that you would enter heaven without Allah testing those of you who fought hard (in His cause) and remained steadfast?

143. You did indeed wish for death before you met it: now you have seen it with your own eyes, (and you flinch!)

144. Muhammad is no more than a messenger: many were the messengers that passed away before him. If he died or were slain, will you then turn back on your heels? If any did turn back on his heels, not the least harm will he do to Allah; but Allah (on the other hand) will swiftly reward those who (serve Him) with gratitude.

145. Nor can a soul die except by Allah's permission, the term being fixed as by writing. If any do desire a reward in this life, We shall give it to him; and if any do desire a reward in the hereafter, We shall give it to him. And swiftly shall We reward those that (serve Us with) gratitude.

146. How many of the prophets fought (in Allah's way), and with them (fought) large bands of godly men? But they never lost heart if they met with disaster in Allah's way, nor did they weaken (in will) nor give in. And Allah loves those who are firm and steadfast.

147. All that they said was: "Our Lord! Forgive us our sins and anything we may have done that transgressed our duty: establish our feet firmly, and help us against those that resist faith."

148. And Allah gave them a reward in this world, and the excellent reward of the hereafter. For Allah loves those who do good.

149. O you who believe! If you obey the unbelievers, they will drive you back on your heels, and you will turn back (from faith) to your own loss.

150. Nay, Allah is your protector, and He is the best of helpers.

151. Soon shall We cast terror into the hearts of the unbelievers, for that they joined companions with Allah, for which He had sent no authority; their abode will be the fire; and evil is the home of the wrongdoers!

152. Allah did indeed fulfil His promise to you when you, with His permission, were about to annihilate your enemy - until you flinched and fell to disputing about the order, and disobeyed it after He brought you in sight (of the booty) which you covet. Among you are some that hanker after this world and some that desire the hereafter. Then did He divert you from your foes in order to test you. But He forgave you: for Allah is full of grace to those who believe.

153. See! You were climbing up the high ground, without even casting a side glance at anyone, and the messenger in your rear was calling you back. There did Allah give you one distress after another by way of requital, to teach you not to grieve for (the booty) that had escaped you and for (the ill) that had befallen you. For Allah is well aware of all that you do.

154. After (the excitement) of the distress He sent down calm on a band of you overcome with slumber, while another band was stirred to anxiety by their own feelings, moved by wrong suspicions of Allah - suspicions due to ignorance. They said: "What affair is this of ours?" Say you: "Indeed, this affair is wholly Allah's." They hide in their minds what they dare not reveal to you. They say (to themselves): "If we had had anything to do with this affair, we should not have been in the slaughter here." Say: "Even if you had remained in your homes, those for whom death was decreed would certainly have gone out to the place of their death"; but (all this was) that Allah might test what is in your breasts and purge what is in your hearts. For Allah knows well the secrets of your hearts.

155. Those of you who turned back on the day the two hosts met - it was Satan who caused them to fail, because of some (evil) they had done. But Allah has blotted out (their fault): for Allah is Oft-Forgiving, Most Forbearing.

156. O you who believe! Be not like the unbelievers, who say of their brothers, when they are travelling through the earth or engaged in fighting: "If they had stayed with us, they would not have died or been slain." This that Allah may make it a cause of sighs and regrets in their hearts. It is Allah that gives life and death, and Allah sees well all that you do.

157. And if you are slain, or die, in the way of Allah, forgiveness and mercy from Allah are far better than all they could amass.

158. And if you die, or are slain, it is to Allah that you are brought together.

159. It is part of the mercy of Allah that you do deal gently with them. Were you severe or harsh-hearted they would have broken away from you; so pass over (their faults) and ask for (Allah's) forgiveness for them; and consult them in affairs (of moment). Then when you have taken a decision, put your trust in Allah. For Allah loves those who put their trust (in Him).

160. If Allah helps you, none can overcome you: if He forsakes you, who

is there, after that, that can help you? In Allah then, let believers put their trust.

161. No prophet could (ever) be false to his trust. If any person is so false, He shall, on the day of judgement, restore what he misappropriated; then shall every soul receive its due, whatever it earned - and none shall be dealt with unjustly.

162. Is the man who follows the good pleasure of Allah like the man who draws on himself the wrath of Allah, and whose abode is in hell? A woeful refuge!

163. They are in varying grades in the sight of Allah; and Allah sees well all that they do.

164. Allah did confer a great favour on the believers when He sent among them a messenger from among themselves, rehearsing to them the signs of Allah, sanctifying them, and instructing them in Scripture and wisdom, while before that they had been in manifest error.

165. What! When a single disaster strikes you, although you struck (your enemies) with one twice as great, do you say? - " From where is this?" Say (to them): "It is from yourselves: for Allah has power over all things."

166. What you suffered on the day the two armies met, was with the permission of Allah, in order that He might test the believers.

167. And the hypocrites also. These were told: "Come, fight in the way of Allah, or (at least) drive (the foe from your city)." They say: "had we known there would be a fight, we should certainly have followed you. They were that day nearer to unbelief than to Faith, saying with their lips what was not in their hearts. But Allah has full knowledge of all they conceal.

168. (They are) the ones that say, (of their brothers slain), while they themselves sit (at ease): "If only they had listened to us, they would not have been slain." Say: "Avert death from your own selves, if you speak the truth."

169. Think not of those who are slain in Allah's way as dead. Nay, they live, finding their sustenance in the presence of their Lord.

170. They rejoice in the bounty provided by Allah: and with regard to those left behind, who have not yet joined them (in their bliss), the (martyrs) glory in the fact that on them is no fear, nor have they (cause to) grieve.

171. They glory in the grace and the bounty from Allah, and in the fact that Allah suffers not the reward of the faithful to be lost (in the least).

172. Of those who answered the call of Allah and the messenger, even after being wounded, those who do right and refrain from wrong have a great reward -

173. Men said to them: "A great army is gathering against you, so fear them": but it (only) increased their faith. They said: "For us Allah suffices and He is the best disposer of affairs."

174. And they returned with grace and bounty from Allah: no harm ever touched them; for they followed the good pleasure of Allah: and Allah is the Lord of bounties unbounded.

175. It is only the evil one that suggests to you the fear of his supporters: be you not afraid of them, but fear Me, if you have faith.

176. Let not those grieve you who rush headlong into unbelief: not the least harm will they do to Allah: Allah's plan is that He will give them no portion in the hereafter, but a severe punishment.

177. Those who purchase unbelief at the price of faith - not the least harm will they do to Allah, but they will have a grievous punishment.

178. Let not the unbelievers think that Our respite to them is good for themselves: We grant them respite that they may grow in their iniquity: but they will have a shameful punishment.

179. Allah will not leave the believers in the state in which you are now, until He separates what is evil from what is good. Nor will Allah disclose to you the secrets of the unseen. But He chooses of His messengers (for the purpose) whom He pleases. So believe in Allah and His messengers: and if you believe and do right, you have a reward without measure.

180. And let not those who covetously withhold of the gifts which Allah has given them of His grace, think that it is good for them: nay, it will be the worse for them: soon shall the things which they covetously withheld be tied to their necks like a twisted collar, on the day of judgement. To Allah belongs the heritage of the heavens and the earth; and Allah is well acquainted with all that you do.

181. Allah has heard the taunt of those who say: "Truly Allah is needy and we are rich!" - We shall certainly record their word and (their act) of slaying the prophets in defiance of right, and We shall say: "Taste you the penalty of the scorching fire!

182. "This is because of the (unrighteous deeds) which your hands sent on before you: for Allah never harms those who serve Him."

183. They (also) said: "Allah took our promise not to believe in a messenger unless He showed us a sacrifice consumed by fire (from heaven)." Say: "There came to you messengers before me with clear signs and even with what you ask for: why then did you slay them, if you speak the truth?"

184. Then if they reject you, so were rejected messengers before you, who came with clear signs, scriptures and the book of enlightenment.

185. Every soul shall have a taste of death: and only on the day of judgement shall you be paid your full recompense. Only he who is saved far from the fire and admitted to the garden will have attained the object (of life): for the life of this world is but goods and chattels of deception.

186. You shall certainly be tried and tested in your possessions and in your personal selves; and you shall certainly hear much that will grieve you from those who received the book before you and from those who worship many gods. But if you persevere patiently, and guard against evil - then that will be a determining factor in all affairs.

187. And remember Allah took a covenant from the People of the Book to make it known and clear to mankind, and not to hide it; but they threw it away behind their backs, and purchased with it some miserable gain! And vile was the bargain they made!

188. Think not that those who exult in what they have brought about, and love to be praised for what they have not done - think not that they can escape the penalty. For them is a penalty grievous indeed.

189. To Allah belongs the dominion of the heavens and the earth; and Allah has power over all things.

190. See! In the creation of the heavens and the earth and the alternation of night and day - there are indeed signs for men of understanding -

191. Men who celebrate the praises of Allah, standing, sitting, and lying down on their sides, and contemplate the (wonders of) creation in the heavens and the earth, (with the thought): "Our Lord! Not for nothing have You created (all) this! Glory to You! Give us salvation from the penalty of the fire."

192. "Our Lord! Any whom You do admit to the fire, truly You cover with shame, and never will wrongdoers find any helpers!"

193. "Our Lord! We have heard the call of one calling (us) to faith, 'Believe you in the Lord', and we have believed. Our Lord! Forgive us our sins, blot out from us our iniquities, and take to Yourself our souls in the company of the righteous."

194. "Our Lord! Grant us what You did promise to us through Your messengers and save us from shame on the day of judgement: for You never break Your promise."

195. And their Lord has accepted of them, and answered them: "Never will I suffer to be lost the work of any of you, be he male or female: you are members, one of another; those who have left their homes or been driven out from it, and suffered harm in My cause or fought or been slain - verily I will blot out from them their iniquities, and admit them into gardens with rivers flowing beneath - a reward from the presence of Allah and from His presence is the best of rewards."

196. Let not the strutting about of the unbelievers through the land deceive you:

197. Little is it for enjoyment; their ultimate abode is hell: what an evil bed (to lie on)!

198. On the other hand, for those who fear their Lord, are gardens, with rivers flowing beneath, in it are they to dwell (for ever) - a gift from the presence of Allah and that which is in the presence of Allah is the best (bliss) for the righteous.

199. And there are, certainly, among the People of the Book, those who believe in Allah, in the revelation to you, and in the revelation to them, bowing in humility to Allah: they will not sell the signs of Allah for a miserable gain! For them is a reward with their Lord, and Allah is swift in account.

200. O you who believe! Persevere in patience and constancy: vie in such perseverance; strengthen each other; and fear Allah; that you may prosper.

Surah 4: *An-Nisa*
(The Women)

In the name of Allah, Most Gracious, Most Merciful.

1. O mankind! Reverence your Guardian-Lord, Who created you from a single person, created of like nature, his mate and from them both scattered (like seeds) countless men and women - Fear Allah through Whom you demand your mutual (rights), and (respect) the wombs (that bore you): for Allah ever watches over you.

2. To orphans restore their property (when they reach their age), nor substitute (your) worthless things for (their) good ones; and devour not their substance (by mixing it up) with your own. For this is indeed a great sin.

3. If you fear that you shall not be able to deal justly with the orphans, marry women of your choice, two or three or four; but if you fear that you shall not be able to deal justly (with them) then only one, or (a captive) that your right hands possess. That will be more suitable, to prevent you from doing injustice.

4. And give the women (on marriage) their dower as a free gift; but if they, of their own good pleasure, remit any part of it to you, take it and enjoy it with right good cheer.

5. To those weak of understanding make not over your property, which Allah has made a means of support for you, but feed and clothe them with it, and speak to them words of kindness and justice.

6. Make trial of orphans until they reach the age of marriage; if then you find sound judgement in them release their property to them; but consume it not wastefully nor in haste against their growing up. If the guardian is well-off, let him claim no remuneration, but if he is poor, let him have for himself what is just and reasonable. When you release their property to them, take witnesses in their presence: but all-sufficient is Allah in taking account.

7. From what is left by parents and those nearest related there is a share for men and a share for women, whether the property be small or large - a determinate share.

8. But if at the time of division other relatives, or orphans, or poor are present, feed them out of the (property) and speak to them words of kindness and justice.

9. Let those (disposing of an estate) have the same fear in their minds as they would have for their own if they had left a helpless family behind: let them fear Allah and speak words of appropriate (comfort).

10. Those who unjustly eat up the property of orphans, eat up a fire into their own bodies: they will soon be enduring a blazing fire!

11. Allah (thus) directs you as regards your children's (inheritance): to the male, a portion equal to that of two females: if only daughters, two or more, their share is two-thirds of the inheritance; if only one, her share is a half. For parents, a sixth share of the inheritance to each, if the deceased left children; if no children and the parents are the (only) heirs, the mother has a third; if the deceased left brothers (or sisters) the mother has a sixth. (The distribution in all cases is) after the payment of legacies and debts. You know not whether your parents or your children are nearest to you in benefit. These are settled portions ordained by Allah and Allah is All-Knowing, All-Wise.

12. In what your wives leave, your share is a half, if they leave no child; but if they leave a child you get a fourth; after payment of legacies and debts. In what you leave their share is a fourth if you leave no child; but if you leave a child they get an eighth; after payment of legacies and debts. If the man or woman whose inheritance is in question has left neither ascendants nor descendants, but has left a brother or a sister, each one of the two gets a sixth; but if more than two, they share in a third; after payment of legacies and debts; so that no loss is caused (to anyone). Thus is it ordained by Allah, and Allah is All-Knowing, Most Forbearing.

13. Those are limits set by Allah: those who obey Allah and His messenger will be admitted to gardens with rivers flowing beneath, to remain in it (forever) and that will be the supreme achievement.

14. But those who disobey Allah and His messenger and transgress His limits will be admitted to a fire to remain in it: and they shall have a humiliating punishment.

15. If any of your women are guilty of lewdness, take the evidence of four (reliable) witnesses from amongst you against them; and if they testify, confine them to houses until death do claim them, or Allah ordain for them some (other) way.

16. If two men among you are guilty of lewdness, punish them both. If they repent and amend, leave them alone; for Allah is Oft-Returning, Most Merciful.

17. Allah accepts the repentance of those who do evil in ignorance and repent soon afterwards; to them will Allah turn in mercy; for Allah is full of knowledge and wisdom.

18. Of no effect is the repentance of those who continue to do evil, until death faces one of them, and he says "Now have I repented indeed"; nor of those who die rejecting faith: for them have We prepared a punishment most grievous.

19. O you who believe! You are forbidden to inherit women against their will. Nor should you treat them with harshness, that you may take away part of the dower you have given them, except where they have been guilty of open lewdness; on the contrary live with them on a footing of kindness and equity. If you take a dislike to them it may be that you dislike a thing and Allah brings about through it a great deal of good.

20. But if you decide to take one wife in place of another, even if you had given the latter a whole treasure for dower, take not the least bit of it back: would you take it by slander and a manifest wrong?

21. And how could you take it when you have gone in to each other, and they have taken from you a solemn covenant?

22. And marry not women whom your fathers married - except what is past - it was shameful and odious, an abominable custom indeed.

23. Prohibited to you (for marriage) are: your mothers, daughters, sisters; father's sisters, mother's sisters; brother's daughters, sister's daughters; foster-mothers (who suckled you), foster-sisters; your wives' mothers; your step-daughters under your guardianship, born of your wives to whom you have gone in, no prohibition if you have not gone in; (those who have been) wives of your sons proceeding from your loins; and two sisters in wedlock at one and the same time, except for what is past; for Allah is Oft-Forgiving, Most Merciful.

24. Also (prohibited are) women already married, except those whom your right hands possess; thus has Allah ordained (prohibitions) against you: except for these, all others are lawful, provided you seek (them in marriage) with gifts from your property - desiring chastity, not lust. Seeing that you derive benefit from them, give them their dowers (at least) as prescribed; but if, after a dower is prescribed, you agree mutually (to vary it) there is no blame on you and Allah is All-Knowing, All-Wise.

25. If any of you have not the means with which to wed free believing women, they may wed believing girls from among those whom your right hands possess: and Allah has full knowledge about your faith. You are one from another: wed them with the permission of their owners, and give them their dowers, according to what is reasonable: they should be chaste, not lustful, nor taking illicit lovers; when they are taken in wedlock, if they fall into shame, their punishment is half that for free women. This (permission) is for those among you who fear sin; but it is better for you that you practice self-restraint: and Allah is Oft-Forgiving, Most Merciful.

26. Allah does wish to make clear to you and to show you the ordinances of those before you; and (He does wish to) turn to you (in mercy): and Allah is All-Knowing, All-Wise.

27. Allah does wish to turn to you, but the wish of those who follow their lusts is that you should turn away (from Him) - far, far away.

28. Allah does wish to lighten your (difficulties): for man was created weak (in flesh).

29. O you who believe! Eat not up your property among yourselves in vanities; but let there be amongst you traffic and trade by mutual good will; nor kill (or destroy) yourselves; for verily Allah has been to you Most Merciful!

30. If any do that in rancour and injustice - soon shall We cast them into the fire; and easy it is for Allah.

31. If you (but) eschew the most heinous of the things which you are forbidden to do, We shall expel out of you all the evil in you, and admit you to a gate of great honour.

32. And in no way covet those things in which Allah has bestowed His gifts more freely on some of you than on others; to men is allotted what they earn, and to women what they earn; but ask Allah of His bounty: for Allah has full knowledge of all things.

33. To (benefit) every one, We have appointed sharers and heirs to property left by parents and relatives. To those, also, to whom your right hand was pledged, give their due portion: for truly Allah is witness to all things.

34. Men are the protectors and maintainers of women, because Allah has given the one more (strength) than the other, and because they support them from their means. Therefore, the righteous women are devoutly obedient, and guard in (the husband's) absence what Allah would have them guard. As to those women on whose part you fear disloyalty and ill-conduct, admonish them (first), (next), refuse to share their beds, (and last) beat them (lightly); but if they return to obedience, seek not against them means (of annoyance): for Allah is Most High, Great (above you all).

35. If you fear a breach between them both, appoint (two) arbiters, one from his family, and the other from hers; if they wish for peace, Allah will cause their reconciliation: for Allah has full knowledge, and is acquainted with all things.

36. Serve Allah, and join not any partners with Him; and do good -

to parents, relatives, orphans, those in need, neighbours who are near, neighbours who are strangers, the companion by your side, the wayfarer (you meet), and what your right hands possess: for Allah loves not the arrogant, the vainglorious -

37. (Nor) those who are niggardly, or enjoin niggardliness on others, or hide the bounties which Allah has bestowed on them; for We have prepared, for those who resist faith, a punishment that steeps them in contempt -

38. Nor those who spend of their substance, to be seen of men, but have no faith in Allah and the last day: if any take the evil one for their intimate, what a dreadful intimate he is!

39. And what burden were it on them if they had faith in Allah and in the last day, and they spent out of what Allah has given them for sustenance? For Allah has full knowledge of them.

40. Allah is never unjust in the least degree: if there is any good (done), He doubles it, and gives from His own presence a great reward.

41. How then if We brought from each people a witness, and We brought you as a witness against these people!

42. On that day those who reject faith and disobey the messenger will wish that the earth were made one with them; but never will they hide a single fact from Allah!

43. O you who believe! Approach not prayers with a mind befogged, until you can understand all that you say - nor in a state of ceremonial impurity (except when travelling on the road), until after washing your whole body. If you are ill, or on a journey, or one of you comes from offices of nature, or you have been in contact with women, and you find no water, then take for yourselves clean sand or earth, and rub with it your faces and hands. For Allah does blot out sins and forgive again and again.

44. (O Muhammad!) Have you not turned your vision to those who were given a portion of the book? They traffic in error, and wish that you should lose the right path.

45. But Allah has full knowledge of your enemies: Allah is enough for a protector, and Allah is enough for a helper.

46. Of the Jews there are those who displace words from their (right) places, and say: "We hear and we disobey"; and "Hear, may you not hear"; and *"Ra'ina,"* with a twist of their tongues and a slander to faith. If only they had said: "We hear and we obey"; and "Do hear"; and "Do look at us"; it would have been better for them, and more proper; but Allah has cursed them for their unbelief; and but few of them will believe.

47. O you People of the Book! Believe in what We have (now) revealed, confirming what was (already) with you, before We change the face and fame of some (of you) beyond all recognition, and turn them hindwards, or curse them as We cursed the Sabbath-breakers, for the decision of Allah must be carried out.

48. Allah forgives not that partners should be set up with Him; but He forgives anything else, to whom He pleases; to set up partners with Allah is to devise a sin most heinous indeed.

49. Have you not turned your vision to those who claim sanctity for themselves? Nay - but Allah does sanctify whom He pleases. But never will they fail to receive justice in the least little thing.

50. See! How they invent a lie against Allah! But that by itself is a manifest sin!

51. Have you not turned your vision to those who were given a portion of the book? They believe in sorcery and evil, and say to the unbelievers that they are better guided in the (right) way than the believers!

52. They are (men) whom Allah has cursed: and those whom Allah has cursed, you will find, have no one to help.

53. Have they a share in dominion or power? See, they give not a farthing to their fellow-men?

54. Or do they envy mankind for what Allah has given them of His bounty? But We had already given the people of Abraham the book and wisdom, and conferred upon them a great kingdom.

55. Some of them believed, and some of them averted their faces from him; and enough is hell for a burning fire.

56. Those who reject Our signs, We shall soon cast into the fire; as often as their skins are roasted through, We shall change them for fresh skins, that they may taste the penalty; for Allah is Exalted in Power, Wise.

57. But those who believe and do deeds of righteousness, We shall soon admit to gardens, with rivers flowing beneath - their eternal home; in it shall they have companions pure and holy; We shall admit them to shades, cool and ever deepening.

58. Allah does command you to render back your trusts to those to whom they are due; and when you judge between man and man, that you judge with justice; verily how excellent is the teaching which He gives you! For Allah is He Who hears and sees all things.

59. O you who believe! Obey Allah, and obey the messenger, and those charged with authority among you. If you differ in anything among yourselves, refer it to Allah and His messenger, if you do believe in Allah and the last day; that is best, and most suitable for final determination.

60. Have you not turned your vision to those who declare that they believe in the revelations that have come to you and to those before you? Their (real) wish is to resort together for judgement (in their disputes) to the evil one, though they were ordered to reject him. But Satan's wish is to lead them astray, far away (from the right).

61. When it is said to them: "Come to what Allah has revealed, and to the messenger"; you see the hypocrites avert their faces from you in disgust.

62. How then, when they are seized by misfortune, because of the deeds which their hands have sent forward?

Then they come to you, swearing by Allah: "We meant no more than goodwill and conciliation!"

63. Those men - Allah knows what is in their hearts; so keep clear of them, but admonish them, and speak to them a word to reach their very souls.

64. We sent not a messenger, but to be obeyed, in accordance with the will of Allah. If they had only, when they were unjust to themselves, come to you and asked Allah's forgiveness, and the messenger had asked forgiveness for them, they would have found Allah indeed Oft-Returning, Most Merciful.

65. But no, by your Lord, they can have no (real) faith, until they make you judge in all disputes between them, and find in their souls no resistance against your decisions, but accept them with the fullest conviction.

66. If We had ordered them to sacrifice their lives or to leave their homes, very few of them would have done it; but if they had done what they were (actually) told, it would have been best for them, and would have gone farthest to strengthen their (faith).

67. And We should then have given them from Our presence a great reward;

68. And We should have shown them the straight way.

69. All who obey Allah and the messenger are in the company of those on whom is the grace of Allah - of the prophets (who teach), the sincere (lovers of truth), the witnesses (who testify), and the righteous (who do good): Ah! What a beautiful fellowship!

70. Such is the bounty from Allah: and sufficient is it that Allah knows all.

71. O you who believe! Take your precautions, and either go out in parties or go out all together.

72. There are certainly among you men who would stay behind; if a misfortune befalls you, they say: "Allah did favour us in that we were not present among them."

73. But if good fortune comes to you from Allah, they would be sure to say - as if there had never been ties of affection between you and them - "Oh! I wish I had been with them; a fine thing should I then have made of it!"

74. Let those fight in the cause of Allah who sell the life of this world for the hereafter. To him who fights in the cause of Allah - whether he is slain or gets victory - soon shall We give him a reward of great (value).

75. And why should you not fight in the cause of Allah and of those who, being weak, are ill-treated (and oppressed)? - Men, women, and children, whose call is: "Our Lord! Rescue us from this town, whose people are oppressors; and raise for us from You one who will protect; and raise for us from You one who will help!"

76. Those who believe fight in the cause of Allah, and those who reject faith fight in the cause of evil: so fight you against the friends of Satan: feeble indeed is the cunning of Satan.

77. Have you not turned your vision to those who were told to hold back their hands (from fight) but establish regular prayers and spend in regular charity? When (at length) the order for fighting was issued to them, behold! A section of them feared men as - or even more than - they should have feared Allah: they say: "Our Lord! Why have You ordered us to fight? Would You not grant us respite to our (natural) term, near (enough)?" Say: "Short is the enjoyment of this world: the hereafter is the best for those who do right; never will you be dealt with unjustly in the very least!"

78. "Wherever you are, death will find you out, even if you are in towers built up strong and high!" If some good befalls them, they say, "This is from Allah"; but if evil, they say, "this is from you" (O Prophet). Say: "All things are from Allah." But what has come to these people, that they fail to understand a single fact?

79. Whatever good, (O man!) happens to you, is from Allah; but whatever evil happens to you, is from your (own) soul. And We have sent you as a messenger to (instruct) mankind. And enough is Allah for a witness.

80. He who obeys the messenger, obeys Allah: but if any turn away, We have not sent you to watch over their (evil deeds).

81. They have "obedience" on their lips; but when they leave you, a section of them meditate all night on things very different from what you tell them. But Allah records their nightly (plots): so keep clear of them and put your trust in Allah, and enough is Allah as a disposer of affairs.

82. Do they not consider the Qur'an (with care)? Had it been from other than Allah, they would surely have found in it much discrepancy.

83. When there comes to them some matter touching (public) safety or fear, they divulge it. If they had only referred it to the messenger or to those charged with authority among them, the proper investigators would have tested it from them (direct). Were it not for the grace and mercy of Allah to you, all but a few of you would have followed Satan.

84. Then fight in Allah's cause - you are held responsible only for yourself - and rouse the believers. It may be that Allah will restrain the fury of the unbelievers: for Allah is the strongest in might and in punishment.

85. Whoever recommends and helps a good cause becomes a partner in it; and whoever recommends and helps an evil cause, shares in its burden; and Allah has power over all things.

86. When a (courteous) greeting is offered you, meet it with a greeting still more courteous, (at least) of equal courtesy. Allah takes careful account of all things.

87. Allah! There is no god but He; certainly He will gather you together against the day of judgement, about which there is no doubt. And whose word can be truer than Allah's?

88. Why should you be divided into two parties about the hypocrites? Allah has upset them for their (evil) deeds. Would you guide those whom Allah has thrown out of the way? For those whom Allah has thrown out of the way, never shall you find the way.

89. They but wish that you should reject faith, as they do, and thus be on the same footing (as they); but take not friends from their ranks until they flee in the way of Allah (from what is forbidden). But if they turn renegades, seize them and slay them wherever you find them; And (in any case) take no friends or helpers from their ranks -

90. Except those who join a group between whom and you there is a treaty (of peace), or those who approach you with hearts restraining them from fighting you as well as fighting their own people. If Allah had pleased, He could have given them power over you, and they would have fought you; therefore if they withdraw from you but fight you not and (instead) send you (guarantees of) peace, then Allah has opened no way for you (to war against them).

91. Others you will find that wish to gain your confidence as well as that of their people; every time they are sent back to temptation, they succumb to it; if they withdraw not from you nor give you (guarantees) of peace besides restraining their hands, seize them and slay them wherever you get them; in their case We have provided you with a clear argument against them.

92. Never should a believer kill a believer; but (if it so happens) by mistake, (compensation is due); if one (so) kills a believer, it is ordained that he should free a believing slave and pay compensation to the deceased's family, unless they remit it freely. If the deceased belonged to a people at war with you, and he was a believer, the freeing of a believing slave (is enough). If he belonged to a people with whom you have a treaty of mutual alliance, compensation should be paid to his family, and a believing slave be freed. For those who find this beyond their means, (is prescribed) a fast for two months running: by way of repentance to Allah: for Allah has all knowledge and all wisdom.

93. If a man kills a believer intentionally, his recompense is hell, to remain in it (for ever); and the wrath and the curse of Allah are upon him, and a dreadful penalty is prepared for him.

94. O you who believe! When you go abroad in the cause of Allah, investigate carefully, and say not to anyone who offers you a salutation: "You are not a believer!" coveting the perishable goods of this life; with Allah are profits and spoils abundant. Even thus were you yourselves before, till Allah conferred on you His favours; therefore carefully investigate. For Allah is well aware of all that you do.

95. Not equal are those believers who sit (at home) and receive no hurt, and those who strive and fight in the cause of Allah with their goods and their persons. Allah has granted a grade higher to those who strive and fight with their goods and persons than to those who sit (at home). To all (in faith) has Allah promised good: but those who strive and fight has He distinguished above those who sit (at home) by a special reward -

96. Ranks specially bestowed by Him and forgiveness and mercy, for Allah is Oft-Forgiving, Most Merciful.

97. When angels take the souls of those who die in sin against their souls, they say: "In what (plight) were you?" They reply: "Weak and oppressed were we in the earth." They say: "Was not the earth of Allah spacious enough for you to move yourselves away (from evil)?" Such men will find their abode in hell - what an evil refuge! -

98. Except those who are (really) weak and oppressed - men, women and children who have no means in their power, nor (a guide-post) to direct their way.

99. For these, there is hope that Allah will forgive: for Allah does blot out (sins) and forgive again and again.

100. He who forsakes his home in the cause of Allah, finds in the earth many a refuge, wide and spacious; should he die as a refugee from home for Allah and His messenger, his reward becomes due and sure with Allah; and Allah is Oft-Forgiving, Most Merciful.

101. When you travel through the earth, there is no blame on you if you shorten your prayers, for fear the unbelievers may attack you: for the unbelievers are to you open enemies.

102. When you (O messenger) are with them, and stand to lead them in prayer, let one party of them stand up (in prayer) with you, taking their arms with them; when they finish their prostrations, let them take

their positions in the rear. And let the other party come up which has not yet prayed - and let them pray with you, taking all precautions, and bearing arms; the unbelievers wish, if you were negligent of your arms and your baggage, to assault you in a single rush. But there is no blame on you if you put away your arms because of the inconvenience of rain or because you are ill; but take (every) precaution for yourselves. For the unbelievers Allah has prepared a humiliating punishment.

103. When you pass (congregational) prayers, celebrate Allah's praises, standing, sitting down, or lying down on your sides; but when you are free from danger, set up regular prayers; for such prayers are enjoined on believers at stated times.

104. And slacken not in following up the enemy; if you are suffering hardships, they are suffering similar hardships; but you have hope from Allah, while they have none. And Allah is full of knowledge and wisdom.

105. We have sent down to you the book in truth, that you might judge between men, as guided by Allah: so be not (used) as an advocate by those who betray their trust;

106. But seek the forgiveness of Allah; for Allah is Oft-Forgiving, Most Merciful.

107. Contend not on behalf of such as betray their own souls: for Allah loves not one given to perfidy and crime;

108. They may hide (their crimes) from men, but they cannot hide (them) from Allah, seeing that He is in their midst when they plot by night, in words that He cannot approve; and Allah does encompass all that they do.

109. Ah! These are the sort of men on whose behalf you may contend in this world; but who will contend with Allah on their behalf on the day of judgement, or who will carry their affairs through?

110. If anyone does evil or wrongs his own soul but afterwards seeks Allah's forgiveness, he will find Allah Oft-Forgiving, Most Merciful.

111. And if anyone earns sin, he earns it against his own soul: for Allah is full of knowledge and wisdom.

112. But if anyone earns a fault or a sin and throws it on to one that is innocent, he carries (on himself) (both) a falsehood and a flagrant sin.

113. But for the grace of Allah to you and His mercy, a party of them would certainly have plotted to lead you astray. But (in fact) they will only lead their own souls astray, and to you they can do no harm in the least. For Allah has sent down to you the book and wisdom and taught you what you knew not (before); and great is the grace of Allah to you.

114. In most of their secret talks there is no good: but if one exhorts to a deed of charity or justice or conciliation between men, (secrecy is permissible): to him who does this, seeking the good pleasure of Allah, We shall soon give a reward of the highest (value).

115. If anyone contends with the messenger even after guidance has been plainly conveyed to him, and follows a path other than that becoming to men of faith, We shall leave him in the path he has chosen, and land him in hell - what an evil refuge!

116. Allah forgives not (the sin of) joining other gods with Him; but He forgives whom He pleases, other sins than this; one who joins other gods with Allah, has strayed far, far away (from the right).

117. (The pagans), leaving Him, call but upon female deities; they call but upon Satan the persistent rebel!

118. Allah did curse him, but he said: "I will take of Your servants a portion marked off;

119. I will mislead them, and I will create in them false desires; I will order them to slit the ears of cattle, and to deface the (fair) nature created by Allah." Whoever, forsaking Allah, takes Satan for a friend, has of a surety suffered a loss that is manifest.

120. Satan makes them promises, and creates in them false desires; but Satan's promises are nothing but deception.

121. They (his dupes) will have their dwelling in hell, and from it they will find no way of escape.

122. But those who believe and do deeds of righteousness - We shall soon admit them to gardens, with rivers flowing beneath to dwell in it, for ever. Allah's promise is the truth, and whose word can be truer than Allah's?

123. Not your desires, nor those of the People of the Book (can prevail): whoever works evil, will be requited accordingly. Nor will he find, besides Allah, any protector or helper.

124. If any do deeds of righteousness - be they male or female - and have faith, they will enter heaven, and not the least injustice will be done to them.

125. Who can be better in religion than one who submits his whole self to Allah, does good, and follows the way of Abraham the true in faith? For Allah did take Abraham for a friend.

126. But to Allah belong all things in the heavens and on earth; and He it is that encompasses all things.

127. They ask your instruction concerning the women. Say: Allah does instruct you about them; and (remember) what has been rehearsed to you in the book, concerning the orphans of women to whom you give not the portions prescribed, and yet whom you desire to marry, as also concerning the children who are weak and oppressed; that you stand firm for justice to orphans. There is not a good deed which you do, but Allah is well-acquainted with it.

128. If a wife fears cruelty or desertion on her husband's part, there is no blame on them if they arrange an amicable settlement between themselves; and such settlement is best; even though men's souls are swayed by greed. But if you do good and practice self-restraint, Allah is well-acquainted with all that you do.

129. You are never able to be fair and just as between women, even if it is your ardent desire; but turn not away (from a woman) altogether, so as to leave her (as it were) hanging (in the air). If you come to a friendly understanding, and

practice self-restraint, Allah is Oft-Forgiving, Most Merciful.

130. But if they disagree (and must part), Allah will provide abundance for all from His all-reaching bounty: for Allah is He that cares for all and is Wise.

131. To Allah belong all things in the heavens and on earth. Verily We have directed the People of the Book before you, and you (O Muslims) to fear Allah. But if you deny Him, to Allah belong all things in the heavens and on earth, and Allah is free of all wants, worthy of all praise.

132. Yea, to Allah belong all things in the heavens and on earth, and enough is Allah to carry through all affairs.

133. If it were His Will, He could destroy you, O mankind, and create another race; for He has power to do this.

134. If anyone desires a reward in this life, in Allah's (gift) is the reward (both) of this life and of the hereafter; for Allah is He that hears and sees (all things).

135. O you who believe! Stand out firmly for justice, as witnesses to Allah, even as against yourselves, or your parents, or your relatives, and whether it be (against) rich or poor: for Allah can best protect both. Follow not the lusts (of your hearts), lest you swerve, and if you distort (justice), or decline to do justice, verily Allah is well-acquainted with all that you do.

136. O you who believe! Believe in Allah and His messenger, and the scripture which He has sent to His messenger and the scripture which He sent to those before (him). And who denies Allah, His angels, His

Books, His messengers, and the day of judgement, has gone far, far astray.

137. Those who believe, then reject faith, then believe (again) and (again) reject faith, and go on increasing in unbelief - Allah will not forgive them nor guide them on the way.

138. To the hypocrites give the glad tidings that there is for them (but) a grievous penalty-

139. Yea, to those who take for friends unbelievers rather than believers; is it honour they seek among them? Nay - all honour is with Allah.

140. Already has He sent you word in the book, that when you hear the signs of Allah held in defiance and ridicule, you are not to sit with them unless they turn to a different theme; if you did, you would be like them. For Allah will collect the hypocrites and those who defy faith - all in hell -

141. (These are) the ones who wait and watch about you: if you do gain a victory from Allah, they say: "Were we not with you?" - but if the unbelievers gain a success, they say (to them): "Did we not gain an advantage over you, and did we not guard you from the believers?" But Allah will judge between you on the day of judgement. And never will Allah grant to the unbelievers a way (to triumph) over the believers.

142. The hypocrites - they think they are over-reaching Allah but He will over-reach them; when they stand up to prayer, they stand without earnestness, to be seen of men, but little do they hold Allah in remembrance.

143. (They are) distracted in mind even in the midst of it - being (sincerely) for neither one group nor for another. Whom Allah leaves straying - never will you find for him the way.

144. O you who believe! Take not for friends unbelievers rather than believers; do you wish to offer Allah an open proof against yourselves?

145. The hypocrites will be in the lowest depths of the fire; no helper will you find for them -

146. Except for those who repent, mend (their life), hold fast to Allah, and purify their religion as in Allah's sight; if so they will be (numbered) with the believers. And soon will Allah grant to the believers a reward of immense value.

147. What can Allah gain by your punishment, if you are grateful and you believe? Nay, it is Allah that recognises (all good), and knows all things.

148. Allah loves not that evil should be noised abroad in public speech, except where injustice has been done; for Allah is He Who hears and knows all things.

149. Whether you publish a good deed or conceal it or cover evil with pardon, verily Allah does blot out (sins) and has power (in the judgement of values).

150. Those who deny Allah and His messengers, and (those who) wish to separate Allah from His messengers, saying: "We believe in some but reject others"; and (those who) wish to take a course midway -

151. They are in truth (equally) unbelievers; and We have prepared for unbelievers a humiliating punishment.

152. To those who believe in Allah and His messengers and make no distinction between any of the messengers, We shall soon give their (due) rewards: for Allah is Oft-Forgiving, Most Merciful.

153. The People of the Book ask you to cause a book to descend to them from heaven; indeed they asked Moses for an even greater (miracle), for they said: "Show us Allah in public," but they were dazed for their presumption, by thunder and lightning. Yet they worshipped the calf even after clear signs had come to them; even so We forgave them; and gave Moses manifest proofs of authority.

154. And for their covenant We raised over them (the towering height) of mount (Sinai); and (on another occasion) We said: "Enter the gate with humility"; and (once again) We commanded them: "Transgress not in the matter of the Sabbath." And We took from them a solemn covenant.

155. (They have incurred divine displeasure); in that they broke their covenant; that they rejected the signs of Allah; that they slew the messengers in defiance of right; that they said, "Our hearts are the wrappings (which preserve Allah's Word; we need no more)" - nay, Allah has set the seal on their hearts for their blasphemy, and little is it they believe -

156. That they rejected faith: that they uttered against Mary a grave false charge;

157. That they said (in boast), "We killed the Messiah Jesus the son of Mary, the messenger of Allah" - but they killed him not, nor crucified him, but so it was made to appear to them, and those who differ in it are full of doubts, with no (certain) knowledge, but only conjecture to follow, for certainly they killed him not -

158. Nay, Allah raised him up to Himself; and Allah is Exalted in Power, Wise -

159. And there is none of the People of the Book but must believe in him before his death; and on the day of judgement he will be a witness against them -

160. For the iniquity of the Jews We made unlawful for them certain (foods) good and wholesome which had been lawful for them - in that they hindered many from Allah's way -

161. That they took usury, though they were forbidden; and that they devoured men's substance wrongfully - We have prepared for those among them who reject faith a grievous punishment.

162. But those among them who are well-grounded in knowledge, and the believers, believe in what has been revealed to you and what was revealed before you; and (especially) those who establish regular prayer and practice regular charity and believe in Allah and in the last day: to them shall We soon give a great reward.

163. We have sent you inspiration, as We sent it to Noah and the messengers after him; We sent inspiration to Abraham, Ishmael, Isaac, Jacob and the Tribes, to Jesus, Job, Jonah, Aaron, and Solomon, and to David We gave the Psalms.

164. Of some messengers We have already told you the story; of others

We have not - and to Moses Allah spoke direct.

165. Messengers who gave good news as well as warning, that mankind, after (the coming) of the messengers, should have no plea against Allah: for Allah is Exalted in Power, Wise.

166. But Allah bears witness that what He has sent to you, He has sent from His (own) knowledge, and the angels bear witness; but enough is Allah for a Witness.

167. Those who reject faith and keep off (men) from the way of Allah, have verily strayed far, far away from the path.

168. Those who reject faith and do wrong - Allah will not forgive them nor guide them to any way -

169. Except the way of hell, to dwell in it for ever. And this to Allah is easy.

170. O mankind! The messenger has come to you in truth from Allah: believe in him; it is best for you. But if you reject faith, to Allah belong all things in the heavens and on earth: and Allah is All-Knowing, All-Wise.

171. O People of the Book! Commit no excesses in your religion; nor say of Allah anything but truth. The Messiah Jesus the son of Mary was (no more than) a messenger of Allah, and His word which He bestowed on Mary, and a Spirit proceeding from Him: so believe in Allah and His messengers. Say not "trinity"; desist; it will be better for you: for Allah is One God; glory be to Him: (for Exalted is He) above having a son. To Him belong all things in the heavens and on earth. And enough is Allah as a Disposer of affairs.

172. The Messiah disdains not to serve and worship Allah, nor do the angels, those nearest (to Allah): those who disdain His worship and are arrogant - He will gather them all together to Himself to (answer).

173. But those who believe and do deeds of righteousness, He will give their (due) rewards - and more, out of His bounty; but those who are disdainful and arrogant, He will punish with a grievous penalty; nor will they find besides Allah, any to protect or help them.

174. O mankind! Verily there has come to you a convincing proof from your Lord: for We have sent to you a light (that is) manifest.

175. Then those who believe in Allah, and hold fast to Him - soon will He admit them to mercy and grace from Himself, and guide them to Himself by a straight way.

176. They ask you for a legal decision. Say: Allah directs (thus) about those who leave no descendants or ascendants as heirs. If it is a man that dies, leaving a sister but no child, she shall have half the inheritance; if (such a deceased was) a woman, who left no child, her brother takes her inheritance; if there are two sisters, they shall have two-thirds of the inheritance (between them): if there are brothers and sisters, (they share) the male having twice the share of the female. Thus does Allah make clear to you (His law) lest you err. And Allah has knowledge of all things.

Surah 5: *Al-Ma'idah*
(The Table Spread)

In the name of Allah,
Most Gracious, Most Merciful.

1. O you who believe! Fulfil (all) obligations. Lawful to you (for food) are all beasts of cattle with the exceptions named; but animals of the chase are forbidden while you are in the sacred precincts or in pilgrims garb: For Allah does command according to His will and plan.

2. O you who believe! Violate not the sanctity of the symbols of Allah, nor of the sacred month, nor of the animals brought for sacrifice, nor the garlands that mark out such animals, nor the people resorting to the Sacred House, seeking of the bounty and good pleasure of their Lord. But when you are clear of the sacred precincts and of pilgrim garb, you may hunt and let not the hatred of some people in (once) shutting you out of the Sacred Mosque lead you to transgression (and hostility on your part). Help you one another in righteousness and piety, but help you not one another in sin and rancour; fear Allah; for Allah is strict in punishment.

3. Forbidden to you (for food) are: dead meat, blood, the flesh of swine, and that on which has been invoked the name of other than Allah; that which has been killed by strangling, or by a violent blow, or by a headlong fall, or by being gored to death; that which has been (partly) eaten by a wild animal; unless you are able to slaughter it (in due form); that which is sacrificed on stone (altars); (forbidden) also is the division (of meat) by raffling with arrows: that is impiety. This day have those who reject faith given up all hope of your religion: yet fear them not but fear Me. This day have I perfected your religion for you, completed My favour upon you, and have chosen for you Islam as your religion. But if any is forced by hunger, with no inclination to transgression, Allah is indeed Oft-Forgiving, Most Merciful.

4. They ask you what is lawful to them (as food). Say: Lawful to you are (all) things good and pure: and what you have taught your trained hunting animals (to catch) in the manner directed to you by Allah; eat what they catch for you, but pronounce the name of Allah over it; and fear Allah; for Allah is swift in taking account.

5. This day are (all) things good and pure made lawful to you. The food of the People of the Book is lawful to you and yours is lawful to them. (Lawful to you in marriage) are (not only) chaste women who are believers, but chaste women among the People of the Book, revealed before your time - when you give them their due dowers, and desire chastity, not lewdness, nor secret intrigues. If anyone rejects faith, fruitless is his work and in the hereafter he will be in the ranks of those who have lost (all spiritual good).

6. O you who believe! When you prepare for prayer, wash your faces, and your hands (and arms) to the elbows; rub your heads (with water); and (wash) your feet to the ankles. If you are in a state of ceremonial impurity, bathe your whole body. But if you are ill, or on a journey, or one of you comes from offices of nature, or you have been in contact with women, and you find no water, then take for yourselves clean sand or earth, and rub with it your faces and hands. Allah does not wish to place you in a difficulty, but to make you clean, and to complete His favour to you, that you may be grateful.

7. And call in remembrance the favour of Allah to you, and His covenant, which He ratified with you, when you said: "We hear and we obey"; and fear Allah, for Allah knows well the secrets of your hearts.

8. O you who believe! Stand out firmly for Allah, as witnesses to fair dealing, and let not the hatred of others to you make you swerve to wrong and depart from justice. Be just: that is next to Piety: and fear Allah. For Allah is well-acquainted with all that you do.

9. To those who believe and do deeds of righteousness has Allah promised forgiveness and a great reward.

10. Those who reject faith and deny our signs will be companions of hellfire.

11. O you who believe! Call in remembrance the favour of Allah to you when certain men formed the design to stretch out their hands against you, but (Allah) held back their hands from you: so fear Allah. And on Allah let believers put (all) their trust.

12. Allah did before take a covenant from the Children of Israel, and We appointed twelve captains among them. And Allah said: "I am with you: if you (but) establish regular prayers, practice regular charity, believe in My messengers, honour and assist them, and loan to Allah a beautiful loan, verily I will wipe out from you your evils, and admit you to gardens with rivers flowing beneath; but if any of you, after this, resists faith, he has truly wandered from the path of rectitude."

13. But because of their breach of their covenant, We cursed them, and made their hearts grow hard: they change the words from their (right) places and forget a good part of the message that was sent them, nor will you cease to find them - barring a few - ever bent on (new) deceits: but forgive them and overlook (their misdeeds): for Allah loves those who are kind.

14. From those, too, who call themselves Christians, We did take a covenant, but they forgot a good part of the message that was sent them: so We estranged them, with enmity and hatred between the one and the other, to the day of judgement. And soon will Allah show them what it is they have done.

15. O People of the Book! There has come to you Our messenger, revealing to you much that you used to hide in the Book, and passing over much (that is now unnecessary): There has come to you from Allah a (new) light and a perspicuous book -

16. With which Allah guides all who seek His good pleasure to ways of peace and safety, and leads them out of darkness, by His Will, to the light - guides them to a path that is straight.

17. In blasphemy indeed are those that say that Allah is the Messiah the son of Mary. Say: "Who then has the least power against Allah, if His Will were to destroy the Messiah the son of Mary, his mother, and all - everyone that is on the earth? For to Allah belongs the dominion of the heavens and the earth, and all that is between. He creates what He pleases. For Allah has power over all things."

18. (Both) the Jews and the Christians say: "We are sons of Allah, and His beloved." Say: "Why then does He punish you for your sins? Nay, you are but men, - of the men He has created; He forgives whom He pleases. And He punishes whom He pleases; and to Allah belongs the dominion of the heavens and the earth and all that is between: and to Him is the final goal (of all)."

19. O People of the Book! Now has come to you, making (things) clear to you, Our messenger, after the break in (the series of) Our messengers, lest you should say: "There came to us no bringer of glad tidings and no warner (from evil)"; but now has come to you a bringer of glad tidings and a warner (from evil). And Allah has power over all things.

20. Remember Moses said to his people: "O my People! Call in remembrance the favour of Allah to you, when He produced prophets among you, made you kings, and gave you what He had not given to any other among the peoples.

21. "O my people! Enter the holy land which Allah has assigned to you, and turn not back ignominiously, for then will you be overthrown to your own ruin."

22. They said: "O Moses! In this land are a people of exceeding strength; never shall we enter it until they leave it; if (once) they leave, then shall we enter."

23. (But) among (their) God-fearing men were two on whom Allah had bestowed His grace; they said: "Assault them at the (proper) gate; when once you are in, victory will be yours; but on Allah put your trust if you have faith."

24. They said: "O Moses! While they remain there, never shall We be able to enter, to the end of time. Go you, and your Lord, and fight you two, while we sit here (and watch)."

25. He said: "O my Lord! I have power only over myself and my brother; so separate us from this rebellious people!"

26. Allah said: "Therefore, will the land be out of their reach for forty years; in distraction will they wander through the land; but sorrow you not over these rebellious people.

27. Recite to them the truth of the story of the two sons of Adam. See! They each presented a sacrifice (to Allah): it was accepted from one, but not from the other. Said the latter: "Be sure I will slay you." "Surely," said the former, "Allah does accept of the sacrifice of those who are righteous.

28. "If you do stretch your hand against me, to slay me, it is not for me to stretch my hand against you to slay you: for I do fear Allah, the Cherisher of the Worlds.

29. "For me, I intend to let you draw on yourself my sin as well as yours, for you will be among the companions of the fire, and that is the reward of those who do wrong."

30. The (selfish) soul of the other led him to the murder of his brother: he murdered him and became (himself) one of the lost ones.

31. Then Allah sent a raven, who scratched the ground to show him how to hide the shame of his brother. "Woe is me!" said he; "Was I not even able to be as this raven, and to hide the shame of my brother?" Then he became full of regrets -

32. On that account: We ordained for the Children of Israel that if anyone slew a person - unless it be for murder or for spreading mischief in the land - it would be as if he slew the whole people; and if anyone saved a life, it would be as if he saved the life of the whole people. Then although there came to them Our messengers with clear signs, yet, even after that, many of them continued to commit excesses in the land.

33. The punishment of those who wage war against Allah and His messenger, and strive with might and main for mischief through the land is: execution, or crucifixion, or the cutting off of hands and feet from opposite sides, or exile from the land: that is their disgrace in this world, and a heavy punishment is theirs in the hereafter;

34. Except for those who repent before they fall into your power: in that case, know that Allah is Oft-Forgiving, Most Merciful.

35. O you who believe! Do your duty to Allah, seek the means of approach to Him, and strive (with might and main) in His cause; that you may prosper.

36. As to those who reject faith - if they had everything on earth, and twice repeated, to give as ransom for the penalty of the day of judgement, it would never be accepted of them. Theirs will be a grievous penalty.

37. Their wish will be to get out of the fire, but never will they get out from it: their penalty will be one that endures.

38. As to the thief, male or female, cut off his or her hands; a punishment by way of example, from Allah, for their crime; and Allah is Exalted in Power, full of wisdom.

39. But if the thief repents after his crime, and amends his conduct, Allah turns to him in forgiveness; for Allah is Oft-Forgiving, Most Merciful.

40. Do you not know that to Allah (alone) belongs the dominion of the heavens and the earth? He punishes whom He pleases, and He forgives whom He pleases: and Allah has power over all things.

41. O messenger! Let not those grieve you, who race each other into unbelief: (whether it be) among those who say "We believe" with their lips but whose hearts have no faith, or it be among the Jews; men who will listen to any lie, will listen even to others who have never so much as come to you. They change the words from their (right) times and places; they say, "If you are given this, take it, but if not, beware!" If anyone's trial is intended by Allah, you have no authority in the least for him against Allah. For such - it is not Allah's Will to purify their hearts. For them there is disgrace in this world, and in the hereafter a heavy punishment.

42. (They are fond of) listening to falsehood, of devouring anything forbidden. If they do come to you, either judge between them, or decline to interfere. If you decline, they cannot hurt you in the least. If you judge, judge in equity between them. For Allah loves those who judge in equity.

43. But why do they come to you for decision, when they have (their own) law before them? - In it is the (plain) command of Allah; yet even after that, they would turn away. For they are not (really) people of faith.

44. It was We who revealed the law (to Moses): in it was guidance and light. By its standard have been judged the Jews, by the prophets who bowed (as in Islam) to Allah's will, by the rabbis and the doctors of law; for to them was entrusted the protection of Allah's Book, and they were witnesses to it; therefore fear not men, but fear Me, and sell not My signs for a miserable price. If any do fail to judge by (the light of) what Allah has revealed, they are (no better than) unbelievers.

45. We ordained in it for them: "Life for life, eye for eye, nose for nose, ear for ear, tooth for tooth, and wounds equal for equal." But if anyone remits the retaliation by way of charity, it is an act of atonement for himself. And if any fail to judge by what Allah has revealed, they are (no better than) wrongdoers.

46. And in their footsteps We sent Jesus the son of Mary, confirming the law that had come before him; We sent him the Gospel; in it was guidance and light, and confirmation of the law that had come before him: a guidance and an admonition to those who fear Allah.

47. Let the People of the Gospel judge by what Allah has revealed in it. If any do fail to judge by (the light of) what Allah has revealed, they are (no better than) those who rebel.

48. To you We sent the Scripture in truth, confirming the scripture that came before it, and guarding it in safety: so judge between them by what Allah has revealed, and follow not their vain desires, diverging from the truth that has come to you. To each among you have We prescribed a law and an open way. If Allah had so willed, He would have made you a single People, but (His plan is) to test you in what He has given you; so strive as in a race in all virtues. The goal of you all is to Allah; it is He that will show you the truth of the matters in which you dispute;

49. And this (He commands): judge you between them by what Allah has revealed, and follow not their vain desires, but beware of them lest they deceive you from any of that (teaching) which Allah has sent down to you.

And if they turn away, be assured that for some of their crimes it is Allah's purpose to punish them. And truly most men are rebellious.

50. Do they then seek after a judgement of (the Days of) Ignorance? But who, for a people whose faith is assured, can give better judgement than Allah?

51. O you who believe! Take not the Jews and the Christians for your friends and protectors: they are but friends and protectors to each other. And he amongst you that turns to them (for friendship) is of them. Verily Allah guides not a people unjust.

52. Those in whose heart is a disease - you see how eagerly they run about amongst them, saying: "We do fear lest a change of fortune bring us disaster." Ah! Perhaps Allah will give (you) victory, or a decision from Him. Then will they repent of the thoughts which they secretly harboured in their hearts.

53. And those who believe will say: "Are these the men who swore their strongest oaths by Allah, that they were with you?" All that they do will be in vain, and they will fall into (nothing but) ruin.

54. O you who believe! If any from among you turn back from his faith, soon will Allah produce a people whom He will love as they will love Him - lowly with the believers, mighty against the rejecters, fighting in the way of Allah, and never afraid of the reproaches of such as find fault. That is the grace of Allah, which He will bestow on whom He pleases: and Allah encompasses all, and He knows all things.

55. Your (real) friends are (no less than) Allah, His messenger, and the (fellowship of) believers - those who establish regular prayers and regular charity, and they bow down humbly (in worship).

56. As to those who turn (for friendship) to Allah, His messenger, and the (fellowship of) believers, it is the party of Allah that must certainly triumph.

57. O you who believe! Take not for friends and protectors those who take your religion for a mockery or sport - whether among those who received the scripture before you, or among those who reject faith; but fear you Allah, if you have faith (indeed).

58. When you proclaim your call to prayer, they take it (but) as mockery and sport; that is because they are a people without understanding.

59. Say: "O People of the Book! Do you disapprove of us for no other reason than that we believe in Allah, and the revelation that has come to us and that which came before (us), and (perhaps) that most of you are rebellious and disobedient?"

60. Say: "Shall I point out to you something much worse than this, (as judged) by the treatment it received from Allah? Those who incurred the curse of Allah and His wrath, those of whom some He transformed into apes and swine, those who worshipped evil - these are (many times) worse in rank, and far more astray from the even path!"

61. When they come to you, they say: "We believe"; but in fact they enter with a mind against faith, and they go out with the same. But Allah knows fully all that they hide.

62. Many of them do you see, racing each other in sin and transgression and their eating of things forbidden; evil indeed are the things that they do.

63. Why do not the rabbis and the doctors of law forbid them from their (habit of) uttering sinful words and eating things forbidden? Evil indeed are their works.

64. The Jews say: "Allah's hand is tied up." Be their hands tied up and be they accursed for the (blasphemy) they utter. Nay, both His hands are widely outstretched: He gives and spends (of His bounty) as He pleases. But the revelation that comes to you from Allah increases in most of them their obstinate rebellion and blasphemy. Amongst them We have placed enmity and hatred till the day of judgement. Every time they kindle the fire of war Allah does extinguish it; but they (ever) strive to do mischief on earth. And Allah loves not those who do mischief.

65. If only the People of the Book had believed and been righteous, We should indeed have blotted out their iniquities and admitted them to gardens of bliss.

66. If only they had stood fast by the law, the Gospel, and all the revelation that was sent to them from their Lord, they would have enjoyed happiness from every side. There is from among them a party of the right course; but many of them follow a course that is evil.

67. O messenger! Proclaim (the Message) which has been sent to you from your Lord. If you did not, you would not have fulfilled and proclaimed His mission: and Allah will defend you from men (who mean mischief). For Allah guides not those who reject faith.

68. Say: "O People of the Book! You have no ground to stand upon unless you stand fast by the law, the Gospel, and all the revelation that has come to you from your Lord." It is the revelation that comes to you from your Lord, that increases in most of them their obstinate rebellion and blasphemy. But sorrow you not over (these) people without faith.

69. Those who believe (in the Qur'an), those who follow the Jewish (Scriptures) and the Sabians and the Christians - any who believe in Allah and the last day, and work righteousness - on them shall be no fear, nor shall they grieve.

70. We took the covenant of the Children of Israel and sent them messengers. Every time there came to them a messenger with what they themselves desired not - some (of these) they called imposters and some they slay.

71. They thought there would be no trial (or punishment); so they became blind and deaf; yet Allah (in mercy) turned to them; yet again many of them became blind and deaf. But Allah sees well all that they do.

72. They do blaspheme who say: "Allah is the Messiah the son of Mary." But said the Messiah: "O Children of Israel! Worship Allah, my Lord and your Lord." Whoever joins other gods with Allah - Allah will forbid him the garden, and the fire will be his abode. There will for the wrongdoers be no one to help.

73. They do blaspheme who say: Allah is one of three in a trinity; for there is no god except One God. If they desist not from their word (of blasphemy), verily a grievous penalty will befall the blasphemers among them.

74. Why turn they not to Allah and seek His forgiveness? For Allah is Oft-Forgiving, Most Merciful.

75. The Messiah, the son of Mary, was no more than a messenger; many were the messengers that passed away before him. His mother was a woman of truth. They had both to eat their (daily) food. See how Allah does make His signs clear to them; yet see in what ways they are deluded away from the truth!

76. Say: "Will you worship, besides Allah, something which has no power either to harm or benefit you? But Allah - He it is that hears and knows all things."

77. Say: "O People of the Book! Exceed not in your religion the bounds (of what is proper), trespassing beyond the truth, nor follow the vain desires of people who went wrong in times gone by - who misled many, and strayed (themselves) from the even way.

78. Curses were pronounced on those among the Children of Israel who rejected faith, by the tongue of David and of Jesus, the son of Mary, because they disobeyed and persisted in excesses.

79. Nor did they (usually) forbid one another the iniquities which they committed: evil indeed were the deeds which they did.

80. You see many of them turning in friendship to the unbelievers. Evil indeed are (the works) which their souls have sent before them (with the result), that Allah's wrath is on them, and in torment will they remain.

81. If only they had believed in Allah, in the prophet, and in what has been revealed to him, never would they have taken them for friends and protectors, but most of them are rebellious wrongdoers.

82. Strongest among men in enmity to the believers will you find the Jews and pagans; and nearest among them in love to the believers will you find those who say, "We are Christians"; because amongst these are men devoted to learning and men who have renounced the world, and they are not arrogant.

83. And when they listen to the revelation received by the messenger, you will see their eyes overflowing with tears, for they recognise the truth: they pray: "Our Lord! We believe; write us down among the witnesses."

84. "What cause can we have not to believe in Allah and the truth which has come to us, seeing that we long for our Lord to admit us to the company of the righteous?"

85. And for this their prayer, has Allah rewarded them with gardens, with rivers flowing underneath - their eternal home. Such is the recompense of those who do good.

86. But those who reject faith and belie Our signs - they shall be companions of hellfire.

87. O you who believe! Make not unlawful the good things which Allah has made lawful for you, but commit no excess: for Allah loves not those given to excess.

88. Eat of the things which Allah has provided for you, lawful and good: but fear Allah, in Whom you believe.

89. Allah will not call you to account for what is futile in your oaths, but He will call you to account for your deliberate oaths: for expiation, feed ten needy persons, on a scale of the average for the food of your families; or clothe them; or give a slave his freedom. If that is beyond your means, fast for three days. That is the expiation for the oaths you have sworn. But keep to your oaths. Thus does Allah make clear to you His signs, that you may be grateful.

90. O you who believe! Intoxicants and gambling, sacrificing to stones, and (divination by) arrows, are an abomination of Satan's handiwork; eschew such (abomination), that you may prosper.

91. Satan's plan is (but) to excite enmity and hatred between you, with intoxicants and gambling, and hinder you from the remembrance of Allah, and from prayer: will you not then abstain?

92. Obey Allah, and obey the messenger and beware (of evil): if you do turn back, know you that it is Our messenger's duty to proclaim (the Message) in the clearest manner.

93. On those who believe and do deeds of righteousness there is no blame for what they ate (in the past), when they guard themselves from evil, and believe, and do deeds of righteousness - (or) again, guard themselves from evil and believe - (or) again, guard themselves from evil and do good. For Allah loves those who do good.

94. O you who believe! Allah does but make a trial of you in a little matter of game well within reach of your hands and your lances, that He may test who fears Him unseen: any who transgress thereafter, will have a grievous penalty.

95. O you who believe! Kill not game while in the sacred precincts or in pilgrim garb. If any of you does so intentionally, the compensation is an offering, brought to the Ka'bah, of a domestic animal equivalent to the one he killed, as adjudged by two just men among you; or by way of atonement, the feeding of the needy; or its equivalent in fasts: that he may taste of the penalty of his deed. Allah forgives what is past: for repetition Allah will exact from him the penalty. For Allah is Exalted, and Lord of Retribution.

96. Lawful to you is the pursuit of water-game and its use for food - for the benefit of yourselves and those who travel; but forbidden is the pursuit of land-game - as long as you are in the sacred precincts or in pilgrim garb.

And fear Allah, to whom you shall be gathered back.

97. Allah made the Ka'bah, the Sacred House, an asylum of security for men, as also the sacred months, the animals for offerings, and the garlands that mark them: that you may know that Allah has knowledge of what is in the heavens and on earth and that Allah is well acquainted with all things.

98. Know you that Allah is strict in punishment and that Allah is Oft-Forgiving, Most Merciful.

99. The messenger's duty is but to proclaim (the message). But Allah knows all that you reveal and all that you conceal.

100. Say: "Not equal are things that are bad and things that are good, even though the abundance of the bad may dazzle you; so fear Allah, O you that understand! That (so) you may prosper."

101. O you who believe! Ask not questions about things which, if made plain to you, may cause you trouble. But if you ask about things when the Qur'an is being revealed, they will be made plain to you, Allah will forgive those: for Allah is Oft-Forgiving, Most Forbearing.

102. Some people before you did ask such questions, and on that account lost their faith.

103. It was not Allah Who instituted (superstitions like those of) a slit-ear she-camel, or a she-camel let loose for free pasture, or idol sacrifices for twin-births in animals, or stallion-camels freed from work: it is blasphemers who invent a lie against Allah; but most of them lack wisdom.

104. When it is said to them: "Come to what Allah has revealed; come to the messenger"; they say: "Enough for us are the ways we found our fathers following." What! Even though their fathers were void of knowledge and guidance?

105. O you who believe! Guard your own souls: if you follow (right) guidance, no hurt can come to you from those who stray. The goal of you all is to Allah: it is He that will show you the truth of all that you do.

106. O you who believe! When death approaches any of you, (take) witnesses among yourselves when making bequests - two just men of your own (brotherhood) or others from outside if you are journeying through the earth, and the chance of death befalls you (thus). If you doubt (their truth), detain them both after prayer, and let them both swear by Allah: "We wish not in this for any worldly gain, even though the (beneficiary) be our near relation: we shall hide not the evidence before Allah: if we do, then see! The sin be upon us!"

107. But if it gets known that these two were guilty of the sin (of perjury), let two others stand up in their places - nearest in relation from among those who claim a lawful right: let them swear by Allah; "We affirm that our witness is truer than that of those two, and that we have not trespassed (beyond the truth): if we did, see! The wrong will be upon us!"

108. That is most suitable: that they may give the evidence in its true nature and shape, or else they would fear that other oaths would be taken after their oaths. But fear Allah, and listen (to His counsel): for Allah guides not a rebellious people.

109. One day will Allah gather the messengers together, and ask: "What was the response you received (from men to your teaching)?" They will say: "We have no knowledge: it is You who knows in full all that is hidden."

110. Then will Allah say: "O Jesus the son of Mary! Recount My favour to you and to your mother. See! I strengthened you with the holy spirit, so that you did speak to the people in childhood and in maturity. See! I taught you the book and wisdom, the law and the Gospel. And see! You make out of clay, as it were, the figure of a bird, by My permission, and you breathe into it, and it becomes a bird by My permission, and you heal those born blind, and the lepers, by My permission. And see! You bring forth the dead by My permission. And see! I did restrain the Children of Israel from (violence to) you when you did show them the clear signs, and the unbelievers among them said: 'This is nothing but evident magic.'"

111. "And see! I inspired the disciples to have faith in Me and My messenger; they said, 'We have faith, and do you bear witness that we bow to Allah as Muslims.'"

112. See! The disciples said: "O Jesus the son of Mary! Can your Lord send down to us a table set (with viands) from heaven?" Said Jesus: "Fear Allah, if you have faith."

113. They said: "We only wish to eat of it and satisfy our hearts, and to know that you have indeed told us the truth; and that we ourselves may be witnesses to the miracle."

114. Said Jesus the son of Mary: "O Allah our Lord! Send us from heaven a table set (with viands) that there may be for us - for the first and the last of us - a solemn festival and a sign from You; and provide for our sustenance, for You are the best Sustainer (of our needs)."

115. Allah said: "I will send it down to you: but if any of you after that resists faith, I will punish him with a penalty such as I have not inflicted on anyone among all the peoples."

116. And see! Allah will say: "O Jesus the son of Mary! Did you say to men, 'Worship me and my mother as gods in derogation of Allah'?" He will say: "Glory to You! Never could I say what I had no right (to say). Had I said such a thing, You would indeed have known it. You know what is in my heart, though I know not what is in Yours. For You know in full all that is hidden."

117. "Never said I to them anything except what You did command me to say: 'Worship Allah, my Lord and your Lord'; and I was a witness over them whilst I dwelt amongst them; when You did take me up You were the Watcher over them, and You are a Witness to all things."

118. "If You do punish them, they are Your servants: if You do forgive them, You are the Exalted in Power, the Wise."

119. Allah will say: "This is a day on which the truthful will profit from their truth: theirs are gardens, with rivers flowing beneath - their eternal home; Allah well-pleased with them, and they with Allah; that is the great salvation (the fulfilment of all desires)."

120. To Allah does belong the dominion of the heavens and the earth, and all that is in it, and it is He Who has power over all things.

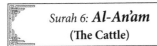

Surah 6: *Al-An'am*
(The Cattle)

In the name of Allah,
Most Gracious, Most Merciful.

1. Praise be to Allah, Who created the heavens and the earth, and made the darkness and the light. Yet those who reject faith hold (others) as equal with their guardian-Lord.

2. He it is Who created you from clay, and then decreed a stated term (for you). And there is in His presence another determined term; yet you doubt within yourselves!

3. And He is Allah in the heavens and on earth. He knows what you hide, and what you reveal, and He knows the (recompense) which you earn (by your deeds).

4. But never did a single one of the signs of their Lord reach them, but they turned away from it.

5. And now they reject the truth when it reaches them; but soon shall learn the reality of what they used to mock at.

6. Do they not see how many of those before them We did destroy? - Generations We had established on the earth, in strength such as We have not given to you - for whom We poured out rain from the skies in abundance, and gave (fertile) streams flowing beneath their (feet): yet for their sins We destroyed them, and raised in their wake fresh generations (to succeed them).

7. If We had sent to you a written (Message) on parchment, so that they could touch it with their hands, the unbelievers would have been sure to say: "This is nothing but obvious magic!"

8. They say: "Why is not an angel sent down to him?" If We did send down an angel, the matter would be settled at once, and no respite would be granted them.

9. If We had made it an angel, We should have sent him as a man, and We should certainly have caused them confusion in a matter which they have already covered with confusion.

10. Mocked were (many) messengers before you; but their scoffers were hemmed in by the thing that they mocked.

11. Say: "Travel through the earth and see what was the end of those who rejected truth."

12. Say: "To whom belongs all that is in the heavens and on earth?" Say: "To Allah. He has inscribed for Himself (the rule of) mercy. That He will gather you together for the day of judgement, there is no doubt whatever. It is they who have lost their own souls, that will not believe.

13. "To Him belongs all that dwells (or lurks) in the night and the day. For He is the One Who hears and knows all things."

14. Say: "Shall I take for my protector any other than Allah, the Maker of the heavens and the earth? And He it is that feeds but is not fed." Say: "Nay! But I am commanded to be the first of those who bow to Allah (in Islam), and be not you of the company of those who join gods with Allah."

15. Say: "I would, if I disobeyed my Lord, indeed have fear of the penalty of a mighty day."

16. "On that day, if the penalty is averted from any, it is due to Allah's mercy; and that would be (salvation), the obvious fulfilment of all desire."

17. "If Allah touches you with affliction, none can remove it but He; and if He touches you with happiness (there is none that can impair it); He has power over all things."

18. "He is the Irresistible, (watching) from above over His worshippers; and He is the Wise, acquainted with all things."

19. Say: "What thing is most weighty in evidence?" Say: "Allah is Witness between me and you; this Qur'an has been revealed to me by inspiration. That I may warn you and all whom it reaches. Can you possibly bear witness that besides Allah there is another God?" Say: "Nay! I cannot bear witness!" Say: "But in truth He is the One God, and I truly am innocent of (your blasphemy of) joining others with Him."

20. Those to whom We have given the book know this as they know their own sons. Those who have lost their own souls refuse therefore to believe.

21. Who does more wrong than he who invents a lie against Allah or rejects His signs? But verily the wrongdoers never shall prosper.

22. One day shall We gather them all together: We shall say to those who ascribed partners (to Us): "Where are the partners whom you (invented and) talked about?"

23. There will then be (left) no subterfuge for them but to say: "By Allah Our Lord, we were not those who joined gods with Allah."

24. See! How they lie against their own souls! But the (lie) which they invented will leave them in the lurch.

25. Of them there are some who (pretend to) listen to you; but We have thrown veils on their hearts, so they understand it not, and deafness in their ears; if they saw every one of the signs, they will not believe in them; in so much that when they come to you, they (but) dispute with you; the unbelievers say: "These are nothing but tales of the ancients."

26. Others they keep away from it, and themselves they keep away; but they only destroy their own souls, and they perceive it not.

27. If you could but see when they are confronted with the fire! They will say: "Would that we were but sent back! Then would we not reject the signs of our Lord, but would be amongst those who believe!"

28. Yea, in their own (eyes) will become manifest what before they concealed. But if they were returned, they would certainly relapse to the things they were forbidden, for they are indeed liars.

29. And they (sometimes) say: "There is nothing except our life on this earth, and never shall we be raised up again."

30. If you could but see when they are confronted with their Lord! He will say: "Is not this the truth?" They will say: "Yea, by our Lord!" He will say: "Taste you then the penalty, because you rejected faith."

31. Lost indeed are they who treat it as a falsehood that they must meet Allah - until on a sudden the hour is on them, and they say: "Ah! Woe to us that we took no thought of it"; for they bear their burdens on their backs, and evil indeed are the burdens that they bear.

32. What is the life of this world but play and amusement? But best is the home in the hereafter, for those who are righteous. Will you not then understand?

33. We know indeed the grief which their words do cause you; it is not you (O Muhammad) they reject; it is the signs of Allah, which the wicked condemn.

34. Rejected were the messengers before you; with patience and constancy they bore their rejection and their wrongs, until Our aid did reach them; there is none that can alter the words (and decrees) of Allah. Already have you received some account of those messengers.

35. If their spurning is hard on your mind, yet if you were able to seek a tunnel in the ground or a ladder to the skies and bring them a sign - (what good?). If it were Allah's Will, He could gather them together to true guidance: so be not you amongst those who are swayed by ignorance (and impatience)!

36. Those who listen (in truth), be sure, will accept; as to the dead, Allah will raise them up; then will they be returned to Him.

37. They say: "Why is not a sign sent down to him from his Lord?" Say: "Allah has certainly power to send down a sign; but most of them understand not."

38. There is not an animal (that lives) on the earth, nor a being that flies on its wings, but (forms part of) communities like you. Nothing have We omitted from the book, and they (all) shall be gathered to their Lord in the end.

39. Those who reject Our signs are deaf and dumb - in the midst of darkness profound: whom Allah wills, He leaves to wander; whom He wills, He places on the way that is straight.

40. Say: "Think you to yourselves, if there come upon you the wrath of Allah, or the hour (that you dread), would you then call upon other than Allah? - (Reply) if you are truthful!"

41. "Nay - On Him would you call, and if it be His Will, He would remove (the distress) which occasioned your call upon Him, and you would forget (the false gods) which you join with Him!"

42. Before you We sent (messengers) to many nations, and We afflicted the nations with suffering and adversity, that they might learn humility.

43. When the suffering reached them from Us, why then did they not learn humility? On the contrary, their hearts became hardened, and Satan made their (sinful) acts seem alluring to them.

44. But when they forget the warning they had received, We opened to them the gates of all (good) things, until, in the midst of their enjoyment of Our gifts, on a sudden, We called them to account, when they were plunged in despair!

45. Of the wrongdoers the last remnant was cut off. Praise be to Allah, the Cherisher of the Worlds.

46. Say: "Think you, if Allah took away your hearing and your sight, and sealed up your hearts, who - a god other than Allah - could restore them to you?" See how We explain the signs by various (symbols); Yet they turn aside.

47. Say: "Think you, if the punishment of Allah comes to you, whether suddenly or openly, will any be destroyed except those who do wrong?"

48. We send the messengers only to give good news and to warn: so those who believe and mend (their lives) - upon them shall be no fear, nor shall they grieve.

49. But those who reject Our signs - them shall punishment touch, for that they ceased not from transgressing.

50. Say: "I tell you not that with me are the Treasures of Allah, nor do I know what is hidden, nor do I tell you I am an angel. I but follow what is revealed to me." Say: "Can the blind be held equal to the seeing?" Will you then not consider?

51. Give the warning to those in whose (hearts) is the fear that they will be brought (to judgement) before their Lord: except for Him they will have no protector nor intercessor; that they may guard (against evil).

52. Send not away those who call on their Lord morning and evening, seeking His Face. In nothing are you accountable for them, and in nothing are they accountable for you, that you should turn them away, and thus be (one) of the unjust.

53. Thus did We try some of them by comparison with others, that they should say: "Is it these then that Allah has favoured from amongst us?" Does not Allah know best those who are grateful?

54. When those come to you who believe in Our signs, say: "Peace be on you"; your Lord has inscribed for Himself (the rule of) mercy: verily, if any of you did evil in ignorance, and thereafter repented, and amended (his conduct), He is Oft-Forgiving, Most Merciful."

55. Thus do We explain the signs in detail: that the way of the sinners may be shown up.

56. Say: "I am forbidden to worship those - other than Allah - whom you call upon." Say: "I will not follow your vain desires; if I did, I would stray from the path, and be not of the company of those who receive guidance."

57. Say: "For me, I (work) on a clear sign from my Lord, but you reject Him. What you would see hastened, is not in my power. The command rests with none but Allah: He declares the truth, and He is the best of judges."

58. Say: "If what you would see hastened were in my power, the matter would be settled at once between you and me. But Allah knows best those who do wrong."

59. With Him are the keys of the unseen, the treasures that none knows but He. He knows whatever there is on the earth and in the sea. Not a leaf does fall but with His knowledge; there is not a grain in the darkness (or depths) of the earth, nor anything fresh or dry (green or withered), but is (inscribed) in a record clear (to those who can read).

60. It is He Who does take your souls by night, and has knowledge of all that you have done by day; by day does He raise you up again; that a term appointed be fulfilled; in the end to Him will be your return; then will He show you the truth of all that you did.

61. He is the Irresistible, (watching) from above over His worshippers, and He sets guardians over you. At length, when death approaches one of you, Our angels take his soul, and they never fail in their duty.

62. Then are men returned to Allah, their true protector, surely His is the command, and He is the swiftest in taking account.

63. Say; "Who is it that delivers you from the dark recesses of land and sea, when you call upon Him in humility and in the secrecy of the heart: 'if He only delivers us from these (dangers), (we vow) we shall truly show our gratitude'?"

64. Say: "It is Allah that delivers you from these and all (other) distresses: and yet you worship false gods!"

65. Say: "He has power to send calamities on you, from above and below, or to cover you with confusion in party strife, giving you a taste of mutual vengeance - each from the other." See how We explain the signs by various (symbols); that they may understand.

66. But your people reject this, though it is the truth. Say: "Not mine is the responsibility for arranging your affairs;

67. For every Message is a limit of time, and soon shall you know it."

68. When you see men engaged in vain discourse about Our signs, turn away from them unless they turn to a different theme. If Satan ever makes you forget, then after recollection, sit not you in the company of those who do wrong.

69. On their account no responsibility falls on the righteous, but (their duty) is to remind them, that they may (learn to) fear Allah.

70. Leave alone those who take their religion to be mere play and amusement, and are deceived by the life of this world. But proclaim (to them) this (truth): that every soul delivers itself to ruin by its own acts; it will find for itself no protector or intercessor except Allah; if it offered every ransom, (or reparation), none will be accepted; such is (the end of) those who deliver themselves to ruin by their own acts: they will have for drink (only) boiling water, and for punishment, one most grievous; for they persisted in rejecting Allah.

71. Say: "Shall we indeed call on others besides Allah - things that can do us neither good nor harm - and turn on our heels after receiving guidance from Allah - like one whom the evil ones have made into a fool, wandering bewildered through the earth, his friends calling 'Come to us,' (vainly) guiding him to the path?" Say: "Allah's guidance is the (only) guidance, and we have been directed to submit ourselves to the Lord of the Worlds -

72. To establish regular prayers and to fear Allah: for it is to Him that we shall be gathered together."

73. It is He Who created the heavens and the earth in true (proportions): the day He says, "Be," see! It is. His word is the truth. His will be the dominion the day the trumpet will be blown. He knows the unseen as well as that which is open. For He is the Wise, well-acquainted (with all things).

74. Abraham said to his father Azar: "Do you take idols for gods? For I see you and your people in manifest error."

75. So also did We show Abraham the power and the laws of the heavens and the earth, that he might (with understanding) have certitude.

76. When the night covered him over, he saw a star: he said: "This is my

Lord." But when it set, he said: "I love not those that set."

77. When he saw the moon rising in splendour, he said: "This is my Lord." But when the moon set, he said: "Unless my Lord guide me, I shall surely be among those who go astray."

78. When he saw the sun rising in splendour, he said: "This is my Lord; this is the greatest (of all)." But when the sun set, he said: "O my people! I am indeed free from your (guilt) of giving partners to Allah."

79. "For me, I have set my face, firmly and truly, towards Him Who created the heavens and the earth, and never shall I give partners to Allah."

80. His people disputed with him. He said: "(Come) you to dispute with me, about Allah, when He (Himself) has guided me? I fear not (the beings) you associate with Allah: unless my Lord wills, (nothing can happen). My Lord comprehends in His knowledge all things: will you not (yourselves) be admonished?"

81. "How should I fear (the beings) you associate with Allah, when you fear not to give partners to Allah without any authority having been given to you? Which of (us) two parties has more right to security? (Tell me) if you know."

82. "It is those who believe and confuse not their beliefs with wrong - that are (truly) in security, for they are on (right) guidance."

83. That was the reasoning about Us, which We gave to Abraham (to use)

against his people; We raise whom We will, degree after degree; for your Lord is full of wisdom and knowledge.

84. We gave him Isaac and Jacob; all (three) We guided; and before him, We guided Noah, and among his progeny, David, Solomon, Job, Joseph, Moses, and Aaron: thus do We reward those who do good:

85. And Zakariya and Yahya, and Jesus and Elias: all in the ranks of the righteous:

86. And Ishmael and Elisha, and Jonah, and Lot: and to all We gave favour above the nations:

87. (To them) and to their fathers, and progeny and brothers: We chose them, And We guided them to a straight way.

88. This is the guidance of Allah: He gives that guidance to whom He pleases of His worshippers. If they were to join other gods with Him, all that they did would be vain for them.

89. These were the men to whom We gave the book, and authority, and prophethood: if these (their descendants) reject them, see! We shall entrust their charge to a new people who reject them not.

90. Those were the (prophets) who received Allah's guidance: copy the guidance they received; Say: "No reward for this do I ask of you: this is no less than a message for the nations."

91. No just estimate of Allah do they make when they say: "Nothing does Allah send down to man (by way of revelation)": Say: "Who then sent down the book which Moses brought?

- A light and guidance to man: but you make it into (separate) sheets for show, while you conceal much (of its contents); in it were you taught that which you knew not - neither you nor your fathers." Say: "Allah (sent it down)": then leave them to plunge in vain discourse and trifling.

92. And this is a book which We have sent down, bringing blessings, and confirming (the revelations) which came before it; that you may warn the mother of cities and all around her. Those who believe in the hereafter, believe in this (book), and they are constant in guarding their prayers.

93. Who can be more wicked than one who invents a lie against Allah, or said, "I have received inspiration," when he has received none, or (again) who says, "I can reveal the like of what Allah has revealed?" If you could but see how the wicked (do fare) in the flood of confusion at death! - the angels stretch forth their hands, (saying), "Yield up your souls: this day shall you receive your reward - a penalty of shame, for that you used to tell lies against Allah, and scornfully to reject of His signs!"

94. "And see! You come to Us bare and alone as We created you for the first time: You have left behind you all (the favours) which We bestowed on you: We see not with you your intercessors whom you thought to be partners in your affairs: so now all relations between you have been cut off, and your (pet) fancies have left you in the lurch!"

95. It is Allah Who causes the seed-grain and the date-stone to split and sprout. He causes the living to issue from the dead, and He is the One to cause the dead to issue from the living. That is Allah; then how are you deluded away from the truth?

96. He it is that cleaves the daybreak (from the dark): He makes the night for rest and tranquillity, and the sun and moon for the reckoning (of time): such is the judgement and ordering of (Him), the Exalted in Power, the Omniscient.

97. It is He Who makes the stars (as beacons) for you, that you may guide yourselves, with their help, through the dark spaces of land and sea: We detail Our signs for people who know.

98. It is He Who has produced you from a single person; here is a place of sojourn and a place of departure; We detail Our signs for people who understand.

99. It is He Who sends down rain from the skies; with it We produce vegetation of all kinds: from some We produce green (crops), out of which We produce grain, heaped up (at harvest); out of the date-palm and its sheaths (or spathes) (come) clusters of dates hanging low and near; and (then there are) gardens of grapes, and olives, and pomegranates, each similar (in kind) yet different (in variety); when they begin to bear fruit, feast your eyes with the fruit and the ripeness of it. See! In these things there are signs for people who believe.

100. Yet they make the Jinns equals with Allah, though Allah did create the Jinns; and they falsely, having no knowledge, attribute to Him sons and daughters. Praise and glory be to Him! (For He is) above what they attribute to Him!

101. To Him is due the primal origin of the heavens and the earth: how can He have a son when He has no consort? He created all things, and He has full knowledge of all things.

102. That is Allah, your Lord! There is no god but He, the Creator of all things; then worship you Him; and He has power to dispose of all affairs.

103. No vision can grasp Him. But His grasp is over all vision: He is above all comprehension, yet is acquainted with all things.

104. "Now have come to you, from your Lord, proofs (to open your eyes): if any will see, it will be for (the good of) his own soul; if any will be blind, it will be to his own (harm): I am not (here) to watch over your doings."

105. Thus do We explain the signs by various (symbols): that they may say, "You have taught (us) diligently," and that We may make the matter clear to those who know.

106. Follow what you are taught by inspiration from your Lord; there is no god but He; and turn aside from those who join gods with Allah.

107. If it had been Allah's plan, they would not have taken false gods; but We made you not one to watch over their doings, nor are you set over them to dispose of their affairs.

108. Revile not you those whom they call upon besides Allah, lest they out of spite revile Allah in their ignorance.

Thus have We made alluring to each people its own doings. In the end will they return to their Lord, and We shall then tell them the truth of all that they did.

109. They swear their strongest oaths by Allah, that if a (special) sign came to them, by it they would believe. Say: "Certainly (all) signs are in the power of Allah; but what will make you (Muslims) realise that even if (special) signs came, they will not believe?"

110. We (too) shall turn to (confusion) their hearts and their eyes, even as they refused to believe in this in the first instance: We shall leave them in their trespasses, to wander in distraction.

111. Even if We did send to them angels, and the dead did speak to them, and We gathered together all things before their very eyes, they are not the ones to believe, unless it is in Allah's plan: but most of them ignore (the truth).

112. Likewise did We make for every messenger an enemy - evil ones among men and Jinns, inspiring each other with flowery discourses by way of deception. If your Lord had so planned, they would not have done it: so leave them and their inventions alone.

113. To such (deceit) let the hearts of those incline, who have no faith in the hereafter: let them delight in it, and let them earn from it what they may.

114. Say: "Shall I seek for judge other than Allah? - When He it is Who has sent to you the book, explained in detail." They know full well, to whom

We have given the book, that it has been sent down from your Lord in truth. Never be then of those who doubt.

115. The word of your Lord does find its fulfilment in truth and in justice: none can change His words: for He is the one Who hears and knows all.

116. Were you to follow the common run of those on earth, they will lead you away from the way of Allah. They follow nothing but conjecture; they do nothing but lie.

117. Your Lord knows best who strays from His way. He knows best who they are that receive His guidance.

118. So eat of (meats) on which Allah's name has been pronounced, if you have faith in His signs.

119. Why should you not eat of (meats) on which Allah's name has been pronounced, when He has explained to you in detail what is forbidden to you - except under compulsion of necessity? But many do mislead (men) by their appetites unchecked by knowledge. Your Lord knows best those who transgress.

120. Eschew all sin, open or secret: those who earn sin will get due recompense for their "earnings."

121. Eat not of (meats) on which Allah's name has not been pronounced: that would be impiety. But the evil ones ever inspire their friends to contend with you; if you were to obey them, you would indeed be pagans.

122. Can he who was dead, to whom We gave life, and a light by which he can walk amongst men, be like him who is in the depths of darkness, from which he can never come out? Thus to those without faith their own deeds seem pleasing.

123. Thus have We placed leaders in every town, its wicked men, to plot (and burrow) in it: but they only plot against their own souls, and they perceive it not.

124. When there comes to them a sign (from Allah), they say: "We shall not believe until we receive one (exactly) like those received by Allah's messengers." Allah knows best where (and how) to carry out His mission. Soon will the wicked be overtaken by humiliation before Allah, and a severe punishment, for all their plots.

125. Those whom Allah (in His plan) wills to guide - He opens their breast to Islam; those whom He wills to leave straying - He makes their breast close and constricted, as if they had to climb up to the skies; thus does Allah (heap) the penalty on those who refuse to believe.

126. This is the way of your Lord, leading straight: We have detailed the signs for those who receive admonition.

127. For them will be a home of peace in the presence of their Lord: He will be their Friend, because they practised (righteousness).

128. One day will He gather them all together, (and say): "O you assembly of Jinns! Much (toll) did you take of men." Their friends amongst men will say: "Our Lord! We made profit from each other: but (alas!) we reached our term - which You did appoint for us." He will say: "The fire be your dwelling-place: you will dwell in it forever, except as Allah wills." For your Lord is full of wisdom and knowledge.

129. Thus do We make the wrongdoers turn to each other, because of what they earn.

130. O you assembly of Jinns and men! Came there not to you messengers from amongst you, setting forth to you My signs, and warning you of the meeting of this day of yours?" They will say: "We bear witness against ourselves." It was the life of this world that deceived them. So against themselves will they bear witness that they rejected faith.

131. (The messengers were sent) thus, for your Lord would not destroy, for their wrongdoing, men's habitations whilst their occupants were unwarned.

132. To all are degrees (or ranks) according to their deeds: for your Lord is not unmindful of anything that they do.

133. Your Lord is Self-sufficient, full of mercy: if it were His will, He could destroy you, and in your place appoint whom He will as your successors, even as He raised you up from the posterity of other people.

134. All that has been promised to you will come to pass; nor can you frustrate it (in the least bit).

135. Say: "O my people! Do whatever you can; I will do (my part); soon will you know who it is whose end will be (best) in the hereafter: Certain it is that the wrongdoers will not prosper."

136. Out of what Allah has produced in abundance in tilth and in cattle, they assigned Him a share: They say, according to their fancies: "This is for Allah, and this - for our 'partners'"! But the share of their 'partners' reaches not Allah, whilst the share of Allah reaches their 'partners'! Evil (and unjust) is their assignment!

137. Even so, in the eyes of most of the pagans their "partners" made alluring the slaughter of their children, in order to lead them to their own destruction, and cause confusion in their religion. If Allah had willed, they would not have done so: but leave alone them and their inventions.

138. And they say that such and such cattle and crops are taboo, and none should eat of them except those whom - so they say - We wish; further, there are cattle forbidden to yoke or burden, and cattle on which, (at slaughter), the name of Allah is not pronounced - inventions against Allah's name: soon will He repay them for their inventions.

139. They say: "What is in the wombs of such and such cattle is specially reserved (for food) for our men, and forbidden to our women; but if it is stillborn, then all have shares in it. For their (false) attribution (of superstitions to Allah), He will soon punish them: for He is full of wisdom and knowledge.

140. Lost are those who slay their children, from folly, without knowledge, and forbid food which Allah has provided for them, inventing

(lies) against Allah. They have indeed gone astray and heeded no guidance.

141. It is He Who produces gardens, with trellises and without, and dates, and tilth with produce of all kinds, and olives and pomegranates, similar (in kind) and different (in variety): eat of their fruit in their season, but render the dues that are proper on the day that the harvest is gathered. But waste not by excess: for Allah loves not the wasters.

142. Of the cattle are some for burden and some for meat: eat what Allah has provided for you, and follow not the footsteps of Satan; for he is to you an avowed enemy.

143. (Take) eight (head of cattle) in (four) pairs: of sheep a pair, and of goats a pair; say, has He forbidden the two males, or the two females, or (the young) which the wombs of the two females enclose? Tell me with knowledge if you are truthful.

144. Of camels a pair, and of oxen a pair; say, has He forbidden the two males, or the two females, or (the young) which the wombs of the two females enclose? - Were you present when Allah ordered you such a thing? But who does more wrong than one who invents a lie against Allah, to lead astray men without knowledge? For Allah guides not people who do wrong.

145. Say: "I find not in the message received by me by inspiration any (meat) forbidden to be eaten by one who wishes to eat it, unless it be dead meat, or blood poured out, or the flesh of swine - for it is an abomination - or what is impious, (meat) on which a name has been invoked other than Allah's." But (even so), if a person is forced by necessity, without wilful disobedience, nor transgressing due limits - your Lord is Oft-Forgiving, Most Merciful.

146. For those who followed the Jewish law, We forbade every (animal) with undivided hoof, and We forbade them the fat of the ox and the sheep, except what adheres to their backs or their entrails, or is mixed up with a bone; this in recompense for their wilful disobedience: for We are True (in Our ordinances).

147. If they accuse you (O Muhammad) of falsehood, say: "Your Lord is full of mercy, All-Embracing;" but from people in guilt never will His wrath be turned back.

148. Those who give partners to Allah will say: "If Allah had wished, we should not have given partners to Him, nor would our fathers; nor should we have had any taboos." So did their ancestors argue falsely, until they tasted of Our wrath. Say: "Have you any (certain) knowledge? If so, produce it before us. You follow nothing but conjecture: You do nothing but lie."

149. Say: "With Allah is the argument that reaches home: if it had been His will, He could indeed have guided you all."

150. Say: "Bring forward your witnesses to prove that Allah did forbid so and so." If they bring such witnesses, be not you amongst them: nor follow you the vain desires of such as treat Our signs as falsehoods, and

such as believe not in the hereafter: for they hold others as equal with their Guardian-Lord.

151. Say: "Come, I will rehearse what Allah has (really) prohibited you from: join not anything as equal with Him; be good to your parents; kill not your children on a plea of want - We provide sustenance for you and for them - come not near to shameful deeds, whether open or secret; take not life, which Allah has made sacred, except by way of justice and law: thus does He command you, that you may learn wisdom.

152. And come not near to the orphan's property, except to improve it until he attain the age of full strength; And give measure and weight with (full) justice - no burden do We place on any soul, but that which it can bear - whenever you speak, speak justly, even if a near relative is concerned; and fulfil the covenant of Allah: thus does He command you, that you may remember.

153. Verily, this is My way leading straight: follow it: follow not (other) paths: they will scatter you about from His (great) path; thus does He command you that you may be righteous.

154. Moreover, We gave Moses the book, completing (Our favour) to those who would do right, and explaining all things in detail - and a guide and a mercy, that they might believe in the meeting with their Lord.

155. And this is a book, which We have revealed as a blessing: so follow it and be righteous, that you may receive mercy;

156. Lest you should say: "The book was sent down to two Peoples before us, and for our part, we remained unacquainted with all that they learned by assiduous study";

157. Or lest you should say: "If the book had only been sent down to us, we should have followed its guidance better than they." Now then has come to you a clear (sign) from your Lord - and a guide and a mercy: then who could do more wrong than one who rejects Allah's signs, and turns away from it? In good time shall We repay those who turn away from Our signs, with a dreadful penalty, for their turning away.

158. Are they waiting to see if the angels come to them, or your Lord (Himself), or certain of the signs of your Lord! The day that certain of the signs of your Lord do come, no good will it do to a soul to believe in them then, if it believed not before, nor earned righteousness through its faith. Say: "Wait you: we too are waiting."

159. As for those who divide their religion and break up into sects, you have no part in them in the least; their affair is with Allah: He will in the end tell them the truth of all that they did.

160. He that does good shall have ten times as much to his credit; he that does evil shall only be recompensed according to his evil; no wrong shall be done to (any of) them.

161. Say: "Verily, my Lord has guided me to a way that is straight - a religion of right - the path (trod) by Abraham the true in faith, and he (certainly) joined not gods with Allah."

162. Say: "Truly, my prayer and my service of sacrifice, my life and my death, are (all) for Allah, the Cherisher of the Worlds;

163. No partner has He: this am I commanded, and I am the first of those who bow to His Will.

164. Say: "Shall I seek for (my) Cherisher other than Allah, when He is the Cherisher of all things (that exist)? Every soul draws the meed of its acts on none but itself: no bearer of burdens can bear the burden of another. Your goal in the end is towards Allah: He will tell you the truth of the things in which you disputed."

165. It is He Who has made you (His) agents, inheritors of the earth: He has raised you in ranks, some above others; that He may try you in the gifts He has given you: for your Lord is quick in punishment; yet He is indeed Oft-Forgiving, Most Merciful.

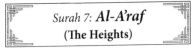

*Surah 7: **Al-A'raf***
(The Heights)

In the name of Allah,
Most Gracious, Most Merciful.

1. *Alif Lam Mim Sad.*

2. A book revealed to you - so let your heart be oppressed no more by any difficulty on that account - that with it you might warn (the erring) and teach the believers.

3. Follow (O men!) the revelation given to you from your Lord, and follow not, as friends or protectors, other than Him. Little it is you remember of admonition.

4. How many towns have We destroyed (for their sins)? Our punishment took them on a sudden by night or while they slept for their afternoon rest.

5. When (thus) Our punishment took them, no call did they utter but this: "Indeed we did wrong."

6. Then shall We question those to whom Our Message was sent and those by whom We sent it.

7. And verily We shall recount their whole story with knowledge, for We were never absent (at any time or place).

8. The balance that day will be true (to a nicety); those whose scale (of good) will be heavy, will prosper;

9. Those whose scale will be light, will find their souls in perdition, for that they wrongfully treated Our signs.

10. It is We who have placed you with authority on earth, and provided you in it with means for the fulfilment of your life; small are the thanks that you give!

11. It is We who created you and gave you shape; then We asked the angels to bow down to Adam, and they bowed down; not so Iblis; he refused to be of those who bow down.

12. (Allah) said: "What prevented you from bowing down when I commanded you?" He said: "I am better than he: You did create me from fire, and him from clay."

13. (Allah) said: "Get you down from this; it is not for you to be arrogant here; get out, for you are of the meanest (of creatures)."

14. He said: "Give me respite till the day they are raised up."

15. (Allah) said: "Be you among those who have respite."

16. He said: "Because You have thrown me out of the way, I will lie in wait for them on Your straight way."

17. "Then will I assault them from before them and behind them, from their right and their left; nor will You find, in most of them, gratitude (for Your mercies)."

18. (Allah) said: "Get out from this, disgraced and expelled. If any of them follow you - hell will I fill with you all.

19. O Adam! Dwell you and your wife in the garden, and enjoy (its good things) as you wish; but approach not this tree, or you run into harm and transgression."

20. Then began Satan to whisper suggestions to them, in order to reveal to them their shame that was hidden from them (before); he said: "Your Lord only forbade you this tree, lest you should become angels or such beings as live for ever."

21. And he swore to them both, that he was their sincere adviser.

22. So by deceit he brought about their fall: when they tasted of the tree, their shame became manifest to them, and they began to sew together the leaves of the garden over their bodies. And their Lord called to them: "Did I not forbid you that tree, and tell you that Satan was an avowed enemy to you?"

23. They said: "Our Lord! We have wronged our own souls; if You forgive us not and bestow not upon us Your mercy, we shall certainly be lost."

24. (Allah) said: "Get you down, with enmity between yourselves. On earth will be your dwelling-place and your means of livelihood - for a time."

25. He said: "In it shall you live, and in it shall you die; but from it shall you be taken out (at last)."

26. O you Children of Adam! We have bestowed garment upon you to cover your shame, as well as to be an adornment to you. But the garment of righteousness - that is the best. Such are among the signs of Allah, that they may receive admonition!

27. O you Children of Adam! Let not Satan seduce you, in the same manner as he got your parents out of the garden, stripping them of their garment, to expose their shame; for he and his tribe watch you from a position where you cannot see them; We made the evil ones friends (only) to those without faith.

28. When they do anything that is shameful, they say: "We found our fathers doing so"; and "Allah commanded us thus"; say: "Nay, Allah never commands what is shameful: Do you say of Allah what you know not?"

29. Say: "My Lord has commanded justice; and that you set your whole selves (to Him) at every time and place of prayer, and call upon Him, making your devotion sincere as in His sight; such as He created you in the beginning, so shall you return."

30. Some He has guided: others have (by their choice) deserved the loss of their way; in that they took the evil ones, in preference to Allah, for their friends and protectors, and think that they receive guidance.

31. O Children of Adam! Wear your beautiful apparel at every time and place of prayer; eat and drink; but waste not by excess, for Allah loves not the wasters.

32. Say: "Who has forbidden the beautiful (gifts) of Allah, which He has produced for His servants, and the things, clean and pure, (which He has provided) for sustenance? Say: They are in the life of this world, for those who believe, (and) purely for them on the day of judgement. Thus do We explain the signs in detail for those who understand."

33. Say: "The things that my Lord has indeed forbidden are: shameful deeds, whether open or secret; sins and trespasses against truth or reason; assigning of partners to Allah, for which He has given no authority; and saying things about Allah of which you have no knowledge."

34. To every People is a term appointed: when their term is reached, not an hour can they cause delay, nor (an hour) can they advance (it in anticipation).

35. O you Children of Adam! Whenever there come to you messengers from amongst you, rehearsing My signs to you - those who are righteous and mend (their lives) - on them shall be no fear nor shall they grieve.

36. But those who reject Our signs and treat them with arrogance - they are companions of the fire, to dwell in it (for ever).

37. Who is more unjust than one who invents a lie against Allah or rejects His signs? For such, their portion appointed must reach them from the book (of decrees); until, when Our messengers (of death) arrive and take their souls, they say: "Where are the things that you used to invoke besides Allah?" They will reply, "they have left us in the lurch," and they will bear witness against themselves, that they had rejected Allah.

38. He will say: "Enter you in the company of the peoples who passed away before you - men and Jinns - into the fire. Every time a new people enters, it curses its sister-people (that went before), until they follow each other all into the fire. Says the last about the first: "Our Lord! It is these that misled us: so give them a double penalty in the fire." He will say: "Doubled for all": but this You do not understand.

39. Then the first will say to the last: "See then! No advantage have you over us; so taste you of the penalty for all that you did!"

40. To those who reject Our signs and treat them with arrogance, no opening will there be of the gates of heaven, nor will they enter the garden, until the camel can pass through the eye of the needle: such is Our reward for those in sin.

41. For them there is hell, as a couch (below) and folds and folds of covering above: such is Our requital of those who do wrong.

42. But those who believe and work righteousness - no burden do We place on any soul, but that which it can bear - they will be companions of the garden, in it to dwell (for ever).

43. And We shall remove from their hearts any lurking sense of injury - beneath them will be rivers flowing - and they shall say: "Praise be to Allah, Who has guided us to this (felicity); never could we have found guidance, had it not been for the guidance of Allah; indeed it was the truth that the messengers of our Lord brought to us." And they shall hear the call: "See! The garden before you! You have been made its inheritors for your deeds (of righteousness)."

44. The companions of the garden will call out to the companions of the fire: "We have indeed found the promises of our Lord to us true; have you also found your Lord's promises true?" They shall say, "Yes"; but a Caller shall proclaim between them: "The curse of Allah is on the wrongdoers -

45. Those who would hinder (men) from the path of Allah and would seek in it something crooked; they were those who denied the hereafter."

46. Between them shall be a veil, and on the heights will be men who would know everyone by his marks: they will call out to the companions of the garden, "Peace on you": they will not have entered, but they will have an assurance (of it.)

47. When their eyes shall be turned towards the companions of the fire, they will say: "Our Lord! Send us not to the company of the wrongdoers."

48. The men on the heights will call to certain men whom they will know from their marks, saying: "Of what profit to you were you hoards and your arrogant ways?"

49. "See! Are these not the men whom you swore that Allah with His mercy would never bless? Enter you the garden: no fear shall be on you, nor shall you grieve."

50. The companions of the fire will call to the companions of the garden; "Pour down to us water or anything that Allah does provide for your sustenance." They will say: "Both these things has Allah forbidden to those who rejected Him -

51. Such as took their religion to be mere amusement and play, and were deceived by the life of the world." That day shall We forget them as they forgot the meeting of this day of theirs, and as they used to reject Our signs.

52. For We had certainly sent to them a book, based on knowledge, which We explained in detail - a guide and a mercy to all who believe.

53. Do they just wait for the final fulfilment of the event? On the day the event is finally fulfilled, those who disregarded it before will say: "The messengers of our Lord did indeed bring true (tidings). Have we no intercessors now to intercede on our behalf? Or could we be sent back? Then should we behave differently from our behaviour in the past." In fact, they will have lost their souls, and the things they invented will leave them in the lurch.

54. Your Guardian-Lord is Allah, Who created the heavens and the earth in six Days, and is firmly established on the throne (of authority); He draws the night as a veil over the day, each seeking the other in rapid succession; He created the sun, the moon, and the stars (all) governed by laws under His command. Is it not His to create and to govern? Blessed be Allah, the Cherisher and Sustainer of the Worlds!

55. Call on your Lord with humility and in private: for Allah loves not those who trespass beyond bounds.

56. Do no mischief on the earth, after it has been set in order, but call on Him with fear and longing (in your hearts): for the mercy of Allah is (always) near to those who do good.

57. It is He Who sends the winds like heralds of glad tidings, going before His mercy; when they have carried the heavy-laden clouds, We drive them to a land that is dead, make rain to descend on it, and produce every kind of harvest with it; thus shall We raise up the dead; perhaps you may remember.

58. From the land that is clean and good, by the will of its Cherisher, springs up produce, (rich) after its kind; but from the land that is bad, spring up nothing but that which is niggardly; thus do We explain the signs by various (symbols) to those who are grateful.

59. We sent Noah to his people. He said: "O my people! Worship Allah! You have no other god but Him. I fear for you the punishment of a dreadful day!"

60. The leaders of his people said: "Ah! We see you evidently wandering (in mind)."

61. He said: "O my people! No wandering is there in my (mind): on the contrary, I am a messenger from the Lord and Cherisher of the Worlds!"

62. "I but fulfil towards you the duties of my Lord's mission: sincere is my advice to you, and I know from Allah something that you know not."

63. "Do you wonder that there has come to you a message from your Lord, through a man of your own people, to warn you - so that you may fear Allah and perhaps receive His mercy?"

64. But they rejected him, and We delivered him, and those with him in the Ark; But We overwhelmed in the flood those who rejected Our signs. They were indeed a blind people!

65. To the 'Ad people, (We sent) Hud, one of their (own) brothers: he said: "O my people! Worship Allah! You have no other god but Him. Will you not fear (Allah)?"

66. The leaders of the unbelievers among his people said: "Ah! We see you are an imbecile!" And "We think you are a liar!"

67. He said: "O my people! I am no imbecile, but (I am) a messenger from the Lord and Cherisher of the Worlds!"

68. "I but fulfil towards you the duties of my Lord's mission: I am to you a sincere and trustworthy adviser."

69. "Do you wonder that there has come to you a message from your Lord through a man of your own people, to warn you? Call in remembrance that He made you inheritors after the people of Noah, and gave you a stature tall among the nations. Call in remembrance the benefits (you have received) from Allah; so that you may prosper."

70. They said: "Do you come to us, that we may worship Allah alone, and give up the cult of our fathers? Bring us what you threaten us with, if so be that you tell the truth!"

71. He said: "Punishment and wrath have already come upon you from your Lord; dispute you with me over names which you have devised - you and your fathers - without authority from Allah? Then wait: I am amongst you, also waiting."

72. We saved him and those who adhered to him, by Our mercy and We cut off the roots of those who rejected Our signs and did not believe.

73. To the Thamud people (We sent) Salih, one of their own brothers: he said: "O my people! Worship Allah; you have no other god but Him. Now has come to you a clear (sign) from your Lord! This she-camel of Allah is a sign to you: so leave her to graze in Allah's earth, and let her come to no harm, or you shall be seized with a grievous punishment."

74. "And remember how He made you inheritors after the 'Ad people and gave you habitations in the land: you build for yourselves palaces and castles in (open) plains, and carve out homes in the mountains; so bring to remembrance the benefits (you have received) from Allah, and refrain from evil and mischief on the earth."

75. The leaders of the arrogant party among his people said to those who were reckoned powerless - those among them who believed: "Do you know that Salih is a messenger from his Lord?" They said: "We do indeed believe in the revelation which has been sent through him."

76. The arrogant party said: "For our part, we reject what you believe in."

77. Then they hamstrung the she-camel, and insolently defied the order of their Lord, saying: "O Salih! Bring about your threats, if you are a messenger (of Allah)!"

78. So the earthquake took them unawares, and they lay prostrate in their homes in the morning!

79. So Salih left them, saying: "O my people! I did indeed convey to you the message for which I was sent by my Lord: I gave you good counsel, but you love not good counsellors!"

80. We also (sent) Lot: he said to his people: "Do you commit lewdness such as no people in creation (ever) committed before you?"

81. "For you practice your lusts on men in preference to women: you are indeed a people transgressing beyond bounds."

82. And his people gave no answer but this: they said, "Drive them out of your city: these are indeed men who want to be clean and pure!"

83. But We saved him and his family, except his wife: she was of those who lagged behind.

84. And We rained down on them a shower (of brimstone): then see what was the end of those who indulged in sin and crime!

85. To the Madyan people We sent Shu'ayb, one of their own brothers: he said: "O my people! Worship Allah; You have no other god but Him. Now has come to you a clear (sign) from your Lord! Give just measure and weight, nor withhold from the people the things that are their due; and do no mischief on the earth after it has been set in order: that will be best for you, if you have faith."

86. "And squat not on every road, breathing threats, hindering from the path of Allah those who believe in Him, and seeking in it something crooked; but remember how you were little, and He gave you increase. And hold in your mind's eye what was the end of those who did mischief."

87. "And if there is a party among you who believes in the message with which I have been sent, and a party which does not believe, hold yourselves in patience until Allah does decide between us: for He is the best to decide."

88. The leaders, the arrogant party among his people, said: "O Shu'ayb! We shall certainly drive you out of our city - (you) and those who believe with you; or else you (you and they) shall have to return to our ways and religion." He said: "What! Even though we do detest (them)?"

89. "We should indeed invent a lie against Allah, if we returned to your ways after Allah has rescued us from it; nor could we by any manner of means return to it unless it be as in the will and plan of Allah, Our Lord. Our Lord can reach out to the utmost recesses of things by His knowledge. In Allah is our trust. Our Lord! Decide You between us and our people in truth, for You are the best to decide."

90. The leaders, the unbelievers among his people, said: "If you follow Shu'ayb, be sure then you are ruined!"

91. But the earthquake took them unawares, and they lay prostrate in their homes before the morning!

92. The men who rejected Shu'ayb became as if they had never been in the homes where they had flourished: the men who rejected Shu'ayb - it was they who were ruined!

93. So Shu'ayb left them, saying: "O my people! I did indeed convey to you the messages for which I was sent by my Lord: I gave you good counsel, but how shall I lament over a people who refuse to believe!"

94. Whenever We sent a prophet to a town, We took up its people in suffering and adversity, in order that they might learn humility.

95. Then We changed their suffering into prosperity, until they grew and multiplied, and began to say: "Our fathers (too) were touched by suffering and affluence." See! We called them to account of a sudden, while they realised not (their peril).

96. If the people of the towns had but believed and feared Allah, We should indeed have opened out to them (all kinds of) blessings from heaven and earth; but they rejected (the truth), and We brought them to book for their misdeeds.

97. Did the people of the towns feel secure against the coming of Our wrath by night while they were asleep?

98. Or else did they feel secure against its coming in broad daylight while they played about (carefree)?

99. Did they then feel secure against the plan of Allah? - But no one can feel secure from the plan of Allah, except those (doomed) to ruin!

100. To those who inherit the earth in succession to its (previous) possessors, is it not a guiding (lesson) that, if We so willed, We could punish them (too) for their sins, and seal up their hearts so that they could not hear?

101. Such were the towns whose story We (thus) relate to you: there came indeed to them their messengers with clear (signs); but they would not believe what they had rejected before. Thus does Allah seal up the hearts of those who reject faith.

102. Most of them We found not men (true) to their covenant; but most of them We found rebellious and disobedient.

103. Then after them We sent Moses with Our signs to Pharaoh and his chiefs, but they wrongfully rejected them: so see what was the end of those who made mischief.

104. Moses said: "O Pharaoh! I am a messenger from the Lord of the Worlds -

105. One for whom it is right to say nothing but truth about Allah. Now have I come to you (people), from your Lord, with a clear (sign): so let the Children of Israel depart along with me."

106. (Pharaoh) said: "If indeed you have come with a sign, show it now - if you tell the truth."

107. Then (Moses) threw his rod and see! It was a serpent, plain (for all to see)!

108. And he drew out his hand, and see! It was white to all onlookers!

109. Said the Chiefs of the people of Pharaoh: "This is indeed a sorcerer well-versed."

110. "His plan is to get you out of your land: then what is it you counsel?"

111. They said: "Keep him and his brother in suspense (for a while); and send to the cities men to collect -

112. And bring up to you all (our) sorcerers well-versed."

113. So there came the sorcerers to Pharaoh: they said, "Of course, we shall have a (suitable) reward if we win!"

114. He said: "Yea, (and more) - for you shall in that case be (raised to posts) nearest (to my person)."

115. They said: "O Moses! Will you throw (first), or shall we have the (first) throw?"

116. Said Moses: "Throw you (first)." So when they threw, they bewitched the eyes of the people, and struck terror into them; for they showed a great (feat of) magic.

117. We put it into Moses's mind by inspiration: "Throw (now) your rod"; and see! It swallowed up straightaway all the falsehoods which they faked!

118. Thus truth was confirmed. And all that they did was made of no effect.

119. So the (great ones) were vanquished there and then, and were made to look small.

120. But the sorcerers fell down prostrate in adoration.

121. Saying: "We believe in the Lord of the Worlds."

122. "The Lord of Moses and Aaron."

123. Said Pharaoh: "Believe you in Him before I give you permission? Surely this is a trick which you have planned in the city to drive out its people; but soon shall you know (the consequences)."

124. "Be sure I will cut off your hands and your feet on opposite sides, and I will cause you all to die on the cross."

125. They said: "For us, we are but sent back to our Lord:

126. But you do wreak your vengeance on us simply because we believed in the signs of our Lord when they reached us! Our Lord! Pour out on us patience and constancy, and take our souls to you as Muslims (who bow to Your will)!"

127. Said the chiefs of Pharaoh's people: "Will you leave Moses and his people, to spread mischief in the land, and to abandon you and your gods?" He said: "Their male children will we slay; (only) their females will we save alive; and we have over them (power) irresistible."

128. Said Moses to his people: "Pray for help from Allah and (wait) in patience and constancy: for the earth is Allah's, to give as a heritage to such of His servants as He pleases; and the end is (best) for the righteous."

129. They said: "We have had (nothing but) trouble, both before and after you came to us." He said: "It may be that your Lord will destroy your enemy and make you inheritors in the earth; that so He may try you by your deeds."

130. We punished the people of Pharaoh with years (of drought) and shortness of crops; that they might receive admonition.

131. But when good (times) came, they said, "This is due to us"; when gripped by calamity, they ascribed it to evil omens connected with Moses and those with him! See! In truth, the omens of evil are theirs in Allah's sight, but most of them do not understand!

132. They said (to Moses): "Whatever be the signs you bring, to work with it the sorcery on us, we shall never believe in you."

133. So We sent (plagues) on them wholesale death, locusts, lice, frogs, and blood: signs openly self-explained; but they were steeped in arrogance, a people given to sin.

134. Every time the penalty fell on them, they said: "O Moses! On our behalf call on your Lord in virtue of His promise to you; if you will remove the penalty from us, we shall truly believe in you, and we shall send away the Children of Israel with you."

135. But every time We removed the penalty from them according to a fixed term which they had to fulfil - See! They broke their word!

136. So We exacted retribution from them: We drowned them in the sea, because they rejected Our signs, and failed to take warning from them.

137. And We made a people, considered weak (and of no account), inheritors of lands in both east and west - lands upon which We sent down Our blessings. The fair promise of your Lord was fulfilled for the Children of Israel, because they had patience and constancy, and We levelled to the ground the great works and fine buildings which Pharaoh and his people erected (with such pride).

138. We took the Children of Israel (with safety) across the sea. They came upon a people devoted entirely to some idols they had. They said: "O Moses! Fashion for us a god like the gods they have." He said: "Surely you are a people without knowledge."

139. "As to these folk - the cult they are in is (but) a fragment of a ruin, and vain is the (worship) which they practice."

140. He said: "Shall I seek for you a god other than the (true) God, when it is Allah who has endowed you with gifts above the nations?"

141. And remember We rescued you from Pharaoh's people, who afflicted you with the worst of penalties, who slew your male children and saved alive your females: in that was a momentous trial from your Lord.

142. We appointed for Moses thirty nights, and completed (the period) with ten (more): thus was completed the term (of communion) with his Lord, forty nights. And Moses had charged his brother Aaron (before he went up): "Act for me amongst my people; do right, and follow not the way of those who do mischief."

143. When Moses came to the place appointed by Us, and his Lord addressed him, He said: "O my Lord! Show (Yourself) to me, that I may look upon You." Allah said: "By no means can you see Me (direct); but look upon the Mount; if it remain in its place, then shall you see Me." When his Lord manifested His glory on the Mount, He made it as dust, and Moses fell down in a swoon. When he recovered his senses he said: "Glory be to You! To You I turn in repentance, and I am the first to believe."

144. (Allah) said: "O Moses! I have chosen you above (other) men, by the mission I (have given you) and the words I (have spoken to you): Take then the (revelation) which I give you, and be of those Who give thanks."

145. And We ordained laws for him in the tablets in all matters, both commanding and explaining all things, (and said): "Take and hold these with firmness, and enjoin your people to hold fast by the best in the precepts: soon shall I show you the homes of the wicked - (how they lie desolate)."

146. Those who behave arrogantly on the earth in defiance of right - them will I turn away from My signs, they will not believe in them; and if they see the way of right conduct, they will not adopt it as the way; but if they see the way of error, that is the way they will adopt; for they have rejected Our signs, and failed to take warning from them.

147. Those who reject Our signs and the meeting in the hereafter - vain are their deeds: can they expect to be rewarded except as they have wrought?

148. The people of Moses made, in his absence, out of their ornaments, the image of a calf, (for worship); it seemed to low: did they not see that it could neither speak to them, nor show them the way? They took it for worship and they did wrong.

149. When they repented, and saw that they had erred, they said: "If our Lord have not mercy upon us and forgive us, we shall indeed be of those who perish."

150. When Moses came back to his people, angry and grieved, he said: "Evil it is that you have done in my place in my absence; did you make haste to bring on the judgement of your Lord?" He put down the tablets, seized his brother by (the hair of) his head, and dragged him to him. Aaron said: "Son of my mother! The people did indeed reckon me as nothing, and went near to slaying me! Make not the enemies rejoice over my misfortune, nor count you me amongst the people of sin."

151. Moses prayed: "O my Lord! Forgive me and my brother! Admit us to Your mercy! For You are the Most Merciful of those who show mercy!"

152. Those who took the calf (for worship) will indeed be overwhelmed with wrath from their Lord, and with shame in this life; thus do We recompense those who invent (falsehoods).

153. But those who do wrong but repent afterwards and (truly) believe - verily Your Lord is afterwards Oft-Forgiving, Most Merciful.

154. When the anger of Moses was appeased, he took up the tablets: in the writing on them was guidance and mercy for such as fear their Lord.

155. And Moses chose seventy of his people for Our place of meeting; when they were seized with violent quaking, he prayed; "O my Lord! If it had been Your will You could have destroyed, long before, both them and me; would You destroy us for the deeds of the foolish ones among us? This is no more than Your trial; by it You cause whom You will to stray and You lead whom You will into the right path. You are our protector: so forgive us and give us Your mercy; for You are the best of those who forgive."

156. "And ordain for us that which is good, in this life and in the hereafter: for we have turned to You." He said: "With My punishment I visit whom I will; but My mercy extends to all things. That (mercy) I shall ordain

for those who do right, and practice regular charity, and those who believe in Our signs -

157. Those who follow the messenger, the unlettered prophet, whom they find mentioned in their own (scriptures) - in the law and the Gospel - for he commands them what is just and forbids them what is evil; he allows them as lawful what is good (and pure) and prohibits them from what is bad (and impure); he releases them from their heavy burdens and from the yokes that are upon them. So it is those who believe in him, honour him, help him, and follow the light which is sent down with him - it is they who will prosper."

158. Say: "O men! I am sent to you all, as the messenger of Allah, to Whom belongs the dominion of the heavens and the earth; there is no god but He; it is He that gives both life and death. So believe in Allah and His messenger, the unlettered prophet, who believes in Allah and His words: follow him (so) that you may be guided."

159. Of the people of Moses there is a section who guide and do justice in the light of truth.

160. We divided them into twelve tribes or nations. We directed Moses by inspiration, when his (thirsty) people asked him for water: "Strike the rock with your staff": out of it there gushed forth twelve springs; each group knew its own place for water. We gave them the shade of clouds, and sent down to them manna and quails, (saying): "Eat of the good things We have provided for you"; (but they rebelled); to Us they did no harm, but they harmed their own souls.

161. And remember it was said to them: "Dwell in this town and eat in it as you wish, but say the word of humility and enter the gate in a posture of humility; We shall forgive you your faults; We shall increase (the portion of) those who do good."

162. But the transgressors among them changed the word from that which had been given them; so We sent on them a plague from heaven for that they repeatedly transgressed.

163. Ask them concerning the town standing close by the sea. See! They transgressed in the matter of the Sabbath. For on the day of their Sabbath their fish did come to them openly holding up their heads, but on the day they had no Sabbath, they came not: thus did We make a trial of them, for they were given to transgression.

164. When some of them said: "Why do you preach to a people whom Allah will destroy or visit with a terrible punishment?" - Said the preachers: "To discharge our duty to your Lord, and perhaps they may fear Him."

165. When they disregarded the warnings that had been given them, We rescued those who forbade evil; but We visited the wrongdoers with a grievous punishment, because they were given to transgression.

166. When in their insolence they transgressed (all) prohibitions, We said to them: "Be you apes, despised and rejected."

167. See! Your Lord did declare that He would send against them to the day of judgement, those who would afflict them with grievous penalty. Your Lord is quick in retribution, but He is also Oft-Forgiving, Most Merciful.

168. We broke them up into sections on this earth. There are among them some that are the righteous, and some that are the opposite. We have tried them with both prosperity and adversity: in order that they might turn (to Us).

169. After them succeeded an (evil) generation; they inherited the book, but they chose (for themselves) the vanities of this world, saying (for excuse): "(Everything) will be forgiven us." (Even so), if similar vanities came their way, they would (again) seize them. Was not the covenant of the book taken from them, that they would not ascribe to Allah anything but the truth? And they study what is in the book. But best for the righteous is the home in the hereafter: will you not understand?

170. As to those who hold fast by the book and establish regular prayer - never shall We suffer the reward of the righteous to perish.

171. When We shook the Mount over them, as if it had been a canopy, and they thought it was going to fall on them (We said): "Hold firmly to what We have given you, and bring (ever) to remembrance what is in it; perhaps you may fear Allah."

172. When your Lord brought out from the Children of Adam from their loins their descendants, and made them testify concerning themselves (saying): "Am I not your Lord (who cherishes and sustains you)?" They said: "Yea! We do testify!" (This), lest you should say on the day of judgement: "Of this we were never mindful."

173. Or lest you should say: "Our fathers before us may have taken false gods, but we are (their) descendants after them: will You then destroy us because of the deeds of men who were futile?"

174. Thus do We explain the signs in detail! And perhaps they may turn (to Us).

175. Relate to them the story of the man to whom We sent Our signs, but he passed them by: so Satan followed him up, and he went astray.

176. If it had been Our Will, We should have elevated him with Our signs; but he inclined to the earth, and followed his own vain desires. His similitude is that of a dog: if you attack him, he lolls out his tongue, or if you leave him alone, he (still) lolls out his tongue. That is the similitude of those who reject Our signs; so relate the story; perhaps they may reflect.

177. Evil as an example are people who reject Our signs and wrong their own souls.

178. Whom Allah does guide - he is on the right path: whom He rejects from His guidance - such are the persons who perish.

179. Many are the Jinns and men We have made for hell: They have hearts

with which they understand not, eyes with which they see not, and ears with which they hear not. They are like cattle - nay more misguided: for they are heedless (of warning).

180. The most beautiful names belong to Allah: so call on Him by them; but shun such men as use profanity in His names: for what they do, they will soon be requited.

181. Of those We have created are people who direct (others) with truth, and dispense justice with it.

182. Those who reject Our signs, We shall gradually visit with punishment, in ways they perceive not.

183. Respite will I grant to them: for My scheme is strong (and unfailing).

184. Do they not reflect? Their companion is not seized with madness: he is but a perspicuous warner.

185. Do they see nothing in the government of the heavens and the earth and all that Allah has created? (Do they not see) that it may well be that their term is near drawing to an end? In what message after this will they then believe?

186. To such as Allah rejects from His guidance, there can be no guide; He will leave them in their trespasses, wandering in distraction.

187. They ask you about the (final) hour - when will be its appointed time? Say: "The knowledge of it is with my Lord (alone): none but He can reveal as to when it will occur. Heavy were its burdens through the heavens and the earth. Only all of a sudden will

it come to you." They ask you as if you were eager in search of it: Say: "The knowledge of it is with Allah (alone), but most men know not."

188. Say: "I have no power over any good or harm to myself except as Allah wills. If I had knowledge of the unseen, I should have multiplied all good, and no evil should have touched me: I am but a warner, and a bringer of glad tidings to those who have faith."

189. It is He Who created you from a single person, and made his mate of like nature, in order that he might dwell with her (in love). When they are united, she bears a light burden and carries it about (unnoticed). When she grows heavy, they both pray to Allah their Lord, (saying): "If You give us a goodly child, we vow we shall (ever) be grateful."

190. But when He gives them a goodly child, they ascribe to others a share in the gift they have received: but Allah is exalted high above the partners they ascribe to Him.

191. Do they indeed ascribe to Him as partners things that can create nothing, but are themselves created?

192. No aid can they give them, nor can they aid themselves!

193. If you call them to guidance, they will not obey: for you it is the same whether you call them or you hold your peace!

194. Verily those whom you call upon besides Allah are servants like to you: call upon them, and let them listen to your prayer, if you are (indeed) truthful!

195. Have they feet to walk with? Or hands to lay hold with? Or eyes to see with? Or ears to hear with? Say: "Call your 'god-partners', scheme (your worst) against me, and give me no respite!"

196. "For my protector is Allah, Who revealed the book (from time to time), and He will choose and befriend the righteous."

197. "But those you call upon besides Him, are unable to help you, and indeed to help themselves."

198. If you (Muslims) call them to guidance, they hear not. You (O Muhammad) will see them looking at you, but they see not.

199. Hold to forgiveness; command what is right; but turn away from the ignorant.

200. If a suggestion from Satan assail your (mind), seek refuge with Allah; for He hears and knows (all things).

201. Those who fear Allah, when a thought of evil from Satan assaults them, bring Allah to remembrance, when they see (aright)!

202. But their brothers (the evil ones) plunge them deeper into error, and never relax (their efforts).

203. If you bring them not a revelation, they say: "Why have you not got it together?" Say: "I but follow what is revealed to me from my Lord: This is (nothing but) lights from your Lord, and guidance and mercy, for any who have faith."

204. When the Qur'an is read, listen to it with attention, and hold your peace; that you may receive mercy.

205. And do you (O reader!) Bring your Lord to remembrance in your (very) soul, with humility and in reverence, without loudness in words, in the mornings and evenings; and be not you of those who are unheedful.

206. Those who are near to your Lord, disdain not to do Him worship: They celebrate His praises, and bow down before Him.

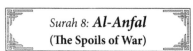

Surah 8: *Al-Anfal*
(The Spoils of War)

In the name of Allah,
Most Gracious, Most Merciful.

1. They ask you (O Muhammad) concerning (things taken as) spoils of war. Say: "(Such) spoils are at the disposal of Allah and the messenger: so fear Allah, and keep straight the relations between yourselves: obey Allah and His messenger, if you do believe."

2. For, believers are those who, when Allah is mentioned, feel a tremor in their hearts, and when they hear His signs rehearsed, find their faith strengthened, and put (all) their trust in their Lord.

3. Who establish regular prayers and spend (freely) out of the gifts We have given them for sustenance:

4. Such in truth are the believers: they have grades of dignity with their Lord, and forgiveness, and generous sustenance.

5. Just as your Lord ordered you (O Muhammad) out of your house in truth, even though a party among the believers disliked it.

6. Disputing with you concerning the truth after it was made manifest, as if they were being driven to death and they (actually) saw it.

7. See! Allah promised you one of the two (enemy) parties, that it should be yours: you wished that the one unarmed should be yours, but Allah willed to justify the truth according to His words, and to cut off the roots of the unbelievers -

8. That He might justify truth and prove falsehood false, distasteful though it be to those in guilt.

9. Remember you implored the assistance of your Lord, and He answered you: "I will assist you with a thousand of the angels, ranks on ranks."

10. Allah made it but a message of hope, and an assurance to your hearts: (in any case) there is no help except from Allah; and Allah is Exalted in Power, Wise.

11. Remember He covered you with a sort of drowsiness, to give you calm as from Himself, and He caused rain to descend on you from heaven, to clean you with it, to remove from you the stain of Satan, to strengthen your hearts, and to plant your feet firmly with it.

12. Remember your Lord inspired the angels (with the message): "I am with you; give firmness to the believers; I will instil terror into the hearts of the unbelievers: strike you above their necks and strike all their finger tips off them."

13. This because they contended against Allah and His messenger: if any contend against Allah and His messenger, Allah is strict in punishment.

14. Thus (will it be said): "Taste you then of the (punishment): for those who resist Allah, is the penalty of the fire."

15. O you who believe! When you meet the unbelievers in hostile array, never turn your backs to them.

16. If any do turn his back to them on such a day - unless it be in a stratagem of war, or to retreat to a troop (of his own) - he draws on himself the wrath of Allah, and his abode is hell - an evil refuge (indeed)!

17. It is not you (O believers) who slew them; it was Allah; when you (O Muhammad) threw (a handful of dust), it was not your act, but Allah's; in order that He might test the believers by a gracious trial from Himself: for Allah is He Who hears and knows (all things).

18. That, and also because Allah is He Who makes feeble the plans and stratagems of the unbelievers.

19. (O unbelievers!) If you prayed for victory and judgement, now has the judgement come to you: if you desist (from wrong), it will be best for you: if you return (to the attack), so shall We. Not the least good will your forces be to you even if they were multiplied; for verily Allah is with those who believe!

20. O you who believe! Obey Allah and His messenger, and turn not away from him when you hear (him speak).

21. Nor be like those who say, "we hear," but listen not;

22. For the worst of beasts in the sight of Allah are the deaf and the dumb - those who understand not.

23. If Allah had found in them any good, He would indeed have made them listen; (as it is), if He had made them listen, they would but have turned back and declined (faith).

24. O you who believe! Give your response to Allah and His messenger, when He calls you to that which will give you life; and know that Allah comes in between a man and his heart, and that it is He to whom You shall (all) be gathered.

25. And fear tumult or oppression, which affects not in particular (only) those of you who do wrong: and know that Allah is strict in punishment.

26. Call to mind when you were a small (band), despised through the land, and afraid that men might despoil and kidnap you; but He provided a safe asylum for you, strengthened you with His aid, and gave you good things for sustenance: that you might be grateful.

27. O you who believe! Betray not the trust of Allah and the messenger, nor misappropriate knowingly things entrusted to you.

28. And know you that your possessions and your progeny are but a trial; and that it is Allah with whom lies your highest reward.

29. O you who believe! If you fear Allah, He will grant you a criterion (to judge between right and wrong), remove from you (all) evil (that may afflict) you, and forgive you; for Allah is the Lord of grace unbounded.

30. Remember how the unbelievers plotted against you (O Muhammad), to keep you in bonds, or slay you, or get you out (of your home). They plot and plan, and Allah too plans, but the best of planners is Allah.

31. When Our signs are rehearsed to them, they say: "We have heard this (before); if we wished, we could say (words) like these; these are nothing but tales of the ancients."

32. Remember how they said: "O Allah! If this is indeed the truth from You, rain down on us a shower of stones from the sky, or send us a grievous penalty."

33. But Allah was not going to send them a penalty whilst you were amongst them; nor was He going to send it whilst they could ask for pardon.

34. But what plea have they that Allah should not punish them, when they keep out (men) from the Sacred Mosque - and they are not its guardians? No men can be its guardians except the righteous; but most of them do not understand.

35. Their prayer at the House (of Allah) is nothing but whistling and clapping of hands: (its only answer can be), "Taste you the penalty because you blasphemed."

36. The unbelievers spend their wealth to hinder (men) from the path of Allah, and so will they continue to spend; but in the end they will have (only) regrets and sighs; at length they will be overcome: and the unbelievers will be gathered together to hell -

37. In order that Allah may separate the impure from the pure, put the impure, one on another, heap them together, and cast them into hell. They will be the ones to have lost.

38. Say to the unbelievers, if (now) they desist (from unbelief), their past would be forgiven them; but if they persist, the punishment of those before them is already (a matter of warning for them).

39. And fight them on until there is no more tumult or oppression, and there prevail justice and faith in Allah altogether and everywhere; but if they cease, verily Allah does see all that they do.

40. If they refuse, be sure that Allah is your protector - the best to protect and the best to help.

41. And know that out of all the booty that you may acquire (in war), a fifth share is assigned to Allah and to the messenger, and to near relatives, orphans, the needy, and the wayfarer - if you do believe in Allah and in the revelation We sent down to Our servant on the day of testing - the day of the meeting of the two forces. For Allah has power over all things.

42. Remember you were on the near side of the valley, and they on the far side, and the caravan on lower ground than you. Even if you had made a mutual appointment to meet, you would certainly have failed in the appointment: but (thus you met), that Allah might accomplish a matter already enacted; that those who died might die after a clear sign (had been given), and those who lived might live after a clear sign (had been given). And verily Allah is He Who hears and knows (all things).

43. Remember in your dream Allah showed them to you (O Muhammad) as few; if He had shown them to you as many, you would surely have been discouraged, and you would surely have disputed in (your) decision; but Allah saved (you): for He knows well the (secrets) of (all) hearts.

44. And remember when you met, He showed them to you as few in your eyes, and He made you appear as contemptible in their eyes; That Allah might accomplish a matter already enacted: for to Allah do all questions go back (for decision).

45. O you who believe! When you meet a force, be firm, and call Allah in remembrance much (and often); that you may prosper.

46. And obey Allah and His messenger; and fall into no disputes, lest you lose heart and your power depart; and be patient and persevering: for Allah is with those who patiently persevere.

47. And be not like those who started from their homes insolently and to be seen of men, and to hinder (men) from the path of Allah; for Allah encompasses all that they do.

48. Remember Satan made their (sinful) acts seem alluring to them, and said: "No one among men can overcome you this day, while I am near to you"; but when the two forces came in sight of each other, he turned on his heels, and said: "I am clear of you; I

see what you see not; I fear Allah; for Allah is strict in punishment."

49. The hypocrites say, and those in whose hearts is a disease: "These people - their religion has misled them." But if any trust in Allah, behold! Allah is Exalted in Might, Wise.

50. If you could see, when the angels take the souls of the unbelievers (at death), (how) they strike their faces and their backs, (saying): "Taste the penalty of the blazing fire -

51. Because of (the deeds) which your (own) hands sent before: for Allah is never unjust to His servants:

52. (Deeds) after the manner of the people of Pharaoh and of those before them: they rejected the signs of Allah and Allah punished them for their crimes: for Allah is Strong, and Strict in punishment:

53. Because Allah will never change the grace which He has bestowed on a people until they change what is in their (own) souls: and verily Allah is He Who hears and knows (all things)."

54. "(Deeds) after the manner of the people of Pharaoh and those before them": they treated as false the signs of their Lord; so We destroyed them for their crimes, and We drowned the People of Pharaoh: for they were all oppressors and wrongdoers.

55. For the worst of beasts in the sight of Allah are those who reject Him; They will not believe.

56. They are those with whom you did make a covenant, but they break their covenant every time, and they have not the fear (of Allah).

57. If you gain the mastery over them in war, disperse, with them, those who follow them, that they may remember.

58. If you fear treachery from any group, throw back (their covenant) to them, (so as to be) on equal terms: for Allah loves not the treacherous.

59. Let not the unbelievers think that they can get the better (of the Godly): they will never frustrate (them).

60. Against them make ready your strength to the utmost of your power, including steeds of war, to strike terror into (the hearts of) the enemies of Allah and your enemies, and others besides, whom you may not know, but whom Allah does know. Whatever you shall spend in the cause of Allah, shall be repaid to you, and you shall not be treated unjustly.

61. But if the enemy incline towards peace, do you (also) incline towards peace, and trust in Allah: for He is the One that hears and knows (all things).

62. Should they intend to deceive you - verily Allah suffices you: He it is that has strengthened you with His aid and with (the company of) the believers;

63. And (moreover) He has put affection between their hearts: not if you had spent all that is in the earth, could you have produced that affection, but Allah has done it: for He is Exalted in might, Wise.

64. O Prophet! Sufficient to you is Allah - (to you) and to those who follow you among the believers.

65. O Prophet! Rouse the believers to the fight. If there are twenty amongst you, patient and persevering, they will vanquish two hundred; if a hundred, they will vanquish a thousand of the unbelievers; for these are a people without understanding.

66. For the present, Allah has lightened your (task) for He knows that there is a weak spot in you: but (even so), if there are a hundred of you, patient and persevering, they will vanquish two hundred, and if a thousand, they will vanquish two thousand, with the leave of Allah; for Allah is with those who patiently persevere.

67. It is not fitting for a prophet that he should have prisoners of war until he has thoroughly subdued the land. You look for the temporal goods of this world; but Allah looks to the hereafter; and Allah is Exalted in might, Wise.

68. Had it not been for a previous ordainment from Allah, a severe penalty would have reached you for the (ransom) that you took.

69. But (now) enjoy what you took in war, lawful and good; but fear Allah; for Allah is Oft-Forgiving, Most Merciful.

70. O Prophet! Say to those who are captives in your hands: "If Allah finds any good in your hearts, He will give you something better than what has been taken from you, and He will forgive you; for Allah is Oft-Forgiving, Most Merciful."

71. But if they have treacherous designs against you, (O messenger!), they have already been in treason against Allah, and so has He given (you) power over them. And Allah is He Who has (full) knowledge and wisdom.

72. Those who believed, and adopted exile, and fought for the faith, with their property and their persons, in the cause of Allah, as well as those who gave (them) asylum and aid - these are (all) friends and protectors, one of another. As to those who believed but came not into exile; you owe no duty of protection to them until they come into exile; but if they seek your aid in religion, it is your duty to help them, except against a people with whom you have a treaty of mutual alliance. And (remember) Allah sees all that you do.

73. The unbelievers are protectors, one of another: unless you do this, (protect each other), there would be tumult and oppression on earth, and great mischief.

74. Those who believe, and adopt exile, and fight for the faith, in the cause of Allah, as well as those who give (them) asylum and aid - these are (all) in very truth the believers: for them is the forgiveness of sins and a provision most generous.

75. And those who accept faith subsequently, and adopt exile, and fight for the faith in your company - they are of you. But relations by blood have prior rights against each other in the book of Allah. Verily Allah is well-acquainted with all things.

Surah 9: *At-Taubah*
(The Repentance)

1. A (declaration) of immunity from Allah and His messenger, to those of the pagans with whom you have contracted mutual alliances -

2. Go you, then, for four months, backwards and forwards, (as you will), throughout the land, but know you that you cannot frustrate Allah (by your falsehood) but that Allah will cover with shame those who reject Him.

3. And an announcement from Allah and His messenger, to the people (assembled) on the day of the great pilgrimage - that Allah and His messenger dissolve (treaty) obligations with the pagans. If, then, you repent, it were best for you; but if you turn away, know you that you cannot frustrate Allah. And proclaim a grievous penalty to those who reject faith.

4. (But the treaties are) not dissolved with those pagans with whom You have entered into alliance and who have not subsequently failed you in anything, nor aided anyone against you. So fulfil your engagements with them to the end of their term: for Allah loves the righteous.

5. But when the forbidden months are past, then fight and slay the pagans wherever you find them, and seize them, beleaguer them, and lie in wait for them, in every stratagem (of war); but if they repent, and establish regular prayers and practice regular charity, then open the way for them: for Allah is Oft-Forgiving, Most Merciful.

6. If one amongst the pagans ask you for asylum, grant it to him, so that he may hear the word of Allah; and then escort him to where he can be secure. That is because they are men without knowledge.

7. How can there be a league, before Allah and His messenger, with the pagans, except those with whom you made a treaty near the Sacred Mosque? As long as these stand true to you, stand you true to them: For Allah does love the righteous.

8. How (can there be such a league), seeing that if they get an advantage over you, they respect not in you the ties either of relationship or of covenant? With (fair words from) their mouths they entice you, but their hearts are averse from you; and most of them are rebellious and wicked.

9. The signs of Allah have they sold for a miserable price, and (many) have they hindered from His Way: evil indeed are the deeds they have done.

10. In a believer they respect not the ties either of relationship or of covenant! It is they who have transgressed all bounds.

11. But (even so), if they repent, establish regular prayers, and practice regular charity - they are your brothers in faith: (thus) do We explain the signs in detail, for those who understand.

12. But if they violate their oaths after their covenant, and taunt you for your faith - fight you the chiefs of unfaith: for their oaths are nothing to them: that thus they may be restrained.

13. Will you not fight people who violated their oaths, plotted to expel the messenger, and took the aggressive by being the first (to assault) you? Do you fear them? Nay, it is Allah whom you should more justly fear, if you believe!

14. Fight them, and Allah will punish them by your hands; cover them with shame; help you (to victory) over them, heal the breasts of believers,

15. And still the indignation of their hearts. For Allah will turn (in mercy) to whom He will; and Allah Is All-Knowing, All-Wise.

16. Or do you think that you shall be abandoned, as though Allah did not know those among you who strive with might and main, and take none for friends and protectors except Allah, His messenger, and the (community of) believers? But Allah is well-acquainted with (all) that you do.

17. It is not for such as join gods with Allah, to visit or maintain the mosques of Allah while they witness against their own souls to infidelity. The works of such bear no fruit: in fire shall they dwell.

18. The mosques of Allah shall be visited and maintained by such as believe in Allah and the last day, establish regular prayers, and practice regular charity, and fear none (at all) except Allah. It is they who are expected to be on true guidance.

19. Do you make the giving of drink to pilgrims, or the maintenance of the Sacred Mosque, equal to (the pious service of) those who believe in Allah and the last day, and strive with might and main in the cause of Allah? They are not comparable in the sight of Allah: and Allah guides not those who do wrong.

20. Those who believe, and suffer exile and strive with might and main, in

Allah's cause, with their goods and their persons, have the highest rank in the sight of Allah: They are the people who will achieve (salvation).

21. Their Lord does give them glad tidings of a mercy from Himself, of His good pleasure, and of gardens for them, in which are delights that endure:

22. They will dwell in it forever. Verily in Allah's presence is a reward, the greatest (of all).

23. O you who believe! Take not for protectors your fathers and your brothers, if they love infidelity above faith: if any of you do so, they do wrong.

24. Say: If it be that your fathers, your sons, your brothers, your mates, or your relations; the wealth that you have gained; the commerce in which you fear a decline; or the dwellings in which you delight - are dearer to you than Allah, or His messenger, or the striving in His cause - then wait until Allah brings about His decision: and Allah guides not the rebellious.

25. Assuredly Allah did help you in many battlefields and on the day of Hunayn: See! Your great numbers elated you, but they availed you nothing; the land, for all that it is wide, did constrain you, and you turned back in retreat.

26. But Allah did pour His calm on the messenger and on the believers, and sent down forces which you saw not; He punished the unbelievers: thus does He reward those without faith.

27. Again will Allah, after this, turn (in mercy) to whom He will: for Allah is Oft-Forgiving, Most Merciful.

28. O you who believe! Truly the pagans are unclean; so let them not, after this year of theirs, approach the Sacred Mosque. And if you fear poverty, soon will Allah enrich you, if He wills, out of His bounty, for Allah is All-Knowing, All-Wise.

29. Fight those who believe not in Allah nor the last day, nor hold that forbidden which has been forbidden by Allah and His messenger, nor acknowledge the religion of truth, (even if they are) of the People of the Book, until they pay the *Jizyah* with willing submission, and feel themselves subdued.

30. The Jews call 'Uzayr a son of God, and the Christians call the Messiah the son of God. That is a saying from their mouths; (in this) they but imitate what the unbelievers of old used to say. Allah's curse be on them: how they are deluded away from the truth!

31. They take their priests and their anchorites to be their lords in derogation of Allah, and (they take as their Lord) the Messiah the son of Mary; Yet they were commanded to worship but One God: there is no god but He. Praise and glory to Him: (far is He) from having the partners they associate (with Him).

32. They would like to extinguish Allah's light with their mouths, but Allah will not allow but that His light should be perfected, even though the unbelievers may detest (it).

33. It is He Who has sent His messenger with guidance and religion of truth, to proclaim it over all religion, even though the pagans may detest (it).

34. O you who believe! There are indeed many among the priests and anchorites, who in falsehood devour the substance of men and hinder (them) from the way of Allah. And there are those who bury gold and silver and spend it not in the way of Allah: announce to them a most grievous penalty -

35. On the day when heat will be produced out of that (wealth) in the fire of hell, and with it will be branded their foreheads, their flanks, and their backs - "This is the (treasure) which you buried for yourselves: taste you, then, the (treasures) you buried!"

36. The number of months in the sight of Allah is twelve (in a year) - so ordained by Him the day He created the heavens and the earth; of them four are sacred; that is the straight usage. So wrong not yourselves in it, and fight the pagans all together as they fight you all together. But know that Allah is with those who restrain themselves.

37. Verily the transposing (of a prohibited month) is an addition to unbelief: the unbelievers are led to wrong thereby; for they make it lawful one year, and forbidden another year, in order to adjust the number of months forbidden by Allah and make such forbidden ones lawful. The evil of their course seems pleasing to them. But Allah guides not those who reject faith.

38. O you who believe! What is the matter with you, that, when you are asked to go out in the cause of Allah, you cling heavily to the earth? Do you prefer the life of this world to the hereafter? But little is the comfort of this life, as compared with the hereafter.

39. Unless you go out, He will punish you with a grievous penalty, and put others in your place; but Him you would not harm in the least. For Allah has power over all things.

40. If you help not (your leader) (it is no matter): for Allah did indeed help him, when the unbelievers drove him out; he had no more than one companion; they two were in the Cave, and he said to his companion, "Have no fear for Allah is with us"; then Allah sent down His peace upon him, and strengthened him with forces which you saw not, and humbled to the depths the word of the unbelievers. But the word of Allah is exalted to the heights: for Allah is Exalted in Might, Wise.

41. Go you out, (whether equipped) lightly or heavily, and strive and struggle, with your goods and your persons, in the cause of Allah. That is best for you, if you (but) knew.

42. If there had been immediate gain (in sight), and the journey easy, they would (all) without doubt have followed you, but the distance was long, (and weighed) on them. They would indeed swear by Allah, "If only could we should certainly have come out with you": they would destroy their own souls; for Allah does know that they are certainly lying.

43. Allah give you grace! Why did you grant them exemption until those who told the truth were seen by you in a clear light, and you had proved the liars?

44. Those who believe in Allah and the last day ask you for no exemption from fighting with their goods and persons. And Allah knows well those who do their duty.

45. Only those ask you for exemption who believe not in Allah and the last day, and whose hearts are in doubt, so that they are tossed in their doubts to and fro.

46. If they had intended to come out, they would certainly have made some preparation for it; but Allah was averse to their being sent out; so He made them lag behind, and they were told, "sit you among those who sit (inactive)."

47. If they had come out with you, they would not have added to your (strength) but only (made for) disorder, hurrying to and fro in your midst and sowing sedition among you, and there would have been some among you who would have listened to them. But Allah knows well those who do wrong.

48. Indeed they had plotted sedition before, and upset matters for you - until the truth arrived, and the decree of Allah became manifest, much to their disgust.

49. Among them is (many) a man who says: "Grant me exemption and draw me not into trial." Have they not fallen into trial already? And indeed hell surrounds the unbelievers (on all sides).

50. If good befalls you, it grieves them; but if a misfortune befalls you, they say, "We took indeed our precautions beforehand," and they turn away rejoicing.

51. Say: "Nothing will happen to us except what Allah has decreed for us; He is our protector": and on Allah let the believers put their trust.

52. Say: "Can you expect for us (any fate) other than one of two glorious things - (martyrdom or victory)? But we can expect for you either that Allah will send His punishment from Himself, or by our hands. So wait (expectant); we too will wait with you."

53. Say: "Spend (for the cause) willingly or unwillingly; not from you will it be accepted; for you are indeed a people rebellious and wicked."

54. The only reasons why their contributions are not accepted are: that they reject Allah and His messenger; that they come to prayer without earnestness; and that they offer contributions unwillingly.

55. Let not their wealth nor their (following in) sons dazzle you (O Muhammad): in reality Allah's plan is to punish them with these things in this life, and that their souls may perish in their (very) denial of Allah.

56. They swear by Allah that they are indeed of you; but they are not of you; yet they are afraid (to appear in their true colours).

57. If they could find a place to flee to, or caves or a place of concealment, they would turn straightway to it, with an obstinate rush.

58. And among them are men who slander you in the matter of (the distribution of) the alms. If they are given part of it, they are pleased, but if not, see! They are indignant!

59. If only they had been content with what Allah and His messenger gave them, and had said, "Sufficient to us is Allah! Allah and His messenger will soon give us of His bounty: to Allah do we turn our hopes!" (That would have been the right course).

60. Alms are for the poor and the needy, and those employed to administer the (funds); for those whose hearts have been (recently) reconciled (to the truth); for those in bondage and in debt; in the cause of Allah; and for the wayfarer: (thus is it) ordained by Allah, and Allah is full of knowledge and wisdom.

61. Among them are men who molest the prophet and say, "He is (all) ear." Say, "He listens to what is best for you; he believes in Allah, has faith in the believers and is a mercy to those of you who believe." But those who molest the messenger will have a grievous penalty.

62. To you they swear by Allah. In order to please you: but it is more fitting that they should please Allah and His messenger if they are believers.

63. Do they not know that for those who oppose Allah and His messenger, is the fire of hell? - in which they shall dwell. That is the supreme disgrace.

64. The hypocrites are afraid lest a Surah should be sent down about them, showing them, what is (really passing) in their hearts. Say: "Mock you! But verily Allah will bring to light all that you fear (should be revealed)."

65. If you do question them, they declare (with emphasis): "We were only talking idly and in play." Say: "Was it at Allah, and His signs, and His messenger, that you were mocking?"

66. Make you no excuses: you have rejected faith after you had accepted it. If We pardon some of you, We will punish others amongst you, for that they are in sin.

67. The hypocrites, men and women, (have an understanding) with each other: they enjoin evil, and forbid what is just, and are close with their hands. They have forgotten Allah; so He has forgotten them. Verily the hypocrites are rebellious and perverse.

68. Allah has promised the hypocrites men and women, and the rejecters of faith, the fire of hell; in it shall they dwell; sufficient is it for them: for them is the curse of Allah, and an enduring punishment -

69. As in the case of those before you: they were mightier than you in power and more flourishing in wealth and children. They had their enjoyment of their portion; and you have of yours, as did those before you; and you indulge in idle talk as they did. They! -

Their works are fruitless in this world and in the hereafter, and they will lose (all spiritual good).

70. Has not the story reached them of those before them? - The people of Noah, and 'Ad, and Thamud; the people of Abraham, the men of Madyan, and the cities overthrown. To them came their messengers with clear signs. It is not Allah who wrongs them, but they wrong their own souls.

71. The believers, men and women, are protectors, one of another: they enjoin what is just, and forbid what is evil: they observe regular prayers, practice regular charity, and obey Allah and His messenger. On them will Allah pour His mercy: for Allah is Exalted in Power, Wise.

72. Allah has promised to believers - men and women - gardens under which rivers flow, to dwell in it, and beautiful mansions in gardens of everlasting bliss. But the greatest bliss is the good pleasure of Allah: that is the supreme felicity.

73. O Prophet! Strive hard against the unbelievers and the hypocrites, and be firm against them. Their abode is hell - an evil refuge indeed.

74. They swear by Allah that they said nothing (evil), but indeed they uttered blasphemy, and they did it after accepting Islam; and they meditated a plot which they were unable to carry out; this revenge of theirs was (their) only return for the bounty with which Allah and His messenger had enriched them! If they repent, it will be best for them; but if they turn back (to their evil ways), Allah will punish them with a grievous penalty in this life and in the hereafter: they shall have none on earth to protect or help them.

75. Amongst them are men who made a covenant with Allah, that if He bestowed on them of His bounty, they would give (largely) in charity, and be truly amongst those who are righteous.

76. But when He did bestow of His bounty, they became covetous, and turned back (from their covenant), averse (from its fulfilment).

77. So He has put as a consequence hypocrisy into their hearts, (to last) till the day on which they shall meet Him: because they broke their covenant with Allah, and because they lied (again and again).

78. Do they not know that Allah does know their secret (thoughts) and their secret counsels, and that Allah knows well all things unseen?

79. Those who slander such of the believers as give themselves freely to (deeds of) charity, as well as such as can find nothing to give except the fruits of their labour - and throw ridicule on them - Allah will throw back their ridicule on them; and they shall have a grievous penalty.

80. Whether you ask for their forgiveness, or not, (their sin is unforgivable); if you ask seventy times for their forgiveness, Allah will not forgive them; because they have rejected Allah and His messenger; and Allah guides not those who are perversely rebellious.

81. Those who were left behind (in the Tabuk expedition) rejoiced in their inaction behind the back of the messenger of Allah; they hated to strive and fight, with their goods and their persons, in the cause of Allah; they said, "Do not go out in the heat." Say, "The fire of hell is fiercer in heat." If only they could understand!

82. Let them laugh a little; much will they weep: a recompense for the (evil) that they do.

83. If then, Allah brings you back to any of them, and they ask your permission to come out (with you), say: "Never shall you come out with me, nor fight an enemy with me; for you preferred to sit inactive on the first occasion; then sit you (now) with those who lag behind."

84. Nor do you (O Muhammad) ever pray for any of them that dies, nor stand at his grave: for they rejected Allah and His messenger, and died in a state of perverse rebellion.

85. Nor let their wealth nor their (following in) sons dazzle you (O Muhammad): Allah's Plan is to punish them with these things in this world, and that their souls may perish in their (very) denial of Allah.

86. When a Surah comes down, enjoining them to believe in Allah and to strive and fight along with His messenger, those with wealth and influence among them ask you for exemption, and say: "Leave us (behind); we would be with those who sit (at home)."

87. They prefer to be with (the women), who remain behind (at home): their hearts are sealed and so they understand not.

88. But the messenger, and those who believe with him, strive and fight with their wealth and their persons: for them are (all) good things; and it is they who will prosper.

89. Allah has prepared for them gardens under which rivers flow, to dwell in it: that is the supreme felicity.

90. And there were, among the desert Arabs (also), men who made excuses and came to claim exemption; and those who were false to Allah and His messenger (merely) sat inactive. Soon will a grievous penalty seize the unbelievers among them.

91. There is no blame on those who are infirm, or ill, or who find no resources to spend (on the cause), if they are sincere (in duty) to Allah and His messenger; no ground (of complaint) can there be against such as do right; and Allah is Oft-Forgiving, Most Merciful.

92. Nor (is there blame) on those who came to you to be provided with mounts, and when you said, "I can find no mounts for you," they turned back, their eyes streaming with tears of grief that they had no resources with which to provide the expenses.

93. The ground (of complaint) is against such as claim exemption while they are rich. They prefer to stay with the (women) who remain behind: Allah has sealed their hearts; so they know not (what they miss).

94. They will present their excuses to you when you return to them. Say you: "Present no excuses: we shall not believe you: Allah has already informed us of the true state of matters concerning you; it is your actions that Allah and His messenger will observe; in the end will you be brought back to Him who knows what is hidden and what is open: then will He show you the truth of all that you did."

95. They will swear to you by Allah, when you return to them, that you may leave them alone. So leave them alone: for they are an abomination, and hell is their dwelling place - a fitting recompense for the (evil) that they did.

96. They will swear to you, that you may be pleased with them. But if you are pleased with them, Allah is not pleased with those who disobey.

97. The Arabs of the desert are the worst in unbelief and hypocrisy, and most fitted to be in ignorance of the command which Allah has sent down to His messenger: but Allah is All-Knowing, All-Wise.

98. Some of the desert Arabs look upon their payments as a fine, and watch for disasters for you: on them be the disaster of evil; for Allah is He that hears and knows (all things).

99. But some of the desert Arabs believe in Allah and the last day, and look on their payments as pious gifts bringing them nearer to Allah and obtaining the prayers of the messenger. Yes, indeed they bring them nearer (to Him); soon will Allah admit them to His mercy: for Allah is Oft- Forgiving, Most Merciful.

100. The vanguard (of Islam) - the first of those who forsook (their homes) and of those who gave them aid, and (also) those who follow them in (all) good deeds - well-pleased is Allah with them, as are they with Him: for them has He prepared gardens under which rivers flow, to dwell in it for ever: that is the supreme felicity.

101. Certain of the desert Arabs round about you are hypocrites, as well as (desert Arabs) among the Madinah folk: they are obstinate in hypocrisy; you do not know them; We know them; twice shall We punish them: and in addition shall they be sent to a grievous penalty.

102. Others (there are who) have acknowledged their wrongdoings: they have mixed an act that was good with another that was evil. Perhaps Allah will turn to them (in mercy): for Allah is Oft-Forgiving, Most Merciful.

103. Of their goods take alms, so that you might purify and sanctify them; and pray on their behalf, verily your prayers are a source of security for them: and Allah is One who hears and knows.

104. Do they not know that Allah does accept repentance from His supporters and receives their gifts of charity, and that Allah is verily He, the Oft-Returning, Most-Merciful?

105. And say: "Work (righteousness): soon will Allah observe your work, and His messenger, and the believers: soon will you be brought back to the Knower of what is hidden and what is open: then will He show you the truth of all that you did."

106. There are (yet) others, held in suspense for the command of Allah, whether He will punish them, or turn in mercy to them: and Allah is All-Knowing, Wise.

107. And there are those who put up a mosque by way of mischief and infidelity - to disunite the believers - and in preparation for one who warred against Allah and His messenger before. They will indeed swear that their intention is nothing but good; but Allah does declare that they are certainly liars.

108. Never stand you up in it. There is a mosque whose foundation was laid from the first day on piety; it is more worthy of you standing up (for prayer) in it. In it are men who love to be purified; and Allah loves those who make themselves pure.

109. Which then is best? - he that lays his foundation on piety to Allah and His good pleasure? - or he that lays his foundation on an undermined sand cliff ready to crumble to pieces? And it does crumble to pieces with him, into the fire of hell. And Allah guides not people that do wrong.

110. The foundation of those who so build is never free from suspicion and shakiness in their hearts, until their hearts are cut to pieces. And Allah is All-Knowing, Wise.

111. Allah has purchased of the believers their persons and their goods; for theirs (in return) is the garden (of paradise): they fight in His cause, and slay and are slain: a promise binding on Him in truth, through the law, the Gospel, and the Qur'an: and who is more faithful to his covenant than Allah? Then rejoice in the bargain which you have concluded: that is the achievement supreme.

112. Those that turn (to Allah) in repentance; that serve Him, and praise Him; that wander in devotion to the cause of Allah; that bow down and prostrate themselves in prayer; that enjoin good and forbid evil; and observe the limits set by Allah - (these do rejoice). So proclaim the glad tidings to the believers.

113. It is not fitting, for the prophet and those who believe that they should pray for forgiveness for pagans, even though they be of kin, after it is clear to them that they are companions of the fire.

114. And Abraham prayed for his father's forgiveness only because of a promise he had made to him. But when it became clear to him that he was an enemy to Allah, he dissociated himself from him: for Abraham was most tender-hearted, forbearing.

115. And Allah will not mislead a people after He has guided them, in order that He may make clear to them what to fear (and avoid) - for Allah has knowledge of all things.

116. To Allah belongs the dominion of the heavens and the earth. He gives life and He takes it. Except for Him you have no protector nor helper.

117. Allah turned with favour to the prophet, the Muhajirs, and the Ansar - who followed him in a time of distress, after that the hearts of a part of them had nearly swerved (from duty); but He turned to them (also); for He is to them Most Kind, Most Merciful.

118. (He turned in mercy also) to the three who were left behind; (they felt guilty) to such a degree that the earth seemed constrained to them, for all its spaciousness, and their (very) souls seemed straitened to them - and they perceived that there is no fleeing from Allah (and no refuge) but to Himself. Then He turned to them, that they might repent: for Allah is Oft-Returning, Most Merciful.

119. O you who believe! Fear Allah and be with those who are true (in word and deed).

120. It was not fitting for the people of Madinah and the Bedouin Arabs of the neighbourhood, to refuse to follow Allah's messenger, nor to prefer their own lives to his; because nothing could they suffer or do, but was reckoned to their credit as a deed of righteousness - whether they suffered thirst, or fatigue or hunger, in the cause of Allah, or trod paths to raise the ire of the unbelievers, or received any injury whatever from an enemy: for Allah suffers not the reward to be lost of those who do good -

121. Nor could they spend anything (for the cause) - small or great - nor cut across a valley, but the deed is inscribed to their credit; that Allah might repay their deed with the best (possible reward).

122. Nor should the believers all go forth together: if a contingent from every expedition remained behind, they could devote themselves to studies in religion, and admonish the people when they return to them - that thus they (may learn) to guard themselves (against evil).

123. O you who believe! Fight the unbelievers who surround you, and let them find firmness in you; and know that Allah is with those who fear Him.

124. Whenever there comes down a Surah, some of them say: "Which of you has had his faith increased by it?" Yea, those who believe - their faith is increased, and they do rejoice.

125. But those in whose hearts is a disease - it will add doubt to their doubt, and they will die in a state of unbelief.

126. Do they not see that they are tried every year once or twice? Yet they turn not in repentance, and they take no heed.

127. Whenever there comes down a Surah, they look at each other, (saying) "Does anyone see you?" Then they turn aside: Allah has turned their hearts (from the light); for they are a people that understand not.

128. Now has come to you a messenger from amongst yourselves; it grieves him that you should perish; ardently anxious is he over you; to the believers is he most kind and merciful.

129. But if they turn away say: "Allah suffices me: There is no god but He: On Him is my trust - He is the Lord of the throne (of glory) supreme!

Surah 10: **Yunus**
(Jonah)

In the name of Allah,
Most Gracious, Most Merciful.

1. *Alif Lam Ra.* These are the Ayat of the book of wisdom.

2. It is a matter of wonderment to men that We have sent Our inspiration to a man from among themselves - that he should warn mankind (of their danger), and give the good news to the believers that they have before their Lord the lofty rank of truth. (But) say the unbelievers: "This is indeed an evident sorcerer!"

3. Verily your Lord is Allah, Who created the heavens and the earth in six Days, and He established Himself on the throne (of authority), regulating and governing all things. No intercessor (can plead with Him) except after His leave (has been obtained). This is Allah your Lord; Him therefore serve you: will you not receive admonition?

4. To Him will be your return - of all of you. The promise of Allah is true and sure. It is He Who begins the process of creation, and repeats it, that He may reward with justice those who believe and work righteousness; but those who reject Him will have draughts of boiling fluids, and a penalty grievous, because they did reject Him.

5. It is He Who made the sun to be a shining glory and the moon to be a light (of beauty), and measured out stages for it: that you might know the number of years and the count (of time). No way did Allah create this but in truth and righteousness. (Thus) does He explain His signs in detail, for those who understand.

6. Verily, in the alternation of the night and the day, and in all that Allah has created, in the heavens and the earth, are signs for those who fear Him.

7. Those who rest not their hope on their meeting with Us, but are pleased and satisfied with the life of the present, and those who heed not Our signs -

8. Their abode is the fire, because of the (evil) they earned.

9. Those who believe, and work righteousness - their Lord will guide them because of their faith: beneath them will flow rivers in gardens of bliss.

10. (This will be) their call in it: "Glory to You, O Allah!" and "Peace" will be their greeting in it! And the close of their call will be: "Praise be to Allah, the Cherisher and Sustainer of the Worlds!"

11. If Allah were to hasten for men the ill (they have earned) as they would fain hasten on the good - then would their respite be settled at once. But We leave those who rest not their hope of their meeting with Us, in their trespasses, wandering in distraction to and fro.

12. When trouble touches a man, he calls to Us (in all postures) - lying down on his side, or sitting, or standing. But when We have solved his trouble, he passes on his way as if he had never called to Us for a trouble that touched him! Thus do the deeds of transgressors seem fair in their eyes!

13. Generations before you We destroyed when they did wrong: their messengers came to them with clear signs, but they would not believe! Thus do We requite those who sin!

14. Then We made you heirs in the land after them, to see how you would behave!

15. But when Our clear signs are rehearsed to them, those who rest not their hope on their meeting with Us, say: "Bring us a reading other than this, or change this." Say: "It is not for me, of my own accord, to change it: I follow nothing but what is revealed to me: if I were to disobey my Lord, I should myself fear the penalty of a great day (to come)."

16. Say: "If Allah had so willed, I should not have rehearsed it to you, or would He have made it known to you. A whole lifetime before this have I stayed amongst you: will you not then understand?"

17. Who does more wrong than such as forge a lie against Allah, or deny His signs? But never will prosper those who sin.

18. They serve, besides Allah, things that hurt them not nor profit them, and they say: "These are our intercessors with Allah." Say: "Do you indeed inform Allah of something He knows not, in the heavens or on earth? - Glory to Him! And far is He above the partners they ascribe (to Him)!"

19. Mankind was but one nation, but differed (later). Had it not been for a word that went before from your Lord, their differences would have been settled between them.

20. They say: "Why is not a sign sent down to him from his Lord?" Say: "The unseen is only for Allah (to know). Then wait you: I too will wait with you."

21. When We make mankind taste of some mercy after adversity has touched them, see! They take to plotting against Our signs! Say: "Swifter to plan is Allah!" Verily Our messengers record all the plots that you make!

22. He it is Who enables you to traverse through land and sea; so that you even board ships - they sail with them with a favourable wind, and they rejoice thereat; then comes a stormy wind and the waves come to them from all sides, and they think they are being overwhelmed; they call to Allah, sincerely offering (their) duty to Him, saying "If You do deliver us from this, we shall truly show our gratitude!"

23. But when He delivers them, see! They transgress insolently through the earth in defiance of right! O mankind! Your insolence is against your own souls - an enjoyment of the life of the present; in the end, to Us is your return, and We shall show you the truth of all that you did.

24. The likeness of the life of the present is as the rain which We send down from the skies; by its mingling arises the produce of the earth - which provides food for men and animals; (it grows) till the earth is clad with its golden ornaments and is decked out (in beauty); the people to whom it belongs think they have all powers of disposal over it; there reaches it Our command by night or by day, and We make it like a harvest clean-mown, as if it had not flourished only the day before! Thus do We explain the signs in detail for those who reflect.

25. But Allah does call to the home of Peace: He does guide whom He pleases to a way that is straight.

26. To those who do right is a goodly (reward) - yea, more (than in measure)! No darkness nor shame shall cover their faces! They are companions of the garden; they will remain in it (forever)!

27. But those who have earned evil will have a reward of like evil; disgrace will cover their (faces); no defender will they have from (the wrath of) Allah; their faces will be covered, as it were, with pieces from the depth of the darkness of night; they are companions of the fire; they will remain in it (forever)!

28. One day shall We gather them all together. Then shall We say to those who joined gods (with Us): "To your place! You and those you joined as 'partners.'" We shall separate them, and their 'partners' shall say: "It was not us that you worshipped!"

29. "Enough is Allah for a witness between us and you: we certainly knew nothing of your worship of us!"

30. There will every soul prove (the fruits of) the deeds it sent before: they will be brought back to Allah their rightful Lord, and their invented falsehoods will leave them in the lurch.

31. Say: "Who is it that sustains you (in life) from the sky and from the earth? Or who is it that has power over hearing and sight? And who is it that brings out the living from the dead and the dead from the living? And who is it that rules and regulates all affairs?" They will soon say, "Allah." Say, "Will you not then show piety (to Him)?"

32. Such is Allah, your real Cherisher and Sustainer: apart from truth, what (remains) but error? How then are you turned away?

33. Thus is the word of your Lord proved true against those who rebel; verily they will not believe.

34. Say: "Of your 'partners', can any originate creation and repeat it?" Say: "It is Allah Who originates creation and repeats it: then how are you deluded away (from the truth)?"

35. Say: "Of your 'partners' is there any that can give any guidance towards truth?" Say: "It is Allah Who gives guidance towards truth. Is then He Who gives guidance to truth more worthy to be followed, or he who finds not guidance (himself) unless he is guided? What then is the matter with you? How do you judge?"

36. But most of them follow nothing but fancy: truly fancy can be of no benefit against truth. Verily Allah is well aware of all that they do.

37. This Qur'an is not such as can be produced by other than Allah; on the contrary, it is a confirmation of (revelations) that went before it, and a fuller explanation of the book - in which there is no doubt - from the Lord of the Worlds.

38. Or do they say "He forged it"? Say: "Bring then a Surah like it, and call (to your aid) anyone you can, besides Allah, if it be you speak the truth!"

39. Nay, they charge with falsehood that whose knowledge they cannot encompass, even before the elucidation of it has reached them; thus did those before them make charges of falsehood; but see what was the end of those who did wrong!

40. Of them there are some who believe in it, and some who do not: and your Lord knows best those who are out for mischief.

41. If they charge you with falsehood, say: "My work to me, and yours to you! You are free from responsibility for what I do, and I for what you do!"

42. Among them are some who (pretend to) listen to you: but can you make the deaf to hear - even though they are without understanding?

43. And among them are some who look at you: but can you guide the blind - even though they will not see?

44. Verily Allah will not deal unjustly with man in anything: it is man that wrongs his own soul.

45. One day He will gather them together; (it will be) as if they had stayed but an hour of a day; they will recognise each other: surely those will be lost who denied the meeting with Allah and refused to receive true guidance.

46. Whether We show you (realised in your lifetime) some part of what We promise them - or We take your soul (to Our mercy) (before that) - in any case, to Us is their return: ultimately Allah is witness to all that they do.

47. To every people (was sent) a messenger: when their messenger comes (before them), the matter will be judged between them with justice, and they will not be wronged.

48. They say: "When will this promise come to pass - if you speak the truth?"

49. Say: "I have no power over any harm or profit to myself except as Allah Wills. To every people is a term appointed: when their term is reached not an hour can they cause delay, nor (an hour) can they advance (it in anticipation)."

50. Say: "Do you see - if His punishment should come to you by night or by day, what portion of it would the sinners wish to hasten?"

51. "Would you then believe in it at last, when it actually comes to pass?" (It will then be said): 'Ah! Now? And you wanted (before) to hasten it on!'

52. "At length will be said to the wrongdoers: 'Taste you the enduring punishment! You get but the recompense of what you earned!'"

53. They seek to be informed by you: "Is that true?" Say: "Aye! By my Lord! It is the very truth! And you cannot frustrate it!"

54. Every soul that has sinned, if it possessed all that is on earth, would like to give it in ransom: they would declare (their) repentance when they see the penalty: but the judgement between them will be with justice, and no wrong will be done to them.

55. Is it not (the case) that to Allah belongs whatever is in the heavens and on earth? Is it not (the case) that Allah's promise is assuredly true? Yet most of them understand not.

56. It is He Who gives life and who takes it, and to Him shall you all be brought back.

57. O mankind! There has come to you a direction from your Lord and a healing for the (diseases) in your hearts - and for those who believe, a guidance and a mercy.

58. Say: "In the bounty of Allah, and in His mercy - in that let them rejoice": that is better than the (wealth) they hoard.

59. Say: "See you what things Allah has sent down to you for sustenance? Yet you hold forbidden some things of it and (some things) lawful." Say: "Has Allah indeed permitted you, or do you invent (things) to attribute to Allah?"

60. And what think those who invent lies against Allah, of the day of judgement? Verily Allah is full of bounty to mankind, but most of them are ungrateful.

61. In whatever business you may be, and whatever portion you may be reciting from the Qur'an - and whatever deed you (mankind) may be doing - We are Witnesses of it when you are deeply engrossed in it. Nor is hidden from your Lord (so much as) the weight of an atom on the earth or in heaven. And not the least and not the greatest of these things but are recorded in a clear record.

62. See! Verily on the friends of Allah there is no fear, nor shall they grieve;

63. Those who believe and (constantly) guard against evil -

64. For them are glad tidings, in the life of the present and in the hereafter: no change can there be in the words of Allah. This is indeed the supreme felicity.

65. Let not their speech grieve you: for all power and honour belong to Allah: it is He Who hears and knows (all things).

66. See! Verily to Allah belong all creatures, in the heavens and on earth. What do they follow who worship as His 'partners' other than Allah? They follow nothing but fancy, and they do nothing but lie.

67. He it is that has made you the night that you may rest in it, and the day to make things visible (to you). Verily in this are signs for those who listen (to His message).

68. They say "Allah has begotten a son!" - Glory be to Him! He is self-sufficient! His are all things in the heavens and on earth! No authority have you for this! Do you say about Allah what you do not know?

69. Say: "Those who invent a lie against Allah will never prosper."

70. A little enjoyment in this world! - And then, to Us will be their return. Then shall We make them taste the severest penalty for their blasphemies.

71. Relate to them the story of Noah. See! He said to his people: "O my people, if it be hard on your (mind) that I should stay (with you) and commemorate the signs of Allah - yet I put my trust in Allah. Get you then an agreement about your plan and among your partners, so your plan be not to you dark and dubious. Then pass your sentence on me, and give me no respite.

72. "But if you turn back, (consider): no reward have I asked of you: my reward is only due from Allah, and I have been commanded to be of those who submit to Allah's will (in Islam)."

73. They rejected him, but We delivered him, and those with him in the ark, and We made them inherit (the earth) while We overwhelmed in the flood those who rejected Our signs. Then see what was the end of those who were warned (but heeded not)!

74. Then after him We sent (many) messengers to their peoples: they brought them clear signs, but they would not believe what they had already rejected beforehand. Thus do We seal the hearts of the transgressors.

75. Then after them sent We Moses and Aaron to Pharaoh and his chiefs with Our signs. But they were arrogant: they were a people in sin.

76. When the truth did come to them from Us, they said: "This is indeed evident sorcery!"

77. Said Moses: "Do you say (this) about the truth when it has (actually) reached you? Is sorcery (like this? But sorcerers will not prosper."

78. They said: "Have you come to us to turn us away from the ways We found our fathers following - in order

that you and your brother may have greatness in the land? But we shall not believe in you!"

79. Said Pharaoh: "Bring me every sorcerer well-versed."

80. When the sorcerers came, Moses said to them: "Throw you what you (wish) to throw!"

81. When they had had their throw, Moses said: "What you have brought is sorcery: Allah will surely make it of no effect: for Allah prospers not the work of those who make mischief."

82. "And Allah by His words does prove and establish His truth, however much the sinners may hate it!"

83. But none believed in Moses except some children of his people, because of the fear of Pharaoh and his chiefs, lest they should persecute them; and certainly Pharaoh was mighty on the earth and one who transgressed all bounds.

84. Moses said: "O my people! If you do (really) believe in Allah, then in Him put your trust, if you submit (your will to His)."

85. They said: "In Allah do we put our trust. Our Lord! Make us not a trial for those who practice oppression;

86. And deliver us by Your mercy from those who reject (You)."

87. We inspired Moses and his brother with this message: "Provide dwellings for your people in Egypt, make your dwellings into places of worship, and establish regular prayers: and give glad tidings to those who believe!"

88. Moses prayed: "Our Lord! You have indeed bestowed on Pharaoh and his chiefs splendour and wealth in the life of the present, and so, our Lord, they mislead (men) from Your path. Deface, our Lord, the features of their wealth, and send hardness to their hearts, so they will not believe until they see the grievous penalty."

89. Allah said: "Accepted is your prayer (O Moses and Aaron)! So stand you straight, and follow not the path of those who know not."

90. We took the Children of Israel across the sea: Pharaoh and his forces followed them in insolence and spite. At length, when overwhelmed with the flood, he said: "I believe that there is no god except Him Whom the Children of Israel believe in: I am of those who submit (to Allah in Islam)."

91. (It was said to him): "Ah now! - But a little while before, were you in rebellion! - And you did mischief (and violence)!"

92. "This day shall We save you in your body, that you may be a sign to those who come after you! But verily, many among mankind are heedless of Our signs!"

93. We settled the Children of Israel in a beautiful dwelling-place, and provided for them sustenance of the best; it was after knowledge had been granted to them, that they fell into schisms. Verily Allah will judge between them as to the schisms amongst them on the day of judgement.

94. If you are in doubt as to what We have revealed to you, then ask those who have been reading the book from before you; the truth has indeed come to you from your Lord: so be in no way of those in doubt.

95. Nor be of those who reject the signs of Allah, or you shall be of those who perish.

96. Those against whom the word of your Lord has been verified would not believe -

97. Even if every sign was brought to them - until they see (for themselves) the grievous penalty.

98. Why was there not a single township (among those We warned), which believed - so its faith should have profited it - except the people of Yunus? When they believed, We removed from them the penalty of disgrace in the life of the present, and permitted them to enjoy (their life) for a while.

99. If it had been the Lord's will, they would all have believed - all who are on earth! Will you then compel mankind, against their will, to believe!

100. No soul can believe, except by the will of Allah, and He will place doubt (or obscurity) on those who will not understand.

101. Say: "See all that is in the heavens and on earth"; but neither signs nor warners profit those who believe not.

102. Do they then expect (anything) but (what happened in) the days of the men who passed away before them?

Say: "Wait you then: for I, too, will wait with you."

103. In the end We deliver Our messengers and those who believe: thus is it fitting on Our part that We should deliver those who believe!

104. Say: "O you men! If you are in doubt as to my religion, (see!) I worship not what you worship other than Allah! But I worship Allah - Who will take your souls (at death): I am commanded to be (in the ranks) of the believers."

105. And further (thus): "Set your face towards religion with true piety, and never in any way be of the unbelievers;

106. Nor call on any, other than Allah - such will neither profit you nor hurt you: if you do, see! You shall certainly be of those who do wrong."

107. If Allah touches you with hurt, there is none who can remove it but He: if He designs some benefit for you, there is none who can keep back His favour: He causes it to reach whomsoever of His servants He pleases. And He is the Oft-Forgiving, Most Merciful.

108. Say: "O you men! Now truth has reached you from your Lord! Those who receive guidance, do so for the good of their own souls; those who stray, do so to their own loss: and I am not (set) over you to arrange your affairs."

109. Follow you the inspiration sent to you, and be patient and constant, till Allah does decide: for He is the best to decide.

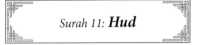

Surah 11: **Hud**

In the name of Allah, Most Gracious, Most Merciful.

1. *Alif Lam Ra.* (This is) a book with verses basic or fundamental (of established meaning) - further explained in detail - from One Who is Wise and Well-Acquainted (with all things):

2. (It teaches) that you should worship none but Allah. (Say:) "Verily I am (sent) to you from Him to warn and to bring glad tidings:"

3. ("And to preach thus), 'Seek you the forgiveness of your Lord, and turn to Him in repentance; that He may grant you enjoyment, good (and true), for a term appointed, and bestow His abounding grace on all who abound in merit! But if you turn away, then I fear for you the penalty of a great day:

4. 'To Allah is your return and He has power over all things.'"

5. See! They fold up their hearts, that they may lie hidden from Him! Ah! Even when they cover themselves with their garments, He knows what they conceal and what they reveal: for He knows well the (inmost secrets) of the hearts.

6. There is no moving creature on earth but its sustenance depends on Allah; He knows the time and place of its temporary deposit: all is in a clear record.

7. He it is Who created the heavens and the earth in six days - and His throne was over the waters - that He might try you, which of you is best in conduct. But if you were to say to them, "You shall indeed be raised up after death," the unbelievers would be sure to say, "This is nothing but obvious sorcery!"

8. If We delay the penalty for them for a definite term, they are sure to say, "What keeps it back?" Ah! On the day it (actually) reaches them, nothing will turn it away from them, and they will be completely encircled by that which they used to mock at!

9. If We give man a taste of mercy from Ourselves, and then withdraw it from him, See! He is in despair and (falls into) blasphemy.

10. But if We give him a taste of (Our) favours after adversity has touched him, he is sure to say, "All with evil has departed from me"; see! He falls into exultation and pride.

11. Not so do those who show patience and constancy, and work righteousness; for them is forgiveness (of sins) and a great reward.

12. Perhaps you may (feel the inclination) to give up a part of what is revealed to you, and your heart feels straitened lest they say, "Why is not a treasure sent down to him, or why does not an angel come down with him?" But you are there only to warn! It is Allah that arranges all affairs!

13. Or they may say, "He forged it." Say "Bring you then ten Surahs forged, like it, and call (to your aid) whomsoever you can, other than Allah! If you speak the truth!"

14. "If then they (your false gods) answer not your (call), know you that this revelation is sent down (replete) with the knowledge of Allah, and that there is no god but He! Will you even then submit (to Islam)?"

15. Those who desire the life of the present and its glitter - to them We shall pay (the price of) their deeds in it - without diminution.

16. They are those for whom there is nothing in the hereafter but the fire: vain are the designs they frame in it, and of no effect are the deeds that they do!

17. Can they be (like) those who accept a clear (sign) from their Lord, and whom a witness from Himself does teach, as did the book of Moses before it - a guide and a mercy? They believe in it; but those of the sects that reject it - the fire will be their promised meeting place. Be not then in doubt about it; for it is the truth from your Lord; yet many among men do not believe!

18. Who does more wrong than those who invent a lie against Allah? They will be turned back to the presence of their Lord, and the witnesses will say, "These are the ones who lied against their Lord! See! The curse of Allah is on those who do wrong! -

19. Those who would hinder (men) from the path of Allah and would seek in it something crooked: these were they who denied the hereafter!"

20. They will in no way frustrate (His design) on earth, nor have they protectors besides Allah! Their penalty will be doubled! They lost the power to hear, and they did not see!

21. They are the ones who have lost their own souls; and the (fancies) they invented have left them in the lurch!

22. Without a doubt, these are the very ones who will lose most in the hereafter!

23. But those who believe and work righteousness, and humble themselves before their Lord - they will be companions of the garden, to dwell in it for ever!

24. These two kinds (of men) may be compared to the blind and deaf, and those who can see and hear well. Are they equal when compared? Will you not then take heed?

25. We sent Noah to his People (with a mission): "I have come to you with a clear Warning:

26. That you serve none but Allah: verily I do fear for you the penalty of a grievous day."

27. But the chiefs of the unbelievers among his people said: "We see (in) you nothing but a man like ourselves: nor do we see that any follow you but the meanest among us, in judgement immature: nor do we see in you (all) any merit above us: in fact we think you are liars!"

28. He said: "O my people! See you if (it be that) I have a clear sign from my Lord, and that He has sent mercy to me from His own presence, but that the mercy has been obscured from your sight? Shall we compel you to accept it when you are averse to it?

29. And O my people! I ask you for no wealth in return: my reward is from none but Allah: but I will not drive away (in contempt) those who believe: for verily they are to meet their Lord, and you, I see, are the ignorant ones!

30. And O my people! Who would help me against Allah if I drove them away? Will you not then take heed?

31. I tell you not that with me are the treasures of Allah, nor do I know what is hidden, nor claim I to be an angel. Nor yet do I say, of those whom your eyes do despise that Allah will not grant them (all) that is good: Allah knows best what is in their souls: I should, if I did, indeed be a wrongdoer."

32. They said: "O Noah! You have disputed with us, and (much) have you prolonged the dispute with us: now bring upon us what you threaten us with, if you speak the truth!"

33. He said: "Truly, Allah will bring it on you if He wills - and then you will not be able to frustrate it!

34. "Of no profit will be my counsel to you, much as I desire to give you (good) counsel, if it be that Allah wills to leave you astray: He is your Lord! And to Him will you return!"

35. Or do they say, "He has forged it?" Say: "If I had forged it, on me were my sin! And I am free of the sins of which you are guilty!"

36. It was revealed to Noah: "None of your people will believe except those who have believed already! So grieve no longer over their (evil) deeds.

37. But construct an ark under Our eyes and Our inspiration, and address Me no (further) on behalf of those who are in sin: for they are about to be overwhelmed (in the flood)."

38. Forthwith he (started) constructing the ark: every time that the chiefs of his people passed by him, they threw ridicule on him. He said: "If you ridicule us now, we (in our turn) can look down on you with ridicule likewise!

39. But soon will you know who it is on whom will descend a penalty that will cover them with shame - on whom will be unloosed a penalty lasting:"

40. At length, see! There came Our command, and the fountains of the earth gushed forward! We said: "Embark in it, of each kind two, male and female, and your family - except those against whom the word has already gone before - and the believers." But only a few believed with him.

41. So he said: "Embark you on the ark in the name of Allah, whether it move or be at rest! For my Lord is, be sure, Oft-Forgiving, Most Merciful!"

42. So the Ark floated with them on the waves (towering) like mountains, and Noah called out to his son, who had separated himself (from the rest): "O my son! Embark with us, and be not with the unbelievers!"

43. The son replied: "I will betake myself to some mountain: it will save me from the water." Noah said: "This day nothing can save, from the command of Allah, any but those on whom He has mercy!" - and the waves came between them, and the son was among those overwhelmed in the flood.

44. Then the word went out: "O earth! Swallow up your water, and O sky! Withhold (your rain)!" And the water abated, and the matter was ended. The ark rested on mount Judi, and the word went forth: "Away with those who do wrong!"

45. And Noah called upon his Lord, and said: "O my Lord! Surely my son is of my family! And Your promise is true, and You are the justest of judges!"

46. He said: "O Noah! He is not of your family: for his conduct is unrighteous. So ask not of Me that of which you have no knowledge! I give you counsel lest you act like the ignorant!"

47. Noah said: "O my Lord! I do seek refuge with You, lest I ask You for that of which I have no knowledge. And unless You forgive me and have mercy on me, I should indeed be lost!"

48. The word came: "O Noah! Come down (from the ark) with peace from Us, and blessing on you and on some of the peoples (who will spring) from those with you: but (there will be other) peoples to whom We shall grant their pleasures (for a time), but in the end will a grievous penalty reach them from Us."

49. Such are some of the stories of the unseen, which We have revealed to you: before this, neither you nor your people knew them. So persevere patiently: for the end is for those who are righteous.

50. To the 'Ad people (We sent) Hud, one of their own brothers. He said: "O my people! Worship Allah! You have no other god but Him. (Your other gods) you do nothing but invent!"

51. "O my people! I ask of you no reward for this (message). My reward is from none but Him Who created me: will you not then understand?

52. "And O my people! Ask forgiveness of your Lord, and turn to Him (in repentance): He will send you the skies pouring abundant rain, and add strength to your strength: so turn you not back in sin!"

53. They said: "O Hud! No clear (sign) have you brought us, and we are not the ones to desert our gods on your word! Nor shall we believe in you!

54. "We say nothing but that (perhaps) some of our gods may have seized you with imbecility." He said: "I call Allah to witness, and do you bear witness, that I am free from the sin of ascribing, to Him,

55. Other gods as partners! So scheme (your worst) against me, all of you, and give me no respite.

56. I put my trust in Allah, my Lord and your Lord! There is not a moving creature, but He has grasp of its forelock. Verily, it is my Lord that is on a straight path.

57. If you turn away - I (at least) have conveyed the message with which I was sent to you. My Lord will make another people to succeed you, and you will not harm Him in the least. For my Lord has care and watch over all things."

58. So when Our decree issued, We saved Hud and those who believed with him, by (special) grace from Ourselves: We saved them from a severe penalty.

59. Such were the 'Ad people: they rejected the signs of their Lord and Cherisher; disobeyed His messengers; and followed the command of every powerful, obstinate transgressor.

60. And they were pursued by a curse in this life - and on the day of judgement. Ah! See! For the 'Ad rejected their Lord and Cherisher! Ah! See! Removed (from sight) were 'Ad, the people of Hud!

61. To the Thamud people (We sent) Salih, one of their own brothers. He said: "O my people! Worship Allah: you have no other god but Him. It is He Who has produced you from the earth and settled you in it: then ask forgiveness of Him, and turn to Him (in repentance): for my Lord is (always) near, ready to answer."

62. They said: "O Salih! You have been of us! - A centre of our hopes so far! Do you (now) forbid us the worship of what our fathers worshipped? But we are really in suspicious (disquieting) doubt as to that to which you invite us."

63. He said: "O my people! Do you see? - If I have a clear (sign) from my Lord and He has sent mercy to me from Himself - who then can help me against Allah if I were to disobey Him? What then would you add to my (portion) but perdition?

64. And O my people! This she-camel of Allah is a symbol to you: leave her to feed on Allah's (free) earth, and inflict no harm on her, or a swift penalty will seize you!"

65. But they did hamstring her. So he said: "Enjoy yourselves in your homes for three days: (then will be your ruin): there a promise not to be belied!"

66. When Our decree issued, We saved Salih and those who believed with him, by (special) grace from Ourselves - and from the disgrace of that day. For your Lord - He is the Strong One, and Able to enforce His Will.

67. The (mighty) blast overtook the wrongdoers, and they lay prostrate in their homes before the morning -

68. As if they had never dwelt and flourished there. Ah! See! For the Thamud rejected their Lord and Cherisher! Ah! See! Removed (from sight) were the Thamud!

69. There came Our messengers to Abraham with glad tidings. They said, "Peace!" He answered, "Peace!" And hastened to entertain them with a roasted calf.

70. But when he saw their hands went not towards the (meal), he felt some mistrust of them, and conceived a fear of them. They said: "Fear not: we have been sent against the people of Lot."

71. And his wife was standing (there), and she laughed: but We gave her glad tidings of Isaac, and after him, of Jacob.

72. She said: "Alas for me! Shall I bear a child, seeing I am an old woman, and my husband here is an old man? That would indeed be a wonderful thing!"

73. They said: "Do you wonder at Allah's decree? The grace of Allah and His blessings on you, O you people of

the house! For He is indeed worthy of all praise, full of all glory!"

74. When fear had passed from (the mind of) Abraham and the glad tidings had reached him, he began to plead with Us for Lot's people.

75. For Abraham was, without doubt, forbearing (of faults), compassionate, and given to look to Allah.

76. O Abraham! Seek not this. The decree of your Lord has gone out: for them there comes a penalty that cannot be turned back!

77. When Our messengers came to Lot, he was grieved on their account and felt himself powerless (to protect) them. He said: "This is a distressful day."

78. And his people came rushing towards him, and they had been long in the habit of practising abominations. He said: "O my people! Here are my daughters: they are purer for you (if you marry)! Now fear Allah, and cover me not with shame about my guests! Is there not among you a single right-minded man?"

79. They said: "Well do you know we have no need of your daughters: indeed you know quite well what we want!"

80. He said: "Would that I had power to suppress you or that I could betake myself to some powerful support."

81. (The messengers) said, "O Lot! We are messengers from your Lord! By no means shall they reach you! Now travel with your family while yet a part of the night remains, and let not any of you look back; but your wife (will remain behind); to her will happen what happens to the people. Morning is their time appointed: is not the morning near?"

82. When Our decree issued, We turned (the cities) upside down, and rained down on them brimstones hard as baked clay, spread layer on layer -

83. Marked as from your Lord: nor are they ever far from those who do wrong!

84. To the Madyan people (We sent) Shu'ayb, one of their own brothers: he said: "O my people! Worship Allah: you have no other god but Him. And give not short measure or weight: I see you in prosperity, but I fear for you the penalty of a day that will compass (you) all round."

85. "And O my people! Give just measure and weight, nor withhold from the people the things that are their due: commit not evil in the land with intent to do mischief.

86. That which is left you by Allah is best for you, if you (but) believed! But I am not set over you to keep watch!"

87. They said: "O Shu'ayb! Does your (religion of) prayer command you that we leave off the worship which our fathers practised, or that we leave off doing what we like with our property? Truly, you are the one that forbears with faults and is right-minded!"

88. He said: "O my people! See you whether I have a clear (sign) from my Lord, and He has given me sustenance (pure and) good as from Himself? I wish not, in opposition to you, to do that which I forbid you to do. I only

desire (your) betterment to the best of my power; and my success (in my task) can only come from Allah: in Him I trust, and to Him I look.

89. "And O my people! Let not my dissent (from you) cause you to sin, lest you suffer a fate similar to that of the people of Noah or of Hud or of Salih, nor are the people of Lot far off from you!

90. But ask forgiveness of you Lord, and turn to Him (in repentance): for my Lord is indeed Full of mercy and loving-kindness."

91. They said: "O Shu'ayb! Much of what you say we do not understand! In fact, among us we see that you have no strength! Were it not for your family, we should certainly have stoned you! For you have among us no great position!"

92. He said: "O my people! Is then my family of more consideration with you than Allah? For you cast Him away behind your backs (with contempt). But verily my Lord encompasses on all sides all that you do!

93. And O my people! Do whatever you can: I will do (my part): soon will you know who it is on whom descends the penalty of disgrace, and who is a liar! And watch you! For I too am watching with you!"

94. When Our decree issued, We saved Shu'ayb and those who believed with him, by (special) mercy from Ourselves: but the (mighty) blast did seize the wrongdoers, and they lay prostrate in their homes by the morning -

95. As if they had never dwelt and flourished there! Ah! See! How the Madyan were removed (from sight) as were removed the Thamud!

96. And We sent Moses with Our clear (signs) and an authority manifest,

97. To Pharaoh and his chiefs: but they followed the command of Pharaoh, and the command of Pharaoh was no right (guide).

98. He will go before his people on the day of judgement, and lead them into the fire (as cattle are led to water): but woeful indeed will be the place to which they are led!

99. And they are followed by a curse in this (life) and on the day of judgement: and woeful is the gift which shall be given (to them)!

100. These are some of the stories of communities which We relate to you: of them some are standing, and some have been mown down (by the sickle of time).

101. It was not We that wronged them: they wronged their own souls: the deities, other than Allah, whom they invoked, profited them not at all when there issued the decree of your Lord nor did they add anything (to their lot) but perdition!

102. Such is the chastisement of your Lord when He chastises communities in the midst of their wrong: grievous, indeed, and severe is His chastisement.

103. In that is a sign for those who fear the penalty of the hereafter; that is a day for which mankind will be gathered together; that will be a day of testimony.

104. Nor shall We delay it but for a term appointed.

105. The day it arrives, no soul shall speak except by His permission; of those (gathered) some will be wretched and some will be blessed.

106. Those who are wretched shall be in the fire; there will be for them in it (nothing but) the heaving of sighs and sobs;

107. They will dwell in it for all the time that the heavens and the earth endure, except as your Lord wills: for your Lord is the (sure) Accomplisher of what He plans.

108. And those who are blessed shall be in the garden; they will dwell in it for all the time that the heavens and the earth endure, except as your Lord wills: a gift without break.

109. Be not then in doubt as to what these men worship. They worship nothing but what their fathers worshipped before (them): but verily We shall pay them back (in full) their portion without (the least) abatement.

110. We certainly gave the book to Moses, but differences arose in it; had it not been that a word had gone before from your Lord, the matter would have been decided between them; but they are in suspicious doubt concerning it.

111. And of a surety, to all will your Lord pay back (in full the recompense) of their deeds: for He knows well all that they do.

112. Therefore, stand firm (in the straight path) as you are commanded - you and those who with you turn (to Allah); and transgress not (from the path): for He sees well all that you do.

113. And incline not to those who do wrong, or the fire will seize you; and you have no protectors other than Allah, nor shall you be helped.

114. And establish regular prayers at the two ends of the day and at the approaches of the night; for those things that are good remove those that are evil; be that the word of remembrance to those who remember (their Lord);

115. And be steadfast in patience; for verily Allah will not suffer the reward of the righteous to perish.

116. Why were there not, among the generations before you, persons possessed of balanced good sense, prohibiting (men) from mischief in the earth - except a few among them whom We saved (from harm)? But the wrongdoers pursued the enjoyment of the good things of life which were given them, and persisted in sin.

117. Nor would your Lord be the One to destroy communities for a single wrongdoing if its members were likely to mend.

118. If your Lord had so willed, He could have made mankind one people: but they will not cease to dispute,

119. Except those on whom your Lord has bestowed His mercy: and for this did He create them: and the word of your Lord shall be fulfilled: "I will fill hell with jinns and men all together."

120. All that We relate to you of the stories of the messengers - with it We make firm your heart: in them there comes to you the truth, as well as an exhortation and a message of remembrance to those who believe.

121. Say to those who do not believe: "Do whatever you can: we shall do our part;

122. And wait you! We too shall wait."

123. To Allah do belong the unseen (secrets) of the heavens and the earth, and to Him goes back every affair (for decision): then worship Him, and put your trust in Him; and your Lord is not unmindful of anything that you do.

Surah 12: *Yusuf*
(Joseph)

In the name of Allah,
Most Gracious, Most Merciful.

1. *Alif Lam Ra.* These are the symbols (or verses) of the perspicuous book.

2. We have sent it down as an Arabic Qur'an, in order that you may learn wisdom.

3. We do relate to you the most beautiful of stories, in that We reveal to you this (portion of the) Qur'an; before this, you too were among those who knew it not.

4. See, Joseph said to his father: "O my father! I did see eleven stars and the sun and the moon; I saw them prostrate themselves to me!"

5. Said (the father): "My (dear) little son! Relate not your vision to your brothers, lest they concoct a plot against you; for Satan is to man an avowed enemy!"

6. "Thus will your Lord choose you and teach you the interpretation of stories (and events) and perfect His favour to you and to the posterity of Jacob - even as He perfected it to your fathers Abraham and Isaac before! For your Lord is full of knowledge and wisdom."

7. Verily in Joseph and his brothers are signs (or symbols) for seekers (after truth).

8. They said: "Truly Joseph and his brother are loved more by our father than we; but we are a goodly body! Really our father is obviously wandering (in his mind)!

9. Slay you Joseph or cast him out to some (unknown) land, that so the favour of your father may be given to you alone: (There will be time enough) for you to be righteous after that!"

10. Said one of them: "Slay not Joseph, but if you must do something, throw him down to the bottom of the well: he will be picked up by some caravan of travellers."

11. They said: "O our father! Why do you not trust us with Joseph - seeing we are indeed his sincere well-wishers?"

12. "Send him with us tomorrow to enjoy himself and play, and we shall take every care of him."

13. (Jacob) said: "Really it saddens me that you should take him away: I fear lest the wolf should devour him while you attend not to him."

14. They said: "If the wolf were to devour him while we are (so large) a

party, then should we indeed (first) have perished ourselves!"

15. So they did take him away, and they all agreed to throw him down to the bottom of the well; and We put into his heart (this message): "Certainly you shall (one day) tell them the truth of this their affair while they know (you) not."

16. Then they came to their father in the early part of the night, weeping.

17. They said: "O our father! We went racing with one another and left Joseph with our things; and the wolf devoured him. But you will never believe us even though we tell the truth."

18. They stained his shirt with false blood. He said: "Nay, but your minds have made up a tale (that may pass) with you. (For me) patience is most fitting: against that which you assert, it is Allah (alone) whose help can be sought."

19. Then there came a caravan of travellers: they sent their water-carrier (for water), and he let down his bucket (into the well). He said: "Ah there! Good news! Here is a (fine) young man!" So they concealed him as a treasure! But Allah knows well all that they do!

20. The (Brothers) sold him for a miserable price - for a few dirhams counted out: in such low estimation did they hold him!

21. The man in Egypt who bought him, said to his wife: "Make his stay (among us) honourable: maybe he will bring us much good, or we shall adopt him as a son." Thus did We establish

Joseph in the land, that We might teach him the interpretation of stories (and events). And Allah has full power and control over His affairs; but most among mankind know it not.

22. When Joseph attained his full manhood, We gave him power and knowledge: thus do We reward those who do right.

23. But she in whose house he was, sought to seduce him from his (true) self; she fastened the doors and said: "Now come you (dear one)!" He said: "Allah forbid! Truly (your husband) is my lord! He made my sojourn agreeable! Truly to no good come those who do wrong!"

24. And (with passion) did she desire him, and he would have desired her, but that he saw the evidence of his Lord; thus (did We order) that We might turn away from him (all) evil and shameful deeds; for he was one of Our servants sincere and purified.

25. So they both raced each other to the door, and she tore his shirt from the back; they both found her lord near the door. She said: "What is the (fitting) punishment for one who formed an evil design against your wife, but prison or a grievous chastisement?"

26. He said: "It was she that sought to seduce me - from my (true) self." And one of her household saw (this) and bore witness, (thus) - "If it be that his shirt is torn from the front, then is her tale true, and he is a liar!"

27. "But if it be that his shirt is torn from the back, then is she the liar, and he is telling the truth!"

28. So when he saw his shirt - that it was torn at the back - (her husband) said: "See! It is a snare of you women! Truly, mighty is your snare!"

29. "O Joseph, pass this over! (O wife), ask forgiveness for your sin, for truly you have been at fault!"

30. Ladies said in the city: "The wife of the (great) Aziz is seeking to seduce her slave from his (true) self; truly has he inspired her with violent love; we see she is evidently going astray."

31. When she heard of their malicious talk, she sent for them and prepared a banquet for them: she gave each of them a knife; and she said (to Joseph) "Come out before them. When they saw him, they did extol him, and (in their amazement) cut their hands: they said, "Allah preserve us! No mortal is this! This is none other than a noble angel!"

32. She said: "There before you is the man about whom you did blame me! I did seek to seduce him from his (true) self but he did firmly save himself guiltless! And now if he does not my bidding he shall certainly be cast into prison and (what is more) be in the company of the vilest!"

33. He said: "O my Lord! The prison is more to my liking than that to which they invite me: unless you turn away their snare from me, I should (in my youthful folly) feel inclined towards them and join the ranks of the ignorant."

34. So his Lord listened to him (in his prayer) and turned away from him their snare; verily He hears and knows (all things).

35. Then it occurred to the men after they had seen the signs, (that it was best) to imprison him for a time.

36. Now with him there came into the prison two young men. Said one of them: "I see myself (in a dream) pressing wine." Said the other: "I see myself (in a dream) carrying bread on my head, and birds are eating of it." "Tell us," (they said), "the truth and meaning of it: for we see you are one that does good (to all)."

37. He said: "Before any food comes (in due course) to feed either of you I will surely reveal to you the truth and meaning of this before it befall you: that is part of the (duty) which my Lord has taught me. I have (I assure you) abandoned the ways of a people that believe not in Allah and that (even) deny the hereafter."

38. "And I follow the ways of my fathers - Abraham, Isaac and Jacob; and never could we attribute any partners whatever to Allah; that (comes) of the grace of Allah to us and to mankind; yet most men are not grateful.

39. "O my two companions of the prison! (I ask you): are many lords differing among themselves better, or Allah, the One, Supreme and Irresistible?"

40. "If not Him, you worship nothing but names which you have named - you and your fathers - for which Allah has sent down no authority; the command is for none but Allah; He has commanded that you worship none but Him: that is the right religion, but most men understand not."

41. "O my two companions of the prison! As to one of you, he will pour out the wine for his lord to drink: as for the other, he will hang from the cross, and the birds will eat from off his head. (So) has been decreed that matter of which you two do enquire."

42. And of the two, to that one whom he considered about to be saved, he said: "Mention me to your lord." But Satan made him forget to mention him to his lord: and (Joseph) lingered in prison a few (more) years.

43. The king (of Egypt) said: "I do see (in a vision) seven fat cows, whom seven lean ones devour - and seven green ears of corn, and seven (others) withered. O you chiefs! Explain to me my vision, if it be that you can interpret visions."

44. They said: "A confused medley of dreams; and we are not skilled in the interpretation of dreams."

45. But the man who had been released, one of the two (who had been in prison) and who now remembered him after (so long) a space of time, said: "I will tell you the truth of its interpretation; send you me (therefore)."

46. "O Joseph!" (he said) "O man of truth! Explain to us (the dream) of seven fat cows whom seven lean ones devour, and of seven green ears of corn and (seven) others withered: that I may return to the people and that they may understand."

47. (Joseph) said: "For seven years shall you diligently sow as is your habit; and the harvests that you reap, you shall leave them in the ear except a little, of which you shall eat.

48. Then will come after that (period) seven dreadful (years), which will devour what you shall have laid by in advance for them - (all) except a little which you shall have (specially) guarded.

49. "Then will come after that (period) a year in which the people will have abundant water, and in which they will press (wine and oil)."

50. So the king said: "Bring you him to me." But when the messenger came to him, (Joseph) said: "Go you back to your lord, and ask him, 'What is the state of mind of the ladies who cut their hands?' For my Lord is certainly well aware of their snare."

51. (The king) said (to the ladies): "What was your affair when you did seek to seduce Joseph from his (true) self?" The ladies said: "Allah preserve us! No evil know we against him!" Said the Aziz's wife: "Now is the truth manifest (to all): it was I who sought to seduce him from his (true) self; he is indeed of those who are (ever) true (and virtuous)."

52. "This (say I), in order that he may know that I have never been false to him in his absence, and that Allah will never guide the snare of the false ones."

53. "Nor do I absolve my own self (of blame); the (human) soul is certainly prone to evil, unless my Lord do bestow His mercy: but surely certainly my Lord is Oft-Forgiving, Most Merciful."

54. So the king said: "Bring him to me; I will take him specially to serve about my own person." Therefore, when he had spoken to him, he said: "Be assured this day, you are, before our own presence, with rank firmly established, and fidelity fully proved!"

55. (Joseph) said: "Set me over the storehouses of the land: I will indeed guard them, as one that knows (their importance)."

56. Thus did We give established power to Joseph in the land, to take possession in it as, when, or where he pleased. We bestow of Our mercy on whom We please, and We suffer not, to be lost, the reward of those who do good.

57. But verily the reward of the hereafter is the best, for those who believe, and are constant in righteousness.

58. Then came Joseph's brothers: they entered his presence, and he knew them, but they knew him not.

59. And when he had furnished them with provisions (suitable) for them he said: "Bring to me a brother you have, of the same father as yourselves, (but a different mother); see you not that I pay out full measure, and that I do provide the best hospitality?"

60. "Now if you bring him not to me, you shall have no measure (of corn) from me, nor shall you (even) come near me."

61. They said: "We shall certainly seek to get our wish about him from his father; indeed we shall do it."

62. And (Joseph) told his servants to put their stock in trade (with which they had bartered) into their saddlebags, so they should know it only when they returned to their people, in order that they might come back.

63. Now when they returned to their father, they said: "O our father! No more measure of grain shall we get (unless we take our brother): so send our brother with us that we may get our measure; and we will indeed take every care of him."

64. He said: "Shall I trust you with him with any result other than when I trusted you with his brother before? But Allah is the best to take care (of him), and He is the Most Merciful of those who show mercy!"

65. Then when they opened their baggage, they found their stock in trade had been returned to them. They said: "O our father! What (more) can we desire? This our stock in trade has been returned to us; so we shall get (more) food for our family; we shall take care of our brother; and add (at the same time) a full camel's load (of grain to our provisions); this is but a small quantity."

66. (Jacob) said: "Never will I send him with you until you swear a solemn oath to me, in Allah's name, that you will be sure to bring him back to me unless you are yourselves hemmed in (and made powerless)." And when they had sworn their solemn oath, he said: "Over all that we say be Allah the Witness and Guardian!"

67. Further he said; "O my sons! Enter not all by one gate; enter you by different gates. Not that I can profit you anything against Allah (with my advice); none can command except Allah; on Him do I put my trust and let all that trust put their trust on Him."

68. And when they entered in the manner their father had enjoined, it did not profit them in the least against (the plan of) Allah; it was but a necessity of Jacob's soul, which he discharged. For he was, by Our instruction, full of knowledge (and experience); but most men know not.

69. Now when they came into Joseph's presence he received his (full) brother to stay with him. He said (to him): "See! I am your (own) brother; so grieve not at any of their doings."

70. At length when he had furnished them with provisions (suitable) for them, he put the drinking cup into his brother's saddlebag. Then shouted out a caller: "O you (in) the caravan! See! You are thieves, without doubt!"

71. They said, turning towards them: "What is it that you miss?"

72. They said: "We miss the great beaker of the king; for him who produces it is (the reward of) a camel-load; I will be bound by it."

73. (The brothers) said: "By Allah! Well you know that we came not to make mischief in the land, and we are no thieves!"

74. (The Egyptians) said: "What then shall be the penalty of this, if you are (proved) to have lied?"

75. They said: "The penalty should be that he in whose saddle bag it is found, should be held (as bondman) to atone for the (crime). Thus it is we punish the wrongdoers!"

76. So he began (the search) with their baggage, before (he came to) the baggage of his brother; at length he brought it out of his brother's baggage. Thus did We plan for Joseph. He could not take his brother by the law of the king except that Allah willed it (so). We raise to degrees (of wisdom) whom We please: but over all endued with knowledge is One, the All-Knowing.

77. They said: "If he steals, there was a brother of his who did steal before (him)." But these things did Joseph keep locked in his heart, revealing not the secrets to them. He (simply) said (to himself): "You are the worse situated; and Allah knows best the truth of what you assert!"

78. They said: "O exalted one! See! He has a father, aged and venerable, (who will grieve for him); so take one of us in his place; for we see that you are (gracious) in doing good."

79. He said: "Allah forbid that we take other than him with whom we found our property; indeed (if we did so), we should be acting wrongfully."

80. Now when they saw no hope of his (yielding), they held a conference in private. The leader among them said: "Do you not know that your father did take an oath from you in Allah's name, and how before this, you did fail in your duty with Joseph? Therefore, I will not leave this land until my father permits me, or Allah commands me; and He is the best to command."

81. "Turn you back to your father, and say, 'O our father! See! Your son committed theft: we bear witness only to what we know, and we could not well guard against the unseen!'

82. "'Ask at the town where we have been and the caravan in which we returned, and (you will find) we are indeed telling the truth.'"

83. Jacob said: "Nay, but you have yourselves contrived a story (good enough) for you. So patience is most fitting (for me). Maybe Allah will bring them (back) all to me (in the end); for He is indeed full of knowledge and wisdom."

84. And he turned away from them, and said: "How great is my grief for Joseph!" And his eyes became white with sorrow, and he fell into silent melancholy.

85. They said: "By Allah! (Never) will you cease to remember Joseph until you reach the last extremity of illness, or until you die!"

86. He said: "I only complain of my distraction and anguish to Allah, and I know from Allah that which you know not."

87. "O my sons! Go you and enquire about Joseph and his brother, and never give up hope of Allah's soothing mercy; truly no one despairs of Allah's soothing mercy, except those who have no faith."

88. Then, when they came (back) into (Joseph's) presence they said: "O exalted one! Distress has seized us and our family; we have (now) brought but scanty capital: so pay us full measure, (we pray you) and treat it as charity to us; for Allah does reward the charitable."

89. He said: "Know you how you dealt with Joseph and his brother, not knowing (what you were doing)?"

90. They said: "Are you indeed Joseph?" He said: "I am Joseph, and this is my brother: Allah has indeed been gracious to us (all); see, he that is righteous and patient - never will Allah suffer the reward to be lost, of those who do right."

91. They said: "By Allah! Indeed has Allah preferred you above us, and we certainly have been guilty of sin!"

92. He said: "This day let no reproach be (cast) on you: Allah will forgive you, and He is the Most Merciful of those who show mercy!"

93. "Go with this my shirt, and cast it over the face of my father: he will come to see (clearly). Then come you (here) to me together with all your family."

94. When the caravan left (Egypt) their father said: "I do indeed scent the presence of Joseph; nay, think me not a senile."

95. They said: "By Allah! Truly you are in your old wandering mind."

96. Then when the bearer of the good news came, he cast (the shirt) over his face, and he forthwith regained clear sight. He said: "Did I not say to you, 'I know from Allah that which you know not?'"

97. They said: "O our father! Ask for us forgiveness for our sins, for we were truly at fault."

98. He said: "Soon will I ask my Lord for forgiveness for you; for He is indeed Oft-Forgiving, Most Merciful."

99. Then when they entered the presence of Joseph, he provided a home for his parents with himself, and said: "Enter you Egypt (all) in safety if it please Allah."

100. And he raised his parents high on the throne (of dignity), and they fell down in prostration, (all) before him. He said: "O my father! This is the fulfilment of my vision of old! Allah has made it come true! He was indeed good to me when He took me out of prison and brought you (all here) out of the desert, (even) after Satan had sown enmity between me and my brothers. Verily my Lord understands best the mysteries of all that He plans to do. For verily He is full of knowledge and wisdom."

101. "O my Lord! You have indeed bestowed on me some power, and taught me something of the interpretation of dreams and events - O You Creator of the heavens and the earth! You are my protector in this world and in the hereafter. Take You my soul (at death) as one submitting to Your Will (as a Muslim), and unite me with the righteous."

102. Such is one of the stories of what happened unseen, which We reveal by inspiration to you; nor were you (present) with them when they concerted their plans together in the process of weaving their plots.

103. Yet no faith will the greater part of mankind have, however ardently you do desire it.

104. And no reward do you ask of them for this: it is no less than a Message for all creatures.

105. And how many signs in the heavens and the earth do they pass by? Yet they turn (their faces) away from them!

106. And most of them believe not in Allah without associating (others as partners) with Him!

107. Do they then feel secure from the coming against them of the covering veil of the wrath of Allah - or of the coming against them of the (final) hour all of a sudden while they perceive not?

108. Say you: "This my way: I do invite to Allah - on evidence clear as the seeing with one's eyes - I and whoever follows me: Glory to Allah! And never will I join gods with Allah!"

109. Nor did We send before you (as messengers) any but men, whom We did inspire - (men) living in human habitations. Do they not travel through the earth, and see what was the end of those before them? But the home of the hereafter is best, for those who do right. Will you not then understand?

110. (Respite will be granted) until, when the messengers give up hope (of their people) and (come to) think that they were treated as liars, there reaches them Our help, and those whom We will, are delivered into safety. But never will be warded off Our punishment from those who are in sin.

111. There is, in their stories, instruction for men endued with understanding. It is not a tale invented, but a confirmation of what went before it - a detailed exposition of all things, and a guide and a mercy to any such as believe.

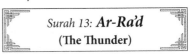

Surah 13: **Ar-Ra'd**
(The Thunder)

In the name of Allah,
Most Gracious, Most Merciful.

1. *Alif Lam Mim Ra'.* These are the signs (or verses) of the book; that which has been revealed to you from your Lord is the truth; but most men believe not.

2. Allah is He Who raised the heavens without any pillars that you can see; then He established Himself on the throne (of authority); He has subjected the sun and the moon (to His law)! Each one runs (its course) for a term appointed. He does regulate affairs explaining the signs in detail, that you may believe with certainty in the meeting with your Lord.

3. And it is He Who spread out the earth, and set on it mountains standing firm, and (flowing) rivers; and fruit of every kind He made in pairs, two and two; He draws the night as a veil over the day. See, verily in these things there are signs for those who consider!

4. And in the earth are tracts (diverse though) neighbouring, and gardens of vines and fields sown with corn, and palm trees - growing out of single roots or otherwise; watered with the same water, yet some of them We make more excellent than others to eat. See, verily in these things there are signs for those who understand!

5. If you do marvel (at their want of faith), strange is their saying: "When we are (actually) dust, shall we indeed then be in a creation renewed?" They are those who deny their Lord! They are those around whose necks will be yokes (of servitude): they will be companions of the fire, to dwell in it (forever)!

6. They ask you to hasten on the evil in preference to the good; yet have come to pass, before them, (many) exemplary punishments! But verily your Lord is full of forgiveness for mankind for their wrongdoing. And verily your Lord is (also) strict in punishment.

7. And the unbelievers say: "Why is not a sign sent down to him from his Lord?" But you are truly a warner, and to every people a guide.

8. Allah does know what every female (womb) does bear, by how much the wombs fall short (of their time or number) or do exceed. Every single thing is before His sight, in (due) proportion.

9. He knows the unseen and that which is open: He is the Great, the Most High.

10. It is the same (to Him) whether any of you conceal his speech or declare it openly; whether he lie hidden by night or walk freely by day.

11. For each (such person) there are (angels) in succession, before and behind him; they guard him by command of Allah. Verily never will Allah change the condition of a people until they change it themselves (with their own souls). But when (once) Allah wills a people's punishment, there can be no turning it back, nor will they find besides Him, any to protect.

12. It is He Who does show you the lightning, by way both of fear and of hope; it is He Who does raise up the clouds, heavy with (fertilising) rain!

13. Nay, thunder repeats His praises, and so do the angels, with awe; He flings the loud-voiced thunderbolts, and with it He strikes whomsoever He will. Yet these (are the men) who (dare to) dispute about Allah, with the strength of His power (supreme)!

14. For Him (alone) is prayer in truth: any others that they call upon besides Him hear them no more than if they were to stretch forth their hands for water to reach their mouths, but it reaches them not: for the prayer of those without faith is nothing but (futile) wandering (in the mind).

15. Whatever beings there are in the heavens and the earth, do prostrate themselves to Allah (acknowledging subjection) - with goodwill or in spite of themselves; so do their shadows in the mornings and evenings.

16. Say: "Who is the Lord and Sustainer of the heavens and the earth?" Say: "It is Allah." Say: "Do you then take (for worship) protectors other than Him, such as have no power either for good or for harm to themselves?" Say: "Are the blind equal with those who see?

Or the depths of darkness equal with light?" Or do they assign to Allah partners who have created (anything) as He has created, so that the creation seemed to them similar? Say: "Allah is the Creator of all things: He is the One, the Supreme and Irresistible."

17. He sends down water from the skies, and the channels flow, each according to its measure; but the torrent bears away the foam that mounts up to the surface. Even so, from that (ore) which they heat in the fire, to make ornaments or utensils from it, there is a scum likewise. Thus does Allah (by parables) show truth and vanity. For the scum disappears like froth cast out; while that which is for the good of mankind remains on the earth. Thus does Allah set out parables.

18. For those who respond to their Lord, are (all) good things. But those who respond not to Him - even if they had all that is in the heavens and on earth, and as much more, (in vain) would they offer it for ransom. For them will the reckoning be terrible; their abode will be hell - what a bed of misery!

19. Is then one who does know that that which has been revealed to these from your Lord is the truth, like one who is blind? It is those who are endued with understanding that receive admonition -

20. Those who fulfil the covenant of Allah and fail not in their promised word;

21. Those who join together those things which Allah has commanded to be joined, hold their Lord in awe, and fear the terrible reckoning;

22. Those who patiently persevere, seeking the countenance of their Lord; establish regular prayers; spend, out of (the gifts) We have bestowed for their sustenance, secretly and openly; and turn off evil with good: for such there is the final attainment of the (eternal) home -

23. Gardens of perpetual bliss; they shall enter there, as well as the righteous among their fathers, their spouses, and their offspring and angels shall enter to them from every gate (with the salutation):

24. "Peace to you for that you persevered in patience! Now how excellent is the final home!"

25. But those who break the covenant of Allah, after having promised their word to it, and cut apart those things which Allah has commanded to be joined, and work mischief in the land - on them is the curse; for them is the terrible home!

26. Allah does enlarge, or grant by (strict) measure, the sustenance (which He gives) to whom so He pleases. (The worldly) rejoice in the life of this world; but the life of this world is but little comfort in the hereafter.

27. The unbelievers say: "Why is not a sign sent down to him from his Lord?" Say: "Truly Allah leaves, to stray, whom He will; but He guides to Himself those who turn to Him in penitence -

28. Those who believe, and whose hearts find satisfaction in the remembrance of Allah: for without doubt in the remembrance of Allah do hearts find satisfaction.

29. For those who believe and work righteousness, is (every) blessedness, and a beautiful place of (final) return."

30. Thus have We sent you amongst a people before whom (long since) have (other) peoples (gone and) passed away; in order that you might rehearse to them what We send down to you by inspiration; yet do they reject (Him) the Most Gracious! Say: "He is my Lord! There is no god but He! On Him is my trust, and to Him do I turn!"

31. If there were a Qur'an with which mountains were moved, or the earth were cloven asunder, or the dead were made to speak, (this would be the one!) But, truly, the command is with Allah in all things! Do not the believers know, that, had Allah (so) willed, He could have guided all mankind (to the right)? But the unbelievers - never will disaster cease to seize them for their (ill) deeds, or to settle close to their homes, until the promise of Allah come to pass, for, verily, Allah will not fail in His promise.

32. Mocked were (many) messengers before you: but I granted respite to the unbelievers, and finally I punished them; then how (terrible) was My requital!

33. Is then He Who stands over every soul (and knows) all that it does, (like any others)? And yet they ascribe partners to Allah. Say: "But name them! Is it that you will inform Him of something He knows not on earth, or

is it (just) a show of words?" Nay! To those who believe not, their pretence seems pleasing, but they are kept back (thereby) from the path. And those whom Allah leaves to stray, no one can guide.

34. For them is a penalty in the life of this world, but harder, truly, is the penalty of the hereafter; and defender have they none against Allah.

35. The parable of the garden which the righteous are promised! - Beneath it flow rivers; perpetual is the enjoyment of it and the shade in it; such is the end of the righteous; and the end of unbelievers is the fire.

36. Those to whom We have given the book rejoice at what has been revealed to you: but there are among the clans those who reject a part of it. Say: "I am commanded to worship Allah, and not to join partners with Him. To Him do I call, and to Him is my return."

37. Thus have We revealed it to be a judgement of authority in Arabic. Were you to follow their (vain) desires after the knowledge which has reached you, then would you find neither protector nor defender against Allah.

38. We did send messengers before you, and appointed for them wives and children; and it was never the part of a messenger to bring a sign except as Allah permitted (or commanded). For each period is a book (revealed).

39. Allah does blot out or confirm what He pleases: with Him is the mother of the book.

40. Whether We shall show you (within your lifetime) part of what We promised them, or take to Ourselves your soul (before it is all accomplished), your duty is to (make the message) reach them; it is Our part to call them to account.

41. Do they not see that We gradually reduce the land (in their control) from its outlying borders? (Where) Allah commands, there is none to put back His command: and He is Swift in calling to account.

42. Those before them did (also) devise plots; but in all things the master-planning is Allah's. He knows the doings of every soul; and soon will the unbelievers know who gets home in the end.

43. The unbelievers say: "No messenger are you." Say: "Enough for a witness between me and you is Allah, and such as have knowledge of the book."

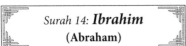

Surah 14: *Ibrahim*
(Abraham)

In the name of Allah,
Most Gracious, Most Merciful.

1. *Alif Lam Ra.* A book which We have revealed to you, in order that you might lead mankind out of the depths of darkness into light - by the leave of their Lord - to the way of (Him) Exalted in Power, Worthy of all Praise! -

2. Of Allah, to Whom do belong all things in the heavens and on earth! But alas for the unbelievers, for a terrible penalty (their unfaith will bring them)! -

3. Those who love the life of this world more than the hereafter, who hinder (men) from the path of Allah and seek in it something crooked; they are astray by a long distance.

4. We sent not a messenger except (to teach) in the language of his (own) people, in order to make (things) clear to them. Now Allah leaves straying those whom He pleases and guides whom He pleases; and He is Exalted in Power, Full of Wisdom.

5. We sent Moses with Our signs (and the command): "Bring out your people from the depths of darkness into light, and teach them to remember the Days of Allah." Verily in this there are signs for such as are firmly patient and constant - grateful and appreciative.

6. Remember! Moses said to his people: "Call to mind the favour of Allah to you when He delivered you from the people of Pharaoh; they set you hard tasks and punishments, slaughtered your sons, and let your womenfolk live; in it was a tremendous trial from your Lord."

7. And remember! Your Lord caused to be declared (publicly): "If you are grateful, I will add more (favours) to you; but if you show ingratitude, truly My punishment is terrible indeed!"

8. And Moses said: "If you show ingratitude, you and all on earth together - yet is Allah Free of all wants, Worthy of all praise."

9. Has not the story reached you, (O people!), of those who (went) before you? - Of the people of Noah, and 'Ad, and Thamud? And of those who (came) after them? None knows them but Allah. To them came messengers with clear (signs); but they put their hands up to their mouths, and said: "We do deny (the mission) on which you have been sent, and we are really in suspicious (disquieting) doubt as to that to which you invite us."

10. Their messengers said: "Is there a doubt about Allah, the Creator of the heavens and the earth? It is He Who invites you, in order that He may forgive you your sins and give you respite for a term appointed!" They said: "Ah! You are no more than human, like ourselves! You wish to turn us away from the (gods) our fathers used to worship: then bring us some clear authority."

11. Their messengers said to them: "True, we are human like yourselves, but Allah does grant His grace to such of His servants as He pleases. It is not for us to bring you an authority except as Allah permits. And on Allah let all men of faith put their trust."

12. "No reason have we why we should not put our trust on Allah. Indeed He has guided us to the ways we (follow). We shall certainly bear with patience all the hurt you may cause us; for those who put their trust should put their trust on Allah."

13. And the unbelievers said to their messengers: "Be sure we shall drive you out of our land, or you shall return to our religion." But their Lord inspired (this Message) to them: "Verily We shall cause the wrongdoers to perish!

14. "And verily We shall cause you to remain in the land, and succeed them. This for such as fear the time when they shall stand before My tribunal - such as fear the punishment denounced."

15. But they sought victory and decision (there and then), and frustration was the lot of every powerful obstinate transgressor.

16. In front of such a one is hell, and he is given for drink, boiling fetid water.

17. In gulps will he sip it, but never well he be near swallowing it down his throat: death will come to him from every quarter, yet will he not die; and in front of him will be a chastisement unrelenting.

18. The parable of those who reject their Lord is that their works are as ashes, on which the wind blows furiously on a tempestuous day; no power have they over anything that they have earned; that is the straying far, far (from the goal).

19. Do you not see that Allah created the Heavens and the earth in truth? If He so will, He can remove you and put (in your place) a new Creation?

20. Nor is that for Allah any great matter.

21. They will all be marshalled before Allah together: then will the weak say to those who were arrogant: "For us, we but followed you; can you then benefit us at all against the wrath of Allah?" They will reply, "If we had received the guidance of Allah, we should have given it to you; to us it makes no difference

(now) whether we rage, or bear (these torments) with patience: for ourselves there is no way of escape."

22. And Satan will say when the matter is decided: "It was Allah Who gave you a promise of truth; I too promised, but I failed in my promise to you. I had no authority over you except to call you, but you listened to me; then reproach not me, but reproach your own souls. I cannot listen to your cries, nor can you listen to mine. I reject your former act in associating me with Allah. For wrongdoers there must be a grievous penalty."

23. But those who believe and work righteousness will be admitted to gardens beneath which rivers flow - to dwell in it for ever with the permission of their Lord; their greeting in it will be: "Peace!"

24. Do you not see how Allah sets out a parable? - A goodly word like a goodly tree, whose root is firmly fixed, and its branches (reach) to the heavens -

25. It brings out its fruit at all times, by the permission of its Lord. So Allah sets out parables for men, in order that they may receive admonition.

26. And the parable of an evil word is that of an evil tree. It is torn up by the root from the surface of the earth; it has no stability.

27. Allah will establish in strength those who believe, with the word that stands firm, in this world and in the hereafter; but Allah will leave, to stray, those who do wrong: Allah does what He wills.

28. Have you not turned your vision to those who have changed the favour of Allah into blasphemy and caused their people to descend to the house of perdition -

29. Into hell? They will burn in it - an evil place to stay in!

30. And they set up (idols) as equal to Allah, to mislead (men) from the path! Say: "Enjoy (your brief power)! But verily you are making straightway for hell!"

31. Speak to My servants who have believed, that they may establish regular prayers, and spend (in charity) out of the sustenance We have given them, secretly and openly, before the coming of a day in which there will be neither mutual bargaining nor befriending.

32. It is Allah Who has created the heavens and the earth and sends down rain from the skies, and with it brings out fruits with which to feed you; it is He Who has made the ships subject to you, that they may sail through the sea by His command; and the rivers (also) has He made subject to you.

33. And He has made subject to you the sun and the moon, both diligently pursuing their courses; and the night and the day has He (also) made subject you.

34. And He gives you of all that you ask for. But if you count the favours of Allah, never will you be able to number them; verily, man is given up to injustice and ingratitude.

35. Remember Abraham said: "O my Lord! Make this city one of peace and security and preserve me and my sons from worshipping idols.

36. "O my Lord! They have indeed led astray many among mankind: he then who follows my (ways) is of me, and he that disobeys me - but You are indeed Oft-Forgiving, Most Merciful."

37. "O our Lord! I have made some of my offspring to dwell in a valley without cultivation, by your Sacred House; in order, O our Lord, that they may establish regular prayer: so fill the hearts of some among men with love towards them, and feed them with fruits; so that they may give thanks."

38. "O our Lord! Truly You do know what we conceal and what we reveal: for nothing whatever is hidden from Allah, whether on earth or in heaven."

39. "Praise be to Allah who has granted to me in old age Ishmael and Isaac: for truly my Lord is He, the Hearer of prayer!"

40. "O my Lord! Make me one who establishes regular prayer, and also (raise such) among my offspring O our Lord! And accept You my prayer."

41. "O our Lord! Cover (us) with Your forgiveness - me, my parents, and (all) believers, on the day that the reckoning will be established!"

42. Do not think that Allah does not heed the deeds of those who do wrong. He but gives them respite against a day when the eyes will fixedly stare in horror -

43. They are running forward with necks outstretched, their heads uplifted, their gaze returning not towards them, and their hearts a (gaping) void!

44. So warn mankind of the day when the wrath will reach them; then will the wrongdoers say: "Our Lord! respite us (if only) for a short term; we will answer Your call, and follow the messengers!" "What! Were you not used to swear before that you should suffer no decline?

45. And you dwelt in the dwellings of men who wronged their own souls; you were clearly shown how We dealt with them; and We put out many parables in your behalf!"

46. Mighty indeed were the plots which they made, but their plots were (well) within the sight of Allah, even though they were such as to shake the hills!

47. Never think that Allah would fail His messengers in His promise; for Allah is Exalted in Power - the Lord of Retribution.

48. One day the earth will be changed to a different earth, and so will be the heavens, and (men) will be marshalled forward, before Allah, the One, the Irresistible;

49. And you will see the sinners that day bound together in fetters -

50. Their garments of liquid pitch, and their faces covered with fire;

51. That Allah may repay each soul according to its due; and verily Allah is Swift in calling to account.

52. Here is a message for mankind; let them take warning from it, and let them know that He is (no other than) One God; let men of understanding take heed.

Surah 15: *Al-Hijr*
(The Rocky Tracts)

In the name of Allah,
Most Gracious, Most Merciful.

1. *Alif Lam Ra.* These are the *Ayat* of revelation - of a Qur'an that makes things clear.

2. Again and again will those who disbelieve wish that they had bowed (to Allah's will) in Islam.

3. Leave them alone, to enjoy (the good things of this life) and to please themselves; let (false) hope amuse them; soon will knowledge (undeceive them).

4. Never did We destroy a population that had not a term decreed and assigned beforehand.

5. Neither can a people anticipate its term, nor delay it.

6. They say: "O you to whom the message is being revealed! Truly you are mad (or possessed)!"

7. "Why do you not bring angels to us if it be that you have the truth?"

8. We send not the angels down except for just cause; if they came (to the ungodly), see! No respite would they have!

9. We have, without doubt, sent down the message; and We will assuredly guard it (from corruption).

10. We did send messengers before you amongst the religious sects of old;

11. But never came a messenger to them but they mocked him.

12. Even so do We let it creep into the hearts of the sinners -

13. That they should not believe in the (message); but the ways of the ancients have passed away.

14. Even if We opened out to them a gate from heaven, and they were to continue (all day) ascending in it,

15. They would only say: "Our eyes have been intoxicated: nay, we have been bewitched by sorcery."

16. It is We who have set out the Zodiacal signs in the heavens, and made them fair-seeming to (all) beholders;

17. And (moreover) We have guarded them from every evil spirit accursed;

18. But any that gains a hearing by stealth, is pursued by a flaming fire, bright (to see).

19. And the earth We have spread out (like a carpet); set on it mountains firm and immovable; and produced in it all kinds of things in due balance.

20. And We have provided in it means of subsistence - for you and for those for whose sustenance you are not responsible.

21. And there is not a thing but its (sources and) treasures (inexhaustible) are with Us; but We only send down of it in due and ascertainable measures.

22. And We send the fecundating winds, then cause the rain to descend from the sky, with it providing you with water (in abundance), though you are not the guardians of its stores.

23. And verily, it is We Who give life, and Who give death; it is We Who remain Inheritors (after all else passes away).

24. To Us are known those of you who hasten forward, and those who lag behind.

25. Assuredly it is your Lord Who will gather them together; for He is Perfect in wisdom and knowledge.

26. We created man from sounding clay, from mud moulded into shape;

27. And the Jinn race, We had created before, from the fire of a scorching wind.

28. See! Your Lord said to the angels: "I am about to create man from sounding clay from mud moulded into shape;

29. When I have fashioned him (in due proportion) and breathed into him of My spirit, fall you down in obeisance to him."

30. So the angels prostrated themselves, all of them together:

31. Not so Iblis: he refused to be among those who prostrated themselves.

32. (Allah) said: "O Iblis! What is your reason for not being among those who prostrated themselves?"

33. (Iblis) said: "I am not one to prostrate myself to man, whom You did create from sounding clay, from mud moulded into shape."

34. (Allah) said: "Then get you out from here; for you are rejected, accursed."

35. "And the curse shall be on you till the day of judgement."

36. (Iblis) said: "O my Lord! Give me then respite till the day the (dead) are raised."

37. (Allah) said: "Respite is granted you -

38. Till the day of the time appointed."

39. (Iblis) said: "O my Lord! Because You have put me in the wrong, I will make (wrong) fair-seeming to them on the earth, and I will put them all in the wrong -

40. Except Your servants among them, sincere and purified (by Your grace)."

41. (Allah) said: "This (way of My sincere servants) is indeed a way that leads straight to Me.

42. For over My servants no authority shall you have, except such as put themselves in the wrong and follow you."

43. And verily, hell is the promised abode for them all!

44. To it are seven gates: for each of those gates is a (special) class (of sinners) assigned.

45. The righteous (will be) amid gardens and fountains (of clear-flowing water).

46. (Their greeting will be): "Enter you here in peace and security."

47. And We shall remove from their hearts any lurking sense of injury: (they will be) brothers (joyfully) facing each other on thrones (of dignity).

48. There, no sense of fatigue shall touch them, nor shall they (ever) be asked to leave.

49. Tell My servants that I am indeed the Oft-Forgiving, Most Merciful;

50. And that My penalty will be indeed the most grievous penalty.

51. Tell them about the guests of Abraham.

52. When they entered his presence and said, "Peace!" He said, "We feel afraid of you!"

53. They said: "Fear not! We give you glad tidings of a son endowed with wisdom."

54. He said: "Do you give me glad tidings that old age has seized me? Of what then, is your good news?"

55. They said: "We give you glad tidings in truth; be not then in despair!"

56. He said: "And who despairs of the mercy of his Lord, but such as go astray?"

57. (Abraham) said: "What then is the business on which you (have come), O you messengers (of Allah)?"

58. They said: "We have been sent to a people (deep) in sin.

59. Excepting the adherents of Lot: them we are certainly (charged) to save (from harm) - all -

60. Except his wife, who, we have ascertained, will be among those who will lag behind."

61. At length, when the messengers arrived among the adherents of Lot,

62. He said: "You appear to be uncommon folk."

63. They said: "Yea, we have come to you to accomplish that of which they doubt."

64. "We have brought to you that which is inevitably due, and assuredly we tell the truth."

65. "Then travel by night with your household, when a portion of the night (yet remains), and do you

bring up the rear; let no one amongst you look back, but pass on where you are ordered."

66. And We made known this decree to him, that the last remnants of those (sinners) should be cut off by the morning.

67. The inhabitants of the city came in (mad) joy (at news of the young men).

68. Lot said: "These are my guests: disgrace me not;

69. But fear Allah and shame me not."

70. They said: "Did we not forbid you (to speak) for all and sundry?"

71. He said: "There are my daughters (to marry), if you must act (so)."

72. Verily, by your life (O Prophet), in their wild intoxication, they wandered in distraction, to and fro.

73. But the (mighty) blast overtook them before morning,

74. And We turned (the cities) upside down, and rained down on them brimstones hard as baked clay.

75. See! In this are signs for those who by signs do understand.

76. And the (cities were) right on the highroad.

77. See! In this is a sign for those who believe!

78. And the companions of the wood were also wrongdoers;

79. So We exacted retribution from them. They were both on an open highway, plain to see.

80. The companions of the rocky Tract also rejected the messengers:

81. We sent them Our signs, but they persisted in turning away from them.

82. Out of the mountains did they hew (their) edifices, (feeling themselves) secure.

83. But the (mighty) blast seized them of a morning,

84. And of no benefit to them was all that they did (with such art and care)!

85. We created not the heavens, the earth, and all between them, but for just ends. And the hour is surely coming (when this will be manifest). So overlook (any human faults) with gracious forgiveness.

86. For verily it is your Lord Who is the Master-Creator, knowing all things.

87. And We have bestowed upon you the seven oft-repeated (verses) and the grand Qur'an.

88. Strain not your eyes (wistfully) at what We have bestowed on certain classes of them, nor grieve over them; but lower your wing (in gentleness) to the believers.

89. And say: "I am indeed he that warns openly and without ambiguity" -

90. (Of just such wrath) as We sent down on those who divided (Scripture into arbitrary parts) -

91. (So also on such) as have made the Qur'an into shreds (as they please).

92. Therefore, by your Lord, We will, of a surety, call them to account,

93. For all their deeds.

94. Therefore, explain openly what you are commanded, and turn away from those who join false gods with Allah.

95. For sufficient are We to you against those who scoff -

96. Those who adopt, with Allah, another god; but soon will they come to know.

97. We do indeed know how your heart is distressed at what they say.

98. But celebrate the praises of your Lord, and be of those who prostrate themselves in adoration.

99. And serve your Lord until there come to you the hour that is certain.

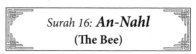

Surah 16: *An-Nahl*
(The Bee)

In the name of Allah,
Most Gracious, Most Merciful.

1. (Inevitably) comes (to pass) the command of Allah; seek you not then to hasten it; glory to Him, and far is He above having the partners they ascribe to Him!

2. He does send down His angels with inspiration of His command, to such of His servants as He pleases, (saying): "Warn (man) that there is no god but I; so do your duty to Me."

3. He has created the heavens and the earth for just ends; far is He above having the partners they ascribe to Him!

4. He has created man from a sperm-drop; and see this same (man) becomes an open disputer!

5. And cattle He has created for you (men); from them you derive warmth, and numerous benefits, and of their (meat) you eat.

6. And you have a sense of pride and beauty in them as you drive them home in the evening, and as you lead them out to pasture in the morning.

7. And they carry your heavy loads to lands that you could not (otherwise) reach except with souls distressed; for your Lord is indeed Most Kind, Most Merciful.

8. And (He has created) horses, mules, and donkeys, for you to ride and use for show; and He has created (other) things of what you have no knowledge.

9. And to Allah leads straight the way, but there are ways that turn aside; if Allah had willed, He could have guided all of you.

10. It is He Who sends down rain from the sky. From it you drink, and out of it (grows) the vegetation on which you feed your cattle.

11. With it He produces for you corn, olives, date palms, grapes, and every kind of fruit; verily in this is a sign for those who give thought.

12. He has made subject to you the night and the day; the sun and the moon; and the stars are in subjection by His command; verily in this are signs for men who are wise.

13. And the things on this earth which He has multiplied in varying colours (and qualities): verily in this is a sign for men who celebrate the praises of Allah (in gratitude).

14. It is He Who has made the sea subject, that you may eat of it flesh that is fresh and tender, and that you may extract from it ornaments to wear, and

you see the ships in it that plough the waves, that you may seek (thus) of the bounty of Allah and that you may be grateful.

15. And He has set up on the earth mountains standing firm, lest it should shake with you; and rivers and roads; that you may guide yourselves,

16. And marks and signposts; and by the stars (men) guide themselves.

17. Is then He Who creates like one that creates not? Will you not receive admonition?

18. If you would count up the favours of Allah, never would you be able to number them; for Allah is Oft-Forgiving, Most Merciful.

19. And Allah does know what you conceal, and what you reveal.

20. Those whom they invoke besides Allah create nothing and are themselves created.

21. (They are things) dead, lifeless; nor do you know when they will be raised up.

22. Your God is One God; as to those who believe not in the hereafter, their hearts refuse to know, and they are arrogant.

23. Undoubtedly, Allah does know what they conceal, and what they reveal; verily He loves not the arrogant.

24. When it is said to them, "What is it that your Lord has revealed?" They say, "Tales of the ancients!"

25. Let them bear, on the day of judgement, their own burdens in full, and also (something) of the burdens of those without knowledge, whom they misled. Alas, how grievous the burdens they will bear!

26. Those before them did also plot (against Allah's way); but Allah took their structures from their foundations, and the roof fell down on them from above; and the wrath seized them from directions they did not perceive.

27. Then, on the day of judgement, He will cover them with shame, and say: "Where are My 'partners' concerning whom you used to dispute (with the godly)?" Those endued with knowledge will say: "This day, indeed, are the unbelievers covered with shame and misery -

28. (Namely) those whose lives the angels take in a state of wrongdoing to their own souls. Then would they offer submission (with the pretence), 'We did no evil (knowingly).'" (The angels will reply), "Nay, but verily Allah knows all that you did;

29. So enter the gates of hell, to dwell in it. Thus evil indeed is the abode of the arrogant."

30. To the righteous (when) it is said, "What is it that your Lord has revealed?" They say, "All that is good." To those who do good, there is good in this world, and the home of the hereafter is even better. And excellent indeed is the home of the righteous -

31. Gardens of eternity which they will enter; beneath them flow (pleasant) rivers; they will have in it all that they wish; thus does Allah reward the righteous -

32. (Namely) those whose lives the angels take in a state of purity, saying (to them), "Peace be on you; enter you the garden, because of the good which you did (in the world)."

33. Do the (ungodly) wait until the angels come to them, or there comes the command of your Lord (for their doom)? So did those who went before them. But Allah wronged them not; nay, they wronged their own souls.

34. But the evil results of their deeds overtook them, and that very (wrath) at which they had scoffed hemmed them in.

35. The worshippers of false gods say: "If Allah had so willed, we should not have worshipped any but Him - neither we nor our fathers - nor should we have prescribed prohibitions other than His." So did those who went before them. But what is the mission of messengers but to preach the clear message?

36. For We assuredly sent amongst every people a messenger, (with the command), "Serve Allah, and eschew evil"; of the people were some whom Allah guided, and some on whom error became inevitably (established). So travel through the earth, and see what was the end of those who denied (the truth).

37. If you are anxious for their guidance, yet Allah guides not such as He leaves to stray. And there is none to help them.

38. They swear their strongest oaths by Allah, that Allah will not raise up those who die; nay, but it is a promise (binding) on Him in truth; but most among mankind realise it not.

39. (They must be raised up), in order that He may manifest to them the truth of that in which they differ, and that the rejecters of truth may realise that they had indeed (surrendered to) falsehood.

40. For to anything which We have willed, We but say the word, "Be", and it is.

41. To those who leave their homes in the cause of Allah, after suffering oppression - We will assuredly give a goodly home in this world; but truly the reward of the hereafter will be greater if they only realise (this)!

42. (They are) those who persevere in patience, and put their trust on their Lord.

43. And before you also, the messengers We sent were but men, to whom We granted inspiration; if you realise this not, ask of those who possess the message.

44. (We sent them) with clear signs and scriptures and We have sent down to you (also, O Muhammad) the message; that you may explain clearly to men what is sent for them, and that they may give thought.

45. Do then those who devise evil (plots) feel secure that Allah will not cause the earth to swallow them up, or that the wrath will not seize them from directions they little perceive? -

46. Or that He may not call them to account in the midst of their goings

to and fro, without a chance of their frustrating Him? -

47. Or that He may not call them to account by a process of slow wastage - for your Lord is indeed full of kindness and mercy.

48. Do they not look at Allah's creation, (even) among (inanimate) things - how their (very) shadows turn round, from the right and the left, prostrating themselves to Allah, and that in the humblest manner?

49. And to Allah does obeisance all that is in the heavens and on earth, whether moving (living), creatures or the angels; for none are arrogant (before their Lord).

50. They all revere their Lord, high above them, and they do all that they are commanded.

51. Allah has said: "Take not (for worship) two gods; for He is just One God; then fear Me (and Me alone)."

52. To Him belongs whatever is in the heavens and on earth. And to Him is duty due always; then will you fear other than Allah?

53. And you have no good thing but is from Allah and moreover when you are touched by distress, to Him you call with groans;

54. Yet, when He removes the distress from you, see! Some of you turn to other gods to join with their Lord -

55. (As if) to show their ingratitude for the favours We have bestowed on them! Then enjoy (your brief day); but soon will you know (your folly)!

56. And they (even) assign, to things they do not know, a portion out of that which We have bestowed for their sustenance! By Allah, you shall certainly be called to account for your false inventions.

57. And they assign daughters for Allah! - Glory be to Him! - And for themselves (sons - the issue) they desire!

58. When news is brought to one of them, of (the birth of) a female (child), his face darkens, and he is filled with inward grief!

59. With shame does he hide himself from his people, because of the bad news he has had! Shall he retain it on (sufferance and) contempt, or bury it in the dust? Ah! What an evil (choice) they decide on!

60. To those who believe not in the hereafter, applies the similitude of evil; to Allah applies the highest similitude; for He is the Exalted in Power, Full of wisdom.

61. If Allah were to punish men for their wrongdoing, He would not leave, on the (earth), a single living creature; but He gives them respite for a stated term: when their term expires, they would not be able to delay (the punishment) for a single hour, just as they would not be able to anticipate it (for a single hour).

62. They attribute to Allah what they hate (for themselves). And their tongues assert the falsehood that all good things are for themselves: without doubt for them is the fire, and they will be the first to be hastened on into it!

63. By Allah, We (also) sent (our prophets) to peoples before you; but Satan made, (to the wicked), their own acts seem alluring: he is also their patron today, but they shall have a most grievous penalty.

64. And We sent down the book to you for the express purpose, that you should make clear to them those things in which they differ, and that it should be a guide and a mercy to those who believe.

65. And Allah sends down rain from the skies, and gives with it life to the earth after its death: verily in this is a sign for those who listen.

66. And verily in cattle (too) will you find an instructive sign. From what is within their bodies, between excretions and blood, We produce for your drink, milk, pure and agreeable to those who drink it.

67. And from the fruit of the date-palm and the vine, you get out wholesome drink, and food: see, in this also is a sign for those who are wise.

68. And your Lord taught the Bee to build its cells in hills, on trees, and in (men's) habitations;

69. Then to eat of all the produce (of the earth), and find with skill the spacious paths of its Lord: there issues from within their bodies a drink of varying colours, in which is healing for men: verily in this is a sign for those who give thought.

70. It is Allah who creates you and takes your souls at death; and of you there are some who are sent back to a feeble age, so that they know nothing after having known (much): for Allah is All-Knowing, All-Powerful.

71. Allah has bestowed His gifts of sustenance more freely on some of you than on others: those more favoured are not going to throw back their gifts to those whom their right hands possess, so as to be equal in that respect. Will they then deny the favours of Allah?

72. And Allah has made for you mates (and companions) of your own nature, and made for you, out of them, sons and daughters and grandchildren. And provided for your sustenance of the best; will they then believe in vain things, and be ungrateful for Allah's favours? -

73. And worship others than Allah - such as have no power of providing them, for sustenance, with anything in heavens or earth, and cannot possibly have such power?

74. Invent not similitudes for Allah; for Allah knows, and you know not.

75. Allah sets out the parable (of two men: one) a slave under the dominion of another; he has no power of any sort; and (the other) a man on whom We have bestowed goodly favours from Ourselves. And he spends of it (freely), privately and publicly; are the two equal? (By no means); praise be to Allah. But most of them understand not.

76. Allah sets out (another) parable of two men: one of them dumb, with no power of any sort: a wearisome burden is he to his master; whichever way he

directs him, he brings no good: is such a man equal with one who commands justice, and is on a straight way?

77. To Allah belongs the mystery of the heavens and the earth. And the decision of the hour (of judgement) is as the twinkling of an eye, or even quicker: for Allah has power over all things.

78. It is He Who brought you out from the wombs of your mothers when you knew nothing; and He gave you hearing and sight and intelligence and affection; that you may give thanks (to Allah).

79. Do they not look at the birds, held poised in the midst of (the air and) the sky? Nothing holds them up but (the power of) Allah. Verily in this are signs for those who believe.

80. It is Allah who made your habitations homes of rest and quiet for you; and made for you, out of the skins of animals, (tents for) dwellings, which you find so light (and handy) when you travel and when you stop (in your travels), and out of their wool, and their soft fibres (between wool and hair), and their hair, rich stuff and articles of convenience (to serve you) for a time.

81. It is Allah who made out of the things He created, some things to give you shade; of the hills He made some for your shelter; He made you garments to protect you from heat, and coats of mail to protect you from your (mutual) violence. Thus does He complete His favours on you, that you may bow to His will (in Islam).

82. But if they turn away, your duty is only to preach the clear message.

83. They recognise the favours of Allah; then they deny them; and most of them are (creatures) ungrateful.

84. One day We shall raise from all peoples a witness: then will no excuse be accepted from unbelievers, nor will they receive any favours.

85. When the wrongdoers (actually) see the penalty, then will it in no way be mitigated, nor will they then receive respite.

86. When those who gave partners to Allah will see their 'partners', they will say: "Our Lord! These are our 'partners', those whom we used to invoke besides You." But they will throw back their word at them (and say): "Indeed you are liars!"

87. That day shall they (openly) show (their) submission to Allah; and all their inventions shall leave them in the lurch.

88. Those who reject Allah and hinder (men) from the path of Allah - for them will We add penalty to penalty; for that they used to spread mischief.

89. One day We shall raise from all peoples a witness against them, from amongst themselves: and We shall bring you as a witness against these (your people); and We have sent down to you the book explaining all things, a guide, a mercy, and glad tidings to Muslims.

90. Allah commands justice, the doing of good, and generosity to relatives,

and He forbids all shameful deeds, and injustice and rebellion: He instructs you, that you may receive admonition.

91. Fulfil the covenant of Allah when you have entered into it, and break not your oaths after you have confirmed them; indeed you have made Allah your surety; for Allah knows all that you do.

92. And be not like a woman who breaks into untwisted strands the yarn which she has spun after it has become strong. Nor take your oaths to practice deception between yourselves, lest one party should be more numerous than another; for Allah will test you by this; and on the day of judgement He will certainly make clear to you (the truth of) that in which you disagree.

93. If Allah so willed, He could make you all one people; but He leaves straying whom He pleases, and He guides whom He pleases; but you shall certainly be called to account for all your actions.

94. And take not your oaths, to practice deception between yourselves, with the result that someone's foot may slip after it was firmly planted, and you may have to taste the evil (consequences) of having hindered (men) from the path of Allah, and a mighty wrath descend on you.

95. Nor sell the covenant of Allah for a miserable price: for with Allah is (a prize) far better for you, if you only knew.

96. What is with you must vanish; what is with Allah will endure. And We will certainly bestow, on those who patiently persevere, their reward according to the best of their actions.

97. Whoever works righteousness, man or woman, and has faith, verily, to him will We give a new life, a life that is good and pure, and We will bestow on such their reward according to the best of their actions.

98. When you do read the Qur'an, seek Allah's protection from Satan the rejected one.

99. No authority has he over those who believe and put their trust in their Lord.

100. His authority is over those only, who take him as patron and who join partners with Allah.

101. When We substitute one revelation for another - and Allah knows best what He reveals (in stages) - they say, "You are but a forger": but most of them understand not.

102. Say, the Holy Spirit has brought the revelation from your Lord in truth, in order to strengthen those who believe, and as a guide and glad tidings to Muslims.

103. We know indeed that they say, "It is a man that teaches him." The tongue of him they wickedly point to is notably foreign, while this is Arabic, pure and clear.

104. Those who believe not in the signs of Allah - Allah will not guide them, and theirs will be a grievous penalty.

105. It is those who believe not in the signs of Allah, that forge falsehood; it is they who lie!

106. Anyone who, after accepting faith in Allah, utters unbelief - except under compulsion, his heart remaining firm in faith - but such as open their breast to unbelief - on them is wrath from Allah, and theirs will be a dreadful penalty.

107. This because they love the life of this world better than the hereafter: and Allah will not guide those who reject faith.

108. Those are they whose hearts, ears, and eyes Allah has sealed up and they take no heed.

109. Without doubt, in the hereafter they will perish.

110. But verily your Lord - to those who leave their homes after trials and persecutions - and who after that strive and fight for the faith and patiently persevere - your Lord, after all this is Oft-Forgiving, Most Merciful.

111. One day every soul will come up struggling for itself, and every soul will be recompensed (fully) for all its actions, and none will be unjustly dealt with.

112. Allah sets out a parable: a city enjoying security and quiet, abundantly supplied with sustenance from every place: yet was it ungrateful for the favours of Allah: so Allah made it taste of hunger and terror (in extremes) (closing in on it) like a garment (from every side), because of the (evil) which (its people) wrought.

113. And there came to them a messenger from among themselves, but they falsely rejected him; so the wrath seized them even in the midst of their iniquities.

114. So eat of the sustenance which Allah has provided for you, lawful and good; and be grateful for the favours of Allah, if it is He Whom you serve.

115. He has only forbidden you dead meat, and blood, and the flesh of swine, and any (food) over which the name of other than Allah has been invoked. But if one is forced by necessity, without wilful disobedience, nor transgressing due limits - then Allah is Oft-Forgiving, Most Merciful.

116. But say not - for any false thing that your tongues may put out - "This is lawful, and this is forbidden," so as to ascribe false things to Allah. For those who ascribe false things to Allah, will never prosper.

117. (In such falsehood) is but a paltry profit; but they will have a most grievous penalty.

118. To the Jews We prohibited such things as We have mentioned to you before; We did them no wrong, but they were used to doing wrong to themselves.

119. But verily your Lord - to those who do wrong in ignorance, but who after that repent and make amends - your Lord, after all this, is Oft- Forgiving, Most Merciful.

120. Abraham was indeed a model. Devoutly obedient to Allah, (and) true in faith, and he joined not gods with Allah:

121. He showed his gratitude for the favours of Allah, Who chose him, and guided him to a straight way.

122. And We gave him good in this world, and he will be, in the hereafter, in the ranks of the righteous.

123. So We have taught you the inspired (message), "Follow the ways of Abraham the True in faith, and he joined not gods with Allah."

124. The Sabbath was only made (strict) to those who disagreed (as to its observance); but Allah will judge between them on the day of judgement, as to their differences.

125. Invite (all) to the way of your Lord with wisdom and beautiful preaching; and argue with them in ways that are best and most gracious: for your Lord knows best, who have strayed from His path, and who receive guidance.

126. And if you do catch them out, catch them out no worse than they catch you out; but if you show patience, that is indeed the best (course) for those who are patient.

127. And do you be patient, for your patience is but from Allah; nor grieve over them; and distress not yourself because of their plots.

128. For Allah is with those who restrain themselves, and those who do good.

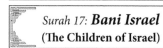

Surah 17: **Bani Israel**
(The Children of Israel)

In the name of Allah,
Most Gracious, Most Merciful.

1. Glory to (Allah) Who did take His servant for journey by night from the Sacred Mosque to the Farthest Mosque, whose precincts We did bless - in order that We might show him some of Our signs: for He is the One Who hears and sees (all things).

2. We gave Moses the book, and made it a guide to the Children of Israel, (commanding): "Take not other than Me as Disposer of (your) affairs."

3. O you that are sprung from those whom We carried (in the ark) with Noah! Verily he was a devotee most grateful.

4. And We gave (clear) warning to the Children of Israel in the book, that twice would they do mischief on the earth and be elated with mighty arrogance, (and twice would they be punished)!

5. When the first of the warnings came to pass, We sent against you Our servants given to terrible warfare. They entered the very inmost parts of your homes; and it was a warning (completely) fulfilled.

6. Then did We grant you the return as against them; We gave you increase in resources and sons, and made you the more numerous in manpower.

7. If you did well, you did well for yourselves; if you did evil, (you did it) against yourselves. So when the second of the warnings came to pass, (We permitted your enemies) to disfigure your faces, and to enter your temple as they had entered it before, and to visit with destruction all that fell into their power.

8. It may be that your Lord may (yet) show mercy to you; but if you revert (to your sins) We shall revert (to Our punishments); and We have made hell a prison for those who reject (all faith).

9. Verily this Qur'an does guide to that which is most right (or stable), and gives the glad tidings to the believers who work deeds of righteousness, that they shall have a magnificent reward;

10. And to those who believe not in the hereafter, (it announces) that We have prepared for them a penalty grievous (indeed).

11. The prayer that man should make for good, he makes for evil; for man is given to hasty (deeds).

12. We have made the night and the day as two (of Our) signs: the sign of the night have We obscured, while the sign of the day We have made to enlighten you; that you may seek bounty from your Lord, and that you may know the number and count of the years; all things have We explained in detail.

13. Every man's fate We have fastened on his own neck: on the day of judgement We shall bring out for him a scroll, which he will see spread open.

14. (It will be said to him:) "Read your (own) record: sufficient is your soul this day to make out an account against you."

157

15. Who receives guidance, receives it for his own benefit; who goes astray, does so to his own loss; no bearer of burdens can bear the burden of another; nor would We visit with Our wrath until We had sent a messenger (to give warning).

16. When We decide to destroy a population, We (first) send a definite order to those among them who are given the good things of this life and yet transgress; so that the word is proved true against them; then (it is) We destroy them utterly.

17. How many generations have We destroyed after Noah? And enough is your Lord to note and see the sins of His servants.

18. If any do wish for the transitory things (of this life), We readily grant them - such things as We will, to such persons as We will: in the end have We provided hell for them: they will burn in it, disgraced and rejected.

19. Those who do wish for the (things of) the hereafter, and strive for it with all due striving, and have faith - they are the ones whose striving is acceptable (to Allah).

20. Of the bounties of your Lord We bestow freely on all - these as well as those; the bounties of your Lord are not closed (to anyone).

21. See how We have bestowed more on some than on others but verily the hereafter is more in rank and gradation and more in excellence.

22. Take not with Allah another object of worship; or you (O man!) will sit in disgrace and destitution.

23. Your Lord has decreed that you worship none but Him, and that you be kind to parents. Whether one or both of them attain old age in your life, say not to them a word of contempt, nor repel them, but address them in terms of honour.

24. And, out of kindness, lower to them the wing of humility, and say: "My Lord! Bestow on them Your mercy even as they cherished me in childhood."

25. Your Lord knows best what is in your hearts; if you do deeds of righteousness, verily He is Most Forgiving to those who turn to Him again and again (in true penitence).

26. And render to the relations their due rights, as (also) to those in want, and to the wayfarer; but squander not (your wealth) in the manner of a spendthrift.

27. Verily spendthrifts are brothers of the evil ones; and the evil one is to his Lord (Himself) ungrateful.

28. And even if you have to turn away from them in pursuit of the mercy from your Lord which you do expect, yet speak to them a word of easy kindness.

29. Make not your hand tied (like a niggard's) to your neck, nor stretch it out to its utmost reach, so that you become blameworthy and destitute.

30. Verily your Lord does provide sustenance in abundance for whom

He pleases, and He provides in a just measure, for He does know and regard all His servants.

31. Kill not your children for fear of want; We shall provide sustenance for them as well as for you. Verily the killing of them is a great sin.

32. Nor come near to adultery for it is a shameful (deed) and an evil, opening the road (to other evils).

33. Nor take life - which Allah has made sacred - except for just cause. And if anyone is slain wrongfully, We have given his heir authority (to demand *Qisas* or to forgive): but let him not exceed bounds in the matter of taking life: for he is helped (by the law).

34. Come not near to the orphan's property except to improve it, until he attains the age of full strength; and fulfil (every) engagement, for (every) engagement will be enquired into (on the day of reckoning).

35. Give full measure when you measure, and weigh with a balance that is straight; that is the most fitting and the most advantageous in the final determination.

36. And pursue not that of which you have no knowledge; for every act of hearing, or of seeing, or of (feeling in) the heart, will be enquired into (on the day of reckoning).

37. Nor walk on the earth with insolence; for you can not split the earth apart, nor reach the mountains in height.

38. Of all such things, the evil is hateful in the sight of your Lord.

39. These are among the (precepts of) wisdom, which your Lord has revealed to you. Take not, with Allah, another object of worship, lest you should be thrown into hell, blameworthy and rejected.

40. Has then your Lord, (O pagans!) preferred for you sons, and taken for Himself daughters among the angels? Truly you utter a most dreadful saying!

41. We have explained (things) in various (ways) in this Qur'an, in order that they may receive admonition, but it only increases their flight (from the truth)!

42. Say: if there had been (other) gods with Him - as they say - see, they would certainly have sought out a way to the Lord of the Throne!

43. Glory to him! He is high above all that they say! - Exalted and Great (beyond measure)!

44. The seven heavens and the earth, and all beings in it, declare His glory: there is not a thing but celebrates His praise; and yet you understand not how they declare His glory! Verily He is Oft-Forbearing, Most Forgiving!

45. When you do recite the Qur'an, We put, between you and those who believe not in the hereafter, a veil invisible;

46. And We put coverings over their hearts (and minds) lest they should understand the Qur'an, and deafness into their ears; when you do commemorate your Lord - and Him alone - in the Qur'an, they turn on their backs, fleeing (from the truth).

47. We know best why it is they listen, when they listen to you; and when they meet in private conference, behold, the wicked say, "You follow none other than a man bewitched!"

48. See what similes they strike for you; but they have gone astray, and never can they find a way.

49. They say: "What! When we are reduced to bones and dust, should we really be raised up (to be) a new creation?"

50. Say: "(Nay!) Be you stones or iron,

51. Or created matter which, in your minds, is hardest (to be raised up) - (yet shall you be raised up)!" Then will they say: "Who will cause us to return?" Say: "He Who created you first!" Then will they wag their heads towards you and say, "When will that be?" Say, "Maybe it will be quite soon!"

52. "It will be on a day when He will call you, and you will answer (His call) with (words of) His praise, and you will think that you stayed but a little while!"

53. Say to My servants that they should (only) say those things that are best; for Satan does sow dissensions among them; for Satan is to man an avowed enemy.

54. It is your Lord that knows you best; if He please, He grants you mercy, or if He please, punishment; We have not sent you to be a disposer of their affairs for them.

55. And it is your Lord that knows best all beings that are in the heavens and on earth; We did bestow on some prophets more (and other) gifts than on others; and We gave to David (the gift of) the Psalms.

56. Say: "Call on those - besides Him - whom you fancy; they have neither the power to remove your troubles from you nor to change them."

57. Those whom they call upon do desire (for themselves) means of access to their Lord - even those who are nearest; they hope for His mercy and fear His wrath; for the wrath of your Lord is something to take heed of.

58. There is not a population but We shall destroy it before the day of judgement or punish it with a dreadful penalty; that is written in the (eternal) record.

59. And We refrain from sending the signs, only because the men of former generations treated them as false; We sent the she-camel to the Thamud to open their eyes, but they treated her wrongfully; We only send the signs by way of terror (and warning from evil).

60. See! We told you that your Lord does encompass mankind; We granted the vision which We showed you, but as a trial for men - as also the cursed tree (mentioned) in the Qur'an: We put terror (and warning) into them, but it only increases their inordinate transgression!

61. See! We said to the angels: "Bow down to Adam": they bowed down except Iblis: he said, "Shall I bow down to one whom You did create from clay?"

62. He said, "See You (O Allah)? This is the one whom You have honoured above me! If You will but respite me to the day of judgement, I will surely bring his descendants under my sway - all but a few!"

63. Allah said: "Go your way; if any of them follow you, verily hell will be the recompense of you (all) - an ample recompense."

64. "Lead to destruction those whom you can among them, with your (seductive) voice; make assaults on them with your cavalry and your infantry; mutually share with them wealth and children; and make promises to them. But Satan promises them nothing but deceit."

65. "As for My servants, no authority shall you have over them." Enough is your Lord for a Disposer of affairs.

66. Your Lord is He that makes the ship go smoothly for you through the sea, in order that you may seek of His bounty. For He is to you Most Merciful.

67. When distress seizes you at sea, those that you call upon - besides Himself - leave you in the lurch! But when He brings you back safe to land, you turn away (from Him), Most ungrateful is man!

68. Do you then feel secure that He will not cause you to be swallowed up beneath the earth when you are on land, or that He will not send against you a violent tornado (with showers of stones) so that you shall find no one to carry out your affairs for you?

69. Or do you feel secure that He will not send you back a second time to sea and send against you a heavy gale to drown you because of your ingratitude, so that you find no helper in it against Us?

70. We have honoured the sons of Adam; provided them with transport on land and sea; given them for sustenance things good and pure; and conferred on them special favours, above a great part of Our creation.

71. One day We shall call together all human beings with their (respective) Imams; those who are given their record in their right hand will read it (with pleasure), and they will not be dealt with unjustly in the least.

72. But those who were blind in this world, will be blind in the hereafter, and most astray from the path.

73. And their purpose was to tempt you away from that which We had revealed to you, to substitute in Our name something quite different: (in that case), see! They would certainly have made you (their) friend!

74. And had We not given you strength you would nearly have inclined to them a little.

75. In that case We should have made you taste an equal portion (of punishment) in this life, and an equal portion in death and moreover you would have found none to help you against Us!

76. Their purpose was to scare you off the land, in order to expel you; but in that case they would not have stayed (in it) after you, except for a little while.

77. (This was Our) way with the messengers We sent before you; you will find no change in Our ways.

78. Establish regular prayers - at the sun's decline till the darkness of the night, and the morning prayer and reading: for the prayer and reading in the morning carry their testimony.

79. And pray in the small watches of the morning; (it would be) an additional prayer (or spiritual profit) for you: soon will your Lord raise you to a station of praise and glory!

80. Say: "O my Lord! Let my entry be by the gate of truth and honour, and likewise my exit by the gate of truth and honour; and grant me from Your presence an authority to aid (me)."

81. And say: "Truth has (now) arrived, and falsehood perished: for falsehood is (by its nature) bound to perish."

82. We send down (stage by stage) in the Qur'an that which is a healing and a mercy to those who believe; to the unjust it causes nothing but loss after loss.

83. Yet when We bestow Our favours on man, he turns away and becomes remote on his side (instead of coming to Us), and when evil seizes him he gives himself up to despair!

84. Say: "Everyone acts according to his own disposition; but your Lord knows best who it is that is best guided on the way."

85. They ask you concerning the spirit (of inspiration). Say: "The spirit (comes) by command of my Lord: of knowledge it is only a little that is communicated to you, (O men!)"

86. If it were Our will, We could take away that which We have sent you by inspiration; then would you find none to plead your affair in that matter as against Us -

87. Except for mercy from your Lord: for His bounty is to you (indeed) great.

88. Say: "If the whole of mankind and Jinns were to gather together to produce the like of this Qur'an, they could not produce the like of it, even if they backed up each other with help and support."

89. And We have explained to man, in this Qur'an, every kind of similitude; yet the greater part of men refuse (to receive it) except with ingratitude!

90. They say: "We shall not believe in you, until you cause a spring to gush out for us from the earth,

91. Or (until) you have a garden of date trees and vines, and cause rivers to gush out in their midst, carrying abundant water,

92. Or you cause the sky to fall in pieces, as you say (will happen), against us, or you bring Allah and the angels before (us) face to face;

93. Or you have a house adorned with gold, or you mount a ladder right into the skies. No, we shall not even believe in your mounting until you send down to us a book that we can read." Say: "Glory to my Lord! I am nothing but a man - a messenger?"

94. What kept men back from belief when guidance came to them, was nothing but this: they said, "Has Allah sent a man (like us) to be (His) messenger?"

95. Say, "If there were settled, on earth, angels walking about in peace and quiet, We should certainly have sent them down from the heavens an angel for a messenger."

96. Say: "Enough is Allah for a witness between me and you; for He is well-acquainted with His servants, and He sees (all things)."

97. It is he whom Allah guides, that is on true guidance; but he whom He leaves astray - for such will you find no protector besides Him. On the day of judgement We shall gather them together, prone on their faces, blind, dumb, and deaf; their abode will be hell: every time it shows abatement, We shall increase for them the fierceness of the fire.

98. That is their recompense, because they rejected Our signs, and said, "When we are reduced to bones and broken dust, should we really be raised up (to be) a new creation?"

99. Do they not see that Allah, Who created the heavens and the earth, has power to create the like of them (anew)? Only He has decreed a term appointed, of which there is no doubt. But the unjust refuse (to receive it) except with ingratitude.

100. Say: "If you had control of the treasures of the mercy of my Lord, behold you would keep them back, for fear of spending them; for man is (ever) niggardly!"

101. To Moses We did give nine clear signs: ask the Children of Israel; when he came to them, Pharaoh said to him:

"O Moses! I consider you, indeed, to have been worked upon by sorcery!"

102. Moses said, "You know well that these things have been sent down by none but the Lord of the heavens and the earth as eye-opening evidence; and I consider you indeed, O Pharaoh, to be one doomed to destruction!"

103. So he resolved to remove them from the face of the earth: but We did drown him and all who were with him.

104. And We said thereafter to the Children of Israel, "Dwell securely in the land (of promise)"; but when the second of the warnings came to pass, We gathered you together in a mingled crowd.

105. We sent down the (Qur'an) in truth, and in truth has it descended; and We sent you but to give glad tidings and to warn (sinners).

106. (It is) a Qur'an which We have divided (into parts from time to time), in order that you might recite it to men at intervals; We have revealed it by stages.

107. Say: "Whether you believe in it or not, it is true that those who were given knowledge beforehand, when it is recited to them, fall down on their faces in humble prostration,

108. And they say: 'Glory to our Lord! Truly has the promise of our Lord been fulfilled!'"

109. They fall down on their faces in tears, and it increases their (earnest) humility.

110. Say: "Call upon Allah, or call upon ar-Rahman: by whatever name you call upon Him, (it is well); for to Him belong the most beautiful Names. Neither speak your prayer aloud, nor speak it in a low tone, but seek a middle course between."

111. Say: "Praise be to Allah, Who begets no son, and has no partner in (His) dominion; nor (needs) He any to protect Him from humiliation; yea, magnify Him for His greatness and glory!"

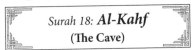

Surah 18: *Al-Kahf*
(The Cave)

In the name of Allah,
Most Gracious, Most Merciful.

1. Praise be to Allah, Who has sent to His servant the book, and has allowed in it no crookedness:

2. (He has made it) straight (and clear) in order that He may warn (the godless) of a terrible punishment from Him, and that He may give glad tidings to the believers who work righteous deeds, that they shall have a goodly reward,

3. In which they shall remain forever:

4. Further, that He may warn those (also) who say, "Allah has begotten a son":

5. No knowledge have they of such a thing, nor had their fathers. It is a grievous thing that issues from their mouths as a saying. What they say is nothing but falsehood!

6. You would only, perhaps, fret yourself to death, following after them, in grief, if they believe not in this message.

7. That which is on earth We have made but as a glittering show for the earth, in order that We may test them - as to which of them are best in conduct.

8. Verily what is on earth We shall make but as dust and dry soil (without growth or herbage).

9. Or do you reflect that the companions of the cave and of the inscription were wonders among Our signs?

10. See, the youths went to the cave: they said, "Our Lord! Bestow on us mercy from Yourself, and dispose of our affair for us in the right way!"

11. Then We drew (a veil) over their ears, for a number of years, in the cave (so that they heard not).

12. Then We roused them, in order to test which of the two parties was best at calculating the term of years they had stayed!

13. We relate to you their story in truth: they were youths who believed in their Lord, and We advanced them in guidance.

14. We gave strength to their hearts: see, they stood up and said: "Our Lord is the Lord of the heavens and of the earth: never shall we call upon any god other than Him: if we did, we should indeed have uttered an enormity!"

15. "These our people have taken for worship gods other than Him: why do they not bring forward an authority clear (and convincing) for what they do? Who does more wrong than such as invent a falsehood against Allah?"

16. "When you turn away from them and the things they worship other than Allah go to the cave; your Lord will shower His mercies on you and dispose of your affair towards comfort and ease."

17. You would have seen the sun, when it rose, declining to the right from their cave, and when it set, turning away from them to the left, while they lay in the open space in the midst of the cave. Such are among the signs of Allah: he whom Allah guides is rightly guided; but he whom Allah leaves to stray - for him will you find no protector to lead him to the Right way.

18. You would have deemed them awake, whilst they were asleep, and We turned them on their right and their left sides; their dog stretching forth his two forelegs on the threshold: if you had come up on to them, you would have certainly turned back from them in flight, and would certainly have been filled with terror of them.

19. Such (being their state), We raised them up (from sleep), that they might question each other. Said one of them, "How long have you stayed (here)?" They said, "We have stayed (perhaps) a day, or part of a day." (At length) they (all) said, "Allah (alone) knows best how long you have stayed here. Now send you then one of you with this money of yours to the town; let him find out which is the best food (to be had) and bring some to you, that (you may) satisfy hunger with it; and let him behave with care and courtesy, and let him not inform anyone about you."

20. "For if they should come upon you, they would stone you or force you to return to their cult, and in that case you would never attain prosperity."

21. Thus did We make their case known to the people, that they might know that the promise of Allah is true, and that there can be no doubt about the hour of judgement. See, they dispute among themselves as to their affair. (Some) said, "Construct a building over them"; their Lord knows best about them; those who prevailed over their affair said, "Let us surely build a place of worship over them."

22. (Some) say they were three, the dog being the fourth among them; (others) say they were five, the dog being the sixth - doubtfully guessing at the unknown; (yet others) say they were seven, the dog being the eighth. Say you; "My Lord knows best their number; it is but few that know their (real case)." Enter not, therefore, into controversies concerning them, except on a matter that is clear, nor consult any of them about (the affair of) the sleepers.

23. Nor say of anything, "I shall be sure to do so and so tomorrow" -

24. Without adding, "So please Allah!" And call your Lord to mind when you forget, and say, "I hope that my Lord will guide me ever closer (even) than this to the right road."

25. So they stayed in their cave three hundred years, and (some) add nine (more).

26. Say: "Allah knows best how long they stayed; with Him is (the knowledge of) the secrets of the heavens and the earth: how clearly He sees, how finely He hears (everything)! They have no protector other than Him; nor does He share His command with any person whatsoever.

27. And recite (and teach) what has been revealed to you of the book of your Lord: none can change His words, and none will you find as a refuge other than Him.

28. And keep your soul content with those who call on their Lord morning and evening, seeking His Face; and let not your eyes pass beyond them seeking the pomp and glitter of this life; nor obey any whose heart We have permitted to neglect the remembrance of Us; one who follows his own desires, whose case has gone beyond all bounds.

29. Say, "The truth is from your Lord"; let him who will, believe, and let him who will, reject (it): for the wrongdoers We have prepared a fire whose (smoke and flames), like the wall and roof of a tent, will hem them in: if they implore relief they will be granted water like melted brass that will scald their faces. How dreadful the drink! How uncomfortable a couch to recline on!

30. As to those who believe and work righteousness, verily We shall not suffer to perish the reward of any who do a (single) righteous deed.

31. For them will be Gardens of Eternity; beneath them rivers will flow; they will be adorned in it with bracelets of gold, and they will wear green garments of fine silk and heavy brocade; they will recline in it on raised thrones. How good the recompense! How beautiful a couch to recline on!

32. Set out to them the parable of two men: for one of them We provided two gardens of grapevines and surrounded them with date-palms; in between the two We placed cornfields.

33. Each of those gardens brought forth its produce, and failed not in the least in it; in the midst of them We caused a river to flow.

34. (Abundant) was the produce, this man had; he said to his companion, in the course of a mutual argument: "More wealth have I than you, and more honour and power in (my following of) men."

35. He went into his garden in a state (of mind) unjust to his soul: He said, "I think not that this will ever perish."

36. "Nor do I think that the hour (of judgement) will (ever) come; even if I am brought back to my Lord, I shall surely find (there) something better in exchange."

37. His companion said to him, in the course of the argument with him: "Do you deny Him Who created you out of dust, then out of a sperm-drop, then fashioned you into a man?

38. But (I think) for my part that He is Allah, my Lord, and none shall I associate with my Lord.

39. Why did you not, as you went into your garden, say: 'Allah's Will (be done)! There is no power but with Allah!' If you do see me less than you in wealth and sons,

40. It may be that my Lord will give me something better than your garden, and that He will send on your garden thunderbolts (by way of reckoning) from heaven, making it (but) slippery sand! -

41. Or the water of the garden will run off underground so that you will never be able to find it."

42. So his fruits (and enjoyment) were encompassed (with ruin), and he remained twisting and turning his hands over what he had spent on his property, which had (now) tumbled to pieces to its very foundations, and he could only say, "Woe is me! Would I had never ascribed partners to my Lord and Cherisher!"

43. Nor had he numbers to help him against Allah, nor was he able to deliver himself.

44. There, the (only) protection comes from Allah, the True One. He is the Best to reward, and the Best to give success.

45. Set out to them the similitude of the life of this world; it is like the rain which We send down from the skies; the earth's vegetation absorbs it, but soon it becomes dry stubble, which the winds do scatter: it is (only) Allah Who prevails over all things.

46. Wealth and sons are allurements of the life of this world; but the things that endure, good deeds, are best in the sight of your Lord, as rewards, and best as (the foundation for) hopes.

47. One day We shall remove the mountains, and you will see the earth as a level stretch, and We shall gather them all together, nor shall We leave out any one of them.

48. And they will be marshalled before your Lord in ranks, (with the announcement) "Now have you come to Us (bare) as We created you first: aye, you thought We shall not fulfil the appointment made to you to meet (Us)!"

49. And the book (of deeds) will be placed (before you); and you will see the sinful in great terror because of what is (recorded) in it; they will say, "Ah! Woe to us! What a book is this! It leaves out nothing small or great, but takes account of it!" They will find all that they did, placed before them, and not one will your Lord treat with injustice.

50. See! We said to the angels, "Bow down to Adam"; they bowed down except Iblis. He was one of the Jinns, and he broke the command of his Lord. Will you then take him and his progeny as protectors rather than Me? And they are enemies to you! Evil would be the exchange for the wrongdoers!

51. I called them not to witness the creation of the heavens and the earth, nor (even) their own creation; nor is it for Me to take as helpers such as lead (men) astray!

52. One day He will say, "Call on those whom you thought to be My partners," and they will call on them, but they will not listen to them; and We shall make for them a place of common perdition.

53. And the sinful shall see the fire and apprehend that they have to fall in it; no means will they find to turn away from it.

54. We have explained in detail in this Qur'an, for the benefit of mankind, every kind of similitude; but man is, in most things, contentious.

55. And what is there to keep back men from believing, now that guidance has come to them, nor from praying for forgiveness from their Lord, but that (they ask that) the ways of the ancients be repeated with them, or the wrath be brought to them face to face?

56. We only send the messengers to give glad tidings and to give warnings: but the unbelievers dispute with vain argument, in order therewith to weaken the truth, and they treat My signs as a jest, as also the fact that they are warned!

57. And who does more wrong than one who is reminded of the signs of his Lord, but turns away from them, forgetting the (deeds) which his hands have sent before? Verily We have set veils over their hearts lest they should understand this, and over their ears, deafness. If you call them to guidance, even then will they never accept guidance.

58. But your Lord is Most Forgiving, full of Mercy. If He were to call them (at once) to account for what they have earned, then surely He would have hastened their punishment: but they have their appointed time, beyond which they will find no refuge.

59. Such were the populations We destroyed when they committed iniquities; but We fixed an appointed time for their destruction.

60. See, Moses said to his attendant, "I will not give up (until) I reach the junction of the two seas or (until) I spend years and years in travel."

61. But when they reached the junction, they forgot (about) their fish, which took its course through the sea (straight) as in a tunnel.

62. When they had passed on (some distance), Moses said to his attendant: "Bring us our early meal; truly we have suffered much fatigue at this (stage of) our journey."

63. He replied: "Did you see (what happened) when we went to the rock? I did indeed forget (about) the fish: none but Satan made me forget to tell (you) about it: it took its course through the sea in a marvellous way!"

64. Moses said: "That was what we were seeking after": so they went back on their footsteps, following (the path they had come).

65. So they found one of Our servants, on whom We had bestowed mercy from Ourselves and whom We had taught knowledge from Our own presence.

66. Moses said to him: "May I follow you, on the footing that you teach me something of the (higher) truth which you have been taught?"

67. (The other) said: "Verily you will not be able to have patience with me!

68. And how can you have patience about things about which your understanding is not complete?"

69. Moses said: "You will find me, if Allah so wills, (truly) patient: nor shall I disobey you in anything."

70. The other said: "If then you would follow me, ask me no questions about anything until I myself speak to you concerning it."

71. So they both proceeded; until, when they were in the boat, he scuttled it. Said Moses: "Have you scuttled it in order to drown those in it? Truly a strange thing have you done!"

72. He answered: "Did I not tell you that you can have no patience with me?"

73. Moses said: "Rebuke me not for forgetting, nor grieve me by raising difficulties in my case."

74. Then they proceeded; until, when they met a young man, he slew him. Moses said: "Have you slain an innocent person who had slain none? Truly a foul (unheard-of) thing have you done!"

75. He answered: "Did I not tell you that you can have no patience with me?"

76. (Moses) said: "If ever I ask you about anything after this, keep me not in your company: then would you have received (full) excuse from my side."

77. Then they proceeded until, when they came to the inhabitants of a town, they asked them for food, but they refused them hospitality. They found there a wall on the point of falling down, but he set it up straight. (Moses) said: "If you had wished,

surely you could have exacted some recompense for it!"

78. He answered: "This is the parting between me and you; now will I tell you the interpretation of (those things) over which you were unable to hold patience.

79. As for the boat, it belonged to certain men in dire want; they plied on the water, I but wished to render it unserviceable, for there was after them a certain king who seized on every boat by force.

80. As for the youth, his parents were people of faith, and we feared that he would grieve them by obstinate rebellion and ingratitude (to Allah and man).

81. So we desired that their Lord would give them in exchange (a son) better in purity (of conduct) and closer in affection.

82. As for the wall, it belonged to two youths, orphans, in the town; there was, beneath it, a buried treasure, to which they were entitled: their father had been a righteous man: so your Lord desired that they should attain their age of full strength and get out their treasure - a mercy (and favour) from your Lord. I did it not of my own accord. Such is the interpretation of (those things) over which you were unable to hold patience."

83. They ask you concerning Dhu al-Qarnayn. Say, "I will rehearse to you something of his story."

84. Verily We established his power on earth, and We gave him the ways and the means to all ends.

85. One (such) way he followed,

86. Until, when he reached the setting of the sun, He found it set in a spring of murky water: near it he found a people; We said: "O Dhu al-Qarnayn! (you have authority) either to punish them, or to treat them with kindness."

87. He said: "Whoever does wrong, him shall we punish; then shall he be sent back to his Lord; and He will punish him with a punishment unheard-of (before)."

88. "But whoever believes, and works righteousness - he shall have a goodly reward, and easy will be his task as we order it by our command."

89. Then followed he (another) way.

90. Until, when he came to the rising of the sun, he found it rising on a people for whom We had provided no covering protection against the sun.

91. (He left them) as they were; We completely understood what was before him.

92. Then followed he (another) way,

93. Until, when he reached (a tract) between two mountains, he found, beneath them, a people who scarcely understood a word.

94. They said: "O Dhu al-Qarnayn! The Gog and Magog (people) do great mischief on earth; shall we then render you tribute in order that you might erect a barrier between us and them?"

95. He said: "(The power) in which my Lord has established me is better (than tribute); help me therefore with strength (and labour); I will erect a strong barrier between you and them;

96. Bring me blocks of iron." At length, when he had filled up the space between the two steep mountainsides, he said, "Blow (with your bellows)." Then when he had made it (red) as fire, he said: "Bring me, that I may pour over it, molten lead."

97. Thus were they made powerless to scale it or to dig through it.

98. He said: "This is a mercy from my Lord; but when the promise of my Lord comes to pass, He will make it into dust; and the promise of My Lord is true."

99. On that day We shall leave them to surge like waves on one another; the trumpet will be blown, and We shall collect them all together.

100. And We shall present hell that day for unbelievers to see, all spread out -

101. (Unbelievers) whose eyes had been under a veil from remembrance of Me, and who had been unable even to hear.

102. Do the unbelievers think that they can take My servants as protectors besides Me? Verily We have prepared hell for the unbelievers for (their) entertainment.

103. Say: "Shall we tell you of those who lose most in respect of their deeds? -

104. Those whose efforts have been wasted in this life. While they thought that they were acquiring good by their works?"

105. They are those who deny the signs of their Lord and the fact of their having to meet Him (in the hereafter): vain will be their works, nor shall We, on the day of judgement, give them any weight.

106. That is their reward, hell; because they rejected faith, and took My signs and My messengers by way of jest.

107. As to those who believe and work righteous deeds, they have, for their entertainment, the gardens of paradise,

108. In which they shall dwell (forever): no change will they wish for from themselves.

109. Say: "If the ocean were ink (with which to write out) the words of my Lord, sooner would the ocean be exhausted than would the words of my Lord, even if we added another ocean like it, for its aid."

110. Say: "I am but a man like yourselves, (but) the inspiration has come to me, that your God is one God: whoever expects to meet his Lord, let him work righteousness and in the worship of his Lord, admit no one as partner."

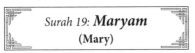

Surah 19: **Maryam**
(Mary)

In the name of Allah,
Most Gracious, Most Merciful.

1. *Kaf, Ha, Ya, Ayn, Sad.*

2. (This is) a recital of the mercy of your Lord to His servant Zakariya.

3. See! He called to his Lord in secret,

4. Praying: "O my Lord! Infirm indeed are my bones, and the hair of my head does glisten with grey; but never am I unblessed, O my Lord, in my prayer to You!"

5. "Now I fear (what) my relatives (and colleagues) (will do) after me: but my wife is barren: so give me an heir as from Yourself -

6. (One that) will (truly) represent me and represent the posterity of Jacob; and make him, O my Lord! One with whom You are well-pleased!"

7. (His prayer was answered): "O Zakariya! We give you good news of a son; his name shall be Yahya; on none by that name have We conferred distinction before."

8. He said: "O my Lord! How shall I have a son, when my wife is barren and I have grown quite infirm from old age?"

9. He said: "So (it will be): your Lord said, 'That is easy for Me: I did indeed create you before when you had been nothing!'"

10. (Zakariya) said, "O my Lord! Give me a sign." "Your sign," was the answer, "shall be that you shall speak to no man for three nights, although you are not dumb."

11. So Zakariya came out to his people from his chamber; he told them by signs to celebrate Allah's praises in the morning and in the evening.

12. (To his son came the command): "O Yahya! Take hold of the book with might": and We gave him wisdom even as a youth.

13. And pity (for all creatures) as from Us, and purity: he was devout,

14. And kind to his parents, and he was not overbearing or rebellious.

15. So peace on him the day he was born, the day that he dies, and the day that he will be raised up to life (again)!

16. Relate in the book (the story of) Mary, when she withdrew from her family to a place in the east.

17. She placed a screen (to screen herself) from them: then We sent to her Our angel, and he appeared before her as a man in all respects.

18. She said: "I seek refuge from you to (Allah) Most Gracious: (come not near) if you do fear Allah."

19. He said: "Nay, I am only a messenger from your Lord, (to announce) to you the gift of a holy son."

20. She said: "How shall I have a son, seeing that no man has touched me, and I am not unchaste?"

21. He said: "So (it will be); your Lord says, 'That is easy for Me: and (We wish) to appoint him as a Sign to men and a mercy from Us'; it is a matter (so) decreed."

22. So she conceived him, and she retired with him to a remote place.

23. And the pains of childbirth drove her to the trunk of a palm-tree; she cried (in her anguish): "Ah! Would that I had died before this! Would that I had been a thing forgotten and out of sight!"

24. But (a voice) called to her from beneath the (palm tree): "Grieve not! For your Lord has provided a rivulet beneath you;

25. And shake towards yourself the trunk of the palm tree; it will let fall fresh ripe dates upon you.

26. So eat and drink and cool (your) eye. And if you do see any man, say, 'I have vowed a fast to (Allah) Most Gracious, and this day will I enter into no talk with any human being.'"

27. At length she brought the (babe) to her people, carrying him (in her arms). They said: "O Mary! Truly an amazing thing have you brought!

28. O sister of Aaron! Your father was not a man of evil, nor your mother a woman unchaste!"

29. But she pointed to the babe. They said: "How can we talk to one who is a child in the cradle?"

30. He said: "I am indeed a servant of Allah; He has given me revelation and made me a prophet;

31. And He has made me blessed wheresoever I be, and has enjoined on me prayer and charity as long as I live."

32. "(He) has made me kind to my mother, and not overbearing or miserable."

33. "So peace is on me the day I was born, the day that I die, and the day that I shall be raised up to life (again)"!

34. Such (was) Jesus the son of Mary; (it is) a statement of truth, about which they (vainly) dispute.

35. It is not befitting to (the majesty of) Allah that He should beget a son. Glory be to Him! When He determines a matter, He only says to it, "Be," and it is.

36. Verily Allah is my Lord and your Lord; Him therefore serve you; this is a way that is straight.

37. But the sects differ among themselves and woe to the unbelievers because of the (coming) judgement of a momentous day!

38. How plainly will they see and hear, the day that they will appear before Us! But the unjust today are in error manifest!

39. But warn them of the day of distress, when the matter will be determined: for (see,) they are negligent and they do not believe!

40. It is We Who will inherit the earth, and all beings thereon: to Us will they all be returned.

41. (Also) mention in the book (the story of) Abraham: he was a man of truth. A prophet.

42. See, he said to his father: "O my father! Why worship that which hears not and sees not and can profit you nothing?"

43. "O my father! To me has come knowledge which has not reached you: so follow me; I will guide you to a way that is even and straight."

44. "O my father! Serve not Satan: for Satan is a rebel against (Allah) Most Gracious."

45. "O my father! I fear lest a penalty afflict you from (Allah) Most Gracious, so that you become to Satan a friend."

46. (The father) replied: "Do you hate my gods, O Abraham? If you forbear not, I will indeed stone you; now get away from me for a good long while!"

47. Abraham said: "Peace be on you; I will pray to my Lord for your forgiveness: for He is to me Most Gracious."

48. "And I will turn away from you (all) and from those whom you invoke besides Allah; I will call on my Lord; perhaps, by my prayer to my Lord, I shall be not unblessed!"

49. When he had turned away from them and from those whom they worshipped besides Allah, We bestowed on him Isaac and Jacob, and each one of them We made a prophet.

50. And We bestowed of Our mercy on them, and We granted them lofty honour on the tongue of truth.

51. Also mention in the book (the story of) Moses: for he was specially chosen, and he was a messenger (and) a prophet.

52. And We called him from the right side of mount (Sinai), and made him draw near to Us, for mystic (converse).

53. And, out of Our mercy, We gave him his brother Aaron, (also) a prophet.

54. Also mention in the book (the story of) Ishmael: He was (strictly) true to what he promised, and he was a messenger (and) a prophet.

55. He used to enjoin on his people prayer and charity, and he was most acceptable in the sight of his Lord.

56. Also mention in the book the case of Idris: he was a man of truth (and sincerity), (and) a prophet:

57. And We raised him to a lofty station.

58. Those were some of the prophets on whom Allah did bestow His grace - of the posterity of Adam, and of those whom We carried (in the ark) with Noah, and of the posterity of Abraham and Israel - of those whom We guided and chose; whenever the signs of (Allah) Most Gracious were rehearsed to them, they would fall down in prostrate adoration and in tears.

59. But after them there followed a posterity who missed prayers and followed after lusts; soon, then, will they face destruction -

60. Except those who repent and believe, and work righteousness; for these will enter the garden and will not be wronged in the least -

61. Gardens of eternity, those which (Allah) Most Gracious has promised to His servants in the unseen; for His promise must (necessarily) come to pass.

62. They will not there hear any vain discourse, but only salutations of peace and they will have in it their sustenance, morning and evening.

63. Such is the garden which We give as an inheritance to those of Our servants who guard against evil.

64. (The angels say:) "We descend not but by command of your Lord; to Him belongs what is before us, and what is behind us, and what is between; and your Lord never does forget" -

65. "Lord of the heavens and of the earth, and of all that is between them; so worship Him, and be constant and patient in His worship; know you of any who is worthy of the same name as He?"

66. Man says: "What! When I am dead, shall I then be raised up alive?"

67. But does not man call to mind that We created him before out of nothing?

68. So, by your Lord, without doubt, We shall gather them together, and (also) the evil ones (with them); then shall We bring them forth on their knees round about hell;

69. Then shall We certainly drag out from every sect all those who were worst in obstinate rebellion against (Allah) Most Gracious.

70. And certainly We know best those who are most worthy of being burned in it.

71. Not one of you but will pass over it; this is, with your Lord, a decree which must be accomplished.

72. But We shall save those who guarded against evil, and We shall leave the wrongdoers in it, (humbled) to their knees.

73. When Our clear signs are rehearsed to them, the unbelievers say to who believe, "Which of the two sides is best in point of position? Which makes the best show in council?"

74. But how many (countless) generations before them have We destroyed, who were even better in equipment and in glitter to the eye?

75. Say: "If any men go astray, (Allah) Most Gracious extends (the rope) to them. Until, when they see the warning of Allah (being fulfilled) - either in punishment or in (the approach of) the hour - they will at length realise who is worst in position, and (who) weakest in forces!"

76. "And Allah does advance in guidance those who seek guidance; and the things that endure, good deeds, are best in the sight of your Lord, as rewards, and best in respect of (their) eventual returns."

77. Have you then seen the (sort of) man who rejects Our signs, yet says: "I shall certainly be given wealth and children?"

78. Has he penetrated to the unseen, or has he taken a contract with (Allah) Most Gracious?

79. Nay! We shall record what he says, and We shall add and add to his punishment.

80. To Us shall return all that he talks of, and he shall appear before Us bare and alone.

81. And they have taken (for worship) gods other than Allah to give them power and glory!

82. Instead, they shall reject their worship, and become adversaries against them.

83. Do you not see that We have set the evil ones on against the unbelievers, to incite them with fury?

84. So make no haste against them, for We but count out to them a (limited) number (of days).

85. The day We shall gather the righteous to (Allah) Most Gracious, like a band presented before a king for honours.

86. And We shall drive the sinners to hell, like thirsty cattle driven down to water -

87. None shall have the power of intercession, but such a one as has received permission (or promise) from (Allah) Most Gracious.

88. They say: "(Allah) Most Gracious has begotten a son!"

89. Indeed you have put forward a thing most monstrous!

90. As if the skies are ready to burst, the earth to split apart, and the mountains to fall down in utter ruin.

91. That they should invoke a son for (Allah) Most Gracious.

92. For it is not consonant with the majesty of (Allah) Most Gracious that He should beget a son.

93. Not one of the beings in the heavens and the earth but must come to (Allah) Most Gracious as a servant.

94. He does take an account of them (all), and has numbered them (all) exactly.

95. And every one of them will come to him singly on the day of judgement.

96. On those who believe and work deeds of righteousness, will (Allah) Most Gracious bestow love.

97. So have We made the (Qur'an) easy in your own tongue, that with it you may give glad tidings to the righteous, and warnings to people given to contention.

98. But how many (countless) generation before them have We destroyed? Can you find a single one of them (now) or hear (so much as) a whisper of them?

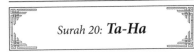

*Surah 20: **Ta-Ha***

In the name of Allah,
Most Gracious, Most Merciful.

1. *Ta Ha.*

2. We have not sent down the Qur'an to you to be (an occasion) for your distress,

3. But only as an admonition to those who fear (Allah) -

4. A revelation from Him Who created the earth and the heavens on high.

5. (Allah) Most Gracious is firmly established on the throne (of authority).

6. To Him belongs what is in the heavens and on earth, and all between them, and all beneath the soil.

7. If you pronounce the word aloud, (it is no matter); for verily He knows what is secret and what is yet more hidden.

8. Allah! There is no god but He! To Him belong the most beautiful names.

9. Has the story of Moses reached you?

10. See, he saw a fire: so he said to his family, "stay you; I perceive a fire; perhaps I can bring you some burning brand from it, or find some guidance at the fire."

11. But when he came to the fire, a voice was heard: "O Moses!"

12. "Verily I am your Lord! Therefore, (in My presence) put off your shoes; you are in the sacred valley Tuwa."

13. "I have chosen you: listen, then to the inspiration (sent to you)."

14. "Verily, I am Allah: there is no god but I; so serve you Me (only), and establish regular prayer for celebrating My praise."

15. "Verily the hour is coming - My design is to keep it hidden - for every soul to receive its reward by the measure of its endeavour."

16. "Therefore, let not such as believe not in it but follow their own lusts, divert you from it, lest you perish!"

17. "And what is that in your right hand, O Moses?"

18. He said, "It is my rod; on it I lean; with it I beat down fodder for my flocks; and in it I find other uses."

19. (Allah) said, "Throw it, O Moses!"

20. He threw it, and see! It was a snake, active in motion.

21. (Allah) said, "Seize it and fear not; We shall return it at once to its former condition".

22. "Now draw your hand close to your side: it shall come out white (and shining), without harm (or stain) - as another sign -

23. In order that We may show you (two) of Our greater signs.

24. Go you to Pharaoh, for he had indeed transgressed all bounds."

25. (Moses) said: "O my Lord! Expand me my breast;

26. Ease my task for me;

27. And remove the impediment from my speech.

28. So they may understand what I say:

29. And give me a minister from my family,

30. Aaron, my brother;

31. Add to my strength through him,

32. And make him share my task:

33. That we may celebrate Your praise aplenty,

34. And remember You aplenty:

35. For You are He that (ever) regards us."

36. (Allah) said: "Granted is your prayer, O Moses!"

37. "And indeed We conferred a favour on you another time (before)."

38. "See! We sent to your mother, by inspiration, the message:

39. 'Throw (the child) into the chest, and throw (the chest) into the river: the river will cast him up on the bank, and he will be taken up by one who is an enemy to Me and an enemy to him': but I cast (the garment of) love over you from Me and (this) in order that you may be reared under my eye.

40. See! Your sister goes out and says, 'Shall I show you one who will nurse and rear the (child)?' So We brought you back to your mother, that her eye might be cooled and she should not grieve. Then you slew a man, but We saved you from trouble, and We tried you in various ways. Then you stayed a number of years with the people of Madyan. Then you came here as ordained, O Moses!

41. And I have prepared you for Myself (for service)"...

42. "Go, you and your brother, with My signs, and slacken not, either of you, in keeping Me in remembrance."

43. "Go, both of you, to Pharaoh for he has indeed transgressed all bounds;

44. But speak to him mildly; perhaps he may take warning or fear (Allah)."

45. They (Moses and Aaron) said: "Our Lord! We fear lest He hasten with insolence against us, or lest he transgress all bounds."

46. He said: "Fear not: for I am with you: I hear and see (everything)."

47. "So go you both to him, and say, 'Verily we are messengers sent by your Lord: send out, therefore the Children of Israel with us and afflict them not: with a sign, indeed, have we come from your Lord! And peace to all who follow guidance!'

48. Verily it has been revealed to us that the penalty (awaits) those who reject and turn away."

49. (When this message was delivered), (Pharaoh) said: "Who then, O Moses, is the Lord of you two?"

50. He said: "Our Lord is He Who gave to each (created) thing its form and nature, and further gave (it) guidance."

51. (Pharaoh) said: "What then is the condition of previous generations?"

52. He replied: "The knowledge of that is with my Lord, duly recorded: my Lord never errs, nor forgets -

53. He Who has made for you the earth like a carpet spread out; has enabled you to go about in it by roads (and channels); and has sent down water from the sky." With it have We produced diverse pairs of plants each separate from the others.

54. Eat (for yourselves) and pasture your cattle: verily, in this are signs, for men endued with understanding.

55. From the (earth) did We create you, and into it shall We return you, and from it shall We bring you out once again.

56. And We showed Pharaoh all Our signs, but he did reject and refuse.

57. He said: "Have you come to drive us out of our land with your magic O Moses?"

58. "But we can surely produce magic to match yours! So make an appointment between us and you, which we shall not fail to keep - neither we nor you - in a place where both shall have even chances."

59. Moses said: "Your appointment is the day of the festival, and let the people be assembled when the sun is well up."

60. So Pharaoh withdrew; he concerted his plan, and then came (back).

61. Moses said to him: "Woe to you! Forge not you a lie against Allah, lest He destroy you (at once) utterly by chastisement; the forger must suffer frustration!"

62. So they disputed, one with another, over their affair, but they kept their talk secret.

63. They said: "These two are certainly (expert) magicians; their object is to drive you out from your land with their magic, and to do away with your most cherished institutions."

64. "Therefore, concert your plan. And then assemble in (ordered) ranks; he wins (all along) today who gains the upper hand."

65. They said: "O Moses! Whether will you that you throw (first) or that we be the first to throw?"

66. He said, "Nay, throw you first!" Then see their ropes and their rods - so it seemed to him on account of their magic - began to be in lively motion!

67. So Moses conceived in his mind a (sort of) fear.

68. We said, "Fear not! For you have indeed the upper hand:

69. "Throw that which is in your right hand: quickly will it swallow up that which they have faked. What they have faked is but a magician's trick and the magician thrives not, (no matter) where he goes."

70. So the magicians were thrown down to prostration; they said, "We believe in the Lord of Aaron and Moses."

71. (Pharaoh) said: "Do you believe in Him before I give you permission? Surely this must be your leader, who has taught you magic! Be sure I will cut off your hands and feet on opposite sides, and I will have you crucified on trunks of palm trees; so shall you know for certain which of us can give the more severe and the more lasting punishment!"

72. They said: "Never shall we regard you as more than the clear signs that have come to us or than Him Who created us! So decree whatever you desire to decree; for you can only decree (touching) the life of this world.

73. For us, we have believed in our Lord; may He forgive us our faults, and the magic to which you did compel us: for Allah is Best and Most Lasting."

74. Verily he who comes to his Lord as a sinner (at judgement) - for him is hell; in it shall he neither die nor live.

75. But such as comes to Him as believers who have worked righteous deeds - for them are ranks exalted -

76. Gardens of eternity, beneath which flow rivers; they will dwell in it forever; such is the reward of those who purify themselves (from evil).

77. We sent an inspiration to Moses: "Travel by night with my servants, and strike a dry path for them through the sea, without fear of being overtaken (by Pharaoh) and without (any other) fear."

78. Then Pharaoh pursued them with his forces, but the waters completely overwhelmed them and covered them up.

79. Pharaoh led his people astray instead of leading them aright.

80. O you Children of Israel! We delivered you from your enemy, and We made a covenant with you on the side of mount (Sinai), and We sent down to you manna and quails:

81. (Saying): "Eat of the good things We have provided for your sustenance, but commit no excess in it, lest My wrath should justly descend on you: and those on whom descends My wrath do perish indeed!"

82. "But, without doubt, I am (also) He that forgives again and again, to those who repent, believe, and do right - who, in fine, are ready to receive true guidance."

83. (When Moses was up on the mount Allah said:) "What made you hasten in advance of your people, O Moses?"

84. He replied: "See, they are close on my footsteps: I hastened to You, O my Lord, to please You."

85. (Allah) said: "We have tested your people in your absence: the Samiri has led them astray."

86. So Moses returned to his people in state of indignation and sorrow. He said: "O my people! Did not your Lord make a handsome promise to you? Did then the promise seem to you long (in coming)? Or did you desire that wrath should descend from your Lord on you, and so you broke your promise to me?"

87. They said: "We broke not the promise to you, as far as lay in our power: but we were made to carry the weight of the ornaments of the (whole) people, and we threw them (into the fire), and that was what the Samiri suggested."

88. "Then he brought out (of the fire) before the (people) the image of a calf: it seemed to low; so they said: 'This is your god, and the god of Moses, but (Moses) has forgotten!'"

89. Could they not see that it could not return them a word (for answer), and that it had no power either to harm them or to do them good?

90. Aaron had already, before this said to them: "O my people! You are being tested in this; for verily your Lord is (Allah) Most Gracious; so follow me and obey my command."

91. They had said: "We will not abandon this cult, but we will devote ourselves to it until Moses returns to us."

92. (Moses) said: "O Aaron! What kept you back when you saw them going wrong,

93. From following me? Did you then disobey my order?"

94. (Aaron) replied: "O son of my mother! Seize (me not) by my beard nor by (the hair of) my head! Truly I feared lest you should say, 'You have caused a division among the Children of Israel, and you did not respect my word!'"

95. (Moses) said: "What then is your case O Samiri?"

96. He replied: "I saw what they saw not, so I took a handful (of dust) from the footprint of the messenger, and threw it (into the calf); thus did my soul suggest to me."

97. (Moses) said: "Go away! But your (punishment) in this life will be that you will say, 'Touch me not'; and moreover (for a future penalty) you have a promise that will not fail; now look at your god, of whom you have become a devoted worshipper; we will certainly (melt) it in a blazing fire and scatter it broadcast in the sea!"

98. But the God of you all is Allah; there is no god but He: all things He comprehends in His knowledge.

99. Thus do We relate to you some stories of what happened before; for

We have sent you a message from Our own presence.

100. If any do turn away from it, verily they will bear a burden on the day of judgement;

101. They will remain in this (state); and grievous will the burden be to them on that day -

102. The day when the trumpet will be sounded; that day, We shall gather the sinful, blear-eyed (with terror),

103. In whispers will they consult each other: "You stayed not longer than ten (days);"

104. We know best what they will say, when their leader most eminent in conduct will say: "You stayed not longer than a day!"

105. They ask you concerning the mountains, say, "My Lord will uproot them and scatter them as dust;"

106. "He will leave them as plains smooth and level;

107. Nothing crooked or curved will you see in their place."

108. On that day will they follow the caller (straight); no crookedness (can they show) him; all sounds shall humble themselves in the presence of (Allah) Most Gracious: nothing shall you hear but the tramp of their feet (as they march).

109. On that day shall no intercession benefit except for those for whom permission has been granted by (Allah) Most Gracious and whose word is acceptable to Him.

110. He knows what (appears to His creatures as) before or after or behind them; but they shall not encompass it with their knowledge.

111. (All) faces shall be humbled before (Him) - the Living, the Self-Subsisting, Eternal: hopeless indeed will be the man that carries iniquity (on his back).

112. But he who works deeds of righteousness, and has faith, will have no fear of harm nor of any curtailment (of what is his due).

113. Thus have We sent this down - an Arabic Qur'an - and explained in it in detail some of the warnings, in order that they may fear Allah, or that it may cause their remembrance (of Him).

114. High above all is Allah, the King, the Truth! Be not in haste with the Qur'an before its revelation to you is completed, but say, "O my Lord! Advance me in knowledge."

115. We had already, beforehand, taken the covenant of Adam, but he forgot; and We found on his part no firm resolve.

116. When We said to the angels, "Prostrate yourselves to Adam", they prostrated themselves but not Iblis; he refused.

117. Then We said: "O Adam! Verily this is an enemy to you and your wife; so let him not get you both out of the garden, so that you are landed in misery."

118. "There is in it (enough provision) for you not to go hungry nor to go naked,"

119. "Nor to suffer from thirst, nor from the sun's heat."

120. But Satan whispered evil to him: he said, "O Adam! Shall I lead you to the tree of eternity and to a kingdom that never decays?"

121. In the result, they both ate of the tree, and so their nakedness appeared to them; they began to sew together, for their covering, leaves from the garden; thus did Adam disobey His Lord, and allow himself to be seduced.

122. But his Lord chose him (for His grace): He turned to him, and gave him guidance.

123. He said: "Get you down, both of you - all together, from the garden, with enmity one to another: but if, as is sure, there comes to you guidance from Me, whosoever follows My guidance, will not lose his way, nor fall into misery."

124. "But whosoever turns away from My message, verily for him is a life narrowed down and We shall raise him up blind on the day of judgement."

125. He will say: "O my Lord! Why have you raised me up blind, while I had sight (before)?"

126. (Allah) will say: "Thus did you, when Our signs came to you, disregard them: so will you, this day, be disregarded."

127. And thus do We recompense him who transgresses beyond bounds and believes not in the signs of his Lord: and the penalty of the hereafter is far more grievous and more enduring.

128. Is it not a warning to such men (to call to mind) how many generations before them We destroyed, in whose haunts they (now) move? Verily, in this are signs for men endued with understanding,

129. Had it not been for a word that went ahead before from your Lord, (their punishment) must necessarily have come; but there is a term appointed (for respite).

130. Therefore, be patient with what they say, and celebrate (constantly) the praises of your Lord before the rising of the sun, and before its setting; yea, celebrate them for part of the hours of the night, and at the sides of the day; that you may have (spiritual) joy.

131. Nor strain your eyes in longing for the things We have given for enjoyment to parties of them, the splendour of the life of this world, through which We test them: but the provision of your Lord is better and more enduring.

132. Enjoin prayer on your people, and be constant in it. We ask you not to provide sustenance; We provide it for you. But the (fruit of) the hereafter is for righteousness.

133. They say: "Why does he not bring us a sign from His Lord?" Has not a clear sign come to them of all that was in the former books of revelation?

134. And if We had inflicted on them a penalty before this, they would have said: "Our Lord! If only You had sent us a messenger, we should certainly have followed Your signs before we were humbled and put to shame."

135. Say: "Each one (of us) is waiting: wait you, therefore, and soon shall you know who it is that is on the straight and even way, and who it is that has received guidance."

Surah 21: *Al-Anbiya*
(The Prophets)

In the name of Allah,
Most Gracious, Most Merciful.

1. Closer and closer to mankind comes their reckoning: yet they heed not and they turn away.

2. Never comes (anything) to them of a renewed message from their Lord, but they listen to it as in jest-

3. Their hearts toying as with trifles. The wrongdoers conceal their private counsels (saying) "Is this (one) more than a man like yourselves? Will you go to witchcraft with your eyes open?"

4. Say: "My Lord knows (every) word (spoken) in the heavens and the earth: He is the One that hears and knows (all things)."

5. "Nay," they say, "(these are) medleys of dreams! Nay he forged it! - Nay he is (but) a poet! Let him then bring us a sign like the ones that were sent to (prophets) of old!"

6. (As to those) before them not one of the populations which We destroyed believed: will these believe?

7. Before you, also, the messengers We sent were but men, to whom We granted inspiration; if you realise this not, ask of those who possess the message.

8. Nor did We give them bodies that ate no food, nor were they exempt from death.

9. In the end We fulfilled to them Our promise, and We saved them and those whom We pleased, but We destroyed those who transgressed beyond bounds.

10. We have revealed for you (O men!) a book in which is a message for you; will you not then understand?

11. How many were the populations We utterly destroyed because of their iniquities, setting up in their places other peoples!

12. Yet, when they felt Our punishment (coming), see they (tried to) flee from it.

13. Flee not, but return to the good things of this life which were given you, and to your homes in order that you may be called to account.

14. They said: "Ah! Woe to us! We were indeed wrongdoers!"

15. And that call of theirs ceased not, till We made them as a field that is mown, as ashes silent and quenched.

16. Not for (idle) sport did We create the heavens and the earth and all that is between!

17. If it had been Our wish to take (just) a pastime, We should surely have taken it from the things nearest to Us, if We would do (such a thing)!

18. Nay We hurl the truth against falsehood and it knocks out its brain and behold falsehood does perish! Ah! Woe be to you for the (false) things you ascribe (to Us).

19. To Him belong all (creatures) in the heavens and on earth; even those who are in His (very) presence are not too proud to serve Him. Nor are they (ever) weary (of His service).

20. They celebrate His praises night and day, nor do they ever flag or intermit.

21. Or have they taken (for worship) gods from the earth who can raise (the dead)?

22. If there were in the heavens and the earth, other gods besides Allah, there would have been confusion in both! But glory to Allah, the Lord of the throne: (high is He) above what they attribute to Him!

23. He cannot be questioned for His acts, but they will be questioned (for theirs).

24. Or have they taken for worship (other) gods besides Him? Say, "Bring your convincing proof; this is the message of those with me and the message of those before me." But most of them know not the truth, and so turn away.

25. Not a messenger did We send before you without this inspiration sent by Us to him: that there is no god but I; therefore worship and serve Me.

26. And they say: "(Allah) Most Gracious has begotten offspring." Glory to Him! They are (but) servants raised to honour.

27. They speak not before He speaks, and they act (in all things) by His command.

28. He knows what is before them, and what is behind them, and they offer no intercession except for those who are acceptable, and they stand in awe and reverence of His (glory).

29. If any of them should say, "I am a god besides Him", such a god We should reward with hell; thus do We reward those who do wrong.

30. Do not the unbelievers see that the heavens and the earth were joined together (as one unit of creation), before We split them apart? We made from water every living thing. Will they not then believe?

31. And We have set on the earth mountains standing firm, lest it should shake with them, and We have made in it broad highways (between mountains) for them to pass through: that they may receive guidance.

32. And We have made the heavens as a canopy well-guarded: yet do they turn away from the signs which these things (point to)!

33. It is He Who created the night and the day, and the sun and the moon; all (the celestial bodies) swim along, each in its rounded course.

34. We granted not to any man before you permanent life (here); if then you should die, would they live permanently?

35. Every soul shall have a taste of death; and We test you by evil and by good by way of trial; to Us must you return.

36. When the unbelievers see you, they treat you not except with ridicule. "Is this," (they say), "the one who talks of your gods?" And they blaspheme at the mention of (Allah) Most Gracious!

37. Man is a creature of haste; soon (enough) will I show you My signs; then you will not ask Me to hasten them!

38. They say: "When will this promise come to pass, if you are telling the truth?"

39. If only the unbelievers knew (the time) when they will not be able to ward off the fire from their faces, nor yet from their backs, and (when) no help can reach them!

40. Nay, it may come to them all of a sudden and confound them; no power will they have then to avert it, nor will they (then) get respite.

41. Mocked were (many) prophets before you; but their scoffers were hemmed in by the thing that they mocked.

42. Say: "Who can keep you safe by night and by day from (the wrath of) (Allah) Most Gracious?" Yet they turn away from the mention of their Lord.

43. Or have they gods that can guard them from Us? They have no power to aid themselves, nor can they be defended from Us.

44. Nay, We gave the good things of this life to these men and their fathers until the period grew long for them; see they not that We gradually reduce the land (in their control) from its outlying borders? Is it then they who will win?

45. Say, "I do but warn you according to revelation": but the deaf will not hear the call, (even) when they are warned!

46. If but a breath of the wrath of your Lord does touch them, they will then say, "Woe to us! We did wrong indeed!"

47. We shall set up scales of justice for the day of judgement, so that not a soul will be dealt with unjustly in the least. And if there be (no more than) the weight of a mustard seed, We will bring it (to account); and enough are We to take account.

48. In the past We granted to Moses and Aaron the criterion (for judgement), and a light and a message for those who would do right

49. Those who fear their Lord in their most secret thoughts, and who hold the hour (of judgement) in awe.

50. And this is a blessed Message which We have sent down; will you then reject it?

51. We bestowed before on Abraham his rectitude of conduct, and well were We acquainted with him.

52. See! He said to his father and his people :"What are these images, to which you are (so assiduously) devoted?"

53. They said, "We found our fathers worshipping them."

54. He said, "Indeed you have been in manifest error - you and your fathers."

55. They said, "Have you brought us the truth, or are you one of those who jest?"

56. He said, "Nay your Lord is the Lord of the heavens and the earth. He Who created them (from nothing): and I am a witness to this (truth).

57. And by Allah, I have a plan for your idols after you go away and turn your backs".

58. So he broke them to pieces, (all) but the biggest of them, that they might turn (and address themselves) to it.

59. They said, "Who has done this to our gods? He must indeed be some man of impiety!"

60. They said, "We heard a youth talk of them: he is called Abraham."

61. They said, "Then bring him before the eyes of the people, that they may bear witness:"

62. They said, "Are you the one that did this with our gods, O Abraham?"

63. He said: "Nay, this was done by this biggest one! Ask them, if they can speak intelligently!"

64. So they turned to themselves and said, "Surely you are the ones in the wrong!"

65. Then were they confounded with shame: (they said) "You know full well that these (idols) do not speak!"

66. (Abraham) said, "Do you then worship, besides Allah, things that can neither be of any good to you nor do you harm?"

67. "Fie upon you, and upon the things that you worship besides Allah! Have you no sense?".

68. They said, "Burn him and protect your gods, if you do (anything at all)!"

69. We said, "O fire! Be you cool, and (a means of)) safety for Abraham!"

70. Then they sought a stratagem against him: but We made them the ones that lost most!

71. But We delivered him and (his nephew) Lot (and directed them) to the land which We have blessed for the nations.

72. And We bestowed on him Isaac and, as an additional gift, (a grandson), Jacob, and We made righteous men of every one (of them).

73. And We made them leaders, guiding (men) by Our command, and We sent them inspiration to do good deeds, to establish regular prayers, and to practice regular charity; and they constantly served Us (and Us only).

74. And to Lot, too, we gave judgement and knowledge, and We saved him from the town which practised abominations: truly they were a people given to evil, a rebellious people.

75. And We admitted him to Our mercy: for he was one of the righteous.

76. (Remember) Noah, when he called (to Us) before: We listened to his (prayer) and delivered him and his family from great distress.

77. We helped him against people who rejected Our signs; truly they were a people given to evil: so We drowned them (in the flood) all together.

78. And remember David and Solomon, when they gave judgement in the matter of the field into which the sheep of certain people had strayed by night: We did witness their judgement.

79. To Solomon We inspired the (right) understanding of the matter; to each (of them) We gave judgement and knowledge; it was Our power that made the hills and the birds celebrate Our praises with David: it was We Who did (these things).

80. It was We Who taught him the making of coats of mail for your benefit, to guard you from each others violence: will you then be grateful?

81. (It was Our power that made) the violent (unruly) wind flow (tamely) for Solomon, to his order, to the land which We had blessed: for We do know all things.

82. And of the evil ones, were some who dived for him, and did other work besides; and it was We Who guarded them.

83. And (remember) Job, when he cried to his Lord, "Truly distress has seized me. But You are the Most Merciful of those that are merciful."

84. So We listened to him: We removed the distress that was on him, and We restored his people to him, and doubled their number as a grace from Ourselves, and a thing for commemoration, for all who serve Us.

85. And (remember) Ishmael, Idris, and Dhu'l-Kifl, all (men) of constancy and patience;

86. We admitted them to Our mercy: for they were of the righteous ones.

87. And remember Dhu'n-Nun, when he departed in wrath: he imagined that We had no power over him! But he cried through the depths of darkness, "There is no god but You: Glory to You; I was indeed wrong!"

88. So We listened to him and delivered him from distress: and thus do We deliver those who have faith.

89. And (remember) Zakariya, when he called to his Lord: "O my Lord! Leave me not without offspring, though You are the best of inheritors."

90. So We listened to him; and We granted him Yahya; We cured his wife's (barrenness) for him. These three were ever quick in emulation in good works: they used to call on Us with love and reverence, and humble themselves before Us.

91. And (remember) her who guarded her chastity: We breathed into her of Our Spirit, and We made her and her son a sign for all peoples.

92. Verily, this brotherhood of yours is a single brotherhood, and I am your Lord and Cherisher: therefore serve Me (and no other).

93. But (later generations) cut off their affair (of unity) one from another: (yet) will they all return to Us.

94. Whoever works any act of righteousness and has faith, his endeavour will not be rejected; We shall record it in his favour.

95. But there is a ban on any population which We have destroyed: that they shall not return.

96. Until the Gog and Magog (people) are let through (their barrier), and they swiftly swarm from every hill.

97. Then will the true promise draw near (of fulfilment): then see! The eyes of the unbelievers will fixedly stare in horror: "Ah! Woe to us! We were indeed heedless of this; nay we truly did wrong!"

98. Verily you, (unbelievers) and the (false) gods that you worship besides Allah, are (but) fuel for hell! To it will you (surely) come!

99. If these had been gods, they would not have got there! But each one will remain in it.

100. There, sobbing will be their lot, nor will they there hear (anything else).

101. Those for whom the good (record) from Us has gone before, will be removed far from it.

102. Not the slightest sound will they hear of hell: what their souls desired, in that will they dwell.

103. The great terror will bring them no grief; but the angels will meet them (with mutual greetings): "This is your day (the day) that you were promised."

104. The day that We roll up the heavens like a scroll rolled up for books (completed) even as We produced the first creation, so shall We produce a new one: a promise We have undertaken: truly shall We fulfil it.

105. Before this We wrote in the Psalms, after the message (given to Moses): My servants, the righteous, shall inherit the earth."

106. Verily in the (Qur'an) is a message for people who would (truly) worship Allah.

107. We sent you not, but as a mercy for all creatures.

108. Say: "What has come to me by inspiration is that your God is One God: will you therefore bow to His will (in Islam)?"

109. But if they turn back, say: "I have proclaimed the message to you all alike and in truth; but I know not whether that which you are promised is near or far."

110. "It is He Who knows what is open in speech and what you hide (in your hearts)."

111. "I know not but that it may be a trial for you, and a grant of (worldly) livelihood (to you) for a time."

112. Say: "O my Lord! Judge You in truth!" "Our Lord Most Gracious is the One Whose assistance should be sought against the blasphemies you utter!"

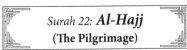

Surah 22: *Al-Hajj*
(The Pilgrimage)

In the name of Allah,
Most Gracious, Most Merciful.

1. O mankind! Fear your Lord! For the convulsion of the hour (of judgement) will be a thing terrible!

2. The day you shall see it, every mother giving suck shall forget her suckling-babe, and every pregnant female shall drop her load (unformed): you shall see mankind as in a drunken riot, yet not drunk; but dreadful will be the wrath of Allah.

3. And yet among men there are such as dispute about Allah, without knowledge, and follow every evil one obstinate in rebellion!

4. About the (evil one) it is decreed that whoever turns to him for friendship, him will he lead astray, and he will guide him to the penalty of the fire.

5. O mankind! If you have a doubt about the resurrection, (consider) that We created you out of dust, then out of sperm, then out of a leech - like clot, then out a morsel of flesh, partly formed and partly unformed, in order

that We may manifest (Our power) to you; and We cause whom We will to rest in the wombs for an appointed term, then do We bring you out as babes, then (foster you) that you may reach your age of full strength; and some of you are called to die, and some are sent back to the feeblest old age, so that they know nothing after having known (much). And (further), you see the earth barren and lifeless, but when We pour down rain on it, it is stirred (to life), it swells, and it puts forth every kind of beautiful growth (in pairs).

6. This is so, because Allah is the reality: it is He Who gives life to the dead, and it is He Who has power over all things.

7. And verily the hour will come: there can be no doubt about it, or about (the fact) that Allah will raise up all who are in the graves.

8. Yet there is among men such a one as disputes about Allah, without knowledge, without guidance, and without a book of enlightenment-

9. (Disdainfully) bending his side, in order to (lead men) astray from the path of Allah; for him there is disgrace in this life, and on the day of judgement We shall make him taste the penalty of burning (fire).

10. (It will be said): "This is because of the deeds which your hands sent before, for verily Allah is not unjust to His servants."

11. There are among men some who serve Allah, as it were, on the verge: if good befalls them, they are with it well content; but if a trial comes to them, they turn on their faces; they lose both this world and the hereafter: that is loss for all to see!

12. They call on such deities, besides Allah, as can neither hurt nor profit them: that is straying far indeed (from the way)!

13. (Perhaps) they call on one whose hurt is nearer than his profit: evil indeed, is the patron, and evil the companion (for help)!

14. Verily Allah will admit those who believe and work righteous deeds, to gardens, beneath which rivers flow: for Allah carries out all that He plans.

15. If any think that Allah will not help him (His messenger) in this world and the hereafter, let him stretch out a rope to the ceiling and cut (himself) off: then let him see whether his plan will remove that which enrages (him)!

16. Thus have We sent down clear signs; and verily Allah does guide whom He will!

17. Those who believe (in the Qur'an), those who follow the Jewish (scriptures), and the Sabians, Christians, Magians and Polytheists - Allah will judge between them on the day of judgement: for Allah is witness of all things.

18. Do you not see that to Allah bow down in worship all things that are in the heavens and on earth - the sun, the moon, the stars; the hills, the trees, the animals; and a great number among mankind? But a great number are (also) such as are fit for punishment; and such as Allah shall disgrace - none

can rise to honour: for Allah carries out all that He wills.

19. These two antagonists dispute with each other about their Lord; but those who deny (their Lord) - for them will be cut out a garment of fire: over their heads will be poured out boiling water.

20. With it will be scalded what is within their bodies, as well as (their) skins.

21. In addition there will be maces of iron (to punish) them.

22. Every time they wish to get away from it, from anguish, they will be forced back in it, and (it will be said), "Taste you the penalty of Burning!"

23. Allah will admit those who believe and work righteous deeds. To gardens beneath which rivers flow: they shall be adorned in it with bracelets of gold and pearls; and their garments there will be of silk.

24. For they have been guided (in this life) to the purest of speeches; they have been guided to the path of Him Who is worthy of (all) praise.

25. As to those who have rejected (Allah), and would keep back (men) from the way of Allah, and from the Sacred Mosque, which We have made (open) to (all) men - equal is the dweller there and the visitor from the country - and any whose purpose in it is profanity or wrongdoing - them will We cause to taste of a most grievous penalty.

26. See! We gave the site to Abraham, of the (Sacred) House (saying): "Associate not any thing (in worship) with Me; and sanctify My House for those who encompass it, or stand up, or bow or prostrate themselves (in it in prayer)."

27. "And proclaim the Pilgrimage among men: they will come to you on foot and (mounted) on every kind of camel, lean on account of journeys through deep and distant mountain highways;

28. That they may witness the benefits (provided) for them, and celebrate the name of Allah, through the Days appointed, over the cattle which He has provided for them (for sacrifice): then eat you of it and feed the distressed ones in want.

29. Then let them complete the rites prescribed for them, perform their vows and (again) circumambulate the Ancient House."

30. Such (is the Pilgrimage): whoever honours the sacred rites of Allah, for him it is good in the sight of his Lord. Lawful to you (for food in pilgrimage) are cattle, except those mentioned to you (as exceptions): but shun the abomination of idols, and shun the word that is false -

31. Being true in faith to Allah, and never assigning partners to Him: if anyone assigns partners to Allah, he is as if he had fallen from heaven and been snatched up by birds, or the wind had swooped (like a bird on its prey) and thrown him into a far-distant place.

32. Such (is his state) and whoever holds in honour the symbols of Allah, (in the sacrifice of animals) such

(honour) should come truly from piety of heart.

33. In them you have benefits for a term appointed: in the end their place of sacrifice is near the Ancient House.

34. To every people did We appoint rites (of sacrifice), that they might celebrate the name of Allah over the sustenance He gave them from animals (fit for food), but your Allah is one Allah: submit then your wills to Him (in Islam) and give you the good news to those who humble themselves -

35. To those whose hearts, when Allah is mentioned, are filled with fear, who show patient perseverance over their afflictions, keep up regular prayer, and spend (in charity) out of what We have bestowed upon them.

36. The sacrificial camels We have made for you as among the symbols from Allah: in them is (much) good for you; then pronounce the name of Allah over them as they line up (for sacrifice); when they are down on their sides (after slaughter), eat you of it, and feed such as (beg not but) live in contentment, and such as beg with due humility: thus have We made animals subject to you, that you may be grateful.

37. It is not their meat nor their blood, that reaches Allah; it is your piety that reaches Him; He has thus made them subject to you, that you may glorify Allah for His guidance to you: and proclaim the good news to all who do right.

38. Verily Allah will defend (from ill) those who believe: verily Allah loves not any that is a traitor to faith, or shows ingratitude.

39. To those against whom war is made, permission is given (to fight), because they are wronged and verily - Allah is Most Powerful for their aid -

40. (They are) those who have been expelled from their homes in defiance of right - (for no cause) except that they say, "Our Lord is Allah." Did not Allah check one set of people by means of another, there would surely have been pulled down monasteries, churches, synagogues, and mosques, in which the name of Allah is commemorated in abundant measure. Allah will certainly aid those who aid His (cause) - for verily Allah is Full of Strength, Exalted in Might (Able to enforce His Will).

41. (They are) those who, if We establish them in the land, establish regular prayer and give regular charity, enjoin the right and forbid wrong: with Allah rests the end (and decision) of (all) affairs.

42. If they treat your (mission) as false, so did the peoples before them (with their prophets) - the people of Noah, and 'Ad and Thamud;

43. Those of Abraham and Lot;

44. And the companions of the Madyan people; and Moses was rejected (in the same way). But I granted respite to the unbelievers and (only) after that did I punish them: but how (terrible) was My rejection (of them)!

45. How many populations have We destroyed, which were given to wrongdoing? They tumbled down on their roofs. And how many wells are lying idle and neglected, and castles lofty and well-built!

46. Do they not travel through the land, so that their hearts (and mind) may thus learn wisdom and their ears may thus learn to hear? Truly it is not their eyes that are blind, but their hearts which are in their breasts.

47. Yet they ask you to hasten on the punishment! But Allah will not fail in His promise. Verily a day in the sight of your Lord is like a thousand years of your reckoning.

48. And to how many populations did I give respite which were given to wrongdoing? In the end I punished them. To Me is the destination (of all).

49. Say: "O men! I am (sent) to you only to give a clear warning;

50. Those who believe and work righteousness, for them is forgiveness and a sustenance most generous.

51. But those who strive against Our signs, to frustrate them - they will be companions of the fire."

52. Never did We send a messenger or a prophet before you, but, when he framed a desire, Satan threw some (vanity) into his desire; but Allah will cancel anything (vain) that Satan throws in, and Allah will confirm (and establish) His signs: for Allah is full of knowledge and wisdom:

53. That He may make the suggestions thrown in by Satan, but a trial for those in whose hearts is a disease and who are hardened of heart: verily the wrongdoers are in a schism far (from the truth):

54. And that those on whom knowledge has been bestowed may learn that the (Qur'an) is the truth from your Lord, and that they may believe in it, and their hearts may be made humbly (open) to it: for verily Allah is the Guide of those who believe, to the straight way.

55. Those who reject faith will not cease to be in doubt concerning (revelation) until the hour (of judgement) comes suddenly upon them, or there comes to them the penalty of a day of disaster.

56. On that day the dominion will be that of Allah; He will judge between them; so those who believe and work righteous deeds will be in gardens of delight.

57. And for those who reject faith and deny Our signs, there will be a humiliating punishment.

58. Those who leave their homes in the cause of Allah, and are then slain or die, on them will Allah bestow verily a goodly provision: truly Allah is He Who bestows the best provision.

59. Verily He will admit them to a place with which they shall be well pleased: for Allah is All-Knowing Most Forbearing.

60. That (is so). And if one has retaliated to no greater extent than the injury he received, and is again set upon inordinately, Allah will help him: for Allah is One that blots out (sins) and forgives (again and again).

61. That is because Allah merges night into day and He merges day into night and verily it is Allah Who hears and sees (all things).

62. That is because Allah He is the Reality; and those besides Him whom they invoke they are but vain falsehood: verily Allah is He Most High Most Great.

63. Do you not see that Allah sends down rain from the sky, and forthwith the earth becomes clothed with green? For Allah is He Who understands the finest mysteries, and is well-acquainted (with them).

64. To Him belongs all that is in the heavens and on earth: for verily Allah He is Free of all wants, Worthy of all praise.

65. Do you not see that Allah has made subject to you (men) all that is on the earth, and the ships that sail through the sea by His command? He withholds the sky (rain) from falling on the earth except by His leave: for Allah is Most Kind and Most Merciful to man.

66. It is He Who gave you life, will cause you to die, and will again give you life: truly man is a most ungrateful creature!

67. To every people have We appointed rites and ceremonies which they must follow, let them not then dispute with you on the matter, but do you invite (them) to your Lord: for you are assuredly on the right way.

68. If they do wrangle with you, say, "Allah knows best what it is you are doing."

69. "Allah will judge between you on the day of judgement concerning the matters in which you differ."

70. Do you not know that Allah knows all that is in heaven and on earth? Indeed it is all in a record, and that is easy for Allah.

71. Yet they worship, besides Allah, things for which no authority has been sent down to them, and of which they have (really) no knowledge: for those that do wrong there is no helper.

72. When Our clear signs are rehearsed to them, you will notice a denial on the faces of the unbelievers! They nearly attack with violence those who rehearse Our signs to them. Say, "Shall I tell you of something (far) worse than these signs? It is the fire (of hell)! Allah has promised it to the unbelievers! And evil is that destination!"

73. O men! Here is a parable set out! Listen to it! Those on whom, besides Allah, you call, cannot create (even) a fly, if they all met together for the purpose! And if the fly should snatch away anything from them they would have no power to release it from the fly: feeble are those who petition and those whom they petition!

74. No just estimate have they made of Allah: for Allah is He Who is strong and able to carry out His Will.

75. Allah chooses prophets from angels and from men: for Allah is He Who hears and sees (all things).

76. He knows what is before them and what is behind them: and to Allah go back all questions (for decision).

77. O you who believe! Bow down, prostrate yourselves, and adore your Lord; and do good; that you may prosper.

78. And strive in His cause as you ought to strive, (with sincerity and under discipline): He has chosen you, and has imposed no difficulties on you

in religion; it is the cult of your father Abraham. It is He Who has named you Muslims, both before and in this (revelation); that the messenger may be a witness for you, and you be witnesses for mankind! So establish regular prayer, give regular charity, and hold fast to Allah! He is your protector, the best to protect and the best to help!

Surah 23: *Al-Mu'minun* (The Believers)

In the name of Allah, Most Gracious, Most Merciful.

1. The Believers must (eventually) win through -

2. Those who humble themselves in their prayers;

3. Who avoid vain talk;

4. Who are active in deeds of charity;

5. Who abstain from sex,

6. Except with those joined to them in the marriage bond, or (the captives) whom their right hands possess - for (in their case) they are free from blame,

7. But those whose desires exceed those limits are transgressors -

8. Those who faithfully observe their trusts and covenants;

9. And who (strictly) guard their prayers -

10. Those will be the heirs,

11. Who will inherit paradise: they will dwell in it (forever).

12. Man We did create from a quintessence (of clay);

13. Then We placed him as (a drop of) sperm in a place of rest, firmly fixed;

14. Then We made the sperm into a clot of congealed blood; then of that clot We made a (foetus) lump; then We made out of that lump bones and clothed the bones with flesh; then We developed out of it another creature. So blessed be Allah, the Best to create!

15. After that, at length you will die.

16. Again, on the day of judgement, will you be raised up.

17. And We have made, above you, seven tracts; and We are never unmindful of (Our) creation.

18. And We send down water from the sky according to (due) measure, and We cause it to soak in the soil; and We certainly are able to drain it off (with ease).

19. With it We grow for you gardens of date palms and vines: in them have you abundant fruits: and of them you eat (and have enjoyment) -

20. Also a tree springing out of mount Sinai, which produces oil, and relish for those who use it for food.

21. And in cattle (too) you have an instructive example: from within their bodies We produce (milk) for you to drink; there are, in them (besides), numerous (other) benefits for you; and of their (meat) you eat;

22. And on them, as well as in ships, you ride.

23. (Further, We sent a long line of prophets for your instruction). We sent Noah to his people: he said, "O my people! Worship Allah! You have

no other god but Him: will you not fear (Him)?"

24. The chiefs of the unbelievers among his people said: "He is no more than a man like yourselves: his wish is to assert his superiority over you: if Allah had wished (to send messengers), He could have sent down angels: never did we hear such a thing (as he says), among our ancestors of old."

25. (And some said:) "He is only a man possessed: wait (and have patience) with him for a time."

26. (Noah) said: "O my Lord! Help me: for that they accuse me of falsehood!"

27. So We inspired him (with this message): "Construct the ark within Our sight and under Our guidance: then when comes Our command, and the fountains of the earth gush out, take you on board pairs of every species, male and female, and your family - except those of them against whom the word has already gone forth: and address Me not in favour of the wrongdoers; for they shall be drowned (in the flood).

28. And when you have embarked on the ark - you and those with you - say: 'Praise be to Allah, Who has saved us from the people who do wrong.'

29. And say: 'O my Lord! Enable me to disembark with Your blessing: for You are the Best to enable (us) to disembark.'"

30. Verily in this there are signs (for men to understand); (thus) do We try (men).

31. Then We raised after them another generation.

32. And We sent to them a messenger from among themselves, (saying) "Worship Allah! You have no other god but Him. Will you not fear (Him)?"

33. And the chiefs of his people, who disbelieved and denied the meeting in the hereafter, and on whom We had bestowed the good things of this life, said: "He is no more than a man like yourselves; he eats of that of which you eat, and drinks of what you drink.

34. If you obey a man like yourselves, see, it is certain you will be lost.

35. Does he promise that when you die and become dust and bones, you shall be brought out (again)?

36. Far, very far, is that which you are promised!

37. There is nothing but our life in this world! We shall die and we live! But we shall never be raised up again!

38. He is only a man who invents a lie against Allah, but we are not the ones to believe in him!"

39. (The prophet) said: "O my Lord! Help me: for that they accuse me of falsehood."

40. (Allah) said: "In but a little while, they are sure to be sorry!"

41. Then the blast overtook them with justice, and We made them as rubbish of dead leaves (floating on the stream of time)! So away with the people who do wrong!

42. Then We raised after them other generations.

43. No people can hasten their term, nor can they delay (it).

44. Then sent We Our messengers in succession: every time there came to a people their messenger, they accused him of falsehood; so We made them follow each other (in punishment); We made them as a tale (that is told); so away with a people that will not believe!

45. Then We sent Moses and his brother Aaron, with Our signs and authority manifest,

46. To Pharaoh and his chiefs: but these behaved insolently: they were arrogant people.

47. They said: "Shall we believe in two men like ourselves? And their people are subject to us!"

48. So they accused them of falsehood, and they became of those who were destroyed.

49. And We gave Moses the book, in order that they might receive guidance.

50. And We made the son of Mary and his mother as a sign: We gave them both shelter on high ground, affording rest and security and furnished with springs.

51. O you messengers! Enjoy (all) things good and pure, and work righteousness: for I am well-acquainted with (all) that you do.

52. And verily this brotherhood of yours is a single brotherhood. And I am your Lord and Cherisher: therefore fear Me (and no other).

53. But people have cut off their affair (of unity), between them, into sects: each party rejoices in that which is with itself.

54. But leave them in their confused ignorance for a time.

55. Do they think that because We have granted them abundance of wealth and sons,

56. We would hasten them on in every good? Nay, they do not understand.

57. Verily those who live in awe for fear of their Lord;

58. Those who believe in the signs of their Lord;

59. Those who join not (in worship) partners with their Lord;

60. And those who dispense their charity with their hearts full of fear, because they will return to their Lord -

61. It is these who hasten in every good work, and these who are foremost in them.

62. On no soul do We place a burden greater than it can bear: before Us is a record which clearly shows the truth. They will never be wronged.

63. But their hearts are in confused ignorance of this; and there are, besides that, deeds of theirs, which they will (continue) to do;

64. Until, when We seize in punishment those of them who received the good things of this world, see, they will groan in supplication!

65. It will be said: "Groan not in supplication this day; for you shall certainly not be helped by Us."

66. "My signs used to be rehearsed to you, but you used to turn back on your heels -

67. In arrogance: talking nonsense about the (Qur'an), like one telling fables by night."

68. Do they not ponder over the word (of Allah), or has anything (new) come to them that did not come to their fathers of old?

69. Or do they not recognise their messenger, that they deny him?

70. Or do they say "He is possessed"? Nay, he has brought them the truth, but most of them hate the truth.

71. If the truth had been in accord with their desires, truly the heavens and the earth, and all beings in it would have been in confusion and corruption! Nay, We have sent them their admonition, but they turn away from their admonition.

72. Or is it that you ask them for some recompense? But the recompense of your Lord is best: He is the Best of those who give sustenance.

73. But verily you call them to the straight way;

74. And verily those who believe not in the hereafter are deviating from that way.

75. If We had mercy on them, and removed the distress which is on them they would obstinately persist in their transgression, wandering in distraction to and fro.

76. We inflicted punishment on them, but they humbled not themselves to their Lord nor do they submissively entreat (Him)! -

77. Until We open on them a gate leading to a severe punishment: then They will be plunged in despair in it!

78. It is He Who has created for you (the faculties of) hearing, sight, feeling, and understanding: little thanks it is you give!

79. And He has multiplied you through the earth, and to Him shall you be gathered back.

80. It is He Who gives life and death, and to Him (is due) the alternation of night and day: will you not then understand?

81. On the contrary they say things similar to what the ancients said.

82. They say: "What! When we die and become dust and bones, could we really be raised up again?

83. Such things have been promised to us and to our fathers before! They are nothing but tales of the ancients!"

84. Say: "To whom belong the earth and all beings in it? (Say) if you know!"

85. They will say "To Allah!" Say: "Yet will you not receive admonition?"

86. Say: "Who is the Lord of the seven heavens, and the Lord of the Throne (of Glory) Supreme?"

87. They will say, "(They belong) to Allah." Say: "Will you not then be filled with awe?"

88. Say: "Who is it in whose hands is the governance of all things - who protects (all), but is not protected (of any)? (Say) if you know."

89. They will say "(It belongs) to Allah." Say: "Then how are you deluded?"

90. We have sent them the truth: but they indeed practice falsehood!

91. No son did Allah beget, nor is there any god along with Him: (if there were many gods), behold, each god would have taken away what be had created, and some would have lorded it over others! Glory to Allah! (He is free) from the (sort of) things they attribute to Him!

92. He knows what is hidden and what is open: too high is He for the partners they attribute to Him!

93. Say: "O my Lord! If You will show me (in my lifetime) that which they are warned against -

94. Then, O my Lord! Put me not amongst the people who do wrong!"

95. And We are certainly able to show you (in fulfilment) that against which they are warned.

96. Repel evil with that which is best: We are well-acquainted with the things they say.

97. And say: "O my Lord! I seek refuge with You from the suggestions of the evil ones.

98. And I seek refuge with You O my Lord! Lest they should come near me."

99. (In falsehood will they be) until, when death comes to one of them, he says: "O my Lord! Send me back (to life) -

100. In order that I may work righteousness in the things I neglected" - "By no means! It is but a word he says"- before them is a partition till the day they are raised up.

101. Then when the trumpet is blown, there will be no more relationships between them that day, nor will one ask after another!

102. Then those whose balance (of good deeds) is heavy - they will attain salvation:

103. But those whose balance is light, will be those who have lost their souls; in hell will they remain.

104. The fire will burn their faces, and they will in it grin, with their lips displaced.

105. "Were not My signs rehearsed to you, and you did but treat them as falsehoods?"

106. They will say: "Our Lord! Our misfortune overwhelmed us, and we became a people astray!"

107. "Our Lord! Bring us out of this: if ever we return (to evil), then shall we be wrongdoers indeed!"

108. He will say: "Be you driven into it (with disgrace)! And speak you not to Me!"

109. "A part of My servants there was, who used to pray, 'Our Lord! We believe; then do You forgive us, and have mercy upon us: for You are the best of those Who show mercy!'

110. But you treated them with ridicule, so much so that (ridicule of) them made you forget My message while you were laughing at them!

111. I have rewarded them this day for their patience and constancy: they are indeed the ones that have achieved bliss."

112. He will say: "What number of years did you stay on earth?"

113. They will say: "We stayed a day or part of a day: but ask those who keep account."

114. He will say: "You stayed not but a little - if you had only known!

115. Did you then think that We had created you in jest, and that you would not be brought back to Us (for account)?"

116. Therefore, exalted be Allah, the King, the Reality; there is no god but He, the Lord of the Throne of Honour!

117. If anyone invokes, besides Allah, any other god, he has no authority therefore; and his reckoning will be only with his Lord! And verily the unbelievers will fail to win through!

118. So say: "O my Lord! Grant You forgiveness and mercy! For You are the Best of those who show mercy!"

Surah 24: *An-Nur* (Light)

In the name of Allah, Most Gracious, Most Merciful.

1. A *Surah* which We have sent down and which We have ordained: in it have We sent down clear signs, in order that you may receive admonition.

2. The woman and the man guilty of adultery or fornication flog each of them with a hundred stripes; let not compassion move you in their case, in a matter prescribed by Allah, if you believe in Allah and the last day;

and let a party of the believers witness their punishment.

3. Let no man guilty of adultery or fornication marry any but a woman similarly guilty, or an Unbeliever; nor let any but such a man or an Unbeliever marry such a woman: to the believers such a thing is forbidden.

4. And those who launch a charge against chaste women, and produce not four witnesses (to support their allegation) - flog them with eighty stripes; and reject their evidence ever after: for such men are wicked transgressors -

5. Unless they repent thereafter and mend (their conduct): for Allah is Oft-Forgiving, Most Merciful.

6. And for those who launch a charge against their spouses, and have (in support) no evidence but their own - their solitary evidence (can be received) if they bear witness four times (with an oath) by Allah that they are solemnly telling the truth;

7. And the fifth (oath) (should be) that they solemnly invoke the curse of Allah on themselves if they tell a lie.

8. But it would avert the punishment from the wife, if she bears witness four times (with an oath) by Allah, that (her husband) is telling a lie;

9. And the fifth (oath) should be that she solemnly invokes the wrath of Allah on herself if (her accuser) is telling the truth.

10. If it were not for Allah's grace and mercy on you and that Allah is Oft-Returning Full of wisdom (you would be ruined indeed).

11. Those who brought forward the lie are a body among yourselves; think it not to be an evil to you; on the contrary it is good for you: to every man among them (will come the punishment) of the sin that he earned, and to him who took on himself the lead among them, will be a penalty grievous.

12. Why did not believers men and women when you heard of the affair, put the best construction on it in their own minds and say, "This (charge) is an obvious lie"?

13. Why did they not bring four witnesses to prove it? When they have not brought the witnesses, such men, in the sight of Allah (stand forth) themselves as liars!

14. Were it not for the grace and mercy of Allah on you, in this world and the hereafter, a grievous penalty would have seized you in that you rushed glibly into this affair.

15. See, you received it on your tongues and said out of your mouths things of which you had no knowledge; and you thought it to be a light matter, while it was most serious in the sight of Allah.

16. And why did you not when you heard it, say "It is not right of us to speak of this: Glory to Allah! This is a most serious slander!"

17. Allah does admonish you, that you may never repeat such (conduct), if you are (true) believers.

18. And Allah makes the signs plain to you: for Allah is full of knowledge and wisdom.

19. Those who love (to see) scandal published broadcast among the believers, will have a grievous penalty in this life and in the hereafter: Allah knows and you know not.

20. Were it not for the grace and mercy of Allah on you, and that Allah is full of kindness and mercy, (you would be ruined indeed).

21. O you who believe! Follow not Satan's footsteps: if any will follow the footsteps of Satan, he will (but) command what is shameful and wrong: and were it not for the grace and mercy of Allah on you, not one of you would ever have been pure; but Allah does purify whom He pleases: and Allah is one Who hears and knows (all things).

22. Let not those among you who are endued with grace and amplitude of means resolve by oath against helping their relatives, those in want, and those who have left their homes in Allah's cause: let them forgive and overlook, do you not wish that Allah should forgive you? For Allah is Oft-Forgiving, Most Merciful.

23. Those who slander chaste women, indiscreet but believing, are cursed in this life and in the hereafter: for them is a grievous penalty -

24. On the day when their tongues, their hands, and their feet will bear witness against them as to their actions.

25. On that day Allah will pay them back (all) their just dues, and they will realise that Allah is the (very) truth, that makes all things manifest.

26. Women impure are for men impure, and men impure are for women impure, and women of purity are for men of purity, and men of purity are for women of purity; these are not affected by what people say: for them there is forgiveness and a provision honourable.

27. O you who believe! Enter not houses other than your own, until you have asked permission and saluted those in them: that is best for you, in order that you may heed (what is seemly).

28. If you find no one in the house, enter not until permission is given to you; if you are asked to go back, go back; that makes for greater purity for yourselves: and Allah knows well all that you do.

29. It is no fault on your part to enter houses not used for living in, which serve some (other) use for you: and Allah has knowledge of what you reveal and what you conceal.

30. Say to the believing men that they should lower their gaze and guard their modesty; that will make for greater purity for them: and Allah is well acquainted with all that they do.

31. And say to the believing women that they should lower their gaze and guard their modesty; that they should not display their beauty and ornaments except what (must ordinarily) appear of it; that they should draw their veils over their bosoms and not display their beauty except to their husbands, their fathers, their husbands' fathers, their sons, their husbands' sons, their brothers or their brothers' sons, or their sisters' sons, or their women, or the slaves whom their right hands possess, or male servants free of physical needs, or small children who have no sense of the shame of sex; and that they should not strike their feet in order to draw attention to their hidden ornaments. And O you believers! Turn you all together towards Allah, that you may attain bliss.

32. Marry those among you who are single or the virtuous ones among your slaves, male or female; if they are in poverty, Allah will give them means out of His grace: for Allah encompasses all and He knows all things.

33. Let those who find not the wherewithal for marriage keep themselves chaste, until Allah gives them means out of His grace. And if any of your slaves ask for a deed in writing (to enable them to earn their freedom for a certain sum) give them such a deed if you know any good in them; yea give them something yourselves out of the means which Allah has given to you. But force not your maids to prostitution when they desire chastity in order that you may make a gain in the goods of this life. But if anyone compels them yet, after such compulsion, is Allah Oft-Forgiving, Most Merciful (to them).

34. We have already sent down to you verses making things clear, an illustration from (the story of) people who passed away before you and an admonition for those who fear (Allah).

35. Allah is the light of the heavens and the earth. The parable of His light is as if there were a niche and within it a lamp; the Lamp enclosed in glass; the glass as it were a brilliant star; lit from a blessed tree an olive, neither of the east nor of the west, whose oil is well-near luminous, though fire scarce touched it: Light upon light! Allah does guide whom He will to His light. Allah does set out parables for men; and Allah does know all things.

36. (Lit is such a light) in houses, which Allah has permitted to be raised to honour; for the celebration, in them of His name: in them, is He glorified in the mornings and in the evenings, (again and again) -

37. By men whom neither traffic nor merchandise can divert from the remembrance of Allah, nor from regular prayer, nor from the practice of regular charity: their (only) fear is for the day when hearts and eyes will be transformed (in a world wholly new) -

38. That Allah may reward them according to the best of their deeds and add even more for them out of His grace: for Allah does provide for those whom He will without measure.

39. But the unbelievers, their deeds are like a mirage in sandy deserts, which the man parched with thirst mistakes for water; until when he comes up to it, he finds it to be nothing; but he finds Allah (ever) with him, and Allah will pay him his account: and Allah is swift in taking account.

40. Or (the unbelievers' state) is like the depths of darkness in a vast deep ocean, overwhelmed with billow topped by billow, topped by (dark) clouds: depths of darkness, one above another; if a man stretches out his hand, he can hardly see it! For any to whom Allah gives not light, there is no light!

41. Do you not see that it is Allah Whose praises all beings in the heavens and on earth do celebrate, and the birds (of the air) with wings outspread? Each one knows its own (mode of) prayer and praise. And Allah knows well all that they do.

42. Yea, to Allah belongs the dominion of the heavens and the earth; and to Allah is the final goal (of all).

43. Do you not see that Allah makes the clouds move gently, then joins them together, then makes them into a heap? Then will you see rain issue forth from their midst. And He sends down from the sky mountain masses (of clouds) in which is hail: He strikes with it whom He pleases and He turns it away from whom He pleases. The vivid flash of His lightning well-near blinds the sight.

44. It is Allah Who alternates the night and the day: verily in these things is an instructive example for those who have vision!

45. And Allah has created every animal from water: of them there are some that creep on their bellies; some that walk on two legs; and some that walk on four. Allah creates what He wills: for verily Allah has power over all things.

46. We have indeed sent down signs that make things manifest: and Allah

guides whom He wills to a way that is straight.

47. They say, "We believe in Allah and in the messenger and we obey": but even after that, some of them turn away: they are not (really) believers.

48. When they are summoned to Allah and His messenger, in order that He may judge between them, see some of them decline (to come).

49. But if the right is on their side, they come to him with all submission.

50. Is it that there is a disease in their hearts? Or do they doubt, or are they in fear, that Allah and His messenger will deal unjustly with them? Nay, it is they themselves who do wrong.

51. The answer of the believers, when summoned to Allah and His messenger, in order that He may judge between them, is no other than this: They say, "We hear and we obey"; it is such as these that will attain felicity.

52. It is such as obey Allah and His messenger, and fear Allah and do right, that will win (in the end).

53. They swear their strongest oaths by Allah that, if only you would command them, they would leave (their homes). Say: "Swear you not; obedience is (more) reasonable: Verily, Allah is well-acquainted with all that you do."

54. Say: "Obey Allah and obey the messenger: but if you turn away, he is only responsible for the duty placed on him and you for that placed on you. If you obey him, you shall be on right guidance. The messenger's duty is only to preach the clear (message)."

55. Allah has promised, to those among you who believe and work righteous deeds, that He will, of a surety, grant them in the land inheritance (of power), as He granted it to those before them; that He will establish in authority their religion - the one which He has chosen for them; and that He will change (their state), after the fear in which they (lived), to one of security and peace: 'They will worship Me (alone) and not associate anything with Me.' If any do reject faith after this, they are rebellious and wicked.

56. So establish regular prayer and give regular charity; and obey the messenger; that you may receive mercy.

57. Never think you that the unbelievers are going to frustrate (Allah's Plan) on earth: their abode is the fire and it is indeed an evil refuge!

58. O you who believe! Let those whom your right hands possess, and the (children) among you who have not come of age ask your permission (before they come to your presence), on three occasions before morning prayer; the while you take off your clothes for the noonday heat; and after the late-night prayer; these are your three times of undress; outside those times it is not wrong for you or for them to move about attending to each other: thus does Allah make clear the signs to you: for Allah is full of knowledge and wisdom.

59. But when the children among you come of age, let them (also) ask for permission, as do those senior to them (in age); thus does Allah make clear His signs to you; for Allah is full of knowledge and wisdom.

60. Such elderly women as are past the prospect of marriage - there is no blame on them if they lay aside their (outer) garments, provided they make not a wanton display of their beauty; but it is best for them to be modest: and Allah is One Who sees and knows all things.

61. It is no fault in the blind nor in one born lame, nor in one afflicted with illness, nor in yourselves, that you should eat in your own houses, or those of your fathers, or your mothers, or your brothers, or your sisters, or your father's brothers, or your father's sisters, or your mother's brothers, or your mother's sisters, or in houses of which the keys are in your possession, or in the house of a sincere friend of yours: there is no blame on you, whether you eat in company or separately. But if you enter houses, salute each other a greeting or blessing and purity as from Allah, thus does Allah make clear the signs to you: that you may understand.

62. Only those are believers, who believe in Allah and His messenger; when they are with him on a matter requiring collective action, they do not depart until they have asked for his leave; those who ask for your leave are those who believe in Allah and His messenger; so when they ask for your leave, for some business of theirs, give leave to those of them whom you will, and ask Allah for their forgiveness: for Allah is Oft-Forgiving, Most Merciful.

63. Think not the summons of the messenger among yourselves like the summons of one of you to another: Allah does know those of you who slip away under shelter of some excuse: then let those beware who withstand the messenger's order, lest some trial befall them, or a grievous penalty be inflicted on them.

64. Be quite sure that to Allah does belong whatever is in the heavens and on earth. Well does He know what you are intent upon; and one day they will be brought back to Him, and He will tell them the truth of what they did: for Allah does know all things.

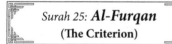

Surah 25: *Al-Furqan*
(The Criterion)

In the name of Allah,
Most Gracious, Most Merciful.

1. Blessed is He Who sent down the criterion to His servant, that it may be an admonition to all creatures-

2. He to Whom belongs the dominion of the heavens and the earth; no son has He begotten, nor has He a partner in His dominion: it is He Who created all things, and ordered them in due proportions.

3. Yet have they taken, besides Him, gods that can create nothing but are themselves created; that have no control of hurt or good to themselves;

nor can they control death nor life nor resurrection.

4. But the unbelievers say: "Nothing is this but a lie which he has forged, and others have helped him at it." In truth it is they who have put forward an iniquity and a falsehood.

5. And they say: "Tales of the ancients, which he has caused to be written: and they are dictated before him morning and evening."

6. Say: "The (Qur'an) was sent down by Him Who knows the mystery (that is) in the heavens and the earth: verily He is Oft-Forgiving, Most Merciful."

7. And they say: "What sort of a messenger is this, who eats food, and walks through the streets? Why has not an angel been sent down to him to give admonition with him?

8. Or (why) has not a treasure been bestowed on him, or why has he (not) a garden for enjoyment?" The wicked say: "You follow none other than a man bewitched."

9. See what kinds of companions they make for you! But they have gone astray, and never a way will they be able to find!

10. Blessed is He Who, if that were His will, could give you better (things) than those gardens beneath which rivers flow; and He could give you palaces (secure to dwell in).

11. Nay, they deny the hour (of the judgement to come): but We have prepared a blazing fire for such as deny the hour:

12. When it sees them from a place far off, they will hear its fury and its raging sigh.

13. And when they are cast, bound together, into a constricted place in it, they will plead for destruction there and then!

14. "This day plead not for a single destruction: plead for destruction oft-repeated!"

15. Say: "Is that best, or the eternal garden, promised to the righteous? For them, that is a reward as well as a goal (of attainment).

16. For them there will be in it all that they wish for: they will dwell (there) for ever; a promise to be prayed for from your Lord."

17. The day He will gather them together as well as those whom they worship besides Allah, He will ask: "Was it you who led these My servants astray or did they stray from the path themselves?"

18. They will say: "Glory to You! Not fit was it for us that we should take for protectors others besides You: but You did bestow on them, and their fathers, good things (in life), until they forgot the message: for they were a people (worthless and) lost."

19. (Allah will say): "Now have they proved you liars in what you say; so you cannot avert (your penalty) nor (get) help." And whoever among you does wrong, him shall We cause to taste of a grievous penalty.

20. And the prophets whom We sent before you were all (men) who ate food and walked through the streets: We have made some of you as a trial for others: will you have patience? For Allah is One Who sees (all things).

21. Such as fear not the meeting with Us (for judgement) say: "Why are not the angels sent down to us, or (why) do we not see our Lord?" Indeed they have an arrogant conceit of themselves, and mighty is the insolence of their impiety!

22. The day they see the angels no joy will there be to the sinners that day; the (angels) will say: "There is a barrier forbidden (to you) altogether!"

23. And We shall turn to whatever deeds they did (in this life), and We shall make such deeds as floating dust scattered about.

24. The companions of the garden will be well, that day, in their abode, and have the fairest of places for repose.

25. The day the heaven shall be rent asunder with clouds, and angels shall be sent down descending (in ranks)-

26. That day, the dominion as of right and truth, shall be (wholly) for (Allah) Most Merciful: it will be a day of dire difficulty for the unbelievers.

27. The day that the wrongdoer will bite at his hands, He will say "Oh! Would that I had taken a (straight) path with the messenger!"

28. "Ah! Woe is me! Would that I had never taken such a one for a friend!

29. He did lead me astray from the message (of Allah) after it had come to me! Ah! The evil one is but a traitor to man!"

30. Then the messenger will say: "O my Lord! Truly my people took this Qur'an for just foolish nonsense."

31. Thus have We made for every prophet an enemy among the sinners: but enough is your Lord to guide and to help.

32. Those who reject faith say: "Why is not the Qur'an revealed to him all at once?" Thus (is it revealed), that We may strengthen your heart by it, and We have rehearsed it to you in slow, well-arranged stages, gradually.

33. And no question do they bring to you but We reveal to you the truth and the best explanation (of it).

34. Those who will be gathered to hell, (prone) on their faces they will be in an evil plight, and as to path, most astray.

35. Before this, We sent Moses the book, and appointed his brother Aaron with him as minister;

36. And We commanded: "Go you both, to the people who have rejected Our signs": and those (people) We destroyed with utter destruction.

37. And the people of Noah when they rejected the messengers, We drowned them, and We made them as a sign for mankind; and We have prepared for (all) wrongdoers a grievous penalty;

38. As also 'Ad and Thamud, and the companions of ar-Rass, and many a generation between them.

39. To teach one We set out parables and examples; and each one We broke to utter annihilation (for their sins).

40. And the (unbelievers) must indeed have passed by the town on which was

rained a shower of evil: did they not then see it (with their own eyes)? But they fear not the resurrection.

41. When they see you they treat you, no otherwise than in mockery: "Is this the one whom Allah has sent as a messenger?"

42. "He indeed would well-near have misled us from our gods, had it not been that we were constant to them!" Soon will they know, when they see the penalty, who it is that is most misled in path!

43. See you such a one as takes for his god his own passion (or impulse)? Could you be a disposer of affairs for him?

44. Or do you think that most of them listen or understand? They are only like cattle; nay, they are worse astray in path.

45. Have you not turned your vision to your Lord? how He does prolong the shadow! If He willed, He could make it stationary! Then do We make the sun its guide;

46. Then We draw it in towards Ourselves - a contraction by easy stages.

47. And He it is Who makes the night as a robe for you, and sleep as repose, and makes the day (as it were) a resurrection.

48. And He it is Who sends the winds as heralds of glad tidings, going before His mercy, and We send down purifying water from the sky -

49. That with it, We may give life to a dead land, and slake the thirst of things We have created cattle and men in great numbers.

50. And We have distributed the (water) amongst them, in order that they may celebrate (Our) praises, but most men are averse (to anything) but (rank) ingratitude.

51. Had it been Our will, We could have sent a warner to every centre of population,

52. Therefore, listen not to the unbelievers, but strive against them with the utmost strenuousness, with the (Qur'an).

53. It is He Who has let free the two bodies of flowing water: one palatable and sweet, and the other salty and bitter; yet has He made a barrier between them, a partition that is forbidden to be passed.

54. It is He Who has created man from water: then has He established relationships of lineage and marriage: for your Lord has power (over all things).

55. Yet do they worship, besides Allah, things that can neither profit them nor harm them: and the unbeliever is a helper (of evil), against his own Lord!

56. But you We only sent to give glad tidings and admonition.

57. Say: "No reward do I ask of you for it but this: that each one who will may take a (straight) path to his Lord."

58. And put your trust in Him Who lives and dies not; and celebrate His praise; and enough is He to be acquainted with the faults of His servants-

59. He Who created the heavens and the earth and all that is between, in six days, and is firmly established on the throne (of authority): Allah, Most Gracious: ask you, then, about Him of any acquainted (with such things).

60. When it is said to them, "Adore you (Allah) Most Gracious!", They say, "And what is (Allah) Most Gracious? Shall we adore that which you command us?" and it increases their flight (from the truth).

61. Blessed is He Who made constellations in the skies, and placed in it a lamp and a moon giving light;

62. And it is He Who made the night and the day to follow each other: for such as have the will to celebrate His praises or to show their gratitude.

63. And the servants of (Allah) Most Gracious are those who walk on the earth in humility, and when the ignorant address them, they say, "Peace!";

64. Those who spend the night in adoration of their Lord prostrate and standing;

65. Those who say: "Our Lord! Avert from us the wrath of hell, for its wrath is indeed an affliction grievous -

66. Evil indeed is it as an abode, and as a place to rest in";

67. Those who, when they spend, are not extravagant and not niggardly, but hold a just (balance) between those (extremes);

68. Those who invoke not, with Allah, any other god, nor slay such life as Allah has made sacred, except for just cause, nor commit fornication - and any that does this (not only) meets punishment.

69. (But) the penalty on the day of judgement will be doubled to him, and he will dwell in it in disgrace -

70. Unless he repents, believes and works righteous deeds, for Allah will change the evil of such persons into good, and Allah is Oft-Forgiving, Most Merciful,

71. And whoever repents and does good has truly turned to Allah with an (acceptable) conversion -

72. Those who witness no falsehood and, if they pass by futility, they pass by it with honourable (avoidance);

73. Those who, when they are admonished with the signs of their Lord, droop not down at them as if they were deaf or blind:

74. And those who pray, "Our Lord! Grant to us wives and offspring who will be the comfort of our eyes, and give us (the grace) to lead the righteous."

75. Those are the ones who will be rewarded with the highest place in heaven, because of their patient constancy; in it shall they be met with salutations and peace,

76. Dwelling in it - how beautiful an abode and place of rest!

77. Say (to the rejecters): "My Lord is not uneasy because of you if you call not on Him, but you have indeed rejected (Him), and soon will come the inevitable (punishment)!"

Surah 26: **Ash-Shu'ara**
(The Poets)

In the name of Allah,
Most Gracious, Most Merciful.

1. *Ta Sin Mim.*

2. These are verses of the book that makes (things) clear.

3. It may be you torment your soul with grief, that they do not become believers.

4. If (such) were Our will We could send down to them from the sky a sign, to which they would bend their necks in humility.

5. But there comes not to them a newly-revealed message from (Allah) Most Gracious, but they turn away from it.

6. They have indeed rejected (the message): so they will know soon (enough) the truth of what they mocked at!

7. Do they not look at the earth how many noble things of all kinds We have produced in it?

8. Verily in this is a sign: but most of them do not believe.

9. And verily, your Lord is He, the Exalted in Might, Most Merciful.

10. See, your Lord called Moses: "Go to the people of iniquity -

11. The people of Pharaoh: will they not fear Allah?"

12. He said: "O my Lord! I do fear that they will charge me with falsehood:

13. My breast will be straitened. And my speech may not go (smoothly): so send to Aaron.

14. And (further), they have a charge of crime against me; and I fear they may slay me."

15. Allah said: "By no means! Proceed then, both of you, with Our signs; We are with you, and will listen (to your call).

16. So go ahead, both of you to Pharaoh, and say: 'We have been sent by the Lord and Cherisher of the Worlds;

17. Send you with us the Children of Israel.'"

18. (Pharaoh) said: "Did we not cherish you as a child among us, and did you not stay in our midst many years of your life?

19. And you did a deed of yours which (you know) you did, and you are an ungrateful (wretch)!"

20. Moses: "I did it then, when I was in error.

21. So I fled from you (all) when I feared you; but my Lord has (since) invested me with judgement (and wisdom) and appointed me as one of the messengers.

22. And this is the favour with which you do reproach me - that you have enslaved the Children of Israel!"

23. Pharaoh said: "And what is the 'Lord and Cherisher of the Worlds?'"

24. (Moses) said: "The Lord and Cherisher of the heavens and the earth, and all between - if you want to be quite sure."

25. (Pharaoh) said to those around: "Do you not listen (to what he says)?"

26. (Moses) said: "Your Lord and the Lord of your fathers from the beginning!"

27. (Pharaoh) said: "Truly your messenger who has been sent to you is a veritable madman!"

28. (Moses) said: "Lord of the east and the west, and all between! If you only had sense!"

29. (Pharaoh) said: "If you do put forward any god other than me, I will certainly put you in prison!"

30. (Moses) said: "Even if I showed you something clear (and) convincing?"

31. (Pharaoh) said: "Show it then if you tell the truth!"

32. So (Moses) threw his rod, and see, it was a serpent, plain (for all to see)!

33. And he drew out his hand, and see, it was white to all onlookers!

34. (Pharaoh) said to the chiefs around him: "This is indeed a sorcerer well-versed:

35. His plan is to get you out of your land by his sorcery; then what is it you counsel?"

36. They said: "Keep him and his brother in suspense (for a while), and dispatch to the cities heralds to collect -

37. And bring up to you all (our) sorcerers well-versed."

38. So the sorcerers were got together for the appointment of a day well-known,

39. And the people were told: "Are you (now) assembled? -

40. That we may follow the sorcerers (in religion) if they win?"

41. So when the sorcerers arrived, they said to Pharaoh: "Of course - shall we have a (suitable) reward if we win?"

42. He said: "Yea (and more) - for you shall in that case be (raised to posts) nearest (to my person)."

43. Moses said to them: "Throw you - that which you are about to throw!"

44. So they threw their ropes and their rods, and said: "By the might of Pharaoh it is we who will certainly win!"

45. Then Moses threw his rod, when, see, it straight away swallows up all the falsehoods which they fake!

46. Then did the sorcerers fall down, prostrate in adoration,

47. Saying: "We believe in the Lord of the Worlds,

48. The Lord of Moses and Aaron."

49. Said (Pharaoh): "Do you believe in him before I give you permission? Surely he is your leader, who has taught you sorcery! But soon shall you know! Be sure I will cut off your hands and your feet on opposite sides, and I will cause you all to die on the cross!"

50. They said: "No matter! For us, we shall but return to our Lord!

51. Only, our desire is that our Lord will forgive us our faults, that we may become foremost among the believers!"

52. By inspiration We told Moses: "Travel by night with My servants; for surely you shall be pursued."

53. Then Pharaoh sent heralds to (all) the cities,

54. (Saying): "These (Israelites) are but a small band,

55. And they are raging furiously against us;

56. But we are a multitude amply fore-warned."

57. So We expelled them from gardens, springs,

58. Treasures, and every kind of honourable position;

59. Thus it was, but We made the Children of Israel inheritors of such things.

60. So they pursued them at sunrise.

61. And when the two bodies saw each other, the people of Moses said: "We are sure to be overtaken."

62. (Moses) said: "By no means! My Lord is with me! Soon will He guide me!"

63. Then We told Moses by inspiration: "Strike the sea with your rod." So it divided, and each separate part become like the huge, firm mass of a mountain.

64. And We made the other party approach there.

65. We delivered Moses and all who were with him;

66. But We drowned the others.

67. Verily in this is a sign: but most of them do not believe.

68. And verily your Lord is He, the Exalted in Might, Most Merciful.

69. And rehearse to them (something of) Abraham's story.

70. See, he said to his father and his people: "What do you worship?"

71. They said: "We worship idols, and we remain constantly in attendance on them."

72. He said: "Do they listen to you when you call (on them),

73. Or do you good or harm?"

74. They said: "Nay, but we found our fathers doing thus (what we do)."

75. He said: "Do you then see whom you have been worshipping -

76. You and your fathers before you? -

77. For they are enemies to me; not so the Lord and Cherisher of the Worlds;

78. Who created me, and it is He Who guides me;

79. Who gives me food and drink.

80. And when I am ill, it is He Who cures me;

81. Who will cause me to die, and then to live (again);

82. And Who, I hope, will forgive me my faults on the day of judgement.

83. O my Lord! Bestow wisdom on me, and join me with the righteous;

84. Grant me honourable mention on the tongue of truth among the latest (generations);

85. Make me one of the inheritors of the garden of bliss;

86. Forgive my father, for that he is among those astray;

87. And let me not be in disgrace on the day when (men) will be raised up -

88. The day on which neither wealth nor sons will benefit,

89. But only he (will prosper) that brings to Allah a sound heart;

90. To the righteous the garden will be brought near,

91. And to those straying in evil, the fire will be placed in full view;

92. And it shall be said to them: 'Where are the (gods) you worshipped -

93. Besides Allah? Can they help you or help themselves?'

94. Then they will be thrown headlong into the (fire) - they and those straying in evil,

95. And the whole hosts of Iblis together.

96. They will say there in their mutual bickerings:

97. 'By Allah, we were truly in an error manifest,

98. When we held you as equals with the Lord of the Worlds;

99. And our seducers were only those who were steeped in guilt.

100. Now then, we have none to intercede (for us),

101. Nor a single friend to feel (for us).

102. Now if we only had a chance of return, we shall truly be of those who believe!'"

103. Verily in this is a sign but most of them do not believe.

104. And verily the Lord is He, the Exalted in Might, Most Merciful.

105. The people of Noah rejected the messengers.

106. See, their brother Noah said to them: "Will you not fear (Allah)?"

107. "I am to you a messenger worthy of all trust:

108. So fear Allah, and obey me."

109. "No reward do I ask of you for it: my reward is only from the Lord of the Worlds:

110. So fear Allah, and obey me."

111. They said: "Shall we believe in you when it is the meanest that follow you?"

112. He said: "And what do I know as to what they do?

113. Their account is only with my Lord, if you could (but) understand.

114. I am not one to drive away those who believe.

115. I am sent only to warn plainly in public."

116. They said: "If you desist not, O Noah! You shall be stoned (to death)."

117. He said: "O my Lord! Truly my people have rejected me.

118. Judge you, then, between me and them openly, and deliver me and those of the believers who are with me."

119. So We delivered him and those with him, in the ark filled (with all creatures).

120. Thereafter We drowned those who remained behind.

121. Verily in this is a sign: but most of them do not believe.

122. And verily your Lord is He, the Exalted in Might, Most Merciful.

123. The 'Ad (people) rejected the prophets.

124. See, their brother Hud said to them: "Will you not fear (Allah)?

125. I am to you a messenger worthy of all trust.

126. So fear Allah and obey me."

127. "No reward do I ask of you for it: my reward is only from the Lord of the Worlds."

128. "Do you build a landmark on every high place to amuse yourselves?

129. And do you get for yourselves fine buildings in the hope of living in it (forever)?

130. And when you exert your strong hand, do you do it like men of absolute power?

131. Now fear Allah, and obey me.

132. Yea, fear Him Who has bestowed on you freely all that you know.

133. Freely has He bestowed on you cattle and sons -

134. And gardens and springs.

135. Truly I fear for you the penalty of a great day."

136. They said: "It is the same to us whether you admonish us or be not among (our) admonishers!

137. This is no other than a customary device of the ancients,

138. And we are not the ones to receive pains and penalties!"

139. So they rejected him, and We destroyed them. Verily in this is a sign: but most of them do not believe.

140. And verily your Lord is He, the Exalted in Might, Most Merciful.

141. The Thamud (people) rejected the messengers.

142. See, their brother Salih said to them: "Will you fear (Allah)?

143. "I am to you a messenger worthy of all trust.

144. So fear Allah, and obey me.

145. No reward do I ask of you for it: my reward is only from the Lord of the Worlds.

146. Will you be left secure, in (the enjoyment of) all that you have here? -

147. Gardens and Springs,

148. And corn-fields and date-palms with spathes near breaking (with the weight of fruit)?

149. And you carve houses out of (rocky) mountains with great skill.

150. But fear Allah and obey me;

151. And follow not the bidding of those who are extravagant -

152. Who make mischief in the land, and mend not (their ways)."

153. They said: "You are only of those bewitched!

154. You are no more than a mortal like us: then bring us a sign, if you tell the truth!"

155. He said: "Here is a she-camel: she has a right of watering, and you have a right of watering, (severally) on a day appointed.

156. Touch her not with harm, lest the penalty of a great day seize you."

157. But they hamstrung her: then did they become full of regrets.

158. But the penalty seized them. Verily in this is a sign: but most of them do not believe.

159. And verily your Lord is He, the Exalted in Might, Most Merciful.

160. The people of Lot rejected the messengers.

161. See, their brother Lot said to them: "Will you not fear (Allah)?

162. I am to you a messenger worthy of all trust.

163. So fear Allah and obey me.

164. No reward do I ask of you for it: my reward is only from the Lord of the Worlds.

165. Of all the creatures in the world, will you approach males,

166. And leave those whom Allah has created for you to be your mates? Nay, you are a people transgressing (all limits)!"

167. They said: "If you desist not O Lot! You will assuredly be cast out!"

168. He said: "I do detest your doings:"

169. "O my Lord! Deliver me and my family from such things as they do!"

170. So We delivered him and his family - all

171. Except an old woman who lingered behind.

172. But the rest We destroyed utterly.

173. We rained down on them a shower (of brimstone): and evil was the shower on those who were admonished (but heeded not)!

174. Verily in this is a sign: but most of them do not believe.

175. And verily your Lord is He, the Exalted in Might, Most Merciful.

176. The Companions of the Wood rejected the prophets.

177. See, Shu'ayb said to them: "Will you not fear (Allah)?

178. I am to you a messenger worthy of all trust.

179. So fear Allah and obey me.

180. No reward do I ask of you for it: my reward is only from the Lord of the Worlds.

181. Give just measure, and cause no loss (to others by fraud).

182. And weigh with scales true and upright.

183. And withhold not things justly due to men, nor do evil in the land, working mischief.

184. And fear Him Who created you and (Who created) the generations before (you)."

185. They said: "You are only one of those bewitched!

186. You are no more than a mortal like us, and indeed we think you are a liar!

187. Now cause a piece of the sky to fall on us, if you are truthful!"

188. He said: "My Lord knows best what you do."

189. But they rejected him. Then the punishment of a day of overshadowing gloom seized them and that was the penalty of a great day.

190. Verily in that is a sign: but most of them do not believe.

191. And verily your Lord is He, the Exalted in Might, Most Merciful.

192. Verily this is a revelation from the Lord of the Worlds:

193. With it came down the spirit of faith and truth -

194. To your heart and mind, that you may admonish -

195. In the perspicuous Arabic tongue.

196. Without doubt it is (announced) in the revealed books of former peoples.

197. Is it not a sign to them that the learned of the Children of Israel knew it (as true)?

198. Had We revealed it to any of the non-Arabs,

199. And had he recited it to them, they would not have believed in it.

200. Thus have We caused it to enter the hearts of the sinners.

201. They will not believe in it until they see the grievous penalty;

202. But the (penalty) will come to them of a sudden, while they perceive it not;

203. Then they will say: "Shall we be respited?"

204. Do they then ask for Our penalty to be hastened on?

205. Do you see? If We do let them enjoy (this life) for a few years,

206. Yet there comes to them at length the (punishment) which they were promised!

207. It will profit them not that they enjoyed (this life)!

208. Never did We destroy a population, but had its warners -

209. By way of reminder; and We never are unjust.

210. No evil ones have brought down this (revelation):

211. It would neither suit them nor would they be able (to produce it).

212. Indeed they have been removed far from even (a chance of) hearing it.

213. So call not on any other god with Allah, or you will be among those under the penalty.

214. And admonish your nearest relatives,

215. And lower your wing to the believers who follow you.

216. Then if they disobey you say: "I am free (of responsibility) for what you do!"

217. And put your trust on the Exalted in Might, the Merciful -

218. Who sees you standing up (in prayer),

219. And your movements among those who prostrate themselves.

220. For it is He Who hears and knows all things.

221. Shall I inform you (O people!), on whom it is that the evil ones descend?

222. They descend on every lying wicked person,

223. (Into whose ears) they pour hearsay vanities, and most of them are liars.

224. And the poets - it is those straying in evil who follow them:

225. Do you not see that they wander distracted in every valley? -

226. And that they say what they practice not? -

227. Except those who believe, work righteousness, engage much in the remembrance of Allah, and defend themselves only after they are unjustly attacked. And soon will the unjust assailants know what vicissitudes their affairs will take!

Surah 27: *An-Naml*
(The Ant)

In the name of Allah,
Most Gracious, Most Merciful.

1. *Ta Sin.* These are verses of the Qur'an - a book that makes (things) clear;

2. A guide; and glad tidings for the believers -

3. Those who establish regular prayers and give in regular charity, and also have (full) assurance of the hereafter.

4. As to those who believe not in the hereafter, We have made their deeds pleasing in their eyes; and so they wander about in distraction.

5. Such are they for whom a grievous penalty is (waiting): and in the hereafter theirs will be the greatest loss.

6. As to you, the Qur'an is bestowed upon you from the presence of One Who is Wise and All-Knowing.

7. See! Moses said to his family: "I perceive a fire; soon will I bring you from there some information, or I will bring you a burning brand to light our fuel, that you may warm yourselves."

8. But when he came to the (fire), a voice was heard: "Blessed are those in the fire and those around: and Glory to Allah, the Lord of the Worlds.

9. O Moses! Verily, I am Allah, the Exalted in Might, the Wise!...

10. Now do you throw your rod!" But when he saw it moving (of its own accord) as if it had been a snake, he turned back in retreat, and retraced not his steps: "O Moses!" (it was said) "Fear not: truly, in My presence, those called as messengers have no fear -

11. But if any have done wrong and have thereafter substituted good to take the place of evil, truly I am Oft-Forgiving, Most Merciful.

12. Now put your hand into your chest, and it will come out white without stain (or harm): (these are) among the nine signs (you will take) to Pharaoh and his people: for they are a people rebellious in transgression."

13. But when our signs came to them, that should have opened their eyes, they said: "This is sorcery manifest!"

14. And they rejected those signs in iniquity and arrogance, though their souls were convinced of it: so see what was the end of those who acted corruptly!

15. We gave (in the past) knowledge to David and Solomon; and they both said: "Praise be to Allah, Who has favoured us above many of His servants who believe!"

16. And Solomon was David's heir. He said: "O you people! We have been taught the speech of birds, and on us has been bestowed (a little) of all things: this is indeed grace manifest (from Allah)."

17. And before Solomon were marshalled his forces - of Jinns and men and birds, and they were all kept in order and ranks.

18. At length, when they came to a (lowly) valley of ants, one of the ants said: "O you ants, get into your habitations, lest Solomon and his forces crush you (under foot) without knowing it."

19. So he smiled, amused at her speech; and he said: "O my Lord! So order me that I may be grateful for Your favours, which You have bestowed on me and on my parents, and that I may work the righteousness that will please You; and admit me, by Your grace, to the ranks of Your righteous servants."

20. And he took a muster of the birds; and he said: "Why is it I see not the Hoopoe? Or is he among the absentees?

21. I will certainly punish him with a severe penalty, or execute him, unless he bring me a clear reason (for absence)."

22. But the Hoopoe tarried not far: I encompassed (territory) which you have not encompassed, and I have come to you from Saba with tidings true.

23. "I found (there) a woman ruling over them and provided with every requisite; and she has a magnificent throne."

24. "I found her and her people worshipping the sun besides Allah: Satan has made their deeds seem pleasing in their eyes, and has kept them away from the path - so they receive no guidance -

25. (Kept them away from the path), that they should not worship Allah, Who brings to light what is hidden in the heavens and the earth, and knows what you hide and what you reveal.

26. Allah! There is no god but He! Lord of the Throne Supreme!"

27. (Solomon) said: "Soon shall we see whether you have told the truth or lied!"

28. "Go you, with this letter of mine, and deliver it to them: then draw back from them, and (wait to) see what answer they return".

29. (The Queen) said: "You chiefs! Here is - delivered to me - a letter worthy of respect.

30. It is from Solomon, and is (as follows): 'In the name of Allah, Most Gracious, Most Merciful:

31. Be you not arrogant against me, but come to me in submission to the true religion.'"

32. She said: "You chiefs! Advise me in (this) my affair: no affair have I decided except in your presence."

33. They said: "We are endued with strength, and given to vehement war: but the command is with you; so consider what you will command."

34. She said: "Kings, when they enter a country, despoil it, and make the noblest of its people its meanest: thus do they behave.

35. But I am going to send him a present, and (wait) to see with what (answer) return (my) ambassadors."

36. How when (the embassy) came to Solomon, he said: "Will you give me abundance in wealth? But that which Allah has given me is better than that which He has given you! Nay, it is you who rejoice in your gift!

37. Go back to them, and be sure we shall come to them with such hosts as they will never be able to meet: we shall expel them from there in disgrace, and they will feel humbled (indeed)."

38. He said (to his own men): "You chiefs! Which of you can bring me her throne before they come to me in submission?"

39. Said an Ifrit, of the Jinns: "I will bring it to you before you rise from your council: indeed I have full strength for the purpose, and may be trusted."

40. Said one who had knowledge of the book: "I will bring it to you within the twinkling of an eye!" Then when (Solomon) saw it placed firmly before him, he said: "This is by the grace of my Lord! To test me whether I am grateful or ungrateful! And if any is grateful, truly his gratitude is (a gain) for his own soul; but if any is ungrateful, truly my Lord is Free of All Needs, Supreme in Honour!"

41. He said: "Transform her throne out of all recognition by her: let us see whether she is guided (to the truth) or is one of those who receive no guidance."

42. So when she arrived, she was asked, "Is this your throne?" She said, "It was just like this" and knowledge was bestowed on us in advance of this, and we have submitted to Allah (in Islam).

43. And he diverted her from the worship of others besides Allah: for she was (sprung) of a people that had no faith.

44. She was asked to enter that lofty palace; but when she saw it, she thought it was a lake of water, and she (tucked up her skirts), uncovering her legs. He said. "This is but a palace paved smooth with slabs of glass." She said: "My Lord! I have indeed wronged my soul: I do (now) submit (in Islam) with Solomon to the Lord of the Worlds."

45. We sent (before), to the Thamud, their brother Salih, saying: "Serve Allah": but see, they became two factions quarrelling with each other.

46. He said: "O my people! Why do you ask to hasten on the evil in preference to the good? If only you ask Allah for forgiveness, you may hope to receive mercy."

47. They said: "Ill omen do we augur from you and those that are with you." He said: "Your ill omen is with Allah, yea, you are a people under trial."

48. There were in the city nine men of a family who made mischief in the land, and would not reform.

49. They said: "Swear a mutual oath by Allah that we shall make a secret night attack on him and his people, and that we shall then say to his heir (when he seeks vengeance): 'We were not present at the slaughter of his people and we are positively telling the truth.'"

50. They plotted and planned, but We too planned, even while they perceived it not.

51. Then see what was the end of their plot! - This, that We destroyed them and their people, all (of them).

52. Now such were their houses - in utter ruin - because they practised wrongdoing. Verily in this is a sign for people of knowledge.

53. And We saved those who believed and practised righteousness.

54. We also sent Lot (as a messenger): behold, he said to his people, "Do you do what is shameful though you see (its iniquity)?

55. Would you really approach men in your lusts rather than women? Nay, you are a people (grossly) ignorant!"

56. But his people gave no other answer but this: they said, "Drive out the followers of Lot from your city: these are indeed men who want to be clean and pure!"

57. But We saved him and his family, except his wife: her We destined to be of those who lagged behind.

58. And We rained down on them a shower (of brimstone): and evil was the shower on those who were admonished (but heeded not)!

59. Say: Praise be to Allah, and peace on His servants whom He has chosen (for his message). (Who) is better? - Allah or the false gods they associate with Him?

60. Or, who has created the heaven and the earth, and who sends you down rain from the sky? Yea, with it We cause to grow well-planted orchards full of beauty and delight: it is not in your power to cause the growth of the trees in them. (Can there be another) god besides Allah? Nay, they are a people who swerve from justice.

61. Or, who has made the earth firm to live in; made rivers in its midst; set thereon mountains immovable, and made a separating bar between the two bodies of flowing water? (Can there be another) god besides Allah? Nay, most of them know not.

62. Or, who listens to the (soul) distressed when it calls on Him, and who relieves its suffering, and makes you (mankind) inheritors of the earth? (Can there be another) god besides Allah? Little it is that you heed!

63. Or, who guides you through the depths of darkness on land and sea, and who sends the winds as heralds of glad tidings, going before his mercy? (Can there be another) god besides Allah? - High is Allah above what they associate with Him!

64. Or, who originates creation, then repeats it, and who gives you sustenance from heaven and earth? (Can there be another) god besides Allah? Say, "Bring forward your argument, if you are telling the truth!"

65. Say: None in the heavens or on earth, except Allah, knows what is hidden: nor can they perceive when they shall be raised up (for judgement).

66. Still less can their knowledge comprehend the hereafter: nay, they are in doubt and uncertainty of it; nay, they are blind to it!

67. The unbelievers say: "What! When we become dust - we and our fathers - shall we really be raised (from the dead)?

68. It is true we were promised this - we and our fathers before (us): these are nothing but tales of the ancients."

69. Say: "Go you through the earth and see what has been the end of those guilty (of sin)."

70. But grieve not over them, nor distress yourself because of their plots.

71. They also say: "When will this promise (come to pass)? (Say) if you are truthful."

72. Say: "It may be that some of the events which you wish to hasten on may be (close) in your pursuit!"

73. But verily your Lord is full of grace to mankind: yet most of them are ungrateful.

74. And verily your Lord knows all that their hearts do hide, as well as all that they reveal.

75. Nor is there anything of the unseen, in heaven or earth, but is (recorded) in a clear record.

76. Verily this Qur'an does explain to the Children of Israel most of the matters in which they disagree.

77. And it certainly is a guide and mercy to those who believe.

78. Verily, your Lord will decide between them by His decree: and He is Exalted in Might, All-Knowing.

79. So put your trust in Allah: for you are on (the path of) manifest truth.

80. Truly you can not cause the dead to listen, nor can you cause the deaf to

hear the call, (especially) when they turn back in retreat.

81. Nor can you be a guide to the blind, (to prevent them) from straying; only those will you get to listen who believe in Our signs, and they will bow in Islam.

82. And when the word is fulfilled against them (the unjust) We shall produce from the earth a beast to (face) them: he will speak to them, for that mankind did not believe with assurance in our signs.

83. One day We shall gather together from every people a troop of those who reject Our signs, and they shall be kept in ranks -

84. Until, when they come (before the judgement-seat), Allah will say: "Did you reject My signs, though you comprehended them not in knowledge, or what was it you did?"

85. And the word will be fulfilled against them, because of their wrongdoing, and they will be unable to speak (in plea).

86. Do they not see that We have made the night for them to rest in and the day to give them light? Verily in this are signs for any people that believe!

87. And the day that the trumpet will be sounded - then will be smitten with terror those who are in the heavens, and those who are on earth, except such as Allah will please (to exempt): and all shall come to His (presence) as beings conscious of their lowliness.

88. You see the mountains and think them firmly fixed: but they shall pass away as the clouds pass away: (such

is) the artistry of Allah, Who disposes of all things in perfect order: for He is well-acquainted with all that you do.

89. If any do good, good will (accrue) to them from it; and they will be secure from terror that day.

90. And if any do evil, their faces will be thrown headlong into the fire: "Do you receive a reward other than that which you have earned by your deeds?"

91. For me, I have been commanded to serve the Lord of this city, Him Who has sanctified it and to Whom (belong) all things: and I am commanded to be of those who bow in Islam to Allah's Will -

92. And to rehearse the Qur'an: and if any accept guidance, they do it for the good of their own souls, and if any stray, say: "I am a warner."

93. And say: "Praise be to Allah, Who will soon show you His signs, so that you shall know them"; and your Lord is not unmindful of all that you do.

Surah 28: **Al-Qasas**
(The Story)

In the name of Allah,
Most Gracious, Most Merciful.

1. *Ta Sin Mim.*

2. These are verses of the book that makes (things) clear.

3. We rehearse to you some of the story of Moses and Pharaoh in truth, for people who believe.

4. Truly Pharaoh elated himself in the land and broke up its people into sections, depressing a small group among them: their sons he slew, but he kept alive their females: for he was indeed a maker of mischief.

5. And We wished to be gracious to those who were being depressed on the land. To make them leaders (in faith) and make them heirs,

6. To establish a firm place for them in the land, and to show Pharaoh, Haman, and their hosts, at their hands, the very things against which they were taking precautions.

7. So We sent this inspiration to the mother of Moses: "Suckle (your child), but when you have fears about him, cast him into the river, but fear not nor grieve: for We shall restore him to you, and We shall make him one of Our prophets."

8. Then the people of Pharaoh picked him up (from the river): (it was intended) that (Moses) should be to them an adversary and a cause of sorrow: for Pharaoh and Haman and (all) their forces were men of sin.

9. The wife of Pharaoh said: "(Here is) a joy of the eye, for me and for you: slay him not. It may be that he will be of use to us, or we may adopt him as a son." And they perceived not (what they were doing)!

10. But there came to be a void in the heart of the mother of Moses: she was going almost to disclose his (case), had We not strengthened her heart (with faith), so that she might remain a (firm) believer.

11. And she said to the sister of (Moses), "Follow him." So she (the sister) watched him in the character of a stranger. And they knew not.

12. And We ordained that he refused suck at first, until (his sister came up and) said: "Shall I point out to you the people of a house that will nourish and bring him up for you and be sincerely attached to him?"

13. Thus did We restore him to his mother, that her eye might be comforted, that she might not grieve and that she might know that the promise of Allah is true; but most of them do not understand.

14. When he reached full age, and was firmly established (in life), We bestowed on him wisdom and knowledge: for thus do We reward those who do good.

15. And he entered the city at a time when its people were not watching: and he found there two men fighting - one of his own people and the other, of his foes. Now the man of his own people appealed to him against his foe, and Moses struck him with his fist and made an end of him. He said: "This is a work of evil (Satan): for he is an enemy that manifestly misleads!"

16. He prayed: "O my Lord! I have indeed wronged my soul! Do You then forgive me!" So (Allah) forgave him: for He is the Oft-Forgiving, Most Merciful.

17. He said: "O my Lord! For that You have bestowed Your grace on me, never shall I be a help to those who sin!"

18. So he saw the morning in the city, looking about, in a state of fear, when behold, the man who had, the day before, sought his help called aloud for his help (again). Moses said to him: "You are truly, it is clear, a quarrelsome fellow!"

19. Then, when he decided to lay hold of the man who was an enemy to both of them, that man said: "O Moses! Is it your intention to slay me as you slew a man yesterday? Your intention is none other than to become a powerful violent man in the land, and not to be one who sets things right!"

20. And there came a man, running, from the furthest end of the city. He said: "O Moses! The chiefs are taking counsel together about you, to slay you: so get you away, for I do give you sincere advice."

21. He therefore got away from it, looking about, in a state of fear. He prayed: "O my Lord! Save me from people given to wrongdoing."

22. Then, when he turned his face towards (the land of) Madyan, he said: "I do hope that my Lord will show me the smooth and straight path."

23. And when he arrived at the watering (place) in Madyan, he found there a group of men watering (their flocks), and besides them he found two women who were keeping back (their flocks). He said: "What is the matter with you?" They said: "We cannot water (our flocks) until the shepherds take back (their flocks): and our father is a very old man."

24. So he watered (their flocks) for them; then he turned back to the shade, and said: "O my Lord! Truly am I in (desperate) need of any good that You do send me!"

25. Afterwards one of the (girls) came (back) to him, walking bashfully. She said: "My father invites you that he may reward you for having watered (our flocks) for us." So when he came to him and narrated the story, he said: "Fear you not: (well) have you escaped from unjust people."

26. Said one of the (girls): "O my (dear) father! Engage him on wages: truly the best of men for you to employ is the (man) who is strong and trusty".

27. He said: "I intended to wed one of these my daughters to you, on condition that you serve me for eight years; but if you complete ten years, it will be (grace) from you. But I intend not to place you under a difficulty: you will find me, indeed, if Allah wills, one of the righteous."

28. He said: "Be that (the agreement) between me and you: whichever of the two terms I fulfil, let there be no ill-will to me. Be Allah a witness to what we say."

29. Now when Moses had fulfilled the term, and was travelling with his family, he perceived a fire in the direction of mount Tur. He said to his family: "Stay you; I perceive a fire; I hope to bring you from there some information, or a burning firebrand, that you may warm yourselves."

30. But when he came to the (fire), a voice was heard from the right bank of the valley, from a tree in sacred ground: "O Moses! Verily I am Allah, the Lord of the Worlds."

31. "Now do you throw your rod!" But when he saw it moving (of its own accord) as if it had been a snake, He turned back in retreat, and retraced not his steps: "O Moses!" (It was said) "Draw near, and fear not: for you are of those who are secure.

32. Move your hand into your chest, and it will come out white without stain (or harm), and draw your hand close to your side (to guard) against fear. Those are the two credentials from your Lord to Pharaoh and his chiefs: for truly they are a people rebellious and wicked."

33. He said: "O my Lord! I have slain a man among them, and I fear lest they slay me.

34. And my brother Aaron - he is more eloquent in speech than I: so send him with me as a helper, to confirm (and strengthen) me; for I fear that they may accuse me of falsehood."

35. He said: "We will certainly strengthen your arm through your brother, and invest you both with authority, so they shall not be able to touch you: with Our signs shall you triumph, you two as well as those who follow you."

36. When Moses came to them with Our clear signs, they said: "This is nothing but sorcery faked up: never did we hear the like among our fathers of old!"

37. Moses said: "My Lord knows best who it is that comes with guidance from Him and whose end will be best in the hereafter: certain it is that the wrongdoers will not prosper."

38. Pharaoh said: "O chiefs! No god do I know for you but myself: therefore, "O Haman! Light me a (kiln to bake bricks) out of clay, and build me a lofty palace, that I may mount up to the god of Moses; but as far as I am concerned, I think (Moses) is a liar!"

39. And he was arrogant and insolent in the land, beyond reason he and his hosts: they thought that they would not have to return to Us!

40. So We seized him and his hosts, and We flung them into the sea: now see what was the end of those who did wrong!

41. And We made them (but) leaders inviting to the fire; and on the day of judgement no help shall they find.

42. In this world We made a curse to follow them: and on the day of judgement they will be among the loathed (and despised).

43. We did reveal to Moses the book after We had destroyed the earlier generations, (to give) insight to men, and guidance and mercy, that they might receive admonition.

44. You were not on the western side when We decreed the commission to Moses, nor were you a witness (of those events).

45. But We raised up (new) generations, and long were the ages that passed over them; but you were not a dweller among the people of Madyan, rehearsing Our signs to them; but it is We Who send prophets (with inspiration).

46. Nor were you at the side of (the mountain of) Tur when We called (to Moses). Yet (are you sent) as a mercy from your Lord, to give warning to a people to whom no warner had come before you; in order that they may receive admonition.

47. If (We had) not (sent you to the Quraysh) - in case a calamity should seize them for (the deeds) that their hands have sent before they might say: "Our Lord! Why did You not send us a messenger? We should then have followed the signs and been amongst those who believe!"

48. But (now), when the truth has come to them from Ourselves, They say "Why are not (signs) sent to him, like those which were sent to Moses?" Do they not then reject (the signs) which were formerly sent to Moses? They say: "Two kinds of sorcery, each assisting the other!" And they say: "For us we reject all (such things)!"

49. Say: "Then bring you a book from Allah, which is a better guide than either of them, that I may follow it! (Do) if you are truthful!"

50. But if they do not listen to you, know that they only follow their own lusts: and who is more astray than one who follows his own lusts, devoid of guidance from Allah? For Allah guides not people given to wrongdoing.

51. Now have We caused the word to reach them themselves, in order that they may receive admonition.

52. Those to whom We sent the book before this - they do believe in this (revelation);

53. And when it is recited to them they say: "We believe in it, for it is the truth from our Lord: indeed we have been Muslims (bowing to Allah's Will) from before this."

54. Twice will they be given their reward, for that they have persevered, that they avert evil with good, and that they spend (in charity) out of what We have given them.

55. And when they hear vain talk, they turn away from it and say: "To us our deeds, and to you yours; peace be to you: we seek not the ignorant."

56. It is true you will not be able to guide everyone whom you love: but Allah guides those whom He will and He knows best those who receive guidance.

57. They say: "If we were to follow the guidance with you we should be snatched away from our land." Have We not established for them a secure sanctuary, to which are brought as tribute fruits of all kinds - a provision from Ourselves? But most of them understand not.

58. And how many populations We destroyed, which exulted in their life (of ease and plenty)! Now those habitations of theirs, after them are deserted - all but a (miserable) few! And We are their heirs!

59. Nor was your Lord the one to destroy a population until He had sent to its centre a messenger, rehearsing to them Our signs: nor are We going to destroy a population except when its members practice iniquity.

60. The (material) things which you are given are but the conveniences of this life and the glitter of it; but that which is with Allah is better and more enduring: will you not then be wise?

61. Are (these two) alike? One to whom We have made a goodly promise and who is going to reach its (fulfilment). And one to whom We have given the good things of this life, but who, on the day of judgement, is to be among those brought up (for punishment)?

62. That day Allah will call to them, and say: "Where are my 'partners'? whom you imagined (to be such)?"

63. Those against whom the charge will be proved, will say: "Our Lord! These are the ones whom we led astray; we led them astray, as we were astray ourselves; we free ourselves (from them) in Your presence! It was not us they worshipped."

64. It will be said (to them): "Call upon your 'partners' (for help)"; they will call upon them but they will not listen to them; and they will see the penalty (before them); (how they will wish) 'If only they had been open to guidance!'

65. That day (Allah) will call to them, and say: "What was the answer you gave to the messengers?"

66. Then the (whole) story that day will seem obscure to them (like light to the blind), and they will not be able (even) to question each other.

67. But any that (in this life) had repented, believed, and worked righteousness, will have hopes to be among those who achieve salvation.

68. Your Lord does create and choose as He pleases: no choice have they (in the matter): Glory to Allah! And far is He above the partners they ascribe (to Him)!

69. And your Lord knows all that their hearts conceal and all that they reveal.

70. And He is Allah: there is no god but He. To Him be praise, at the first and at the last; for Him is the command and to Him shall you (all) be brought back.

71. Say: Do you see? If Allah were to make the night perpetual over you to the day of judgement, what god is there other than Allah, who can give you enlightenment? Will you not then listen?

72. Say: Do you see? If Allah were to make the day perpetual over you to the day of judgement, what god is there other than Allah, who can give you a night in which you can rest? Will you not then see?

73. It is out of His mercy that He has made for you night and day - that you may rest in it, and that you may seek of His grace - and in order that you may be grateful.

74. The day that He will call on them, He will say: "Where are My 'partners' whom you imagined (to be such)?"

75. And from each people shall We draw a witness, and We shall say: "Produce your proof"; then shall they know that the truth is in Allah (alone), and the (lies) which they invented will leave them in the lurch.

76. Qarun was doubtless of the people of Moses; but he acted insolently towards them: such were the treasures We had bestowed on him, that their very keys would have been a burden to a body of strong men: See, his people said to him: "Exult not, for Allah loves not those who exult (in riches).

77. But seek, with the (wealth) which Allah has bestowed on you, the home of the hereafter, nor forget your portion in this world; but do you good, as Allah has been good to you, and seek not (occasions for) mischief in the land: for Allah loves not those who do mischief."

78. He said: "This has been given to me because of a certain knowledge which I have." Did he not know that Allah had destroyed, before him (whole) generations - which were superior to him in strength and greater in amount (of riches) they had collected? But the wicked are not called (immediately) to account for their sins.

79. So he went forth among his people in the (pride of his worldly) glitter. Said those whose aim is the life of this world: "Oh that we had the like of what Qarun has got! For he is truly a lord of mighty good fortune."

80. But those who had been granted (true) knowledge said: "Alas for you! The reward of Allah (in the hereafter) is best for those who believe and work righteousness: but this none shall attain, save those who steadfastly persevere (in good)."

81. Then We caused the earth to swallow him up and his house; and he had not (the least little) party to help him against Allah nor could he defend himself.

82. And those who had envied his position the day before began to say in the morning: "Ah! It is indeed

Allah Who enlarges the provision or restricts it, to any of His servants He pleases! Had it not been that Allah was gracious to us, He could have caused the earth to swallow us up! Ah! Those who reject Allah will assuredly never prosper."

83. That House of the hereafter We shall give to those who intend not high-handedness or mischief on earth: and the end is (best) for the righteous.

84. If any does good, the reward to him is better than his deed; but if any does evil, the doers of evil are only punished (to the extent) of their deeds.

85. Verily He Who ordained the Qur'an for you will bring you back to the place of return. Say: "My Lord knows best who it is that brings true guidance and who is in manifest error."

86. And you had not expected that the book would be sent to you except as a mercy from your Lord: therefore lend not your support in any way to those who reject (Allah's message).

87. And let nothing keep you back from the signs of Allah after they have been revealed to you: and invite (men) to your Lord and be not of the company of those who join gods with Allah.

88. And call not besides Allah on another god. There is no god but He. Everything (that exists) will perish except His own Face. To Him belongs the command and to Him will you (all) be brought back.

Surah 29: *Al-'Ankabut* (The Spider)

In the name of Allah, Most Gracious, Most Merciful.

1. *Alif Lam Mim.*

2. Do men think that they will be left alone on saying, "We believe," and that they will not be tested?

3. We did test those before them, and Allah will certainly know those who are true from those who are false.

4. Do those who practice evil think that they will get the better of Us? Evil is their judgement!

5. For those whose hopes are in the meeting with Allah (in the hereafter, let them strive); for the term (appointed) by Allah is surely coming: and He hears and knows (all things).

6. And if any strive (with might and main), they do so for their own souls: for Allah is free of all needs from all creation.

7. Those who believe and work righteous deeds - from them shall We blot out all evil (that may be) in them, and We shall reward them according to the best of their deeds.

8. We have enjoined on man kindness to parents: but if they (either of them) strive (to force) you to join with Me (in worship) anything of which you have no knowledge, obey them not. You have (all) to return to Me, and I will tell you (the truth) of all that you did.

9. And those who believe and work righteous deeds - them shall We admit to the company of the righteous.

10. Then there are among men such as say: "We believe in Allah"; but when they suffer affliction in (the cause of) Allah, they treat men's oppression as if it were the wrath of Allah! And if help comes (to you) from your Lord, they are sure to say, "We have (always) been with you!" Does not Allah know best all that is in the hearts of all creation?

11. And Allah most certainly knows those who believe, and as certainly those who are hypocrites.

12. And the unbelievers say to those who believe: "Follow our path, and we will bear (the consequences) of your faults." Never in the least will they bear their faults: in fact they are liars!

13. They will bear their own burdens, and (other) burdens along with their own, and on the day of judgement they will be called to account for their falsehoods.

14. We (once) sent Noah to his people, and he stayed among them a thousand years less fifty: but the deluge overwhelmed them while they (persisted in) sin.

15. But We saved him and the companions of the ark, and We made the (ark) a sign for all peoples!

16. And (We also saved) Abraham: See, he said to his people: "Serve Allah and fear Him: that will be best for you - if you understand!

17. For you do worship idols besides Allah, and you invent falsehood. The things that you worship besides Allah have no power to give you sustenance; then seek you sustenance from Allah, serve Him, and be grateful to Him: to Him will be your return.

18. And if you reject (the message) so did generations before you; and the duty of the messenger is only to preach publicly (and clearly)."

19. Do they not see how Allah originates creation, then repeats it: truly that is easy for Allah.

20. Say: "Travel through the earth and see how Allah did originate creation: so will Allah produce a later creation: for Allah has power over all things."

21. "He punishes whom He pleases, and He grants mercy to whom He pleases, and towards Him are you turned."

22. "Not on earth nor in heaven will you be able (fleeing) to frustrate (His plan), nor have you besides Allah, any protector or helper."

23. Those who reject the signs of Allah and the meeting with Him (in the hereafter) - it is they who shall despair of My mercy: it is they who will (suffer) a most grievous penalty.

24. So nothing was the answer of (Abraham's) people except that they said: "Slay him or burn him." But Allah did save him from the fire: verily in this are signs for people who believe.

25. And he said: "For you, you have taken (for worship) idols besides Allah, out of mutual love and regard between yourselves in this life; but on the day of judgement you shall disown each other and curse each other: and

your abode will be the fire, and you shall have none to help.

26. But Lot had faith in him; he said: "I will leave home for the sake of my Lord: for He is Exalted in Might, and Wise."

27. And We gave (Abraham) Isaac and Jacob, and ordained among his progeny prophethood and revelation, and We granted him his reward in this life; and he was in the hereafter (of the company) of the righteous.

28. And (remember) Lot: see, he said to his people: "You do commit lewdness, such as no people in creation (ever) committed before you."

29. "Do you indeed approach men and cut off the highway? - And practice wickedness (even) in your councils?" But his people gave no answer but this: they said: "Bring us the wrath of Allah if you tell the truth."

30. He said: "O my Lord! Help You me against people who do mischief!"

31. When Our messengers came to Abraham with the good news, they said: "We are indeed going to destroy the people of this township: for truly they are (addicted to) crime."

32. He said: "But there is Lot there." They said: "Well do we know who is there; we will certainly save him and his following - except his wife; she is of those who lag behind!"

33. And when Our messengers came to Lot, he was grieved on their account, and felt himself powerless (to protect) them: but they said "Fear you not, nor grieve: we are (here) to save you and your following, except your wife: she is of those who lag behind.

34. For we are going to bring down on the people of this township a punishment from heaven, because they have been wickedly rebellious."

35. And We have left of it an evident sign, for any people who (care to) understand.

36. To the Madyan (people) (We sent) their brother Shu'ayb. Then he said: "O my people! Serve Allah, and fear the last day: nor commit evil on the earth with intent to do mischief."

37. But they rejected him: then the mighty blast seized them, and they lay prostrate in their homes by the morning.

38. Remember also the 'Ad and the Thamud (people): clearly will appear to you from (the traces) of their buildings (their fate): the evil one made their deeds alluring to them, and kept them back from the path, though they were gifted with intelligence and skill.

39. (Remember also) Qarun, Pharaoh, and Haman: there came to them Moses with clear signs, but they behaved with insolence on the earth; yet they could not overreach (Us).

40. Each one of them We seized for his crime: of them, against some We sent a violent tornado (with showers of stones); some were caught by a (mighty) blast; some We caused the earth to swallow up; and some We drowned (in the waters); it was not Allah Who injured (or oppressed) them; they injured (and oppressed) their own souls.

41. The parable of those who take protectors other than Allah is that of the spider who builds (to itself) a house; but truly the flimsiest of houses is the spider's house - if they but knew.

42. Verily Allah does know of (everything) whatever that they call upon besides Him: and He is Exalted (in Power), Wise.

43. And such are the parables We set for mankind, but only those understand them who have knowledge.

44. Allah created the heavens and the earth in true (proportions): verily in that is a sign for those who believe.

45. Recite what is sent of the book by inspiration to you, and establish regular prayer: for prayer restrains from shameful and unjust deeds; and remembrance of Allah is the greatest (thing in life) without doubt. And Allah knows the (deeds) that you do.

46. And do not dispute with the People of the Book, except with means better (than mere disputation), unless it be with those of them who inflict wrong (and injury); but say "We believe in the revelation which has come down to us and in that which came down to you; our God and your God is one; and it is to Him we bow (in Islam)."

47. And thus (it is) that We have sent down the book to you. So the People of the Book believe in it, as also do some of these (pagan Arabs); and none but unbelievers reject Our signs.

48. And you were not (able) to recite a book before this (book came), nor are you (able) to transcribe it with your right hand; in that case, indeed, would the talkers of vanities have doubted.

49. Nay, here are signs self-evident in the hearts of those endowed with knowledge; and none but the unjust rejects Our signs.

50. Yet they say: "Why are not signs sent down to him from his Lord?" Say: "The signs are indeed with Allah; and I am indeed a clear warner."

51. And is it not enough for them that We have sent down to you the book which is rehearsed to them? Verily, in it is mercy and a reminder to those who believe.

52. Say: "Enough is Allah for a witness between me and you: He knows what is in the heavens and on earth. And it is those who believe in vanities and reject Allah, that will perish (in the end)."

53. They ask you to hasten on the punishment (for them): had it not been for a term (of respite) appointed, the punishment would certainly have come to them: and it will certainly reach them - of a sudden while they perceive not!

54. They ask you to hasten on the punishment: but certainly, hell will encompass the rejecters of faith! -

55. On the day that the punishment shall cover them from above them and from below them, and (a voice) shall say: "Taste you (the fruits) of your deeds!"

56. O My servants who believe! Truly spacious is My earth: therefore serve you Me - (and Me alone)!

57. Every soul shall have a taste of death: in the end to Us shall you be brought back.

58. But those who believe and work deeds of righteousness - to them shall We give a home in heaven - lofty mansions beneath which flow rivers

- to dwell in it for ever - an excellent reward for those who do (good)! -

59. Those who persevere in patience, and put their trust in their Lord and Cherisher.

60. How many are the creatures that carry not their own sustenance? It is Allah Who feeds (both) them and you, for He hears and knows (all things).

61. If indeed you ask them who has created the heavens and the earth, and subjected the sun and the moon (to His law); they will certainly reply "Allah." How are they then deluded away (from the truth)?

62. Allah enlarges the sustenance (which He gives) to whichever of His servants He pleases; and He (similarly) grants by (strict) measure, (as He pleases): for Allah has full knowledge of all things.

63. And if indeed you ask them who it is that sends down rain from the sky, and gives life with it to the earth after its death, they will certainly reply, "Allah!" Say, "Praise be to Allah!" But most of them understand not.

64. What is the life of this world but amusement and play? But verily the home in the hereafter - that is life indeed if they but knew.

65. Now, if they embark on a boat, they call on Allah making their devotion sincerely (and exclusively) to Him; but when He had delivered them safely to (dry) land, See, they give a share (of their worship to others)! -

66. Disdaining ungratefully Our gifts, and giving themselves up to (worldly) enjoyment! But soon will they know.

67. Do they not then see that We have made a sanctuary secure, and that men are being snatched away from all around them? Then, do they believe in that which is vain, and reject the grace of Allah!

68. And who does more wrong than he who invents a lie against Allah or rejects the truth when it reaches Him? Is there not a home in hell for those who reject faith?

69. And those who strive in Our (cause) - We will certainly guide them to Our paths: for verily Allah is with those who do right.

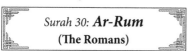

Surah 30: *Ar-Rum*
(The Romans)

In the name of Allah,
Most Gracious, Most Merciful.

1. *Alif Lam Mim.*

2. The Roman empire has been defeated -

3. In a land close by: but they, (even) after (this) defeat of theirs, will soon be victorious -

4. Within a few years. With Allah is the decision, in the past and in the future: on that day shall the believers rejoice -

5. With the help of Allah. He helps whom He will, and He is Exalted in Might, Most Merciful.

6. (It is) the promise of Allah. Never does Allah depart from His promise: but most men understand not.

7. They know but the outer (things) in the life of this world: but of the end of things they are heedless.

8. Do they not reflect in their own minds? Not but for just ends and for a term appointed did Allah create the heavens and the earth, and all between them: yet are there truly many among men who deny the meeting with their Lord (at the resurrection)!

9. Do they not travel through the earth, and see what was the end of those before them? They were superior to them in strength; they tilled the soil and populated it in greater numbers than these have done; there came to them their messengers with clear (signs) (which they rejected to their own destruction): it was not Allah Who wronged them, but they wronged their own souls.

10. In the long run, evil in the extreme will be the end of those who do evil; for that they rejected the signs of Allah, and held them up to ridicule.

11. It is Allah Who begins (the process of) creation; then repeats it; then shall you be brought back to Him.

12. On the day that the hour will be established, the guilty will be struck dumb with despair.

13. No intercessor will they have among their "partners," and they will (themselves) reject their "partners."

14. On the day that the hour will be established that day shall (all men) be sorted out.

15. Then those who have believed and worked righteous deeds, shall be made happy in a mead of delight.

16. And those who have rejected faith and falsely denied Our signs and the meeting of the hereafter - such shall be brought out to punishment.

17. So (give) glory to Allah, when you reach evening and when you rise in the morning;

18. Yea, to Him be praise in the heavens and on earth; and in the late afternoon and when the day begins to decline.

19. It is He Who brings out the living from the dead, and brings out the dead from the living, and Who gives life to the earth after it is dead: and thus shall you be brought out (from the dead).

20. Among His signs is this, that He created you from dust; and then - See, you are men scattered (far and wide)!

21. And among His signs is this, that He created for you mates from among yourselves, that you may dwell in tranquillity with them, and He has put love and mercy between your (hearts): verily in that are signs for those who reflect.

22. And among His signs is the creation of the heavens and the earth, and the variations in your languages and your colours: verily in that are signs for those who know.

23. And among His signs is the sleep that you take by night and by day, and the quest that you (make for livelihood) out of His bounty: verily in that are signs for those who listen.

24. And among His signs, He shows you the lightning, by way both of fear and of hope, and He sends down rain from the sky and with it gives life to the earth after it is dead: verily in that are signs for those who are wise.

25. And among His signs is this, that heaven and earth stand by His command: then when He calls you, by a single call, from the earth, see, you (straight away) come out.

26. To Him belongs every being that is in the heavens and on earth: all are devoutly obedient to Him.

27. It is He Who begins (the process of) creation; then repeats it; and for Him it is most easy. To Him belongs the loftiest similitude (we can think of) in the heavens and the earth: for He is Exalted in Might, Full of wisdom.

28. He does present to you a similitude from your own (experience): do you have partners among those whom your right hands possess, to share as equals in the wealth We have bestowed on you? Do you fear them as you fear each other? Thus do We explain the signs in detail to a people that understand.

29. Nay, the wrongdoers (merely) follow their own lusts, being devoid of knowledge. But who will guide those whom Allah leaves astray? To them there will be no helpers.

30. So set you your face steadily and truly to the faith: (establish) Allah's handiwork according to the pattern on which He has made mankind: no change (let there be) in the work (wrought) by Allah: that is the standard religion: but most among mankind understand not.

31. Turn you back in repentance to Him, and fear Him: establish regular prayers, and be not you among those who join gods with Allah -

32. Those who split up their religion, and become (mere) sects - each party rejoicing in that which is with itself!

33. When trouble touches men, they cry to their Lord, turning back to Him in repentance: but when He gives them a taste of mercy as from Himself, see, some of them pay part-worship to other gods besides their Lord -

34. (As if) to show their ingratitude for the (favours) We have bestowed on them! Then enjoy (your brief day); but soon will you know (your folly).

35. Or have We sent down authority to them, which points out to them the things to which they pay part-worship?

36. When We give men a taste of mercy, they exult at it: and when some evil afflicts them because of what their (own) hands have sent before, see, they are in despair!

37. Do they not see that Allah enlarges the provision and restricts it, to whomsoever He pleases? Verily in that are signs for those who believe.

38. So give what is due to relations, the needy, and the wayfarer. That is best for those who seek the countenance of Allah, and it is they who will prosper.

39. That which you lay out for increase through the property of (other) people, will have no increase with Allah: but that which you lay out for charity, seeking the countenance of Allah, (will increase): it is these who will get a recompense multiplied.

40. It is Allah Who has created you: further, He has provided for your sustenance; then He will cause you to die; and again He will give you life. Are there any of your (false) "partners" who can do any single one of these things? Glory to Him! And High is He above the partners they attribute (to Him)!

41. Mischief has appeared on land and sea because of (the dues) that the hands of men have earned, that (Allah) may give them a taste of some of their deeds: in order that they may turn back (from evil).

42. Say: "Travel through the earth and see what was the end of those before (you): most of them worshipped others besides Allah."

43. But set you your face to the right religion, before there come from Allah the day which there is no chance of averting: on that day shall men be divided (in two).

44. Those who reject faith will suffer from that rejection; and those who work righteousness will spread their couch (of repose) for themselves (in heaven);

45. That He may reward those who believe and work righteous deeds, out of His bounty. For He loves not those who reject faith.

46. Among His signs is this, that He sends the winds, as heralds of glad tidings, giving you a taste of His (grace and) mercy - that the ships may sail (majestically) by His command and that you may seek of His bounty; in order that you may be grateful.

47. We did indeed send, before you messengers to their (respective) peoples, and they came to them with clear signs; then, to those who transgressed, We meted out Retribution; and it was due from Us to aid those who believed.

48. It is Allah Who sends the winds, and they raise the clouds: then does He spread them in the sky as He wills, and break them into fragments, until you see raindrops issue from the midst of it; then when He has made them reach such of His servants as He wills, see they do rejoice! -

49. Even though, before they received (the rain) - just before this - they were dumb with despair!

50. Then contemplate (O man!) the memorials of Allah's mercy! - How He gives life to the earth after its death: verily the Same will give life to the men who are dead: for He has power over all things.

51. And if We (but) send a wind from which they see (their tilth) turn yellow - behold, they become thereafter ungrateful (unbelievers)!

52. So verily you can not make the dead to hear, nor can you make the deaf to hear the call, when they show their backs and turn away.

53. Nor can you lead back the blind from their straying: only those will you make to hear, who believe in Our signs and submit (their wills in Islam).

54. It is Allah Who created you in a state of (helpless) weakness, then gave (you) strength after weakness, then, after strength, gave (you) weakness and a hoary head: He creates as He wills, and it is He Who has all knowledge and power.

55. On the day that the hour (of reckoning) will be established, the transgressors will swear that they stayed not but an hour: thus were they used to being deluded!

56. But those endued with knowledge and faith will say: "Indeed you did stay, within Allah's decree to the day of resurrection and this is the day of resurrection: but you - you were not aware!"

57. So on that day no excuse of theirs will benefit the transgressors, nor will they be invited (then) to seek grace (by repentance).

58. Verily We have presented for men in this Qur'an, every kind of parable: but if you bring to them any sign, the unbelievers are sure to say, "You do nothing but talk vanities."

59. Thus does Allah seal up the hearts of those who understand not.

60. So patiently persevere: for verily the promise of Allah is true: nor let those shake your firmness, who have (themselves) no certainty of faith.

Surah 31: *Luqman*

In the name of Allah,
Most Gracious, Most Merciful.

1. *Alif Lam Mim*

2. These are verses of the wise book -

3. A guide and a mercy to the doers of good -

4. Those who establish regular prayer, and give regular charity, and have (in their hearts) the assurance of the hereafter.

5. These are on (true) guidance from their Lord; and these are the ones who will prosper.

6. But there are, among men, those who purchase idle tales, without knowledge (or meaning), to mislead (men) from the path of Allah and throw ridicule (on the path): for such there will be a humiliating penalty.

7. When Our signs are rehearsed to such a one, he turns away in arrogance, as if he heard them not, as if there were deafness in both his ears: announce to him a grievous penalty.

8. For those who believe and work righteous deeds, there will be gardens of bliss -

9. To dwell in it. The promise of Allah is true: and He is Exalted in Power, Wise.

10. He created the heavens without any pillars that you can see; He set on the earth mountains standing firm, lest it should shake with you; and He scattered through it beasts of all kinds. We send down rain from the sky, and produce on the earth every kind of noble creature, in pairs.

11. Such is the creation of Allah; now show Me what is there that others besides Him have created: nay, but the transgressors are in manifest error.

12. We bestowed (in the past) wisdom on Luqman: "Show (your) gratitude to Allah." Any who is (so) grateful does so to the profit of his own soul: but if any is ungrateful, verily Allah is Free of all Wants, worthy of all praise.

13. See, Luqman said to his son by way of instruction: "O my son! Join

not in worship (others) with Allah: for false worship is indeed the highest wrongdoing."

14. And We have enjoined on man (to be good) to his parents: in travail upon travail did his mother bear him, and in two years was his weaning: (hear the command), "Show gratitude to Me and to your parents: to Me is (your final) goal."

15. "But if they strive to make you join in worship with Me things of which you have no knowledge, obey them not; yet bear them company in this life with justice (and consideration), and follow the way of those who turn to Me (in love): in the end the return of you all is to Me, and I will tell you the truth (and meaning) of all that you did."

16. "O my son," (said Luqman), "if there be (but) the weight of a mustard seed and it were (hidden) in a rock, or (anywhere) in the heavens or on earth, Allah will bring it out: for Allah understands the finest mysteries, (and) is well-acquainted (with them).

17. "O my son! Establish regular prayer, enjoin what is just, and forbid what is wrong: and bear with patient constancy whatever befall you; for this is firmness (of purpose) in (the conduct of) affairs. "

18. "And swell not your cheek (for pride) at men, nor walk in insolence through the earth; for Allah loves not any arrogant boaster."

19. "And be moderate in your pace, and lower your voice; for the harshest of sounds without doubt is the braying of the ass."

20. Do you not see that Allah has subjected to your (use) all things in the heavens and on earth, and has made His bounties flow to you in exceeding measure, (both) seen and unseen? Yet there are among men those who dispute about Allah, without knowledge and without guidance, and without a book to enlighten them!

21. When they are told to follow the (revelation) that Allah has sent down, they say: "Nay, we shall follow the ways that we found our fathers (following)." What! Even if it is Satan beckoning them to the penalty of the (blazing) fire!

22. Whoever submits his whole self to Allah, and is a doer of good, has grasped indeed the most trustworthy handhold: and with Allah rests the end and decision of (all) affairs.

23. But if any reject faith, let not his rejection grieve you; to Us is their return, and We shall tell them the truth of their deeds: for Allah knows well all that is in (men's) hearts.

24. We grant them their pleasure for a little while: in the end shall We drive them to a chastisement unrelenting.

25. If you ask them, who it is that created the heavens and the earth, they will certainly say "Allah." Say: "Praise be to Allah!" But most of them understand not.

26. To Allah belong all things in heaven and earth: verily Allah is He (that is) Free of all Wants, Worthy of all Praise.

27. And if all the trees on earth were pens and the ocean (were ink), with seven oceans behind it to add to its (supply), yet would not the words of Allah be exhausted (in the writing): for Allah is Exalted in Power, Full of wisdom.

28. And your creation or your resurrection is in no way but as an individual soul: for Allah is He Who hears and sees (all things).

29. Do you not see that Allah merges night into day and He merges day into night; that He has subjected the sun and the moon (to His law), each running its course for a term appointed: and that Allah is well acquainted with all that you do?

30. That is because Allah is the (only) Reality, and because whatever else they invoke besides Him is falsehood; and because Allah - He is the Most High, Most Great.

31. Do you not see that the ships sail through the ocean by the grace of Allah? - That He may show you of His signs? Verily in this are signs for all who constantly persevere and give thanks.

32. When a wave covers them like the canopy (of clouds) they call to Allah, offering Him sincere devotion, but when He has delivered them safely to land, there are among them those that halt between (right and wrong). But none reject Our signs except only a perfidious ungrateful (wretch)!

33. O mankind! Do your duty to your Lord, and fear (the coming of) a day when no father can benefit anything for his son, nor a son benefit anything for his father. Verily, the promise of Allah is true: let not then this present life deceive you, nor let the chief deceiver deceive you about Allah.

34. Verily the knowledge of the hour is with Allah (alone). It is He Who sends down rain, and He Who knows what is in the wombs. Nor does anyone know what it is that he will earn the next day; nor does anyone know in what land he is to die. Verily with Allah is full knowledge and He is acquainted (with all things).

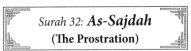

Surah 32: **As-Sajdah**
(The Prostration)

In the name of Allah, Most Gracious, Most Merciful.

1. *Alif Lam Mim*

2. (This is) the revelation of the book in which there is no doubt - from the Lord of the Worlds.

3. Or do they say, "He has forged it"? Nay, it is the truth from your Lord, that you may admonish a people to whom no warner has come before you: in order that they may receive guidance.

4. It is Allah Who has created the heavens and the earth, and all between them, in six days, then He established Himself on the throne (of authority); you have none, besides Him, to protect or intercede (for you): will you not then receive admonition?

5. He rules (all) affairs from the heavens to the earth: in the end will (all affairs) go up to Him, on a day, the

space of which will be (as) a thousand years of your reckoning.

6. Such is He, the Knower of all things, hidden and open, the Exalted (in power), the Merciful -

7. He Who has made everything which He has created most good: He began the creation of man with (nothing more than) clay,

8. And made his progeny from a quintessence of the nature of a fluid despised:

9. But He fashioned him in due proportion, and breathed into him something of His spirit. And He gave you (the faculties of) hearing and sight and feeling (and understanding): little thanks do you give!

10. And they say: "What! When we lie, hidden and lost, in the earth, shall we indeed be in a creation renewed?" Nay, they deny the meeting with their Lord!

11. Say: "The angel of death, put in charge of you, will (duly) take your souls: then shall you be brought back to your Lord."

12. If only you could see when the guilty ones will bend low their heads before their Lord, (saying:) "Our Lord! We have seen and we have heard; now then send us back (to the world); we will work righteousness: for we do indeed (now) believe."

13. If We had so willed, We could certainly have brought every soul its true guidance: but the word from Me will come true. "I will fill hell with Jinns and men all together."

14. "Taste you then - for you forgot the meeting of this day of yours. And We too will forget you - taste you the penalty of eternity for your (evil) deeds!"

15. Only those believe in Our signs, who, when they are recited to them fall down in adoration, and celebrate the praises of their Lord, nor are they (ever) puffed up with pride.

16. Their limbs do forsake their beds of sleep, the while they call on their Lord, in fear and hope: and they spend (in charity) out of the sustenance which We have bestowed on them.

17. Now no person knows what delights of the eye are kept hidden (in reserve) for them - as a reward for their (good) deeds.

18. Is then the man who believes no better than the man who is rebellious and wicked? Not equal are they.

19. For those who believe and do righteous deeds, are gardens as hospitable homes, for their (good) deeds.

20. As to those who are rebellious and wicked, their abode will be the fire: every time they wish to get away from it, they will be forced in it, and it will be said to them: "Taste you the penalty of the fire, which you used to reject as false."

21. And indeed We will make them taste of the penalty of this (life) prior to the supreme penalty, in order that they may (repent and) return.

22. And who does more wrong than one to whom are recited the signs of his Lord and who then turns away from it? Verily from those who transgress We shall exact (due) retribution.

23. We did indeed before give the book to Moses: be not then in doubt of its reaching (you): and We made it a guide to the Children of Israel.

24. And We appointed, from among them, leaders, giving guidance under Our command, so long as they persevered with patience and continued to have faith in Our signs.

25. Verily your Lord will judge between them on the day of judgement, in the matters in which they differ (among themselves).

26. Does it not teach them a lesson, how many generations We destroyed before them, in whose dwellings they (now) go to and fro? Verily in that are signs: do they not then listen?

27. And do they not see that We do drive rain to parched soil (bare of herbage), and produce with it crops, providing food for their cattle and themselves? Have they not the vision?

28. They say: "When will this decision be if you are telling the truth?"

29. Say: "On the day of decision, no profit will it be to unbelievers if they (then) believe! Nor will they be granted a respite."

30. So turn away from them, and wait: they too are waiting.

Surah 33: *Al-Ahzab*
(The Clans)

**In the name of Allah,
Most Gracious, Most Merciful.**

1. O Prophet! Fear Allah, and listen not to the unbelievers and the hypocrites: verily Allah is Full of knowledge and wisdom.

2. But follow that which comes to you by inspiration from your Lord: for Allah is well acquainted with (all) that you do.

3. And put your trust in Allah, and enough is Allah as a Disposer of affairs.

4. Allah has not made for any man two hearts in his (one) body: nor has He made your wives whom you divorce by *zihar* your mothers: nor has He made your adopted sons your sons. Such is (only) your (manner of) speech by your mouths. But Allah tells (you) the truth, and He shows the (right) way.

5. Call them by (the names) of their fathers: that is more just in the sight of Allah. But if you do not know their father's (names, call them) your brothers in faith, or your *Mawlas*. But there is no blame on you if you make a mistake in it; (what counts is) the intention of your hearts: and Allah is Oft-Forgiving, Most Merciful.

6. The Prophet is closer to the believers than their own selves, and his wives are their mothers. Blood-relations among each other have closer personal ties, in the decree of Allah, than (the brotherhood of) believers and Muhajirs; nevertheless do you what is just to your closest friends; such is the writing in the decree (of Allah).

7. And remember We took from the prophets their covenant as (We did) from you; from Noah, Abraham, Moses, and Jesus the son of Mary; We took from them a solemn covenant:

8. That (Allah) may question the (custodians) of truth concerning the truth they (were charged with): and He has prepared for the unbelievers a grievous penalty.

9. O you who believe! Remember the grace of Allah (bestowed) on you, when there came down on you forces (to overwhelm you): but We sent against them a hurricane and force that you saw not. But Allah sees (clearly) all that you do.

10. See! They came on you from above you and from below you, and behold, the eyes became dim and the hearts gaped up to the throats, and you imagined various (vain) thoughts about Allah!

11. In that situation were the believers tried: they were shaken as by a tremendous shaking.

12. And behold! The hypocrites and those in whose hearts is a disease (even) say: "Allah and His messenger promised us nothing but delusions!"

13. See! A party among them said: "You men of Yathrib! You cannot stand (the attack)! Therefore, go back!" And a band of them ask for permission of the prophet saying, "Truly our houses are bare and exposed;" though they were not exposed: they intended nothing but to run away.

14. And if an entry had been effected to them from the sides of the (city), and they had been incited to sedition, they would certainly have brought it to pass, with none but a brief delay!

15. And yet they had already covenanted with Allah not to turn their backs, and a covenant with Allah must (surely) be answered for.

16. Say: "Running away will not profit you if you are running away from death or slaughter; and even if (you do escape) no more than a brief (respite) will you be allowed to enjoy!"

17. Say: "Who is it that can screen you from Allah if it be His wish to give you punishment or to give you mercy?" Nor will they find for themselves, besides Allah, any protector or helper.

18. Verily Allah knows those among you who keep back (men) and those who say to their brothers, "Come along to us," but come not to the fight except for just a little while,

19. Covetous over you (believers). Then when fear comes, you will see them looking to you, their eyes revolving, like (those of) one over whom hovers death; but when the fear is past, they will strike you with sharp tongues, covetous of goods. Such men have no faith, and so Allah has made their deeds of no effect; and that is easy for Allah.

20. They think that the confederates have not withdrawn; and if the confederates should come (again), they would wish they were in the deserts (wandering) among the Bedouins, and seeking news about you (from a

safe distance); and if they were in your midst, they would fight but little.

21. You have indeed in the messenger of Allah a beautiful pattern of (conduct) for anyone whose hope is in Allah and the final day, and who engages much in the praise of Allah.

22. When the believers saw the confederate forces they said: "This is what Allah and His messenger had promised us and Allah and His messenger told us what was true." And it only added to their faith and their zeal in obedience.

23. Among the believers are men who have been true to their covenant with Allah; of them, some have completed their vow to (the extreme) and some (still) wait; but they have never changed (their determination) in the least;

24. That Allah may reward the men of truth for their truth and punish the hypocrites if that be His will or turn to them in mercy: for Allah is Oft-Forgiving, Most Merciful.

25. And Allah turned back the unbelievers for (all) their fury; no advantage did they gain and enough is Allah for the believers in their fight. And Allah is full of strength, Able to enforce His Will.

26. And those of the people of the Book who aided them - Allah did take them down from their strongholds and cast terror into their hearts, (so that) some you slew, and some you made prisoners.

27. And He made you heirs of their lands, their houses, and their goods, and of a land which you had not frequented (before). And Allah has power over all things.

28. O Prophet! Say to your consorts: "If it be that you desire the life of this world, and its glitter, - then come! I will provide for your enjoyment and set you free in a handsome manner."

29. But if you seek Allah and His messenger, and the home of the hereafter, verily Allah has prepared for the well-doers amongst you a great reward.

30. O consorts of the prophet! If any of you were guilty of evident unseemly conduct, the punishment would be doubled to her, and that is easy for Allah.

31. But any of you that is devout in the service of Allah and His messenger, and works righteousness - to her shall We grant her reward twice: and We have prepared for her a generous sustenance.

32. O consorts of the prophet! You are not like any of the (other) women: if you do fear (Allah), be not too complaisant of speech, lest one in whose heart is a disease should be moved with desire: but speak you a speech (that is) just.

33. And stay quietly in your houses, and make not a dazzling display, like that of the former times of ignorance; and establish regular prayer, and give regular charity; and obey Allah and His messenger. And Allah only wishes to remove all abomination from you, you members of the family, and to make you pure and spotless.

34. And recite what is rehearsed to you in your homes of the signs of Allah and His wisdom: for Allah understands the finest mysteries and is well-acquainted (with them).

35. For Muslim men and women - for believing men and women, for devout men and women, for true men and women, for men and women who are patient and constant, for men and women who humble themselves, for men and women who give in charity, for men and women who fast (and deny themselves), for men and women who guard their chastity, and for men and women who engage much in Allah's praise - for them has Allah prepared forgiveness and great reward.

36. It is not fitting for a believer, man or woman, when a matter has been decided by Allah and His messenger, to have any option about their decision: if anyone disobeys Allah and His messenger, he is indeed on a clearly wrong path.

37. See! You did say to one who had received the grace of Allah and your favour: "Retain you (in wedlock) your wife, and fear Allah." But you did hide in your heart that which Allah was about to make manifest: you did fear the people, but it is more fitting that you should fear Allah. Then when Zayd had dissolved (his marriage) with her, with the necessary (formality), We joined her in marriage to you: in order that (in future) there may be no difficulty to the believers in (the matter of) marriage with the wives of their adopted sons, when the latter have dissolved with the necessary (formality) (their marriage) with them. And Allah's command must be fulfilled.

38. There can be no difficulty to the prophet in what Allah has indicated to him as a duty. It was the practice (approved) of Allah amongst those of old that have passed away, and the command of Allah is a decree determined.

39. (It is the practice of those) who preach the messages of Allah, and fear Him, and fear none but Allah. And enough is Allah to call (men) to account.

40. Muhammad is not the father of any of your men, but (he is) the messenger of Allah, and the seal of the prophets: and Allah has full knowledge of all things.

41. O you who believe! Celebrate the praises of Allah, and do this often;

42. And glorify Him morning and evening.

43. He it is Who sends blessings on you, as do His angels, that He may bring you out from the depths of darkness into light: and He is Full of mercy to the believers.

44. Their salutation on the day they meet Him will be "peace!": and He has prepared for them a generous reward.

45. O prophet! Truly We have sent you as a witness, a bearer of glad tidings, and a warner -

46. And as one who invites to Allah's (grace) by His permission, and as a lamp spreading light.

47. Then give the glad tidings to the believers, that they shall have from Allah a very great bounty.

48. And obey not (the behests) of the unbelievers and the hypocrites, and heed not their annoyances, but put your trust in Allah. For enough is Allah as a Disposer of affairs.

49. O you who believe! When you marry believing women, and then divorce them before you have touched them, no period of *Iddah* have you to count in respect of them: so give them a present, and set them free in a handsome manner.

50. O prophet! We have made lawful to you your wives to whom you have paid their dowers; and those whom your right hand possesses out of the prisoners of war whom Allah has assigned to you; and daughters of your paternal uncles and aunts, and daughters of your maternal uncles and aunts, who migrated (from Makkah) with you; and any believing woman who dedicates her soul to the prophet if the prophet wishes to wed her - this only for you, and not for the believers (at large); We know what We have appointed for them as to their wives and the captives whom their right hands possess - in order that there should be no difficulty for you. And Allah is Oft-Forgiving, Most Merciful.

51. You may defer (the turn of) any of them that you please, and you may receive any you please: and there is no blame on you if you invite one whose (turn) you had set aside. This were nearer to the cooling of their eyes, the prevention of their grief, and their satisfaction - that of all of them - with that which you have to give them:

and Allah knows (all) that is in your hearts: and Allah is All-Knowing, Most Forbearing.

52. It is not lawful for you (to marry more) women after this, nor to change them for (other) wives, even though their beauty attract you, except any your right hand should possess (as hand maidens): and Allah does watch over all things.

53. O you who believe! Enter not the prophet's houses - until permission is given you - for a meal, (and then) not (so early as) to wait for its preparation; but when you are invited, enter; and when you have taken your meal, disperse, without seeking familiar talk. Such (behaviour) annoys the prophet: he is ashamed to dismiss you but Allah is not ashamed (to tell you) the truth. And when you ask (his ladies) for anything you want, ask them from before a screen: that makes for greater purity for your hearts and for theirs. Nor is it right for you that you should annoy Allah's messenger, or that you should marry his widows after him at any time. Truly such a thing is in Allah's sight an enormity.

54. Whether you reveal anything or conceal it, verily Allah has full knowledge of all things.

55. There is no blame (on these ladies if they appear) before their fathers or their sons, their brothers, or their brothers' sons, or their sisters' sons, or their women, or the (slaves) whom their right hands possess. And, (ladies), fear Allah: for Allah is Witness to all things.

56. Allah and His angels send blessings on the prophet: O you that believe! Send you blessings on him, and salute him with all respect.

57. Those who annoy Allah and His messenger - Allah has cursed them in this world and in the hereafter, and has prepared for them a humiliating punishment.

58. And those who annoy believing men and women undeservedly, bear (on themselves) a calumny and a glaring sin.

59. O prophet! Tell your wives and daughters, and the believing women, that they should cast their outer garments over their persons (when abroad); that is most convenient, that they should be known (as such) and not molested; and Allah is Oft-Forgiving, Most Merciful.

60. Truly, if the hypocrites and those in whose hearts is a disease, and those who stir up sedition in the city, desist not, We shall certainly stir you up against them: then will they not be able to stay in it as your neighbours for any length of time;

61. They shall have a curse on them; wherever they are found, they shall be seized and slain (without mercy).

62. (Such was) the practice (approved) of Allah among those who lived before: no change will you find in the practice (approved) of Allah.

63. Men ask you concerning the hour: say, "The knowledge thereof is with Allah (alone)": and what will make you understand? - Perhaps the hour is near!

64. Verily Allah has cursed the unbelievers and prepared for them a blazing fire -

65. To dwell in it forever: no protector will they find, nor helper.

66. The day that their faces will be turned upside down in the fire they will say: "Woe to us! Would that we had obeyed Allah and obeyed the messenger!"

67. And they would say: "Our Lord! We obeyed our chiefs and our great ones, and they misled us as to the (right) path.

68. "Our Lord! Give them double penalty and curse them with a very great curse!"

69. O you who believe! Be you not like those who vexed and insulted Moses, but Allah cleared him of the (calumnies) they had uttered: and he was honourable in Allah's sight.

70. O you who believe! Fear Allah, and (always) say a word directed to the right:

71. That He may make your conduct whole and sound and forgive you your sins: he that obeys Allah and His messenger, has already attained the highest achievement.

72. We did indeed offer the trust to the heavens and the earth and the mountains: but they refused to undertake it, being afraid of it: but man undertook it - he was indeed unjust and foolish -

73. (With the result) that Allah has to punish the hypocrites, men and women, and the unbelievers, men and women, and Allah turns in mercy to the believers, men and women: for Allah is Oft-Forgiving, Most Merciful.

Surah 34: **Saba** (Sheba)

In the name of Allah, Most Gracious, Most Merciful.

1. Praise be to Allah, to Whom belong all things in the heavens and on earth: to Him be Praise in the hereafter: and He is Full of wisdom, acquainted with all things.

2. He knows all that goes into the earth, and all that comes out of it: all that comes down from the sky and all that ascends to it: and He is the Most Merciful, the Oft-Forgiving.

3. The unbelievers say, "Never to us will come the hour": say, "Nay! But most surely, by my Lord, it will come upon you - by Him Who knows the unseen - from Whom is not hidden the least little atom in the heavens or on earth: nor is there anything less than that, or greater, but is in the record perspicuous:

4. That He may reward those who believe and work deeds of righteousness: for such is forgiveness and a sustenance Most Generous."

5. But those who strive against Our signs, to frustrate them - for such will be a punishment most humiliating.

6. And those to whom knowledge has come see that the (revelation) sent down to you from your Lord - that is the truth, and that it guides to the path of the Exalted (in Might), Worthy of all praise.

7. The unbelievers say (in ridicule): "Shall we point out to you a man that will tell you, when you are all scattered to pieces in disintegration, that you shall (then be raised) in a new creation?"

8. "Has he invented a falsehood against Allah or has a spirit (seized) him?" - Nay, it is those who believe not in the hereafter, that are in (real) penalty, and in farthest error.

9. Do they not see what is before them and behind them, of the sky and the earth? If We wished, We could cause the earth to swallow them up, or cause a piece of the sky to fall upon them. Verily in this is a sign for every devotee that turns to Allah (in repentance).

10. We bestowed grace before on David from Ourselves: "O you mountains! Sing you back the praises of Allah with him! And you birds (also)! And We made the iron soft for him -

11. (Commanding), "Make you coats of mail, balancing well the rings of chain armour, and work you righteousness; for be sure I see (clearly) all that you do."

12. And to Solomon (We made) the wind (obedient): its early morning (stride) was a month's (journey), and its evening (stride) was a month's (journey); and We made a font of molten brass to flow for him; and there were Jinns that worked in front of him, by the leave of his Lord, and if any of them turned aside from Our command, We made Him taste of the penalty of the blazing fire.

13. They worked for him as he desired, (making) arches, images, basins, as large as reservoirs, and (cooking) cauldrons fixed (in their places): "Work you, sons of David with thanks! But few of My servants are grateful!"

14. Then, when We decreed (Solomon's) death, nothing showed them his death except a little worm of the earth, which kept (slowly) gnawing away at his staff: so when he fell down the Jinns saw plainly that if they had known the unseen, they would not have stayed in the humiliating penalty (of their task).

15. There was for Saba before, a sign in their homeland - two gardens to the right and to the left. Eat of the sustenance (provided) by your Lord, and be grateful to Him: a territory fair and happy, and a Lord Oft-Forgiving!

16. But they turned away (from Allah) and We sent against them the flood (released) from the dams, and We converted their two garden (rows) into "gardens" producing bitter fruit, and tamarisks, and some few (stunted) lote trees.

17. That was the requital We gave them because they ungratefully rejected faith: and never do We give (such) requital except to such as are ungrateful rejecters.

18. Between them and the cities on which We had poured Our blessings, We had placed cities in prominent positions, and between them We had appointed stages of journey in due proportion: "Travel in it, secure by night and by day."

19. But they said: "Our Lord! Place longer distances between our journey-stages." But they wronged themselves (in it). At length We made them as a tale (that is told), and We dispersed them all in scattered fragments. Verily in this are signs for every (soul that is) patiently constant and grateful.

20. And on them did Satan prove true his idea, and they followed him, all but a party that believed.

21. But he had no authority over them - except that We might test the man who believes in the hereafter from him who is in doubt concerning it: and your Lord does watch over all things.

22. Say: "Call upon other (gods) whom you fancy, besides Allah: they have no power - not the weight of an atom - in the heavens or on earth; no (sort of) share have they in it, nor is any of them a helper to Allah."

23. "No intercession can benefit in His presence, except for those for whom He has granted permission. So far (is this the case) that when terror is removed from their hearts (at the day of judgement, then) will they say, 'What is it that your Lord commanded?' They will say: 'That which is true and just; and He is the Most High, Most Great.'"

24. Say: "Who gives you sustenance, from the heavens and the earth?" Say: "It is Allah; and certain it is that either we or you are on right guidance or in manifest error!"

25. Say: "You shall not be questioned as to our sins, nor shall we be questioned as to what you do."

26. Say: "Our Lord will gather us together and will in the end decide the matter between us (and you) in truth and justice: and He is the One to decide, the One Who knows all."

27. Say: "Show me those whom you have joined with Him as partners: by no means (can you). Nay, He is Allah, the Exalted in Power, the Wise."

28. We have not sent you but as a universal (messenger) to men, giving them glad tidings, and warning them (against sin), but most men understand not.

29. They say: "When will this promise (come to pass) if you are telling the truth?"

30. Say: "The appointment to you is for a day, which you cannot put back for an hour nor put forward."

31. The unbelievers say: "We shall neither believe in this scripture nor in (any) that (came) before it." Could you but see when the wrongdoers will be made to stand before their Lord, throwing back the word (of blame) on one another! Those who had been despised will say to the arrogant ones: "Had it not been for you, we should certainly have been believers!"

32. The arrogant ones will say to those who had been despised: "Was it we who kept you back from guidance after it reached you? Nay, rather it was you who transgressed."

33. Those who had been despised will say to the arrogant ones: "Nay! It was a plot (of yours) by day and by night: See! You (constantly) ordered us to be ungrateful to Allah and to attribute equals to Him!" They will declare (their) repentance when they see the penalty: We shall put yokes on the necks of the unbelievers: it would only be a requital for their (ill) deeds.

34. Never did We send a warner to a population, but the wealthy ones among them said: "We believe not in the (message) with which you have been sent."

35. They said: "We have more in wealth and in sons, and we cannot be punished."

36. Say: "Verily my Lord enlarges and restricts the provision to whom He pleases, but most men understand not."

37. It is not your wealth nor your sons, that will bring you nearer to Us in degree; but only those who believe and work righteousness - these are the ones for whom there is a multiplied reward for their deeds, while secure they (reside) in the dwellings on high!

38. Those who strive against Our signs, to frustrate them, will be given over into punishment.

39. Say: "Verily my Lord enlarges and restricts the sustenance to such of His servants as He pleases: and nothing do you spend in the least (in His cause) but He replaces it: for He is the best of those Who grant sustenance.

40. One day, He will gather them all together and say to the angels, "Was it you that these men used to worship?"

41. They will say "Glory to You! Our (tie) is with You - as protector - not with them. Nay, but they worshipped the Jinns: most of them believed in them."

42. So on that day no power shall they have over each other, for profit or harm: and We shall say to the wrongdoers, "Taste you the penalty of the fire - which you used to deny!"

43. When Our clear signs are rehearsed to them, they say, "This is only a man who wishes to hinder you from the (worship) which your fathers practised." And they say, "This is only a falsehood invented!" And the unbelievers say of the truth when it comes to them: "This is nothing but evident magic!"

44. But We had not given them books which they could study, nor sent messengers to them before you as warners.

45. And their predecessors rejected (the truth); these have not received a tenth of what We had granted to those: yet when they rejected My messengers, how (terrible) was My rejection (of them)!

46. Say: "I do admonish you on one point: that you do stand up before Allah - (it may be) in pairs, or (it may be) singly, and reflect (within yourselves): your companion is not possessed: he is no less than a warner to you, in face of a terrible penalty."

47. Say: "No reward do I ask of you: it is (all) in your interest: my reward is only due from Allah: and He is Witness to all things."

48. Say: "Verily my Lord does cast the (mantle of) truth (over His servants) - He that has full knowledge of (all) that is hidden."

49. Say: "The truth has arrived and falsehood neither creates anything new, nor restores anything."

50. Say: "If I am astray, I only stray to the loss of my own soul; but if I receive guidance, it is because of the inspiration of my Lord to me: it is He Who hears all things and is (ever) near."

51. If you could but see when they will quake with terror: but then there will be no escape (for them), and they will be seized from a position (quite) near.

52. And they will say, "We do believe (now) in the (truth)"; but how could they receive (faith) from a position (so) far off -

53. Seeing that they did reject faith (entirely) before, and that they (continually) cast (slanders) on the unseen from a position far off?

54. And between them and their desires, is placed a barrier, as was done in the past with their partisans: for they were indeed in suspicious (disquieting) doubt.

Surah 35: *Fatir* (The Originator of Creation)

In the name of Allah, Most Gracious, Most Merciful.

1. Praise be to Allah, Who created (out of nothing) the heavens and the earth, Who made the angels messengers with wings - two, or three, or four (pairs): He adds to creation as He pleases: for Allah has power over all things.

2. What Allah out of His mercy does bestow on mankind there is none that can withhold: what He does withhold there is none that can grant apart from Him: and He is the Exalted in power, Full of wisdom.

3. O men! Call to mind the grace of Allah to you! Is there a creator, other

than Allah, to give you sustenance from heaven or earth? There is no god but He: how then are you deluded away from the truth?

4. And if they reject you, so were messengers rejected before you: to Allah go back for decision all affairs.

5. O men! Certainly the promise of Allah is true. Let not then this present life deceive you, nor let the chief deceiver deceive you about Allah.

6. Verily Satan is an enemy to you: so treat him as an enemy. He only invites his adherents, that they may become companions of the blazing fire.

7. For those who reject Allah, is a terrible penalty: but for those who believe and work righteous deeds, is forgiveness, and a magnificent reward.

8. Is he, then, to whom the evil of his conduct is made alluring, so that he looks upon it as good, (equal to one who is rightly guided)? For Allah leaves to stray whom He wills, and guides whom He wills. So let not your soul go out in (vainly) sighing after them: for Allah knows well all that they do!

9. It is Allah Who sends ahead the winds, so that they raise up the clouds, and We drive them to a land that is dead, and revive the earth with it after its death: even so (will be) the resurrection!

10. If any do seek for glory and power - to Allah belong all glory and power. To Him mount up (all) words of purity: it is He Who exalts each deed of righteousness. Those that lay plots of evil - for them is a penalty terrible; and the plotting of such will be void (of result).

11. And Allah did create you from dust; then from a sperm-drop; then He made you in pairs. And no female conceives, or lays down (her load), but with His knowledge. Nor is a man long-lived granted length of days, nor is a part cut off from his life, but it is in a decree (ordained). All this is easy for Allah.

12. Nor are the two bodies of flowing water alike - the one palatable, sweet, and pleasant to drink, and the other, salty and bitter. Yet from each (kind of water) do you eat flesh fresh and tender, and you extract ornaments to wear; and you see the ships in it that plough the waves, that you may seek (thus) of the bounty of Allah that you may be grateful.

13. He merges night into day and He merges day into night, and He has subjected the sun and the moon (to His law): each one runs its course for a term appointed. Such is Allah your Lord: to Him belongs all dominion. And those whom you invoke besides Him have not the least power.

14. If you invoke them, they will not listen to your call, and if they were to listen, they cannot answer your (prayer). On the day of judgement they will reject your "partnership." And none, (O man!) can tell you (the truth) like the One Who is acquainted with all things.

15. O you men! It is you that have need of Allah: but Allah is the One Free of all wants, Worthy of all praise.

16. If He so pleased, He could blot you out and bring in a new creation.

17. Nor is that (at all) difficult for Allah.

18. Nor can a bearer of burdens bear another's burden. If one heavily laden should call another to (bear) his load not the least portion of it can be carried (by the other) even though he be nearly related. You can but admonish such as fear their Lord unseen and establish regular prayer. And whoever purifies himself does so for the benefit of his own soul; and the destination (of all) is to Allah.

19. The blind and the seeing are not alike;

20. Nor are the depths of darkness and the light;

21. Nor are the (chilly) shade and the (genial) heat of the sun:

22. Nor are alike those that are living and those that are dead. Allah can make any that He wills to hear; but you can not make those to hear who are (buried) in graves.

23. You are no other than a warner.

24. Verily We have sent you in truth, as a bearer of glad tidings, and as a warner: and there never was a people, without a warner having lived among them (in the past).

25. And if they reject you, so did their predecessors to whom came their messengers with clear signs, scriptures and the book of enlightenment.

26. In the end did I punish those who rejected faith: and how (terrible) was My rejection (of them)!

27. Do you not see that Allah sends down rain from the sky? With it We then bring out produce of various colours. And in the mountains are tracts white and red, of various shades of colour, and black intense in hue.

28. And so amongst men and crawling creatures and cattle, are they of various colours. Those truly fear Allah, among His servants, who have knowledge: for Allah is Exalted in Might, Oft-Forgiving.

29. Those who rehearse the book of Allah, establish regular prayer, and spend (in charity) out of what We have provided for them, secretly and openly, hope for a commerce that will never fail:

30. For He will pay them their reward, nay, He will give them (even) more out of His bounty: for He is Oft-Forgiving, Most Ready to appreciate (service).

31. That which We have revealed to you of the book is the truth - confirming what was (revealed) before it: for Allah is assuredly - with respect to His servants Well Acquainted and Fully-Observant.

32. Then We have given the book for inheritance to such of Our servants as We have chosen: but there are among them some who wrong their own souls; some who follow a middle course; and some who are by Allah's leave, foremost in good deeds; that is the highest grace.

33. Gardens of eternity will they enter: in it will they be adorned with bracelets of gold and pearls; and their garments there will be of silk.

34. And they will say: "Praise be to Allah, Who has removed from us (all) sorrow: for Our Lord is indeed Oft-Forgiving, Ready to appreciate (service).

35. Who has, out of His bounty, settled us in a home that will last: no toil nor sense of weariness shall touch us in it."

36. But those who reject (Allah) for them will be the fire of hell: no term shall be determined for them, so they should die, nor shall its penalty be lightened for them. Thus do We reward every ungrateful one!

37. In it will they call aloud (for assistance): "Our Lord! Bring us out: we shall work righteousness, not the (deeds) we used to do!" - Did We not give you long enough life so that he that would, should receive admonition? And (moreover) the warner came to you. So taste you (the fruits of your deeds): For the wrongdoers there is no helper."

38. Verily Allah knows (all) the hidden things of the heavens and the earth; verily He has full knowledge of all that is in (men's) hearts.

39. He it is that has made you inheritors in the earth; if, then, any do reject (Allah), their rejection (works) against themselves; their rejection but adds to the odium for the unbelievers in the sight of their Lord; their rejection but adds to (their own) undoing.

40. Say: "Have you seen (these) 'partners' of yours whom you call upon besides Allah?" Show me what it is they have created in the (wide) earth. Or have they a share in the heavens? Or have We given them a book from which they (can derive) clear (evidence)? - Nay, the wrongdoers promise each other nothing but delusions.

41. It is Allah Who sustains the heavens and the earth, lest they cease (to function): and if they should fail, there is none - not one - can sustain them thereafter: verily He is Most Forbearing, Oft-Forgiving.

42. They swore their strongest oaths by Allah that if a warner came to them, they would follow his guidance better than any (other) of the peoples: but when a warner came to them, it has only increased their flight (from righteousness) -

43. On account of their arrogance in the land and their plotting of evil. But the plotting of evil will hem in only the authors of it. Now are they but looking for the way the ancients were dealt with? But no change will you find in Allah's way (of dealing): no turning off will you find in Allah's way (of dealing).

44. Do they not travel through the earth, and see what was the end of those before them - though they were superior to them in strength? Nor is Allah to be frustrated by anything whatever in the heavens or on earth: for He is All-Knowing, All-Powerful.

45. If Allah were to punish men according to what they deserve, He would not leave on the back of the (earth) a single living creature; but He gives them respite for a stated term: when their term expires, verily Allah has in His sight all His servants.

Surah 36: *Ya Sin*

In the name of Allah,
Most Gracious, Most Merciful.

1. *Ya-Sin.*

2. By the Qur'an, full of wisdom -

3. You are indeed one of the messengers.

4. On a straight way.

5. It is a revelation sent down by (Him), the Exalted in Might, Most Merciful,

6. In order that you may admonish a people, whose fathers had received no admonition, and who therefore remain heedless (of the signs of Allah).

7. The word is proved true against the greater part of them; for they do not believe.

8. We have put yokes round their necks right up to their chins, so that their heads are forced up (and they cannot see).

9. And We have put a bar in front of them and a bar behind them, and further, We have covered them up; so that they cannot see.

10. The same is it to them whether you admonish them or you do not admonish them: they will not believe.

11. You can but admonish such a one as follows the message and fears the (Lord) Most Gracious, unseen: give such a one, therefore, good tidings of forgiveness and a reward most generous.

12. Verily We shall give life to the dead, and We record that which they sent before and that which they leave behind, and of all things have We taken account in a clear book (of evidence).

13. Set out to them, by way of a parable, the (story of) the companions of the city. See, there came messengers to it.

14. When We (first) sent to them two messengers, they rejected them: but We strengthened them with a third: they said, "Truly, we have been sent on a mission to you."

15. The (people) said: "You are only men like ourselves; and (Allah) Most Gracious sends no sort of revelation: you do nothing but lie."

16. They said: "Our Lord does know that we have been sent on a mission to you:

17. And our duty is only to proclaim the clear message."

18. The (people) said: "For us, we augur an evil omen from you: if you desist not, we will certainly stone you, and a grievous punishment indeed will be inflicted on you by us."

19. They said: "Your evil omens are with yourselves: (think you this an evil omen), if you are admonished? Nay, but you are a people transgressing all bounds!"

20. Then there came running from the farthest part of the city, a man saying, "O my people! Obey the messengers:

21. Obey those who ask no reward of you (for themselves), and who have themselves received guidance.

22. It would not be reasonable in me if I did not serve Him Who created me, and to Whom you shall (all) be brought back.

23. Shall I take (other) gods besides Him? If (Allah) Most Gracious should intend some adversity for me, of no use whatever will be their intercession for me, nor can they deliver me.

24. I would indeed if I were to do so, be in manifest error.

25. For me, I have faith in the Lord of you (all): listen then, to me!"

26. It was said: "Enter you the garden." He said: "Ah me! Would that my people knew (what I know)! -

27. For that my Lord has granted me forgiveness and has enrolled me among those held in honour!"

28. And We sent not down against his people, after him, any forces from heaven, nor was it needful for Us so to do.

29. It was no more than a single mighty blast, and see! They were (like ashes) quenched and silent.

30. Ah! Alas for (My) servants! There comes not a messenger to them but they mock him!

31. Do they not see how many generations before them We destroyed? Not to them will they return:

32. But each one of them all will be brought before Us (for judgement).

33. A sign for them is the earth that is dead: We do give it life and produce grain from it, of which you do eat.

34. And We produce in it orchards with date-palms and vines, and We cause springs to gush out in it;

35. That they may enjoy the fruits of this (artistry); it was not their hands that made this: will they not then give thanks?

36. Glory to Allah, Who created in pairs all things that the earth produces, as well as their own (human) kind and (other) things of which they have no knowledge.

37. And a sign for them is the night: We withdraw from it the day, and behold they are plunged in darkness;

38. And the sun runs its course for a period determined for it: that is the decree of (Him), the Exalted in Might, the All-Knowing.

39. And the moon - We have measured for it mansions (to traverse) till it returns like the old (and withered) lower part of a date stalk.

40. It is not permitted to the sun to catch up the moon, nor can the night outstrip the day: each (just) swims along in (its own) orbit (according to law).

41. And a sign for them is that We bore their race (through the flood) in the loaded ark;

42. And We have created for them similar (vessels) on which they ride.

43. If it were Our will, We could drown them: then would there be no helper (to hear their call), nor could they be delivered.

44. Except by way of mercy from Us, and by way of (worldly) convenience (to serve them) for a time.

45. When they are told, "Fear you that which is before you and that which will be after you, in order that you may receive mercy," (they turn back).

46. Not a sign comes to them from among the signs of their Lord, but they turn away from it.

47. And when they are told, "Spend you of (the bounties) with which Allah has provided you," the unbelievers say to those who believe: "Shall we then feed those whom, if Allah had so willed, He would have fed, (Himself)? - You are in nothing but manifest error."

48. Further, they say, "When will this promise (come to pass), if what you say is true?"

49. They will not (have to) wait for anything but a single blast: it will seize them while they are yet disputing among themselves!

50. No (chance) will they then have, by will, to dispose (of their affairs), nor to return to their own people!

51. The trumpet shall be sounded, when see, from the graves (men) will rush forward to their Lord!

52. They will say: "Ah! Woe to us! Who has raised us up from our beds of rest? (A voice will say:) "This is what (Allah) Most Gracious had promised, and true was the word of the messengers!"

53. It will be no more than a single blast, when lo, they will all be brought up before Us!

54. Then, on that day, not a soul will be wronged in the least, and you shall but be repaid the dues of your past deeds.

55. Verily the companions of the garden shall that day have joy in all that they do;

56. They and their associates will be in groves of (cool) shade, reclining on thrones (of dignity);

57. (Every) fruit (enjoyment) will be there for them; they shall have whatever they call for;

58. "Peace! - A word (of salutation) from a Lord Most Merciful!

59. And O you in sin! Get you apart this day!

60. Did I not enjoin on you, O you children of Adam, that you should not worship Satan; for that he was to you an enemy avowed?-

61. And that you should worship Me, (for that) this was the straight way?

62. But he did lead astray a great multitude of you. Did you not, then, understand?

63. This is the hell of which you were (repeatedly) warned!

64. Embrace you the (fire) this day, for that you (persistently) rejected (truth)."

65. That day shall We set a seal on their mouths. But their hands will speak to Us, and their feet bear witness, to all that they did.

66. If it had been Our will, We could surely have blotted out their eyes; then should they have run about groping for the path, but how could they have seen?

67. And if it had been Our will, We could have transformed them (to remain) in their places; then should they have been unable to move about, nor could they have returned (after error).

68. If We grant long life to any, We cause him to be reversed in nature: will they not then understand?

69. We have not instructed the (prophet) in poetry nor is it befitting for Him: this is no less than a message and a Qur'an making things clear:

70. That it may give admonition to any (who are) alive, and that the charge may be proved against those who reject (truth).

71. Do they not see that it is We Who have created for them - among the things which Our hands have fashioned - cattle, which are under their dominion?-

72. And that We have subjected them to their (use)? Of them some do carry them and some they eat:

73. And they have (other) profits from them (besides), and they get (milk) to drink. Will they not then be grateful?

74. Yet they take (for worship) gods other than Allah, (hoping) that they might be helped!

75. They have not the power to help them: but they will be brought up (before Our judgement seat) as a troop (to be condemned).

76. Let not their speech then grieve you. Verily We know what they hide as well as what they disclose.

77. Does not man see that it is We Who created Him from sperm? Yet see! He (stands up) as an open adversary!

78. And he makes comparisons for Us, and forgets his own (origin and) creation: He says, "Who can give life to (dry) bones and decomposed ones (at that)?"

79. Say, "He will give them life Who created them for the first time! For He is well-versed in every kind of creation!-

80. The same Who produces for you fire out of the green tree, when behold, you kindle with it (your own fires)!

81. Is not He Who created the heavens and the earth able to create the like of it?" Yea, indeed! For He is the Creator Supreme of skill and knowledge (infinite)!

82. Verily, when He intends a thing, His command is, "Be", and it is!

83. So glory to Him in Whose hands is the dominion of all things; and to Him will you be all brought back.

Surah 37: **As-Saffat**
(Those Ranged In Ranks)

**In the name of Allah,
Most Gracious, Most Merciful.**

1. By those who range themselves in ranks,

2. And so are strong in repelling (evil),

3. And thus proclaim the message (of Allah)!

4. Verily, your God is One!-

5. Lord of the heavens and of the earth, and all between them, and Lord of every point at the rising of the sun!

6. We have indeed decked the lower heaven with beauty (in) the stars -

7. (For beauty) and for guard against all obstinate rebellious evil spirits.

8. (So) they should not strain their ears in the direction of the exalted assembly but be cast away from every side,

9. Repulsed for they are under a perpetual penalty,

10. Except such as snatch away something by stealth, and they are pursued by a flaming fire, of piercing brightness.

11. Just ask their opinion: are they the more difficult to create, or the (other) beings We have created? Them have We created out of a sticky clay!

12. Truly do you marvel, while they ridicule,

13. And, when they are admonished, pay no heed -

14. And, when they see a sign, turn it to mockery,

15. And say, "This is nothing but evident sorcery!

16. What! When we die, and become dust and bones, shall we (then) be raised up (again)?

17. And also our fathers of old?"

18. Say you: "Yea, and you shall then be humiliated (on account of your evil)."

19. Then it will be a single (compelling) call; and see, they will begin to see!

20. They will say, "Ah! Woe to us! This is the day of judgement!"

21. (A voice will say,) "This is the day of sorting out, whose truth you (once) denied!"

22. "Bring you up", it shall be said, "The wrongdoers and their wives, and the things they worshipped-

23. Besides Allah, and lead them to the way to the (fierce) fire!

24. But stop them, for they must be asked:

25. 'What is the matter with you that you help not each other?'"

26. Nay, but that day they shall submit (to judgement);

27. And they will turn to one another, and question one another.

28. They will say: "It was you who used to come to us from the right hand (of power and authority)!"

29. They will reply: "Nay, you yourselves had no faith!

30. Nor had we any authority over you. Nay, it was you who were a people in obstinate rebellion!

31. So now has been proved true, against us, the word of our Lord that we shall indeed (have to) taste (the punishment of our sins):

32. We led you astray: for truly, we were ourselves astray."

33. Truly, that day, they will (all) share in the penalty.

34. Verily that is how We shall deal with sinners.

35. For they, when they were told that there is no god except Allah, would puff themselves up with pride,

36. And say: "What! Shall we give up our gods for the sake of a poet possessed?"

37. Nay! He has come with the (very) truth, and he confirms (the message of) the messengers (before Him).

38. You shall indeed taste of the grievous penalty -

39. But it will be no more than the retribution of (the evil) that you have wrought -

40. But the sincere (and devoted) servants of Allah -

41. For them is a sustenance determined,

42. Fruits (delights); and they (shall enjoy) honour and dignity,

43. In gardens of felicity,

44. Facing each other on thrones (of dignity):

45. Round will be passed to them a cup from a clear-flowing fountain,

46. Crystal-white, of a taste delicious to those who drink (of it),

47. Free from headiness; nor will they suffer intoxication from it.

48. And beside them will be chaste women; restraining their glances, with big eyes (of wonder and beauty).

49. As if they were (delicate) eggs closely guarded.

50. Then they will turn to one another and question one another.

51. One of them will start the talk and say: "I had an intimate companion (on the earth),

52. Who used to say, 'What! Are you amongst those who bear witness to the truth (of the message)?

53. When we die and become dust and bones, shall we indeed receive rewards and punishments?'"

54. (A voice) said: "Would you like to look down?"

55. He looked down and saw him in the midst of the fire.

56. He said: "By Allah! You were little short of bringing me to perdition!

57. Had it not been for the grace of my Lord, I should certainly have been among those brought (there)!

58. Is it (the case) that we shall not die,

59. Except our first death, and that we shall not be punished?"

60. Verily this is the supreme achievement!

61. For the like of this let all strive, who wish to strive.

62. Is that the better entertainment or the tree of Zaqqum?

63. For We have truly made it (as) a trial for the wrongdoers.

64. For it is a tree that springs out of the bottom of hellfire;

65. The shoots of its fruit-stalks are like the heads of devils;

66. Truly they will eat of it and fill their bellies with it.

67. Then on top of that they will be given a mixture made of boiling water.

68. Then shall their return be to the (blazing) fire.

69. Truly they found their fathers on the wrong path;

70. So they (too) were rushed down on their footsteps!

71. And truly before them, many of the ancients went astray -

72. But We sent before, among them, (messengers) to admonish them -

73. Then see what was the end of those who were admonished (but heeded not) -

74. Except the sincere (and devoted) servants of Allah.

75. (In the days of old), Noah called to Us, and We are the Best to hear prayer.

76. And We delivered him and his people from the great calamity,

77. And made his progeny to endure (on this earth);

78. And We left (this blessing) for him among generations to come in later times:

79. "Peace and salutation to Noah among the nations!"

80. Thus indeed do We reward those who do right.

81. For he was one of Our believing servants.

82. Then the rest We overwhelmed in the flood.

83. Verily among those who followed his way was Abraham.

84. See, He approached his Lord with a sound heart.

85. See, he said to his father and to his people, "What is that which you worship?

86. Is it a falsehood - gods other than Allah that you desire?

87. Then what is your idea about the Lord of the Worlds?"

88. Then did he cast a glance at the stars.

89. And he said, "I am indeed sick (at heart)!"

90. So they turned away from him, and departed.

91. Then did he turn to their gods and said, "Will you not eat (of the offerings before you)?

92. What is the matter with you that you speak not (intelligently)?"

93. Then did he turn upon them striking (them) with the right hand.

94. Then came (the worshippers) with hurried steps, and faced (him).

95. He said: "Worship you that which you have (yourselves) carved?

96. But Allah has created you and your handiwork!"

97. They said, "Build him a furnace, and throw him into the blazing fire!"

98. (This failing) they then sought a stratagem against him, but We made them the ones most humiliated!

99. He said: "I will go to my Lord! He will surely guide me!

100. O my Lord! Grant me a righteous (son)!"

101. So We gave him the good news of a boy ready to suffer and forbear.

102. Then, when (the son) reached (the age of) (serious) work with him, he said: "O my son! I see in vision that I offer you in sacrifice: now see what is your view!" (The son) said: "O my father! Do as you are commanded: you will find me, if Allah so wills, one practising patience and constancy!"

103. So when they had both submitted their wills (to Allah), and He had laid Him prostrate on his forehead (for sacrifice),

104. We called out to him, "O Abraham!

105. "You have already fulfilled the vision!" - thus indeed do We reward those who do right.

106. For this was obviously a trial -

107. And We ransomed him with a momentous sacrifice:

108. And We left (this blessing) for him among generations (to come) in later times:

109. "Peace and salutation to Abraham!"

110. Thus indeed do We reward those who do right.

111. For he was one of Our believing servants.

112. And We gave him the good news of Isaac - a prophet - one of the righteous.

113. We blessed him and Isaac: but of their progeny are (some) that do right, and (some) that obviously do wrong, to their own souls.

114. Again, (of old), We bestowed Our favour on Moses and Aaron,

115. And We delivered them and their people from (their) great calamity;

116. And We helped them, so they overcame (their troubles);

117. And We gave them the book which helps to make things clear;

118. And We guided them to the straight way.

119. And We left (this blessing) for them among generations (to come) in later times:

120. "Peace and salutation to Moses and Aaron!"

121. Thus indeed do We reward those who do right.

122. For they were two of Our believing servants.

123. So also was Elias among those sent (by Us).

124. See, he said to his people, "Will you not fear (Allah)?

125. Will you call upon Baal and forsake the Best of Creators -

126. Allah, your Lord and Cherisher and the Lord and Cherisher of your fathers of old?"

127. But they rejected him, and they will certainly be called up (for punishment) -

128. Except the sincere and devoted servants of Allah (among them).

129. And We left (this blessing) for him among generations (to come) in later times:

130. "Peace and salutation to such as Elias!"

131. Thus indeed do We reward those who do right.

132. For He was one of Our believing servants.

133. So also was Lot among those sent (by Us).

134. See, We delivered him and his adherents, all

135. Except an old woman who was among those who lagged behind:

136. Then We destroyed the rest.

137. Verily, you pass by their (sites), by day -

138. And by night: will you not understand?

139. So also was Jonah among those sent (by Us).

140. When he ran away (like a slave from captivity) to the ship (fully) laden,

141. He (agreed to) cast lots, and he was condemned:

142. Then the big fish did swallow him, and he had done acts worthy of blame.

143. Had it not been that he (repented and) glorified Allah,

144. He would certainly have remained inside the fish till the day of resurrection.

145. But We cast him out on the naked shore in a state of sickness,

146. And We caused to grow over him, a spreading plant of the gourd kind,

147. And We sent him (on a mission) to a hundred thousand (men) or more.

148. And they believed; so We permitted them to enjoy (their life) for a while.

149. Now ask them their opinion: Is it that your Lord has (only) daughters, and they have sons? -

150. Or that We created the angels female, and they are witnesses (to it)?

151. Is it not that they say, from their own invention,

152. "Allah has begotten children"? But they are liars!

153. Did He (then) choose daughters rather than sons?

154. What is the matter with you? How judge you?

155. Will you not then receive admonition?

156. Or have you an authority manifest?

157. Then bring you your book (of authority) if you be truthful!

158. And they have invented a blood-relationship between Him and the Jinns: but the Jinns know (quite well) that they have indeed to appear (before His judgement seat)!

159. Glory to Allah! (He is free) from the things they ascribe (to Him)!

160. Not (so do) the servants of Allah, sincere and devoted.

161. For, verily, neither you nor those you worship -

162. Can lead (any) into temptation concerning Allah,

163. Except such as are (themselves) going to the blazing fire!

164. (Those ranged in ranks say): "Not one of us but has a place appointed

165. And we are verily ranged in ranks (for service);

166. And we are verily those who declare (Allah's) glory!"

167. And there were those who said,

168. "If only we had had before us a message from those of old,

169. We should certainly have been servants of Allah, sincere (and devoted)!"

170. But (now that the Qur'an has come), they reject it: but soon will they know!

171. Already has Our word been passed before (this) to Our servants sent (by Us),

172. That they would certainly be assisted,

173. And that Our forces - they surely must conquer.

174. So turn you away from them for a little while,

175. And watch them (how they fare), and they soon shall see (how you fare)!

176. Do they wish (indeed) to hurry on Our punishment?

177. But when it descends into the open space before them, evil will be the morning for those who were warned (and heeded not)!

178. So turn you away from them for a little while,

179. And watch (how they fare) and they soon shall see (how you fare)!

180. Glory to your Lord, the Lord of Honour and Power! (He is free) from what they ascribe (to him)!

181. And peace on the messengers!

182. And praise to Allah, the Lord and Cherisher of the Worlds.

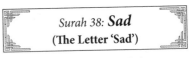

Surah 38: *Sad*
(The Letter 'Sad')

In the name of Allah,
Most Gracious, Most Merciful.

1. *Sad.* By the Qur'an full of admonition: (This is the truth).

2. But the unbelievers (are steeped) in self-glory and separatism.

3. How many generations before them did We destroy? In the end they cried (for mercy) - when there was no longer time for being saved!

4. So they wonder that a warner has come to them from among themselves! And the unbelievers say, "This is a sorcerer telling lies!

5. Has he made the gods (all) into one God? Truly this is a wonderful thing!"

6. And the leaders among them go away (impatiently) (saying), "Walk you away, and remain constant to your gods! For this is truly a thing designed (against you)!

7. We never heard (the like) of this among the people of these latter days: this is nothing but a made-up tale!"

8. "What! Has the message been sent to him - (of all persons) among us?" But they are in doubt concerning My (own) message! Nay, they have not yet tasted My punishment!

9. Or do they have the treasures of the mercy of your Lord - the Exalted in Power, the Grantor of Bounties without measure!

10. Or do they have the dominion of the heavens and the earth and all between? If so, let them mount up with the ropes and means (to reach that end)!

11. But they will be put to flight even a host of confederates.

12. Before them (were many who) rejected messengers - the people of Noah, and 'Ad, and Pharaoh the Lord of stakes,

13. And Thamud, and the people of Lot, and the Companions of the Wood - such were the confederates.

14. Not one (of them) but rejected the messengers, but My punishment came justly and inevitably (on them).

15. These (today) only wait for a single mighty blast, which (when it comes) will tolerate no delay.

16. They say: "Our Lord! Hasten to us our sentence (even) before the day of account!"

17. Have patience at what they say, and remember Our servant David, the man of strength: for he ever turned (to Allah).

18. It was We that made the hills declare, in unison with him, Our praises, at eventide and at break of day,

19. And the birds gathered (in assemblies): all with him did turn (to Allah).

20. We strengthened his kingdom, and gave him wisdom and sound judgement in speech and decision.

21. Has the story of the disputants reached you? See, they climbed over the wall of the private chamber;

22. When they entered the presence of David, and he was terrified of them, they said: "Fear not; we are two disputants, one of whom has wronged the other; decide now between us with truth, and treat us not with injustice, but guide us to the even path.

23. This man is my brother: he has nine and ninety ewes, and I have (but) one: Yet he says, 'Commit her to my care,' and is (moreover) harsh to me in speech."

24. (David) said: "He has undoubtedly wronged you in demanding your (single) ewe to be added to his (flock of) ewes; truly many are the partners (in business) who wrong each other: not so do those who believe and work deeds of righteousness, and how few are they?" And David gathered that We had tried him: he asked forgiveness of his Lord, fell down, bowing (in prostration), and turned (to Allah in repentance).

25. So We forgave him this (lapse): he enjoyed, indeed, a near approach to Us, and a beautiful place of (final) return.

26. O David! We did indeed make you a vicegerent on earth: so judge you between men in truth (and justice): nor follow you the lusts (of your heart), for they will mislead you from the path of Allah: for those who wander astray from the path of Allah, is a penalty grievous, for that they forget the day of account.

27. Not without purpose did We create heaven and earth and all between! That were the thought of unbelievers! But woe to the unbelievers because of the fire (of hell)!

28. Shall We treat those who believe and work deeds of righteousness, the same as those who do mischief on earth? Shall We treat those who guard against evil, the same as those who turn aside from the right?

29. (Here is) a book which We have sent down to you, full of blessings, that they may meditate on its signs, and that men of understanding may receive admonition.

30. To David We gave Solomon (for a son) - how excellent in Our service! Ever did he turn (to Us)!

31. See, there were brought before him, at eventide, coursers of the highest breeding, and swift of foot;

32. And he said, "Truly do I love the love of good, with a view to the glory of my Lord" - until (the sun) was hidden in the veil (of night):

33. "Bring them back to me." Then began he to pass his hand over (their) legs and their necks.

34. And We did try Solomon: We placed on his throne a body (without life): but he did turn (to Us in true devotion):

35. He said: "O my Lord! Forgive me, and grant me a kingdom which, (it may be), suits not another after me: for You are the Grantor of Bounties (without measure)."

36. Then We subjected the wind to his power, to flow gently to his order, which ever way he willed -

37. As also the evil ones, (including) every kind of builder and diver -

38. As also others bound together in fetters.

39. "Such are Our bounties: whether you bestow them (on others) or withhold them, no account will be asked."

40. And he enjoyed, indeed, a near approach to Us, and a beautiful place of (final) return.

41. Commemorate Our servant Job. See, he called to his Lord: "The evil one has afflicted me with distress and suffering!"

42. (The command was given:) "Strike with your foot: here is (water) in which to wash, cool and refreshing and (water) to drink."

43. And We gave him (back) his people and doubled their number - as a grace from Ourselves, and a thing for commemoration, for all who have understanding.

44. "And take in your hand a little grass, and strike with it: and break not (your oath)." Truly We found him full of patience and constancy, how excellent in Our service! Ever did he turn (to Us)!

45. And commemorate Our servants Abraham, Isaac, and Jacob, possessors of power and vision.

46. Verily, We did choose them for a special (purpose) - proclaiming the message of the hereafter.

47. They were, in Our sight, truly, of the company of the elect and the good.

48. And commemorate Ishmael, al-Yasa, and Dhu al-Kifl: each of them was of the company of the good.

49. This is a message (of admonition): and verily, for the righteous is a beautiful place of (final) return -

50. Gardens of Eternity, whose doors will (ever) be open to them;

51. In it will they recline (at ease); in it can they call (at pleasure) for fruit in abundance, and (delicious) drink;

52. And beside them will be chaste women restraining their glances, (companions) of equal age.

53. Such is the promise made to you for the day of account!

54. Truly such will be Our bounty (to you); it will never fail -

55. Yea, such! But - for the wrongdoers will be an evil place of (final) return!

56. Hell! - They will burn in it - an evil bed (indeed to lie on)! -

57. Yea, such! - Then shall they taste it - a boiling fluid, and a fluid dark, murky, intensely cold! -

58. And other penalties of a similar kind, to match them!

59. Here is a troop rushing headlong with you! No welcome for them! Truly they shall burn in the fire!

60. (The followers shall call to the misleaders:) "Nay, you (too)! No welcome for you! It is you who have brought this upon us! Now evil is (this) place to stay in!"

61. They will say: "Our Lord! Whoever brought this upon us - add to him a double penalty in the fire!"

62. And they will say: "What has happened to us that we do not see men whom we used to number among the bad ones?

63. Did we treat them (as such) in ridicule or have (our) eyes failed to perceive them?"

64. Truly that is just and fitting - the mutual recriminations of the people of the fire!

65. Say: "Truly am I a warner: no god is there but the One God, Supreme and Irresistible -

66. The Lord of the heavens and the earth, and all between - Exalted in Might, Able to enforce His will, Forgiving again and again."

67. Say: "That is a message supreme (above all) -

68. From which you do turn away!

69. No knowledge have I of the chiefs on high, when they discuss (matters) among themselves.

70. Only this has been revealed to me: that I am to give warning plainly and publicly."

71. See, your Lord said to the angels: "I am about to create man from clay:

72. When I have fashioned him (in due proportion) and breathed into him of My spirit, fall you down in obeisance to him."

73. So the angels prostrated themselves, all of them together;

74. Not so Iblis: he was haughty, and became one of those who reject faith.

75. (Allah) said: "O Iblis! What prevents you from prostrating yourself to one whom I have created with My hands? Are you haughty? Or are you one of the high (and mighty) ones?"

76. (Iblis) said: "I am better than he: You created me from fire, and him You created from clay."

77. (Allah) said: "Then get you out from here: for you are rejected, accursed.

78. And My curse shall be on you till the day of judgement."

79. (Iblis) said: "O my Lord! Give me then respite till the day the (dead) are raised."

80. (Allah) said: "Respite then is granted you -

81. Till the day of the time appointed."

82. (Iblis) said: "Then, by Your power, I will put them all in the wrong -

83. Except Your servants amongst them, sincere and purified (by Your grace)."

84. (Allah) said: "Then it is just and fitting - and I say what is just and fitting -

85. That I will certainly fill hell with you and those that follow you - everyone."

86. Say: "No reward do I ask of you for this (Qur'an), nor am I a pretender.

87. This is no less than a message to (all) the worlds.

88. And you shall certainly know the truth of it (all) after a while."

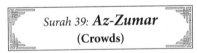

Surah 39: **Az-Zumar**
(Crowds)

In the name of Allah,
Most Gracious, Most Merciful.

1. The revelation of this book is from Allah, the Exalted in power, Full of wisdom.

2. Verily it is We Who have revealed the book to you in truth: so serve Allah, offering Him sincere devotion.

3. Is it not to Allah that sincere devotion is due? But those who take for protectors other than Allah (say): "We only serve them in order that they may bring us nearer to Allah." Truly Allah will judge between them in that in which they differ. But Allah guides not such as are false and ungrateful.

4. Had Allah wished to take to Himself a son, He could have chosen whom He pleased out of those whom He does create: but glory be to Him! (He is above such things.) He is Allah, the One, the Irresistible.

5. He created the heavens and the earth in true (proportions): He makes the night overlap the day, and the day overlap the night: He has subjected the sun and the moon (to His law): each one follows a course for a time appointed. Is not He the Exalted in power - He Who forgives again and again?

6. He created you (all) from a single person: then created, of like nature, his mate; and He sent down for you eight head of cattle in pairs: He makes you, in the wombs of your mothers, in stages, one after another, in three veils of darkness. Such is Allah, your Lord and Cherisher: to Him belongs (all) dominion. There is no god but He: then how are you turned away (from your true centre)?

7. If you reject (Allah), truly Allah has no need of you; but He likes not ingratitude from His servants: if you are grateful, He is pleased with you. No bearer of burdens can bear the burden of another. In the end, to your Lord is your return, when He will tell you the truth of all that you did (in this life). For He knows well all that is in (men's) hearts.

8. When some trouble touches man, he cries to his Lord, turning to Him in repentance: but when He bestows a favour upon him, as from

Himself, (man) does forget what he cried and prayed for before, and he does set up rivals to Allah, thus misleading others from Allah's path. Say, "Enjoy your blasphemy for a little while: verily you are (one) of the companions of the fire!"

9. Is one who worships devoutly during the hours of the night prostrating himself or standing (in adoration), who takes heed of the hereafter, and who places his hope in the mercy of his Lord - (like one who does not)? Say: "Are those equal, those who know and those who do not know? It is those who are endued with understanding that receive admonition."

10. Say: "(Thus speaks God:) O you My servants who believe! Fear your Lord. Good is (the reward) for those who do good in this world. Spacious is Allah's earth! Those who patiently persevere will truly receive a reward without measure!"

11. Say: "Verily, I am commanded to serve Allah with sincere devotion;

12. And I am commanded to be the first of those who bow to Allah in Islam."

13. Say: "I would, if I disobeyed my Lord, indeed have fear of the penalty of a mighty day."

14. Say: "It is Allah I serve, with my sincere (and exclusive) devotion:

15. Serve you what you will besides Him." Say: "Truly, those in loss are those who lose their own souls and their people on the day of judgement: Ah! That is indeed the (real and) evident loss!"

16. They shall have layers of fire above them, and layers (of fire) below them: with this does Allah warn off His servants: "O My servants! Then fear you Me!"

17. Those who eschew evil - and fall not into its worship - and turn to Allah (in repentance) - for them is good news: so announce the good news to My servants -

18. Those who listen to the word, and follow the best (meaning) in it: those are the ones whom Allah has guided, and those are the ones endued with understanding.

19. Is then, one against whom the decree of punishment is justly due (equal to one who eschews evil)? Would you, then, deliver one (who is) in the fire?

20. But it is for those who fear their Lord, that lofty mansions, one above another, have been built; beneath them flow rivers (of delight); (such is) the promise of Allah: never does Allah fail in (His) promise.

21. Do you not see that Allah sends down rain from the sky, and leads it through springs in the earth? Then He causes to grow, with it, produce of various colours; then it withers; you will see it grow yellow; then He makes it dry up and crumble away. Truly, in this, is a message of remembrance to men of understanding.

22. Is one whose heart Allah has opened to Islam, so that he has received enlightenment from Allah, (no better than one hardhearted)? Woe to those whose hearts are hardened against celebrating the praises of Allah! They are manifestly wandering (in error)!

23. Allah has revealed (from time to time) the most beautiful message in the form of a book, consistent with itself, (yet) repeating (its teaching in various aspects); the skins of those who fear their Lord tremble at it; then their skins and their hearts do soften to the celebration of Allah's praises. Such is the guidance of Allah: He guides with it whom He pleases, but such as Allah leaves to stray, can have none to guide.

24. Is, then, one who has to fear the brunt of the penalty on the day of judgement (and receive it) on his face, (like one guarded from it)? It will be said to the wrongdoers: "Taste you (the fruits of) what you earned!"

25. Those before them (also) rejected (revelation) and so the punishment came to them from directions they did not perceive.

26. So Allah gave them a taste of humiliation in the present life, but greater is the punishment of the hereafter, if they only knew!

27. We have put out for men, in this Qur'an every kind of parable, in order that they may receive admonition.

28. (It is) a Qur'an in Arabic, without any crookedness (in it): in order that they may guard against evil.

29. Allah puts out a parable - a man belonging to many partners at variance with each other, and a man belonging entirely to one master: are those two equal in comparison? Praise be to Allah! But most of them have no knowledge.

30. (O prophet!) Truly you will die (one day), and truly they (too) will die (one day).

31. In the end will you (all), on the day of judgement, settle your disputes in the presence of your Lord.

32. Who, then, does more wrong than one who utters a lie concerning Allah, and rejects the truth when it comes to him! Is there not in hell an abode for blasphemers?

33. And he who brings the truth and he who confirms (and supports) it - such are the men who do right.

34. They shall have all that they wish for, in the presence of their Lord: such is the reward of those who do good:

35. So that Allah will turn off from them (even) the worst in their deeds and give them their reward according to the best of what they have done.

36. Is not Allah enough for His servant? But they try to frighten you with other (gods) besides Him! For such as Allah leaves to stray, there can be no guide.

37. And such as Allah does guide there can be none to lead astray. Is not Allah Exalted in power, (able to enforce His will), Lord of retribution?

38. If indeed you ask them who it is that created the heavens and the earth, they would be sure to say, "Allah." Say: "See you then? The things that you invoke besides Allah - can they, if Allah wills some penalty for me, remove His penalty? - Or if He wills some grace for me, can they keep back His grace?" Say:

"Sufficient is Allah for me! In Him trust those who put their trust."

39. Say: "O my people! Do whatever you can: I will do (my part): but soon will you know -

40. Who it is to whom comes a penalty of disgrace, and on whom descends a penalty that lasts."

41. Verily We have revealed the book to you in truth, for (instructing) mankind. He, then, that receives guidance benefits his own soul: but he that strays injures his own soul. Nor are you set over them to dispose of their affairs.

42. It is Allah that takes the souls (of men) at death; and those that die not (He takes) during their sleep: those on whom He has passed the decree of death, He keeps back (from returning to life), but the rest He sends (to their bodies) for a term appointed. Verily in this are signs for those who reflect.

43. What! Do they take for intercessors others besides Allah? Say: "Even if they have no power whatever and no intelligence?"

44. Say: "To Allah belongs exclusively (the right to grant) intercession: to Him belongs the dominion of the heavens and the earth: in the end it is to Him that you shall be brought back."

45. When Allah, the One and Only, is mentioned, the hearts of those who believe not in the hereafter are filled with disgust and horror; but when (gods) other than He are mentioned, behold they are filled with joy!

46. Say: "O Allah! Creator of the heavens and the earth! Knower of all that is hidden and open! It is You that will judge between Your servants in those matters about which they have differed."

47. Even if the wrongdoers had all that there is on earth, and as much more, (in vain) would they offer it for ransom from the pain of the penalty on the day of judgement: but something will confront them from Allah, which they could never have counted upon!

48. For the evils of their deeds will confront them, and they will be (completely) encircled by that which they used to mock at!

49. Now, when trouble touches man, he cries to Us; but when We bestow a favour upon him as from Ourselves, he says, "This has been given to me because of a certain knowledge (I have)!" Nay, but this is but a trial, but most of them understand not!

50. Thus did the (generations) before them say! But all that they did was of no profit to them.

51. Nay, the evil results of their deeds overtook them. And the wrongdoers of this (generation) - the evil results of their deeds will soon overtake them (too), and they will never be able to frustrate (Our plan)!

52. Do they not know that Allah enlarges the provision or restricts it, for any He pleases? Verily, in this are signs for those who believe!

53. Say: "O My servants who have transgressed against their souls! Despair not of the mercy of Allah: for Allah forgives all sins: for He is Oft-Forgiving, Most Merciful.

54. Turn you to your Lord (in repentance) and bow to His (Will), before the penalty comes on you: after that you shall not be helped.

55. And follow the Best of (the courses) revealed to you from your Lord, before the penalty comes on you - of a sudden, while you perceive not! -

56. Lest the soul should (then) say: 'Ah! Woe is me! - In that I neglected (my duty) towards Allah, and was but among those who mocked!' -

57. Or (lest) it should say: 'If only Allah had guided me, I should certainly have been among the righteous!' -

58. Or (lest) it should say when it (actually) sees the penalty: 'If only I had another chance, I should certainly be among those who do good!'"

59. "(The reply will be) Nay, but there came to you My signs, and you did reject them: you were haughty, and became one of those who reject faith!"

60. On the day of judgement will you see those who told lies against Allah - their faces will be turned black; is there not in hell an abode for the haughty?

61. But Allah will deliver the righteous to their place of salvation: no evil shall touch them, nor shall they grieve.

62. Allah is the Creator of all things, and He is the Guardian and Disposer of all affairs.

63. To Him belong the keys of the heavens and the earth: and those who reject the signs of Allah it is they who will be in loss.

64. Say: "Is it someone other than Allah that you order me to worship, O you ignorant ones?"

65. But it has already been revealed to you - as it was to those before you - "If you were to join (gods with Allah) truly fruitless will be your work (in life), and you will surely be in the ranks of those who lose (all spiritual good)."

66. Nay, but worship Allah, and be of those who give thanks.

67. No just estimate have they made of Allah, such as is due to Him: on the day of judgement the whole of the earth will be but His handful and the heavens will be rolled up in His right hand: Glory to Him! High is He above the partners they attribute to Him!

68. The trumpet will (just) be sounded, when all that are in the heavens and on earth will swoon, except such as it will please Allah (to exempt). Then will a second one be sounded, when, see, they will be standing and looking on!

69. And the earth will shine with the glory of its Lord: the record (of deeds) will be placed (open); the prophets and the witnesses will be brought forward: and a just decision pronounced between them; and they will not be wronged (in the least).

70. And to every soul will be paid in full (the fruit) of its deeds; and (Allah) knows best all that they do.

71. The unbelievers will be led to hell in crowds: until, when they arrive there, its gates will be opened, and its keepers will say, "Did not messengers come to you from among yourselves, rehearsing to you the signs of your Lord, and warning you of the meeting of this day of yours?" The answer will be: "True:

but the decree of punishment has been proved true against the unbelievers!"

72. (To them) will be said: "Enter you the gates of hell, to dwell in it: and evil is (this) abode of the arrogant!"

73. And those who feared their Lord will be led to the garden in crowds: until behold they arrive there; its gates will be opened; and its keepers will say: "Peace be upon you! Well have you done! Enter you here, to dwell in it."

74. They will say: "Praise be to Allah, Who has truly fulfilled His promise to us, and has given us (this) land in heritage; we can dwell in the garden as we will; how excellent a reward for those who work (righteousness)!"

75. And you will see the angels surrounding the throne (divine) on all sides, singing glory and praise to their Lord. The decision between them (at judgement) will be in (perfect) justice, and the call (on all sides) will be, "Praise be to Allah, the Lord of the Worlds!"

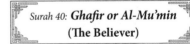

Surah 40: **Ghafir or Al-Mu'min**
(The Believer)

In the name of Allah,
Most Gracious, Most Merciful.

1. *Ha Mim.*

2. The revelation of this book is from Allah, Exalted in power, Full of knowledge -

3. Who forgives sin, accepts repentance, is strict in punishment, and has a long reach (in all things). There is no god but He: to Him is the final goal.

4. None can dispute about the signs of Allah but the unbelievers. Let not, then, their strutting about through the land deceive you!

5. But (there were people) before them, who denied (the signs) - the people of Noah, and the confederates (of evil) after them; and every people plotted against their prophet, to seize him, and disputed by means of vanities, with it to condemn the truth: but it was I that seized them! And how (terrible) was My requital!

6. Thus was the decree of your Lord proved true against the unbelievers; that truly they are companions of fire!

7. Those who sustain the throne (of Allah) and those around it sing glory and praise to their Lord; believe in Him; and implore forgiveness for those who believe: "Our Lord! Your reach is over all things, in mercy and knowledge. Forgive, then, those who turn in repentance, and follow Your path: and preserve them from the penalty of the blazing fire!

8. And grant, our Lord! That they enter the gardens of eternity, which You have promised to them, and to the righteous among their fathers, their wives, and their posterity! For You are (He), the Exalted in Might, Full of wisdom.

9. And preserve them from (all) ills; and any whom You do preserve from ills that day - on them will You have bestowed mercy indeed: and that will be truly (for them) the highest achievement."

10. The unbelievers will be addressed: "Greater was the aversion of Allah to you than (is) your aversion to

yourselves, seeing that you were called to the faith and you used to refuse."

11. They will say: "Our Lord! Twice have You made us without life, and twice have You given us life! Now have we recognised our sins: is there any way out (of this)?"

12. (The answer will be:) "This is because, when Allah was invoked as the only (object of worship), you did reject faith, but when partners were joined to Him, you believed! The command is with Allah, Most High, Most Great!"

13. He it is Who shows you His signs, and sends down sustenance for you from the sky: but only those receive admonition who turn (to Allah).

14. Call you, then, upon Allah with sincere devotion to Him, even though the unbelievers may detest it.

15. Raised high above ranks (or degrees), (He is) the Lord of the Throne (of authority): by His command does He send the spirit (of inspiration) to any of His servants He pleases, that it may warn (men) of the day of mutual meeting -

16. The day on which they will (all) come out: Not a single thing concerning them is hidden from Allah. Whose will be the dominion that day? That of Allah, the One, the Irresistible!

17. That day will every soul be requited for what it earned; no injustice will there be that day, for Allah is swift in taking account.

18. Warn them of the day that is (ever) drawing near, when the hearts will (come) right up to the throats to choke (them); no intimate friend nor intercessor will the wrongdoers have, who could be listened to.

19. (Allah) knows of (the tricks) that deceive with the eyes, and all that hearts (of men) conceal.

20. And Allah will judge with (justice and) truth: but those whom (men) invoke besides Him, will not (be in a position) to judge at all. Verily it is Allah (alone) Who hears and sees (all things).

21. Do they not travel through the earth and see what was the end of those before them? They were even superior to them in strength, and in the traces (they have left) in the land: but Allah did call them to account for their sins, and none had they to defend them against Allah.

22. That was because there came to them their messengers with clear (signs) but they rejected them: So Allah called them to account: for He is Full of Strength, Strict in punishment.

23. Of old We sent Moses, with Our signs and an authority manifest,

24. To Pharaoh, Haman, and Qarun; but they called (him) "A sorcerer telling lies!"

25. Now, when he came to them in truth, from Us, they said, "Slay the sons of those who believe with him, and keep alive their females," but the plots of unbelievers (end) in nothing but errors (and delusions)!

26. Said Pharaoh: "Leave me to slay Moses; and let him call on his Lord! What I fear is lest he should change your religion, or lest he should cause mischief to appear in the land!"

27. Moses said: "I have indeed called upon my Lord and your Lord (for protection) from every arrogant one who believes not in the day of account!"

28. A believer, a man from among the people of Pharaoh, who had concealed his faith, said: "Will you slay a man because he says 'My Lord is Allah'? - When he has indeed come to you with clear (signs) from your Lord? And if he be a liar, on him is (the sin of) his lie; but, if he is telling the truth, then will fall on you something of the (calamity) of which he warns you: truly Allah guides not one who transgresses and lies!"

29. "O my people! Yours is the dominion this day; you have the upper hand in the land; but who will help us from the punishment of Allah, should it befall us?" Pharaoh said: "I but point out to you that which I see (myself); nor do I guide you but to the path of right!"

30. Then said the man who believed: "O my people! Truly I do fear for you something like the day (of disaster) of the confederates (in sin)! -

31. Something like the fate of the people of Noah, the 'Ad, and the Thamud, and those who came after them: but Allah never wishes injustice to His servants.

32. And O my people! I fear for you a day when there will be mutual calling (and wailing) -

33. A day when you shall turn your backs and flee: no defender shall you have from Allah: any whom Allah leaves to stray there is none to guide.

34. And to you there came Joseph in times gone by, with clear signs, but you ceased not to doubt of the (mission) for which he had come: at length, when he died, you said: 'No messenger will Allah send after him.' Thus does Allah leave to stray such as transgress and live in doubt -

35. (Such) as dispute about the signs of Allah, without any authority that has reached them. Grievous and odious (is such conduct) in the sight of Allah and of the believers. Thus does Allah seal up every heart - of arrogant and obstinate transgressors."

36. Pharaoh said: "O Haman! Build me a lofty palace, that I may attain the ways and means -

37. "The ways and means of (reaching) the heavens, and that I may mount up to the God of Moses; but as far as I am concerned, I think (Moses) is a liar!" Thus was made alluring in Pharaoh's eyes, the evil of his deeds, and he was hindered from the path; and the plot of Pharaoh led to nothing but perdition (for him).

38. The man who believed said further: "O my people! Follow me; I will lead you to the path of right.

39. O my people! This life of the present is nothing but (temporary) convenience: it is the hereafter that is the home that will last.

40. He that works evil will not be requited but by the like of it; and he that works a righteous deed - whether man or woman - and is a believer - such will

enter the garden (of bliss): in it will they have abundance without measure.

41. And O my people! How (strange) it is for me to call you to salvation while you call me to the fire!

42. You do call upon me to blaspheme against Allah, and to join with Him partners of whom I have no knowledge; and I call you to the Exalted in Power, Who forgives again and again!"

43. Without doubt you do call me to one who is not fit to be called to, whether in this world or in the hereafter; our return will be to Allah; and the transgressors will be companions of the fire!

44. Soon will you remember what I say to you (now). My (own) affair I commit to Allah: for Allah (ever) watches over His servants."

45. Then Allah saved him from (every) ill that they plotted (against him), but the brunt of the penalty encompassed on all sides the people of Pharaoh.

46. In front of the fire will they be brought, morning and evening: and (the sentence will be) on the day that judgement will be established: "Cast you the people of Pharaoh into the severest penalty!"

47. See, they will dispute with each other in the fire! The weak ones (who followed) will say to those who had been arrogant, "We but followed you: can you then take (on yourselves) from us some share of the fire?"

48. Those who had been arrogant will say: "We are all in this (fire)! Truly Allah has judged between (His) servants!"

49. Those in the fire will say to the keepers of hell: "Pray to your Lord to lighten us the penalty for a day (at least)!"

50. They will say: "Did there not come to you your messengers with clear signs?" They will say "Yes." They will reply, "Then pray (as you like)! But the prayer of those without faith is nothing but (futile wandering) in (mazes of) error!"

51. We will, without doubt, help Our messengers, and those who believe, (both) in this world's life and on the day when the witnesses will stand up -

52. The day when no profit will it be to wrongdoers to present their excuses, but they will (only) have the curse and the home of misery.

53. We did before give Moses the (book of) guidance, and We gave the book in inheritance to the Children of Israel -

54. A guide and a message to men of understanding.

55. Patiently, then, persevere: for the promise of Allah is true: and ask forgiveness for your fault, and celebrate the praises of your Lord in the evening and in the morning.

56. Those who dispute about the signs of Allah without any authority bestowed on them - there is nothing in their breasts but (the quest of) greatness which they shall never attain to: seek refuge, then, in Allah: it is He Who hears and sees (all things).

57. Assuredly the creation of the heavens and the earth is a greater (matter) than the creation of men: Yet most men do not understand.

58. Not equal are the blind and those who (clearly) see: nor are (equal) those who believe and work deeds of righteousness, and those who do evil. Little do you learn by admonition!

59. The hour will certainly come: in it is no doubt: yet most men do not believe.

60. And your Lord says: "Call on Me; I will answer your (prayer): but those who are too arrogant to serve Me will surely find themselves in hell - in humiliation!"

61. It is Allah Who has made the night for you, that you may rest in it, and the day, as that which helps (you) to see. Verily Allah is Full of grace and bounty to men: yet most men give no thanks.

62. Such is Allah, your Lord, the Creator of all things. There is no god but He: then how you are deluded away from the truth!

63. Thus are deluded those who used to reject the signs of Allah.

64. It is Allah Who has made for you the earth as a resting place, and the sky as a canopy, and has given you shape - and made your shapes beautiful - and has provided for you sustenance of things pure and good - such is Allah your Lord. So glory to Allah, the Lord of the Worlds!

65. He is the Living (One). There is no god but He: call upon Him, giving Him sincere devotion. praise be to Allah, Lord of the Worlds!

66. Say: "I have been forbidden to invoke those whom you invoke besides Allah - seeing that the clear signs have come to me from my Lord: and I have been commanded to bow (in Islam) to the Lord of the Worlds."

67. It is He Who has created you from dust, then from a sperm-drop, then from a leech-like clot; then does He get you out (into the light) as a child; then lets you (grow and) reach your age of full strength; then lets you become old - though of you there are some who die before - and lets you reach a term appointed; in order that you may learn wisdom.

68. It is He Who gives life and death; and when He decides upon an affair, He says to it, "Be," and it is.

69. Do you not see those that dispute concerning the signs of Allah? How are they turned away (from reality)? -

70. Those who reject the book and the (revelations) with which We sent Our messengers: but soon shall they know -

71. When the yokes (shall be) round their necks, and the chains; they shall be dragged along -

72. In the boiling fetid fluid; then in the fire shall they be burned;

73. Then shall it be said to them: "Where are the (deities) to which you gave part-worship -

74. In derogation of Allah?" They will reply: "They have left us in the lurch: nay, we invoked not, of old, anything (that had real existence)." Thus does Allah leave the unbelievers to stray.

75. "That was because you used to rejoice on the earth in things other than the truth, and that you used to be insolent.

76. Enter you the gates of hell, to dwell in it: and evil is (this) abode of the arrogant!"

77. So persevere in patience; for the promise of Allah is true: and whether We show you (in this life) some part of what We promise them - or We take your soul (to Our mercy) (before that) - (in any case) it is to Us that they shall (all) return.

78. We did before send messengers before you: of them there are some whose story We have related to you, and some whose story We have not related to you. It was not (possible) for any messenger to bring a sign except by the leave of Allah: but when the command of Allah issued, the matter was decided in truth and justice, and there perished, there and then, those who stood on falsehoods.

79. It is Allah Who made cattle for you, that you may use some for riding and some for food;

80. And there are (other) advantages in them for you (besides); that you may through them attain to any need (there may be) in your hearts; and on them and on ships you are carried.

81. And He shows you always His signs; then which of the signs of Allah will you deny?

82. Do they not travel through the earth and see what was the end of those before them? They were more numerous than these and superior in strength and in the traces (they have left) in the land: yet all that they accomplished was of no profit to them.

83. For when their messengers came to them with clear signs, they exulted in such knowledge (and skill) as they had; but that very (wrath) at which they used to scoff hemmed them in.

84. But when they saw Our punishment, they said: "We believe in Allah - the One God - and we reject the partners we used to join with Him."

85. But their professing the faith when they (actually) saw Our punishment was not going to profit them. (Such has been) Allah's way of dealing with His servants (from the most ancient times). And even thus did the rejecters of Allah perish (utterly)!

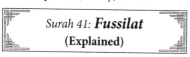

Surah 41: *Fussilat* (Explained)

In the name of Allah, Most Gracious, Most Merciful.

1. *Ha Mim.*

2. A revelation from (Allah), Most Gracious, Most Merciful -

3. A book, of which the verses are explained in detail - a Qur'an in Arabic, for people who understand -

4. Giving good news and admonition: yet most of them turn away, and so they hear not.

5. They say: "Our hearts are under veils, (concealed) from that to which you do invite us, and in our ears is a deafness and between us and you is a screen: so do you (what you will); for us, we shall do (what we will!)."

6. (O prophet!) Say you: "I am but a man like you: it is revealed to me by inspiration, that your God is One God: so stand true to Him and ask for His forgiveness." And woe to those who join gods with Allah -

7. Those who practice not regular charity, and who even deny the hereafter.

8. For those who believe and work deeds of righteousness is a reward that will never fail.

9. Say: "Is it that you deny Him Who created the earth in two Days? And do you join equals with Him? He is the Lord of (all) the Worlds."

10. He set on the (earth) mountains standing firm, high above it, and bestowed blessings on the earth, and measured in it all things to give them nourishment in due proportion, in four days in accordance with (the needs of) those who seek (sustenance).

11. Moreover, He comprehended in His design the sky, and it had been (as) smoke: He said to it and to the earth: "Come you together, willingly or unwillingly." They said: "We do come (together), in willing obedience."

12. So He completed them as seven firmaments in two days and He assigned to each heaven its duty and command. And We adorned the lower heaven with lights, and (provided it) with guard. Such is the decree of (Him) the Exalted in Might, Full of knowledge.

13. But if they turn away, say you: "I have warned you of a stunning punishment (as of thunder and lightning) like that which (overtook) the 'Ad and the Thamud!"

14. See, the messengers came to them, from before them and behind them, (preaching): "Serve none but Allah."

They said, "If our Lord had so pleased He would certainly have sent down angels (to preach): now we reject your mission (altogether)."

15. Now the 'Ad behaved arrogantly through the land, against (all) truth and reason, and said: "Who is superior to us in strength?" What! Did they not see that Allah, Who created them, was superior to them in strength? But they continued to reject Our signs!

16. So We sent against them a furious wind through days of disaster, that We might give them a taste of a penalty of humiliation in this life; but the penalty of the hereafter will be more humiliating still: and they will find no help.

17. As to the Thamud, We gave them guidance, but they preferred blindness (of heart) to guidance; so the stunning punishment of humiliation seized them, because of what they had earned.

18. But We delivered those who believed and practised righteousness.

19. On the day that the enemies of Allah will be gathered together to the fire, they will be marched in ranks.

20. At length, when they reach the (fire), their hearing, their sight, and their skins will bear witness against them, as to (all) their deeds.

21. They will say to their skins: "Why bear you witness against us?" They will say: "Allah has given us speech - (He) Who gives speech to everything: He created you for the first time, and to Him were you to return.

22. You did not seek to hide yourselves, lest your hearing, your sight, and your skins should bear witness against you! But you did think that Allah knew not many of the things that you used to do!

23. But this thought of yours which you did entertain concerning your Lord, has brought you to destruction, and (now) have you become of those utterly lost!"

24. If, then, they have patience, the fire will be a home for them! And if they beg to be received into favour, into favour will they not (then) be received.

25. And We have destined for them intimate companions (of like nature), who made alluring to them what was before them and behind them; and the sentence among the previous generations of Jinns and men, who have passed away, is proved against them; for they are utterly lost.

26. The unbelievers say: "Listen not to this Qur'an, but talk at random in the midst of its (reading), that you may gain the upper hand!"

27. But We will certainly give the unbelievers a taste of a severe penalty, and We will repay them for the worst of their deeds.

28. Such is the requital of the enemies of Allah - the fire: in it will be for them the eternal home: a (fit) requital for that they used to reject Our signs.

29. And the unbelievers will say: "Our Lord! Show us those among Jinns and men who misled us: we shall crush them beneath our feet, so that they become the vilest (before all)."

30. In the case of those who say, "Our Lord is Allah," and, further, stand straight and steadfast, the angels

descend on them (from time to time): "Fear you not!" (they suggest), "Nor grieve! But receive the glad tidings of the garden (of bliss), that which you were promised!

31. We are your protectors in this life and in the hereafter: in it shall you have all that your souls shall desire; in it shall you have all that you ask for! -

32. A hospitable gift from One Oft-Forgiving, Most Merciful!"

33. Who is better in speech than one who calls (men) to Allah, works righteousness, and says, "I am of those who bow in Islam"?

34. Nor can goodness and evil be equal. Repel (evil) with what is better: then will he between whom and you was hatred become as it were your friend and intimate!

35. And no one will be granted such goodness except those who exercise patience, and self-restraint - none but persons of the greatest good fortune.

36. And if (at any time) an incitement to discord is made to you by the evil one, seek refuge in Allah. He is the One Who hears and knows all things.

37. Among His signs are the night and the day, and the sun and moon. Adore not the sun and the moon but adore Allah, Who created them, if it is Him you wish to serve.

38. But if they (unbelievers) are arrogant, (no matter): for in the presence of your Lord are those who celebrate His praises by night and by day. And they never flag (nor feel themselves above it).

39. And among His signs is this: you see the earth barren and desolate; but when We send down rain to it, it is stirred to life and yields increase. Truly, He Who gives life to the (dead) earth can surely give life to (men) who are dead. For He has power over all things.

40. Those who pervert the truth in Our signs are not hidden from Us. Which is better? - he that is cast into the fire, or he that comes safe through, on the day of judgement? Do what you will: verily He sees (clearly) all that you do.

41. Those who reject the message when it comes to them (are not hidden from Us); and indeed it is a book of exalted power.

42. No falsehood can approach it from before or behind it: it is sent down by One Full of wisdom, worthy of all praise.

43. Nothing is said to you that was not said to the messengers before you: that your Lord has at His command (all) forgiveness as well as a most grievous penalty.

44. Had We sent this as a Qur'an (in a language) other than Arabic they would have said: "Why are not its verses explained in detail? What! (a book) not in Arabic and (a prophet) an Arab?" Say: "It is a guide and a healing to those who believe; and for those who believe not, there is a deafness in their ears, and it is blindness in their (eyes); they are (as it were) being called from a place far distant!"

45. We certainly gave Moses the book before: but dispute arose in this. Had it not been for a word that went forth before from your Lord, (their differences) would have been settled between them: but they remained in suspicious disquieting doubt about it.

46. Whoever works righteousness benefits his own soul; whoever works evil, it is against his own soul: nor is your Lord ever unjust (in the least) to His servants.

47. To Him is referred the knowledge of the hour (of judgement: He knows all): no date-fruit comes out of its sheath, nor does a female conceive (within her womb) nor bring out (young), but by His knowledge. The day that (Allah) will propound to them the (question), "Where are the partners (you attributed) to Me?" They will say, "We do assure You not one of us can bear witness!"

48. The (deities) they used to invoke before will leave them in the lurch, and they will perceive that they have no way of escape.

49. Man does not weary of asking for good (things), but if ill touches him, he gives up all hope (and) is lost in despair.

50. When We give him a taste of some mercy from Ourselves after some adversity has touched him, he is sure to say, "This is due to my (merit): I think not that the hour (of judgement) will (ever) be established; but if I am brought back to my Lord, I have (much) good (stored) in His sight!" But We will show the unbelievers the truth of all that they did, and We shall give them the taste of a severe penalty.

51. When We bestow favours on man, he turns away, and gets himself remote on his side (instead of coming to Us);

and when evil seizes him (he comes) full of prolonged prayer!

52. Say: "See you if the (revelation) is (really) from Allah and yet do you reject it? Who is more astray than one who is in a schism far (from any purpose)?"

53. Soon will We show them Our signs in the (furthest) regions (of the earth), and in their own souls, until it becomes manifest to them that this is the truth. Is it not enough that your Lord does witness all things?

54. Ah indeed! Are they in doubt concerning the meeting with their Lord? Ah indeed! It is He that does encompass all things!

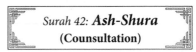

Surah 42: **Ash-Shura**
(Counsultation)

In the name of Allah,
Most Gracious, Most Merciful.

1. *Ha Mim;*

2. *Ayn. Sin. Qaf.*

3. Thus does (He) send inspiration to you as (He did) to those before you - Allah, Exalted in Power, full of wisdom.

4. To Him belongs all that is in the heavens and on earth: and He is Most High, Most Great.

5. The heavens are almost split apart from above them (by His glory): and the angels celebrate the praises of their Lord, and pray for forgiveness for all beings on earth: see! Verily Allah is He, the Oft-Forgiving, Most Merciful.

6. And those who take as protectors others besides Him - Allah does watch over them; and you are not the disposer of their affairs.

7. Thus have We sent by inspiration to you an Arabic Qur'an: that you may warn the mother of cities and all around her - and warn (them) of the day of assembly, of which there is no doubt: (when) some will be in the garden, and some in the blazing fire.

8. If Allah had so willed, He could have made them a single people; but He admits whom He will to His mercy; and the wrongdoers will have no protector nor helper.

9. What! Have they taken (for worship) protectors besides Him? But it is Allah - He is the protector, and it is He Who gives life to the dead: it is He Who has power over all things.

10. Whatever it be in which you differ, the decision of it is with Allah; such is Allah my Lord: in Him I trust, and to Him I turn.

11. (He is) the Creator of the heavens and the earth; He has made for you pairs from among yourselves, and pairs among cattle; by this means does He multiply you: there is nothing whatever like to Him, and He is the One that hears and sees (all things).

12. To Him belong the keys of the heavens and the earth; He enlarges and restricts the sustenance to whom He will; for He knows full well all things.

13. The same religion has He established for you as that which He enjoined on Noah - that which We have sent by inspiration to you - and that which We enjoined on Abraham, Moses, and Jesus: namely, that you should remain steadfast in religion, and make no divisions in it: to those who worship other things than Allah, hard is the (way) to which you call them. Allah chooses to Himself those whom He pleases and guides to Himself those who turn (to Him).

14. And they became divided only after knowledge reached them - through selfish envy as between themselves. Had it not been for a word that went before from your Lord, (tending) to a term appointed, the matter would have been settled between them: but truly those who have inherited the book after them are in suspicious (disquieting) doubt concerning it.

15. Now then, for that (reason) call (them to the faith), and stand steadfast as you are commanded, nor follow you their vain desires; but say: "I believe in the book which Allah has sent down; and I am commanded to judge justly between you. Allah is Our Lord and your Lord. For us (is the responsibility for) our deeds and for you for your deeds. There is no contention between us and you. Allah will bring us together, and to Him is (Our) final goal."

16. But those who dispute concerning Allah after He has been accepted - futile is their dispute in the sight of their Lord: on them is wrath, and for them will be a penalty terrible.

17. It is Allah Who has sent down the book in truth, and the balance (by which to weigh conduct). And what will make you realise that perhaps the hour is close at hand?

18. Only those wish to hasten it who believe not in it: those who believe hold it in awe, and know that it is the truth. See, verily those that dispute concerning the hour are far astray.

19. Gracious is Allah to His servants: He gives sustenance to whom He pleases: and He has power and can carry out His will.

20. To any that desires the tilth of the hereafter, We give increase in his tilth; and to any that desires the tilth of this world, We grant somewhat of it, but he has no share or lot in the hereafter.

21. What! Have they partners (in godhead), who have established for them some religion without the permission of Allah? Had it not been for the decree of judgement, the matter would have been decided between them (at once). But verily the wrongdoers will have a grievous penalty.

22. You will see the wrongdoers in fear on account of what they have earned, and (the burden of) that must (necessarily) fall on them. But those who believe and work righteous deeds will be in the luxuriant meads of the gardens: they shall have, before their Lord, all that they wish for: that will indeed be the magnificent bounty (of Allah).

23. That is (the bounty) of which Allah gives glad tidings to His servants who believe and do righteous deeds. Say: "No reward do I ask of you for this except the love of those near of kin." And if anyone earns any good, We shall give Him an increase of good in respect of it: for Allah is Oft-Forgiving, Most ready to appreciate (service).

24. What! Do they say, "He has forged a falsehood against Allah"? But if Allah willed He could seal up your heart. And Allah blots out vanity, and proves the truth by His words. For He knows well the secrets of all hearts.

25. He is the One that accepts repentance from His servants and forgives sins: and He knows all that you do.

26. And He listens to those who believe and do deeds of righteousness, and gives them increase of His bounty: but for the unbelievers there is a terrible penalty.

27. If Allah were to enlarge the provision for His servants, they would indeed transgress beyond all bounds through the earth; but He sends (it) down in due measure as He pleases: for He is with His servants Well-Acquainted, Watchful.

28. He is the One that sends down rain (even) after (men) have given up all hope, and scatters His mercy (far and wide). And He is the Protector, worthy of all praise.

29. And among His signs is the creation of the heavens and the earth, and the living creatures that He has scattered through them: and He has power to gather them together when He wills.

30. Whatever misfortune happens to you, is because of the things your hands have wrought, and for many (of them) He grants forgiveness.

31. Nor can you frustrate (anything) (fleeing) through the earth; nor have you, besides Allah, anyone to protect or to help.

32. And among His signs are the ships, smooth-running through the ocean, (tall) as mountains.

33. If it be His will, He can still the wind: then would they become motionless on the back of the (ocean). Verily in this are signs for everyone who patiently perseveres and is grateful.

34. Or He can cause them to perish because of the (evil) which (the men) have earned: but much does He forgive.

35. But let those know, who dispute about Our signs, that there is for them no way of escape.

36. Whatever you are given (here) is (but) a convenience of this life; but that which is with Allah is better and more lasting: (it is) for those who believe and put their trust in their Lord;

37. Those who avoid the greater crimes and shameful deeds, and when they are angry even then forgive;

38. Those who listen to their Lord, and establish regular prayer; who (conduct) their affairs by mutual consultation; who spend out of what We bestow on them for sustenance;

39. And those who when an oppressive wrong is inflicted on them, (are not cowed but) help and defend themselves.

40. The recompense for an injury is an injury equal to it (in degree); but if a person forgives and makes reconciliation,

His reward is due from Allah: for (Allah) loves not those who do wrong.

41. But indeed if any do help and defend themselves after a wrong (done) to them, against such there is no cause of blame.

42. The blame is only against those who oppress men with wrongdoing and insolently transgress beyond bounds through the land, defying right and justice: for such there will be a penalty grievous.

43. But indeed if any show patience and forgive, that would truly be an exercise of courageous will and resolution in the conduct of affairs.

44. For any whom Allah leaves astray, there is no protector after that. And you will see the wrongdoers, when in sight of the penalty, say: "Is there any way (to effect) a return?"

45. And you will see them brought forward to the (penalty), in a humble frame of mind because of (their) disgrace, (and) looking with a stealthy glance. And the believers will say: "Those are indeed in loss who have given to perdition their own selves and those belonging to them on the day of judgement. See! Truly the wrongdoers are in a lasting penalty!"

46. And no protectors have they to help them, other than Allah: and for any whom Allah leaves to stray, there is no way (to the goal).

47. Listen you to your Lord, before there come a day which there will be no putting back, because of (the ordainment of) Allah! That day there will be for you no place of refuge nor will there be for you any room for denial (of your sins)!

48. If then they turn away, We have not sent you as a guard over them. Your duty is but to convey (the message). And truly, when We give man a taste of a mercy from Ourselves, he does exult at it, but when some ill happens to him, on account of the deeds which his hands have sent before, truly then is man ungrateful!

49. To Allah belongs the dominion of the heavens and the earth. He creates what He wills (and plans). He bestows (children) male or female according to His will (and plan).

50. Or He bestows both males and females, and He leaves barren whom He will: for He is full of knowledge and power.

51. It is not fitting for a man that Allah should speak to him except by inspiration, or from behind a veil, or by the sending of a messenger to reveal, with Allah's permission, what Allah wills: for He is Most High, Most Wise.

52. And thus have We, by Our command, sent inspiration to you; you knew not (before) what was revelation, and what was faith; but We have made the Qur'an) a light, with which We guide such of Our servants as We will; and verily you do guide (men) to the straight way -

53. The way of Allah to whom belongs whatever is in the heavens and whatever is on earth: see (how) all affairs tend towards Allah!

Surah 43: *Az-Zukhruf* (The Gold Ornaments)

In the name of Allah, Most Gracious, Most Merciful.

1. *Ha Mim.*

2. By the book that makes things clear -

3. We have made it a Qur'an in Arabic, that you may be able to understand (and learn wisdom).

4. And verily, it is in the mother of the book in Our presence, high (in dignity), full of wisdom.

5. Shall We then take away the message from you and repel (you), for that you are a people transgressing beyond bounds?

6. But how many were the prophets We sent amongst the peoples of old?

7. And never came there a prophet to them but they mocked him.

8. So We destroyed (them) - stronger in power than these - and (thus) has passed on the parable of the peoples of old.

9. If you were to question them, "Who created the heavens and the earth?" They would be sure to reply, "They were created by (Him) the Exalted in power, Full of knowledge."

10. (Yea, the same that) has made for you the earth (like a carpet) spread out, and has made for you roads (and channels) in it, in order that you may find guidance (on the way);

11. That sends down (from time to time) rain from the sky in due measure - and We raise to life with it a land that is dead; even so will you be raised (from the dead) -

12. That has created pairs in all things, and has made for you ships and cattle on which you ride,

13. In order that you may sit firm and square on their backs, and when so seated, you may celebrate the (kind) favour of your Lord, and say, "Glory to Him Who has subjected these to our (use), for We could never have accomplished this (by ourselves).

14. And to our Lord, surely, must we turn back!"

15. Yet they attribute to some of His servants a share with Him (in His godhead)! Truly is man a blasphemous ingrate avowed!

16. What! Has He taken daughters out of what He Himself creates, and granted to you sons for choice?

17. When news is brought to one of them of (the birth of) what he sets up as a likeness to (Allah) Most Gracious, his face darkens, and he is filled with inward grief!

18. Is then one brought up among trinkets, and unable to give a clear account in a dispute (to be associated with Allah)?

19. And they make into females angels who themselves serve Allah. Did they witness their creation? Their evidence will be recorded, and they will be called to account!

20. ("Ah!") They say, "If it had been the will of (Allah) Most Gracious, We should not have worshipped such (deities)!" Of that they have no knowledge! They do nothing but lie!

21. What! Have We given them a book before this, to which they are holding fast?

22. Nay! They say: "We found our fathers following a certain religion, and we do guide ourselves by their footsteps."

23. Just in the same way, whenever We sent a warner before you to any people, the wealthy ones among them said: "We found our fathers following a certain religion, and we will certainly follow in their footsteps."

24. He said: "What! Even if I brought you better guidance than that which you found your fathers following?" They said: "For us, We deny that you (prophets) are sent (on a mission at all)."

25. So We exacted retribution from them: now see what was the end of those who rejected (truth)!

26. See! Abraham said to his father and his people: "I do indeed clear myself of what you worship:

27. (I worship) only Him who made me, and He will certainly guide me."

28. And he left it as a word to endure among those who came after him, that they may turn back (to Allah).

29. Yea, I have given the good things of this life to these (men) and their fathers, until the truth has come to them, and a messenger making things clear.

30. But when the truth came to them, they said: "This is sorcery, and We do reject it."

31. Also, they say: "Why is not this Qur'an sent down to some leading man in either of the two (chief) cities?"

32. Is it they who would portion out the mercy of your Lord? It is We Who portion out between them their livelihood in the life of this world: and We raise some of them above others in ranks, so that some may command work from others. But the mercy of your Lord is better than the (wealth) which they amass.

33. And were it not that (all) men might become of one (evil) way of life, We would provide, for everyone that blasphemes against (Allah) Most Gracious, silver roofs for their houses, and (silver) stairways on which to go up,

34. And (silver) doors to their houses, and thrones (of silver) on which they could recline,

35. And also adornments of gold. But all this were nothing but conveniences of the present life: the hereafter, in the sight of your Lord, is for the righteous.

36. If anyone withdraws himself from remembrance of (Allah) Most Gracious, We appoint for him an evil one, to be an intimate companion to him.

37. Such (evil ones) really hinder them from the path, but they think that they are being guided aright!

38. At length, when (such a one) comes to Us, he says (to his evil-companion): "Would that between me and you were the distance of east and west!" Ah! evil is the companion (indeed)!

39. When you have done wrong, it will benefit you nothing, that day, that you shall be partners in punishment!

40. Can you then make the deaf to hear, or give direction to the blind, or to such as (wander) in manifest error?

41. Even if We take you away, We shall be sure to exact retribution from them,

42. Or We shall show you that (accomplished) which We have promised them: for verily We shall prevail over them.

43. So hold you fast to the revelation sent down to you: verily you are on a straight way.

44. The (Qur'an) is indeed the message, for you and for your people; and soon shall you (all) be brought to account.

45. And question you Our messengers whom We sent before you; did We appoint any deities other than (Allah) Most Gracious, to be worshipped?

46. We did send Moses before, with Our signs, to Pharaoh and his chiefs: he said, "I am a messenger of the Lord of the Worlds."

47. But when he came to them with Our signs, behold, they ridiculed them.

48. We showed them sign after sign, each greater then its fellow, and We seized them with punishment, in order that they might turn (to Us).

49. And they said, "O you sorcerer! Invoke your Lord for us according to His covenant with you; for we shall truly accept guidance."

50. But when We removed the penalty from them, see, they broke their word.

51. And Pharaoh proclaimed among his people, saying: "O my people! Does not the dominion of Egypt belong to me, (witness) these streams flowing underneath my (palace)? What! Do you not see then?

52. Am I not better than this (Moses), who is a contemptible wretch and can scarcely express himself clearly?

53. Then why are not gold bracelets bestowed on him, or (why) come (not) with him angels accompanying him in procession?"

54. Thus did he make fools of his people, and they obeyed him: Truly were they a people rebellious (against Allah).

55. When at length they provoked Us, We exacted retribution from them, and We drowned them all.

56. And We made them (a people) of the past and an example to later ages.

57. When (Jesus) the son of Mary is held up as an example, behold your people raise a clamour at it (in ridicule)!

58. And they say, "Are our gods best or He?" This they set out to you, only by way of disputation: yea, they are a contentious people.

59. He was no more than a servant: We granted Our favour to him, and We made him an example to the Children of Israel.

60. And if it were Our will, We could make angels from amongst you succeeding each other on the earth.

61. And (Jesus) shall be a sign (for the coming of) the hour (of judgement): therefore have no doubt about the (hour) but follow you Me: this is a straight way.

62. Let not the evil one hinder you: for he is to you an enemy avowed.

63. When Jesus came with clear signs he said: "Now have I come to you with wisdom and in order to make clear to you some of the (points) on which you dispute: therefore fear Allah and obey me.

64. For Allah; He is my Lord and your Lord: so worship you Him: this is a straight way."

65. But sects from among themselves fell into disagreement: then woe to the wrongdoers from the penalty of a grievous day!

66. Do they only wait for the hour - that it should come on them all of a sudden, while they perceive not?

67. Friends on that day will be foes, one to another - except the righteous.

68. My devotees! No fear shall be on you that day, nor shall you grieve -

69. (Being) those who have believed in Our signs and bowed (their wills to Ours) in Islam.

70. Enter you the garden, you and your wives, in (beauty and) rejoicing.

71. To them will be passed round, dishes and goblets of gold: there will be there all that the souls could desire, all that the eyes could delight in: and you shall remain in it (for ever).

72. Such will be the garden of which you are made heirs for your (good) deeds (in life).

73. You shall have in it abundance of fruit, from which you shall have satisfaction.

74. The sinners will be in the punishment of hell, to dwell in it (for ever):

75. In no way will the (punishment) be lightened for them, and in despair will they be there overwhelmed.

76. In no way shall We be unjust to them: but it is they who have been unjust themselves.

77. They will call: "O Malik! Would that your Lord put and end to us!" He will say, "Nay, but you shall remain!"

78. Verily We have brought the truth to you: but most of you have a hatred for truth.

79. What! Have they settled some plan (among themselves)? But it is We Who settle things.

80. Or do they think that We hear not their secrets and their private counsels? Indeed (We do) and Our messengers are by them, to record.

81. Say: "If (Allah) Most Gracious had a son, I would be the first to worship."

82. Glory to the Lord of the heavens and the earth, the Lord of the throne (of authority)! (He is free) from the things they attribute (to Him)!

83. So leave them to babble and play (with vanities) until they meet that day of theirs, which they have been promised.

84. It is He Who is God in heaven and God on earth; and He is full of wisdom and knowledge.

85. And blessed is He to Whom belongs the dominion of the heavens and the earth, and all between them: with Him is the knowledge of the hour (of judgement): And to Him shall you be brought back.

86. And those whom they invoke besides Allah have no power of intercession - only he who bears witness to the truth, and they know (him).

87. If you ask them, Who created them, they will certainly say, Allah: how then are they deluded away (from the truth)?

88. (Allah has knowledge) of the (prophet's) call, "O my Lord! Truly these are a people who will not believe!"

89. But turn away from them and say, "Peace!" But soon shall they know!

Surah 44: *Ad-Dukhan*
(The Smoke)

In the name of Allah,
Most Gracious, Most Merciful.

1. *Ha Mim.*

2. By the book that makes things clear -

3. We sent it down during a blessed night: for We (ever) wish to warn (against evil).

4. In that (night) is made distinct every affair of wisdom,

5. By command, from Our presence. For We (ever) send (revelations),

6. As a mercy from your Lord: for He hears and knows (all things);

7. The Lord of the heavens and the earth and all between them, if you (but) have an assured faith.

8. There is no god but He: it is He Who gives life and gives death - the Lord and Cherisher to you and your earliest ancestors.

9. Yet they play about in doubt.

10. Then watch you for the day that the sky will bring forth a kind of smoke (or mist) plainly visible,

11. Enveloping the people: this will be a penalty grievous.

12. (They will say:) "Our Lord! Remove the penalty from us, for We do really believe!"

13. How shall the message be (effectual) for them, seeing that a messenger explaining things clearly has (already) come to them -

14. Yet they turn away from him and say: "Tutored (by others), a man possessed!"

15. We shall indeed remove the penalty for a while, (but) truly you will revert (to your ways).

16. One day We shall seize you with a mighty onslaught: We will indeed (then) exact retribution!

17. We did, before them, try the people of Pharaoh: there came to them a messenger most honourable,

18. Saying: "Restore to me the servants of Allah: I am to you a messenger worthy of all trust;

19. And be not arrogant as against Allah: for I come to you with authority manifest.

20. For me, I have sought safety with my Lord and your Lord, against your injuring me.

21. If you believe me not, at least keep yourselves away from me."

22. (But they were aggressive): then he cried to his Lord: "These are indeed a people given to sin."

23. (The reply came): "March out with My servants by night: for you are sure to be pursued.

24. And leave the sea as a furrow (divided). For they are a host (destined) to be drowned."

25. How many were the gardens and springs they left behind,

26. And cornfields and noble buildings,

27. And wealth (and conveniences of life) in which they had taken such delight!

28. Thus (was their end)! And We made other people inherit (those things)!

29. And neither heaven nor earth shed a tear over them: nor were they given a respite (again).

30. We did deliver before the Children of Israel from humiliating punishment,

31. Inflicted by Pharaoh, for he was arrogant (even) among inordinate transgressors.

32. And We chose them before above the nations knowingly,

33. And granted them signs in which there was a manifest trial.

34. As to these (Quraysh) they say:

35. "There is nothing beyond our first death and we shall not be raised again.

36. Then bring (back) our forefathers, if what you say is true!"

37. What! Are they better than the people of Tubba and those who were before them? We destroyed them because they were guilty of sin.

38. We created not the heavens, the earth, and all between them merely in (idle) sport:

39. We created them not except for just ends: but most of them do not understand.

40. Verily the day of sorting out is the time appointed for all of them -

41. The day when no protector can benefit his client in anything, and no help can they receive.

42. Except such as receive Allah's mercy: for He is Exalted in Might, Most Merciful.

43. Verily the tree of Zaqqum

44. Will be the food of the sinful -

45. Like molten brass; it will boil in their insides,

46. Like the boiling of scalding water.

47. (A voice will call:) "Seize you him and drag him into the midst of the blazing fire!

48. Then pour over his head the penalty of boiling water;

49. Taste you (this)! Truly were you mighty, full of honour!

50. Truly this is what you used to doubt!"

51. As to the righteous (they will be) in a position of security,

52. Among gardens and springs;

53. Dressed in fine silk and in rich brocade, they will face each other;

54. Moreover, We shall join them to companions with beautiful, big, and lustrous eyes.

55. There can they call for every kind of fruit in peace and security;

56. Nor will they there taste death, except the first death; and He will preserve them from the penalty of the blazing fire -

57. As a bounty from your Lord! That will be the supreme achievement!

58. Verily, We have made this (Qur'an) easy, in your tongue, in order that they may give heed.

59. So wait you and watch; for they (too) are waiting.

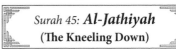

Surah 45: **Al-Jathiyah**
(The Kneeling Down)

In the name of Allah,
Most Gracious, Most Merciful.

1. *Ha Mim.*

2. The revelation of the book is from Allah the Exalted in power, Full of wisdom.

3. Verily in the heavens and the earth, are signs for those who believe.

4. And in the creation of yourselves and the fact that animals are scattered (through the earth), are signs for those of assured faith.

5. And in the alternation of night and day, and the fact that Allah sends down sustenance from the sky, and revives with it the earth after its death, and the change of the winds - are signs for those that are wise.

6. Such are the signs of Allah, which We rehearse to you in truth: then in what exposition will they believe after (rejecting) Allah and His signs?

7. Woe to each sinful dealer in falsehoods:

8. He hears the signs of Allah rehearsed to him, yet is obstinate and lofty, as if he had not heard them: then announce to him a penalty grievous!

9. And when he learns something of Our signs, he takes them in jest: for such there will be a humiliating penalty.

10. In front of them is hell; and of no profit to them is anything they may have earned, nor any protectors they may have taken to themselves besides Allah; for them is a tremendous penalty.

11. This is (true) guidance: and for those who reject the signs of their Lord, is a grievous penalty of abomination.

12. It is Allah Who has subjected the sea to you, that ships may sail through it by His command, that you may seek of His bounty, and that you may be grateful.

13. And He has subjected to you, as from Him, all that is in the heavens and on earth: see in that are signs indeed for those who reflect.

14. Tell those who believe to forgive those who do not look forward to the days of Allah: it is for Him to recompense (for good or ill) each people according to what they have earned.

15. If anyone does a righteous deed, it enures to the benefit of his own soul; if he does evil, it works against (His own soul). In the end will you (all) be brought back to your Lord.

16. We did before grant to the Children of Israel the book, the power of command and prophethood; We gave them, for sustenance, things good and pure; and We favoured them above the nations.

17. And We granted them clear signs in affairs (of religion); it was only after knowledge had been granted to them that they fell into schisms, through insolent envy among themselves. Verily your Lord will judge between them on the day of judgement as to those matters in which they set up differences.

18. Then We put you on the (right) way of religion: so follow you that (way), and follow not the desires of those who know not.

19. They will be of no use to you in the sight of Allah; it is only wrongdoers (that stand as) protectors, one to another; but Allah is the protector of the righteous.

20. These are clear evidences to men, and a guidance and mercy to those of assured faith.

21. What! Do those who seek after evil ways think that We shall hold them equal with those who believe and do righteous deeds - that equal will be their life and their death? Ill is the judgement that they make.

22. Allah created the heavens and the earth for just ends and in order that each soul may find the recompense of what it has earned, and none of them be wronged.

23. Then do you see such a one as takes, as his god, his own vain desire? Allah has, knowing (him as such), left him astray, and sealed his hearing and his heart (and understanding) and put a cover on his sight. Who, then, will guide him after Allah (has withdrawn guidance)? Will you not then receive admonition?

24. And they say: "What is there but our life in this world? We shall die and we live, and nothing but time can destroy us." But of that they have no knowledge: they merely conjecture:

25. And when Our clear signs are rehearsed to them, their argument is nothing but this: they say, "Bring (back) our forefathers, if what you say is true!"

26. Say: "It is Allah Who gives you life, then gives you death; then He will gather you together for the day of judgement about which there is no doubt": but most men do not understand.

27. To Allah belongs the dominion of the heavens and the earth, and the day that the hour of judgement is established - that day will the dealers in falsehood perish!

28. And you will see every sect bowing the knee: every sect will be called to its record: "This day shall you be recompensed for all that you did!

29. "This Our record speaks about you with truth: for We used to put on record all that you did."

30. Then, as to those who believed and did righteous deeds, their Lord will admit them to His mercy: that will be the achievement for all to see.

31. But as to those who reject Allah, (to them will be said): "Were not Our signs rehearsed to you? But you were arrogant, and were a people given to sin!

32. And when it was said that the promise of Allah was true, and that the hour - there was no doubt about its (coming), you used to say, 'We know not what is the hour: we only think it is an idea, and we have no firm assurance.'"

33. Then will appear to them the evil (fruits) of what they did, and they will be completely encircled by that which they used to mock at!

34. It will also be said: "This day We will forget you as you forgot the meeting of this day of yours! And your abode is the fire, and no helpers have you!

35. This, because you used to take the signs of Allah in jest, and the life of the world deceived you." (From) the day, therefore, they shall not be taken out from there, nor shall they be received into grace.

36. Then praise be to Allah Lord of the heavens and Lord of the earth - Lord and Cherisher of all the Worlds!

37. To Him be glory throughout the heavens and the earth: and He is Exalted in Power, Full of Wisdom!

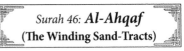

Surah 46: *Al-Ahqaf*
(The Winding Sand-Tracts)

In the name of Allah,
Most Gracious, Most Merciful.

1. *Ha Mim.*

2. The revelation of the book is from Allah the Exalted in Power, Full of Wisdom.

3. We created not the heavens and the earth and all between them but for just ends, and for a term appointed: but those who reject faith turn away from that of which they are warned.

4. Say: "Do you see what it is you invoke besides Allah? Show me what it is they have created on earth, or have they a share in the heavens? Bring me a book (revealed) before this, or any remnant of knowledge (you may have), if you are telling the truth!"

5. And who is more astray than one who invokes, besides Allah, such as will not answer him to the day of judgement, and who (in fact) are unconscious of their call (to them)?

6. And when mankind are gathered together (at the resurrection), they will be hostile to them and reject their worship (altogether)!

7. When Our clear signs are rehearsed to them, the unbelievers say, of the truth when it comes to them: "This is evident sorcery!"

8. Or do they say, "He has forged it"? Say: "Had I forged it, then can you obtain no single (blessing) for me from Allah. He knows best of that of which you talk (so glibly)! Enough is He for a witness between me and you! And He is Oft-Forgiving, Most Merciful."

9. Say: "I am no bringer of new-fangled doctrine among the messengers, nor do I know what will be done with me or with you. I follow but that which is revealed to me by inspiration: I am but a warner, open and clear."

10. Say: "Do you see? If (this teaching) be from Allah, and you reject it and a witness from among the Children of Israel testifies to its similarity (with earlier scriptures), and has believed while you are arrogant, (how unjust you are!) Truly Allah guides not a people unjust."

11. The unbelievers say of those who believe: "If (this message) were a good thing, (such men) would not have gone to it first, before us!" And seeing that they guide not themselves thereby, they will say, "This is an (old) old falsehood!"

12. And before this, was the book of Moses as a guide and a mercy; and this book confirms (it) in the Arabic tongue; to admonish the unjust, and as glad tidings to those who do right.

13. Verily those who say, "Our Lord is Allah," and remain firm (on that path) - on them shall be no fear, nor shall they grieve.

14. Such shall be companions of the garden, dwelling in it (for ever): a recompense for their (good) deeds.

15. We have enjoined on man kindness to his parents: in pain did his mother bear him, and in pain did she give him birth. The carrying of the (child) to his weaning is (a period of) thirty months. At length when he reaches the age of full strength and attains forty years, he says, "O my Lord! Grant me that I may be grateful for Your favour which You have bestowed upon me, and upon both my parents, and that I may work righteousness such as You may approve; and be gracious to me in my issue. Truly have I turned to You and truly do I bow (to You) in Islam."

16. Such are they from whom We shall accept the best of their deeds and pass by their ill deeds; (they shall be) among the companions of the garden: a promise of truth, which was made to them (in this life).

17. But (there is one) who says to his parents, "Fie on you! Do you hold out the promise to me that I shall be raised up, even though generations have passed before me (without rising again)?" And they two seek Allah's aid (and rebuke the son): "Woe to you! Have faith! For the promise of Allah is true." But he says, "This is nothing but tales of the ancients!"

18. Such are they against whom is proved the sentence among the previous generations of Jinns and men, that have passed away; for they will be (utterly) lost.

19. And to all are (assigned) degrees according to the deeds which they (have done), and in order that (Allah) may recompense their deeds, and no injustice be done to them.

20. And on the day that the unbelievers will be placed before the fire, (it will be said to them): "You received your good things in the life of the world, and you took your pleasure out of them; but today shall you be recompensed with a penalty of humiliation; for that you were arrogant on earth without just cause, and that you (ever) transgressed."

21. Mention (Hud) one of 'Ad's (own) brothers: behold, he warned his people about the winding sand-tracts; but there have been warners before him and after him: "Worship you none other than Allah; truly I fear for you the penalty of a mighty day."

22. They said: "Have you come in order to turn us aside from our gods? Then bring upon us the (calamity) with which you do threaten us, if you are telling the truth!"

23. He said: "The knowledge (of when it will come) is only with Allah: I proclaim to you the mission on which I have been sent: but I see that you are a people in ignorance!"

24. Then when they saw the (penalty in the shape of) a cloud traversing the sky coming to meet their valleys, they said, "This cloud will give us rain!" "Nay, it is the (calamity) you were asking to be hastened! - A wind in which is a grievous penalty!

25. Everything will it destroy by the command of its Lord!" Then by the morning they - nothing was to be seen but (the ruins of) their houses! Thus do We recompense those given to sin!

26. And We had firmly established them in a (prosperity and) power which We have not given to you (you Quraysh!) and We had endowed them with (faculties of) hearing, seeing, heart and intellect; but of no profit to them were their (faculties of) hearing, sight, and heart and intellect, when they went on rejecting the signs of Allah; and they were (completely) encircled by that which they used to mock at!

27. We destroyed before populations round about you; and We have shown the signs in various ways that they may turn (to Us).

28. Why then was no help forthcoming to them from those whom they worshipped as gods, besides Allah, as a means of access (to Allah)? Nay, they left them in the lurch: but that was their falsehood and their invention.

29. See, We turned towards you a company of Jinns (quietly) listening to the Qur'an: when they stood in the presence of it, they said, "Listen in silence!" When the (reading) was finished, they returned to their people, to warn (them of their sins).

30. They said, "O our people! We have heard a book revealed after Moses, confirming what came before it: it guides (men) to the truth and to a straight path.

31. O our people, listen to the one who invites (you) to Allah, and believe in him: He will forgive you your faults, and deliver you from a penalty grievous.

32. If any does not listen to the one who invites (us) to Allah, he cannot frustrate (Allah's plan) on earth, and no protectors can he have besides Allah: such men (wander) in manifest error."

33. Do they not see that Allah Who created the heavens and the earth, and never wearied with their creation, is able to give life to the dead? Yea, verily He has power over all things.

34. And on the day that the unbelievers will be placed before the fire, (they will be asked,) "Is this not the truth? " They will say, "Yea, by our Lord!" (One will say:) "Then taste you the penalty, for that you used to deny (truth)!"

35. Therefore, patiently persevere as did (all) messengers of inflexible purpose; and be in no haste about the (unbelievers). On the day that they see the (punishment) promised them, (it will be) as if they had not stayed more than an hour in a single day. (Yours is but) to proclaim the message; but shall any be destroyed except those who transgress?

Surah 47: *Muhammad*

In the name of Allah,
Most Gracious, Most Merciful.

1. Those who reject Allah and hinder (men) from the path of Allah - their deeds will Allah render astray (from their mark).

2. But those who believe and work deeds of righteousness, and believe in the (revelation) sent down to Muhammad - for it is the truth from their Lord - He will remove from them their ills and improve their condition.

3. This because those who reject Allah follow vanities, while those who believe follow the truth from their Lord: thus does Allah set out for men their lessons by similitudes.

4. Therefore, when you meet the unbelievers (in fight), strike at their necks; at length, when you have thoroughly subdued them, bind a bond firmly (on them); thereafter (is the time for) either generosity or ransom; until the war lays down its burdens. Thus (are you commanded); but if it had been Allah's Will He could certainly have exacted retribution from them (Himself); but (He lets you fight) in order to test you, some with others. But those who are slain in the way of Allah - He will never let their deeds be lost.

5. Soon will He guide them and improve their condition,

6. And admit them to the garden which He has announced for them.

7. O you who believe! If you will aid (the cause of) Allah, He will aid you, and plant your feet firmly.

8. But those who reject (Allah) for them is destruction, and (Allah) will render their deeds astray (from their mark).

9. That is because they hate the revelation of Allah; so He has made their deeds fruitless.

10. Do they not travel through the earth, and see what was the end of those before them (who did evil)? Allah brought utter destruction on them, and similar (fates await) those who reject Allah.

11. That is because Allah is the protector of those who believe, but those who reject Allah have no protector.

12. Verily Allah will admit those who believe and do righteous deeds, to gardens beneath which rivers flow; while those who reject Allah will enjoy (this world) and eat as cattle eat; and the fire will be their abode.

13. And how many cities, with more power than your city which has driven you out, have We destroyed (for their sins)? And there was none to aid them.

14. Is then one who is on a clear (path) from his Lord, no better than one to whom the evil of his conduct seems pleasing, and such as follow their own lusts?

15. (Here is) a parable of the garden which the righteous are promised: in it are rivers of water incorruptible; rivers of milk of which the taste never changes; rivers of wine, a joy to those who drink; and rivers of honey pure and clear. In it there are for them all kinds of fruits, and grace from their Lord. (Can those in such bliss) be compared to such as shall dwell forever in the fire, and be given to drink boiling water, so that it cuts up their bowels (to pieces)?

16. And among them are men who listen to you, but in the end, when they go out from you, they say to those who have received knowledge, "What is it he said just then?" Such are men whose hearts Allah has sealed, and who follow their own lusts.

17. But to those who receive guidance, He increases (the light of) guidance, and bestows on them their piety and restraint (from evil).

18. Do they then only wait for the hour - that it should come on them of a sudden? But already have come some signs of it, and when it (actually) is on them, how can they benefit then by their admonition?

19. Know, therefore, that there is no god but Allah, and ask forgiveness for your fault, and for the men and women who believe: for Allah knows how you move about and how you dwell in your homes.

20. Those who believe say, "Why is not a Surah sent down (for us)?" But when a Surah of basic or categorical meaning is revealed and fighting is mentioned in it, you will see those in whose hearts is a disease looking at you with a look of one in swoon at the approach of death. But more fitting for them -

21. Were it to obey and say what is just and when a matter is resolved on, it were best for them if they were true to Allah.

22. Then, is it to be expected of you, if you were put in authority that you will do no mischief in the land, and break your ties of relationship?

23. Such are the men whom Allah has cursed for He has made them deaf and blinded their sight.

24. Do they not then earnestly seek to understand the Qur'an or are their hearts locked up by them?

25. Those who turn back as apostates after guidance was clearly shown to them - the evil one has instigated them and buoyed them up with false hopes.

26. This, because they said to those who hate what Allah has revealed, "We will obey you in part of (this) matter"; but Allah knows their (inner) secrets.

27. But how (will it be) when the angels take their souls at death, and strike their faces and their backs?

28. This because they followed that which called the wrath of Allah, and they hated Allah's good pleasure; so He made their deeds of no effect.

29. Or do those in whose hearts is a disease, think that Allah will not bring to light all their rancour?

30. Had We so willed, We could have shown them up to you, and you should have known them by their marks: but surely you will know them by the tone of their speech! And Allah knows all that you do.

31. And We shall try you until We test those among you who strive their utmost and persevere in patience; and We shall try your reported (mettle).

32. Those who reject Allah, hinder (men) from the path of Allah, and resist the messenger, after guidance has been clearly shown to them, will not injure Allah in the least, but He will make their deeds of no effect.

33. O you who believe! Obey Allah, and obey the messenger, and make not vain your deeds!

34. Those who reject Allah, and hinder (men) from the path of Allah, then die rejecting Allah - Allah will not forgive them.

35. Be not weary and faint-hearted, crying for peace, when you should be uppermost: for Allah is with you, and will never put you in loss for your (good) deeds.

36. The life of this world is but play and amusement: and if you believe and guard against evil, He will grant you your recompense, and will not ask you (to give up) your possessions.

37. If He were to ask you for all of them, and press you, you would covetously withhold, and He would bring out all your ill-feeling.

38. See, you are those invited to spend (of your substance) in the way of Allah; but among you are some that are niggardly. But any who are niggardly are so at the expense of their own souls. But Allah is free of all wants, and it is you that are needy. If you turn back (from the path), He will substitute in your stead another people; then they would not be like you!

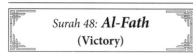

Surah 48: *Al-Fath*
(Victory)

In the name of Allah,
Most Gracious, Most Merciful.

1. Verily We have granted you a manifest victory:

2. That Allah may forgive you your faults of the past and those to follow; fulfil His favour to you; and guide you on the straight way;

3. And that Allah may help you with powerful help.

4. It is He Who sent down tranquillity into the hearts of the believers, that they may add faith to their faith - for to Allah belong the forces of the heavens and the earth; and Allah is full of knowledge and wisdom -

5. That He may admit the men and women who believe, to gardens beneath which rivers flow, to dwell in it for ever, and remove their ills from them - and that is, in the sight of Allah, the highest achievement (for man) -

6. And that He may punish the hypocrites, men and women, and the polytheists, men and women, who imagine an evil opinion of Allah. On them is a round of evil; the wrath of Allah is on them; He has cursed them and got hell ready for them; and evil is it for a destination.

7. For to Allah belong the forces of the heavens and the earth; and Allah is Exalted in Power, Full of Wisdom.

8. We have truly sent you as a witness, as a bringer of glad tidings, and as a warner:

9. In order that you (O men) may believe in Allah and His messenger, that you may assist and honour Him, and celebrate His praises morning and evening.

10. Verily those who pledge their fealty to you do no less than pledge their fealty to Allah: the Hand of Allah is over their hands: then anyone who violates his oath, does so to the harm of his own soul, and anyone who fulfils what he has covenanted with Allah - Allah will soon grant him a great reward.

11. The desert Arabs who lagged behind will say to you: "We were engaged in (looking after) our flocks and herds, and our families; do you then ask forgiveness for us." They say with their tongues what is not in their hearts. Say: "Who then has any power at all (to intervene) on your behalf with Allah, if His will is to give you some loss or to give you some profit? But Allah is well acquainted with all that you do.

12. Nay, you thought that the messenger and the believers would never return to their families; this seemed pleasing in your hearts, and you conceived an evil thought, for you are a people lost (in wickedness)."

13. And if any believe not in Allah and His messenger, We have prepared for those who reject Allah, a blazing fire!

14. To Allah belongs the dominion of the heavens and the earth: He forgives whom He wills, and He punishes whom He wills; but Allah is Oft-Forgiving, Most Merciful.

15. Those who lagged behind (will say), when you (are free to) march and take booty (in war): "Permit us to follow you." They wish to change Allah's decree; say: "Not thus will you follow us; Allah has already declared (this) beforehand"; then they will say, "But you are jealous of us." Nay, but little do they understand (such things).

16. Say to the desert Arabs who lagged behind: "You shall be summoned (to fight) against a people given to vehement war: then shall you fight or they shall submit. Then if you show obedience, Allah will grant you a goodly reward, but if you turn back as you did before, He will punish you with a grievous penalty."

17. No blame is there on the blind, nor is there blame on the lame, nor on one ill (if he joins not the war); but he that obeys Allah and His messenger - (Allah) will admit him to gardens beneath which rivers flow; and he who turns back, (Allah) will punish him with a grievous penalty.

18. Allah's good pleasure was on the believers when they swore allegiance to you under the tree: He knew what was in their hearts and He sent down tranquillity to them and He rewarded them with a speedy victory;

19. And many gains will they acquire (besides): and Allah is Exalted in Power, Full of Wisdom.

20. Allah has promised you many gains that you shall acquire, and He has given you these beforehand; and He has restrained the hands of men from you; that it may be a sign for the

believers, and that He may guide you to a straight path;

21. And other gains (there are) which are not within your power, but which Allah has encompassed: and Allah has power over all things.

22. If the unbelievers should fight you, they would certainly turn their backs; then would they find neither protector nor helper.

23. (Such has been) the practice (approved) of Allah already in the past: no change will you find in the practice (approved) of Allah.

24. And it is He Who has restrained their hands from you and your hand from them in the midst of Makkah, after that He gave you the victory over them. And Allah sees well all that you do.

25. They are the ones who denied revelation and hindered you from the Sacred Mosque and the sacrificial animals, detained from reaching their place of sacrifice. Had there not been believing men and believing women whom you did not know that you were trampling down and on whose account a crime would have accrued to you without (your) knowledge, (Allah would have allowed you to force your way, but He held back your hands) that He may admit to His mercy whom He will. If they had been apart, We should certainly have punished the unbelievers among them with a grievous punishment.

26. While the unbelievers got up in their hearts heat and zeal - the heat and zeal of ignorance - Allah sent down

His tranquillity to His messenger and to the believers, and made them stick close to the command of self-restraint; and well were they entitled to it and worthy of it. And Allah has full knowledge of all things.

27. Truly did Allah fulfil the vision for His messenger: you shall enter the Sacred Mosque, if Allah wills with minds secure, heads shaved, hair cut short, and without fear. For He knew what you knew not and He granted, besides this, a speedy victory.

28. It is He Who has sent His messenger with guidance and the religion of truth, to proclaim it over all religion: and enough is Allah for a witness.

29. Muhammad is the messenger of Allah; and those who are with him are strong against unbelievers, (but) compassionate amongst each other. You will see them bow and prostrate themselves (in prayer), seeking grace from Allah and (His) good pleasure. On their faces are their marks, (being) the traces of their prostration. This is their similitude in the Tawrah; and their similitude in the Gospel is like a seed which sends out its blade, then makes it strong; it then becomes thick, and it stands on its own stem, (filling) the sowers with wonder and delight. As a result, it fills the unbelievers with rage at him. Allah has promised those among them who believe and do righteous deeds forgiveness and a great reward.

Surah 49: *Al-Hujurat*
(The Chambers)

In the name of Allah,
Most Gracious, Most Merciful.

1. O you who believe! Put not yourselves forward before Allah and His messenger: but fear Allah: for Allah is He Who hears and knows all things.

2. O you who believe! Raise not your voices above the voice of the messenger, nor speak aloud to him in talk, as you may speak aloud to one another, lest your deeds become vain and you perceive not.

3. Those that lower their voice in the presence of Allah's messenger - their hearts has Allah tested for piety: for them is forgiveness and a great reward.

4. Those who shout out to you from without the inner apartments - most of them lack understanding.

5. If only they had patience until you could come out to them, it would be best for them: but Allah is Oft-Forgiving, Most Merciful.

6. O you who believe! If a wicked person comes to you with any news, ascertain the truth, lest you harm people unwittingly, and afterwards become full of repentance for what you have done.

7. And know that among you is Allah's messenger: were he, in many matters, to follow your (wishes), you would certainly fall into misfortune; but Allah has endeared the faith to you, and has made it beautiful in your hearts, and He has made hateful to you unbelief, wickedness, and rebellion: such indeed are those who walk in righteousness -

8. A grace and favour from Allah; and Allah is full of Knowledge and Wisdom.

9. If two parties among the believers fall into a quarrel, make you peace between them; but if one of them transgresses beyond bounds against the other, then fight you (all) against the one that transgresses until it complies with the command of Allah; but if it complies, then make peace between them with justice, and be fair: for Allah loves those who are fair (and just).

10. The believers are but a single brotherhood; so make peace and reconciliation between your two (contending) brothers: and fear Allah that you may receive mercy.

11. O you who believe! Let not some men among you laugh at others; it may be that the (latter) are better than the (former); nor let some women laugh at others; it may be that the (latter) are better than the (former); nor defame, nor be sarcastic to each other, nor call each other by (offensive) nicknames: ill-seeming is a name connoting wickedness, (to be used of one) after he has believed; and those who do not desist are (indeed) doing wrong.

12. O you who believe! Avoid suspicion as much (as possible); for suspicion in some cases is a sin; and spy not on each other, nor speak ill of each other behind their backs. Would any of you like to eat the flesh of his dead brother? Nay you would abhor it, but fear Allah: for Allah is Oft-Returning, Most Merciful.

13. O mankind! We created you from a single (pair) of a male and a female and made you into nations and tribes, that you may know each other (not that you may despise each other). Verily the most honoured of you in the sight of Allah is (he who is) the most righteous of you. And Allah has full knowledge and is well acquainted (with all things).

14. The desert Arabs say, "We believe." Say, "You have no faith; but you (should) say, 'We have submitted our wills to Allah,' for not yet has faith entered your hearts. But if you obey Allah and His messenger, He will not belittle anything of your deeds: for Allah is Oft-Forgiving, Most Merciful."

15. Only those are believers who have believed in Allah and His messenger, and have never since doubted, but have striven with their belongings and their persons in the cause of Allah: such are the sincere ones.

16. Say: "What! Will you instruct Allah about your religion?" But Allah knows all that is in the heavens and on earth: He has full knowledge of all things.

17. They impress on you as a favour that they have embraced Islam. Say, "Count not your Islam as a favour upon me: nay, Allah has conferred a favour upon you that He has guided you to the faith, if you be true and sincere.

18. Verily Allah knows the secrets of the heavens and the earth: and Allah sees well all that you do."

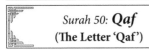

Surah 50: **Qaf**
(The Letter 'Qaf')

In the name of Allah,
Most Gracious, Most Merciful.

1. *Qaf.* By the Glorious Qur'an (You are Allah's messenger).

2. But they wonder that there has come to them a warner from among themselves. So the unbelievers say: "This is a wonderful thing!

3. What! When we die and become dust, (shall we live again?). That is a (sort of) return far (from our understanding)."

4. We already know how much of them the earth takes away: with Us is a record guarding (the full account).

5. But they deny the truth when it comes to them: so they are in a confused state.

6. Do they not look at the sky above them? - How We have made it and adorned it, and there are no flaws in it?

7. And the earth - We have spread it out, and set on it mountains standing firm, and produced in it every kind of beautiful growth (in pairs) -

8. To be observed and commemorated by every devotee turning (to Allah).

9. And We send down from the sky rain charged with blessing, and We produce with it gardens and grain for harvests;

10. And tall (and stately) palm trees, with shoots of fruit-stalks, piled one over another -

11. As sustenance for (Allah's) servants - and We give (new) life therewith to land that is dead: thus will be the resurrection.

12. Before them was denied (the hereafter) by the people of Noah, the companions of ar-Rass, the Thamud,

13. The 'Ad, Pharaoh, the brothers of Lot,

14. The companions of the wood, and the people of Tubba; each one (of them) rejected the messengers, and My warning was duly fulfilled (in them).

15. Were We then weary with the first creation, that they should be in confused doubt about a new creation?

16. It was We Who created man and We know what dark suggestions his soul makes to him: for We are nearer to him than (his) jugular vein.

17. See, two (guardian angels) appointed to learn (his doings) learn (and note them), one sitting on the right and one on the left.

18. Not a word does he utter but there is a sentinel by him ready (to note it).

19. And the stupor of death will bring truth (before his eyes): "This was the thing which you were trying to escape!"

20. And the trumpet shall be blown: that will be the day of which warning (had been given).

21. And there will come out every soul: with each will be an (angel) to drive, and an (angel) to bear witness.

22. (It will be said:) "You were heedless of this; now have We removed your veil and sharp is your sight this day!"

23. And his companion will say: "Here is (his record) ready with me!"

24. (The sentence will be:) "Throw, throw into hell every contumacious rejecter, (of Allah)! -

25. Who forbade what was good, transgressed all bounds, cast doubts and suspicions;

26. Who set up another god besides Allah: throw him into a severe penalty."

27. His companion will say: "Our Lord! I did not make him transgress, but he was (himself) far astray."

28. He will say: "Dispute not with each other in My presence: I had already in advance sent you warning.

29. The word changes not before Me, and I do not the least injustice to My servants."

30. One day We will ask hell, "Are you filled to the full?" It will say, "Are there any more (to come)?"

31. And the garden will be brought near to the righteous - no more a thing distant.

32. (A voice will say:) "This is what was promised for you - for everyone who turned (to Allah) in sincere repentance, who kept (His law).

33. Who feared (Allah) Most Gracious unseen, and brought a heart turned in devotion (to Him):

34. Enter you in it in peace and security; this is a day of eternal life!"

35. There will be for them in it all that they wish and more besides in Our presence.

36. But how many generations before them did We destroy (for their sins) - stronger in power than they? Then did they wander through the land: was there any place of escape (for them)?

37. Verily in this is a message for any that has a heart and understanding or who gives ear and earnestly witnesses (the truth).

38. We created the heavens and the earth and all between them in six days, nor did any sense of weariness touch Us.

39. Bear, then, with patience, all that they say, and celebrate the praises of your Lord, before the rising of the sun and before (its) setting,

40. And during part of the night, (also,) celebrate His praises and (so likewise) after the postures of adoration.

41. And listen for the day when the caller will call out from a place quite near -

42. The day when they will hear a (mighty) blast in (very) truth: that will be the day of resurrection.

43. Verily it is We Who give life and death; and to Us is the final goal -

44. The day when the earth will be split apart, from (men) hurrying out: that will be a gathering together - quite easy for Us.

45. We know best what they say; and you are not one to overawe them by force. So admonish with the Qur'an such as fear My warning!

Surah 51: **Adh-Dhariyat**
(The Winds That Scatter)

In the name of Allah,
Most Gracious, Most Merciful.

1. By the (winds) that scatter broadcast;

2. And those that lift and bear away heavy weights;

3. And those that flow with ease and gentleness;

4. And those that distribute and apportion by command -

5. Verily that which you are promised is true;

6. And verily judgement and justice must indeed come to pass.

7. By the sky with (its) numerous paths,

8. Truly you are in a doctrine discordant,

9. Through which are deluded (away from the truth) such as would be deluded.

10. Woe to the falsehood-mongers -

11. Those who (flounder) heedless in a flood of confusion:

12. They ask, "When will be the day of judgement and justice?"

13. (It will be) a day when they will be tried (and tested) over the fire!

14. "Taste you your trial! This is what you used to ask to be hastened!"

15. As to the righteous, they will be in the midst of gardens and springs,

16. Taking joy in the things which their Lord gives them, because, before then they lived a good life.

17. They were in the habit of sleeping but little by night,

18. And in the hours of early dawn, they (were found) praying for forgiveness;

19. And in their wealth and possessions (was remembered) the right of the (needy), him who asked, and him who (for some reason) was prevented (from asking).

20. On the earth are signs for those of assured faith,

21. As also in your own selves: will you not then see?

22. And in heaven is your sustenance, as (also) that which you are promised.

23. Then, by the Lord of heaven and earth, this is the very truth, as much as the fact that you can speak intelligently to each other.

24. Has the story reached you, of the honoured guests of Abraham?

25. See, they entered his presence, and said: "Peace!" He said: "Peace!" (And thought,) "These seem unusual people."

26. Then he turned quickly to his household, brought out a fatted calf.

27. And placed it before them. He said, "Will you not eat?"

28. (When they did not eat) he conceived a fear of them. They said, "Fear not," and they gave him glad tidings of a son endowed with knowledge.

29. But his wife came forward (laughing) aloud: she struck her forehead and said: "A barren old woman!"

30. They said, "Even so has your Lord spoken: and He is full of Wisdom and Knowledge."

31. (Abraham) said: "And what, O you messengers, is your errand (now)?"

32. They said, "We have been sent to a people (deep) in sin -

33. To bring on, on them, (a shower of) stones of clay (brimstone),

34. Marked as from your Lord for those who trespass beyond bounds."

35. Then We evacuated those of the believers who were there,

36. But We found not there any just (Muslim) persons except in one house:

37. And We left there a sign for such as fear the grievous penalty.

38. And in Moses (was another sign): behold, We sent him to Pharaoh, with authority manifest.

39. But (Pharaoh) turned back with his chiefs, and said, "A sorcerer, or one possessed!"

40. So We took him and his forces, and threw them into the sea: and his was the blame.

41. And in the 'Ad (people) (was another sign): see, We sent against them the devastating wind:

42. It left nothing whatever that it came up against, but reduced it to ruin and rottenness.

43. And in the Thamud (was another sign): see they were told, "Enjoy (your brief day) for a little while!"

44. But they insolently defied the command of their Lord: so the stunning noise (of an earthquake) seized them, even while they were looking on.

45. Then they could not even stand (on their feet), nor could they help themselves.

46. So were the people of Noah before them: for they wickedly transgressed.

47. With the power and skill did We construct the firmament: for it is We Who create the vastness of space.

48. And We have spread out the (spacious) earth: how excellently We do spread out!

49. And of everything We have created pairs: that you may receive instruction.

50. Hasten you then (at once) to Allah: I am from Him a warner to you clear and open!

51. And make not another an object of worship with Allah: I am from Him a warner to you, clear and open!

52. Similarly, no messenger came to the peoples before them, but they said (of him) in like manner, "A sorcerer, or one possessed!"

53. Is this the legacy they have transmitted, one to another? Nay, they are themselves a people transgressing beyond bounds!

54. So turn away from them: not yours is the blame.

55. But teach (your message): for teaching benefits the believers.

56. I have only created jinns and men, that they may serve Me.

57. No sustenance do I require of them, nor do I require that they should feed Me.

58. For Allah is He Who gives (all) sustenance - Lord of Power - steadfast (forever).

59. For the wrongdoers, their portion is like to the portion of their fellows (of earlier generations): then let them not ask Me to hasten (that portion)!

60. Woe, then, to the unbelievers, on account of that day of theirs which they have been promised!

Surah 52: *At-Tur*
(The Mount)

In the name of Allah,
Most Gracious, Most Merciful.

1. By the mount (of revelation);

2. By a decree inscribed,

3. In a scroll unfolded;

4. By the much-frequented fane;

5. By the canopy raised high;

6. And by the ocean filled with swell -

7. Verily, the doom of your Lord will indeed come to pass -

8. There is none that can avert it -

9. On the day when the firmament will be in dreadful commotion.

10. And the mountains will fly here and there.

11. Then woe that day to those that treat (truth) as falsehood -

12. That play (and paddle) in shallow trifles.

13. That day shall they be thrust down to the fire of hell, irresistibly.

14. "This," it will be said, "Is the fire - which you used to deny!

15. Is this then a fake, or is it you that do not see?

16. Burn you in it: the same is it to you whether you bear it with patience, or not: you but receive the recompense of your (own) deeds."

17. As to the righteous, they will be in gardens, and in happiness -

18. Enjoying the (bliss) which their Lord has bestowed on them, and their Lord shall deliver them from the penalty of the fire.

19. (To them will be said:) "Eat and drink you, with profit and health, because of your (good) deeds."

20. They will recline (with ease) on thrones (of dignity) arranged in ranks; and We shall join them to companions, with beautiful big and lustrous eyes.

21. And those who believe and whose families follow them in faith - to them shall We join their families: nor shall We deprive them (of the fruit) of anything of their works: (yet) is each individual in pledge for his deeds.

22. And We shall bestow on them, of fruit and meat, anything they shall desire.

23. They shall there exchange one with another, a (loving) cup free of frivolity, free of all taint of ill.

24. Round about them will serve, (devoted) to them, youths (handsome) as pearls well-guarded.

25. They will advance to each other, engaging in mutual enquiry.

26. They will say: "Before, we were not without fear for the sake of our people.

27. But Allah has been good to us, and has delivered us from the penalty of the scorching wind.

28. Truly, we did call to Him from of old: truly it is He, the Beneficent, the Merciful."

29. Therefore, proclaim you the praises (of your Lord): for by the grace of your Lord, you are no (vulgar) soothsayer, nor are you one possessed,

30. Or do they say - "A poet! We await for him some calamity (hatched) by time!"

31. Say you: "Await you! - I too will wait along with you!"

32. Is it that their faculties of understanding urge them to this, or are they but a people transgressing beyond bounds?

33. Or do they say, "He fabricated the (message)?" Nay, they have no faith!

34. Let them then produce a recital like it - if (it be) they speak the truth!

35. Were they created of nothing, or were they themselves the creators?

36. Or did they create the heavens and the earth? Nay, they have no firm belief.

37. Or are the treasures of your Lord with them, or are they the managers (of affairs)?

38. Or have they a ladder by which they can (climb up to heaven and) listen (to its secrets)? Then let (such a) listener of theirs produce a manifest proof.

39. Or has He only daughters and you have sons?

40. Or is it that you do ask for a reward, so that they are burdened with a load of debt? -

41. Or that the unseen is in their hands, and they write it down?

42. Or do they intend a plot (against you)? But those who defy Allah are themselves involved in a plot!

43. Or have they a god other than Allah? Exalted is Allah far above the things they associate with Him!

44. Were they to see a piece of the sky falling (on them), they would (only) say: "Clouds gathered in heaps!"

45. So leave them alone until they encounter that day of theirs, in which they shall (involuntarily) swoon (with terror) -

46. The day when their plotting will benefit them nothing and no help shall be given them.

47. And verily, for those who do wrong, there is another punishment besides this: but most of them understand not.

48. Now await in patience the command of your Lord: for verily you are in Our eyes: and celebrate the praises of your Lord the while you stand up.

49. And for part of the night also praise you Him and at the retreat of the stars!

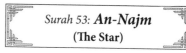

Surah 53: **An-Najm**
(The Star)

In the name of Allah,
Most Gracious, Most Merciful.

1. By the star when it goes down -

2. Your companion is neither astray nor being misled,

3. Nor does he say (anything) of (his own) desire.

4. It is no less than inspiration sent down to him:

5. He was taught by one Mighty in power,

6. Endued with wisdom: for he appeared (in stately form),

7. While he was in the highest part of the horizon:

8. Then he approached and came closer,

9. And was at a distance of but two bow-lengths or (even) nearer;

10. So did (Allah) convey the inspiration to His servant - (conveyed) what He (meant) to convey.

11. The (prophet's) (mind and) heart in no way falsified that which he saw.

12. Will you then dispute with him concerning what he saw?

13. For indeed he saw him at a second descent,

14. Near the lote-tree beyond which none may pass:

15. Near it is the garden of abode.

16. See, the lote-tree was shrouded (in mystery unspeakable!)

17. (His) sight never swerved, nor did it go wrong!

18. For truly did he see, of the signs of his Lord, the Greatest!

19. Have you seen Lat, and Uzza,

20. And another, the third (goddess), Manat?

21. What! For you the male sex, and for Him, the female?

22. See, such would be indeed a division most unfair!

23. These are nothing but names which you have devised - you and your fathers - for which Allah has sent down no authority (whatever). They follow nothing but conjecture and what their own souls desire! - Even though there has already come to them guidance from their Lord!

24. Nay, shall man have (just) anything he hankers after?

25. But it is to Allah that the end and the beginning (of all things) belong.

26. How many so ever be the angels in the heavens, their intercession will benefit nothing except after Allah has given leave for whom He pleases and that he is acceptable to Him.

27. Those who believe not in the hereafter, name the angels with female names.

28. But they have no knowledge in it. They follow nothing but conjecture; and conjecture avails nothing against truth.

29. Therefore, shun those who turn away from Our message and desire nothing but the life of this world.

30. That is as far as knowledge will reach them. Verily your Lord knows best those who stray from His path and He knows best those who receive guidance.

31. Yea, to Allah belongs all that is in the heavens and on earth; so that He rewards those who do evil, according to their deeds, and He rewards those who do good, with what is best.

32. Those who avoid great sins and shameful deeds, only (falling into) small faults - verily your Lord is ample in forgiveness. He knows you well when He brings you out of the earth and when you are hidden in your mothers' wombs. Therefore, justify not yourselves: He knows best who it is that guards against evil.

33. See you one who turns back,

34. Gives a little, then hardens (his heart)?

35. What! Has he knowledge of the unseen so that he can see?

36. Nay, is he not acquainted with what is in the books of Moses -

37. And of Abraham who fulfilled his engagements -

38. Namely, that no bearer of burdens can bear the burden of another;

39. That man can have nothing but what he strives for;

40. That (the fruit of) his striving will soon come in sight;

41. Then will he be rewarded with a reward complete;

42. That to your Lord is the final goal;

43. That it is He Who grants laughter and tears;

44. That it is He Who grants death and life;

45. That He did create in pairs - male and female,

46. From a seed when lodged (in its place);

47. That He has promised a second creation (raising of the dead);

48. That it is He Who gives wealth and satisfaction;

49. That He is the Lord of Sirius (the mighty star);

50. And that it is He Who destroyed the (powerful) ancient 'Ad (people),

51. And the Thamud, nor gave them a lease of perpetual life.

52. And before them, the people of Noah, for that they were (all) most unjust and most insolent transgressors,

53. And He destroyed the overthrown cities (of Sodom and Gomorrah),

54. So that (ruins unknown) have covered them up.

55. Then which of the gifts of your Lord (O man,) will you dispute about?

56. This is a warner, of the (series of) warners of old!

57. The (judgement) ever approaching draws near:

58. No (soul) but Allah can lay it bare.

59. Do you then wonder at this recital?

60. And will you laugh and not weep, -

61. Wasting your time in vanities?

62. But fall you down in prostration to Allah and adore (Him)!

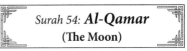

Surah 54: *Al-Qamar*
(The Moon)

In the name of Allah,
Most Gracious, Most Merciful.

1. The hour (of judgement) is near, and the moon is cleft asunder.

2. But if they see a sign, they turn away, and say, "This is (but) transient magic."

3. They reject (the warning) and follow their (own) lusts, but every matter has its appointed time.

4. There have already come to them recitals in which there is (enough) to check (them),

5. Mature wisdom - but (the preaching of) warners profits them not.

6. Therefore, (O prophet), turn away from them. The day that the caller will call (them) to a terrible affair,

7. They will come forth - their eyes humbled - from (their) graves, (torpid) like locusts scattered abroad,

8. Hastening, with eyes transfixed, towards the caller! "Hard is this day!" - The unbelievers will say.

9. Before them the people of Noah rejected (their messenger): they rejected Our servant, and said, "Here is one possessed!" And he was driven out.

10. Then he called on his Lord: "I am one overcome: do You then help (me)!"

11. So We opened the gates of heaven, with water pouring out.

12. And We caused the earth to gush out with springs. So the waters met (and rose) to the extent decreed.

13. But We bore him on an (ark) made of broad planks and caulked with palm-fibre:

14. She floated under Our eyes (and care): a recompense to one who had been rejected (with scorn)!

15. And We have left this as a sign (for all time): then is there any that will receive admonition?

16. But how (terrible) was My penalty and My warning?

17. And We have indeed made the Qur'an easy to understand and remember: then is there any that will receive admonition?

18. The 'Ad (people) (too) rejected (truth): then how terrible was my penalty and my warning!

19. For We sent against them a furious wind, on a day of violent disaster,

20. Plucking out men as if they were roots of palm-trees torn up (from the ground).

21. Yea, how (terrible) was My penalty and My warning!

22. But We have indeed made the Qur'an easy to understand and remember: then is there any that will receive admonition?

23. The Thamud (also) rejected (their) warners.

24. For they said: "What! A man! A solitary one from among ourselves! Shall we follow such a one? Truly should we then be straying in mind, and mad!

25. Is it that the message is sent to him, of all people amongst us? Nay, he is a liar, an insolent one!"

26. Ah! They will know on the morrow which is the liar, the insolent one!

27. For We will send the she-camel by way of trial for them. So watch them, (O Salih) and possess yourself in patience!

28. And tell them that the water is to be divided between them: each one's right to drink being brought forward (by suitable turns).

29. But they called to their companion, and he took a sword in hand, and hamstrung (her).

30. Ah! How (terrible) was My penalty and My warning!

31. For We sent against them a single mighty blast, and they became like the dry stubble used by one who pens cattle.

32. And We have indeed made the Qur'an easy to understand and remember: then is there any that will receive admonition?

33. The people of Lot rejected (his) warning.

34. We sent against them a violent tornado with showers of stones (which destroyed them), except Lot's household: them We delivered by early dawn -

35. As a grace from Us: thus do We reward those who give thanks.

36. And (Lot) did warn them of Our punishment, but they disputed about the warning.

37. And they even sought to snatch away his guests from him, but We blinded their eyes. (They heard:) "Now taste you My wrath and My warning."

38. Early on the morrow a lasting punishment seized them:

39. "So taste you My wrath and My warning."

40. And We have indeed made the Qur'an easy to understand and remember: then is there any that will receive admonition?

41. To the people of Pharaoh, too, before came warners (from Allah).

42. The (people) rejected all Our signs; but We seized them with such penalty (as comes) from One Exalted in Power, able to carry out His will.

43. Are your unbelievers, (O Quraysh), better than they? Or have you an immunity in the sacred books?

44. Or do they say: "We acting together can defend ourselves"?

45. Soon will their multitude be put to flight, and they will show their backs.

46. Nay, the hour (of judgement) is the time promised them (for their full recompense): and that hour will be most grievous and most bitter.

47. Truly those in sin are the ones straying in mind, and mad.

48. The day they will be dragged through the fire on their faces, (they will hear:) "Taste you the touch of hell!"

49. Verily, all things have We created in proportion and measure.

50. And Our command is but a single (Act) - like the twinkling of an eye.

51. And (oft) in the past, have We destroyed gangs like you: then is there any that will receive admonition?

52. All that they do is noted in (their) books (of deeds):

53. Every matter, small and great, is on record.

54. As to the righteous, they will be in the midst of gardens and rivers.

55. In an assembly to truth, in the presence of a sovereign omnipotent.

Surah 55: *Ar-Rahman*
(The Most Gracious)

In the name of Allah,
Most Gracious, Most Merciful.

1. (Allah) Most Gracious!

2. It is He Who has taught the Qur'an.

3. He has created man:

4. He has taught him speech (and Intelligence).

5. The sun and the moon follow courses (exactly) computed;

6. And the herbs and the trees - both (alike) bow in adoration.

7. And the firmament has He raised high, and He has set up the balance (of justice),

8. In order that you may not transgress (due) balance.

9. So establish weight with justice and fall not short in the balance.

10. It is He Who has spread out the earth for (His) creatures:

11. In it is fruit and date-palms, producing spathes (enclosing dates):

12. Also corn, with (its) leaves and stalk for fodder, and sweet-smelling plants.

13. Then which of the favours of your Lord will you deny?

14. He created man from sounding clay like pottery.

15. And He created Jinns from fire free of smoke:

16. Then which of the favours of your Lord will you deny?

17. (He is) Lord of the two easts and Lord of the two wests:

18. Then which of the favours of your Lord will you deny?

19. He has let free the two bodies of flowing water meeting together:

20. Between them is a barrier which they do not transgress:

21. Then which of the favours of your Lord will you deny?

22. Out of them come pearls and coral:

23. Then which of the favours of your Lord will you deny?

24. And His are the ships sailing smoothly through the seas, lofty as mountains:

25. Then which of the favours of your Lord will you deny?

26. All that is on earth will perish:

27. But will remain (forever) the face of your Lord - Full of majesty, bounty and honour.

28. Then which of the favours of your Lord will you deny?

29. Of Him seeks (its needs) every creature in the heavens and on earth: every day in (new) splendour does He (shine)!

30. Then which of the favours of your Lord will you deny?

31. Soon shall We settle your affairs, O both you worlds!

32. Then which of the favours of your Lord will you deny?

33. O you assembly of Jinns and men! If it be you can pass beyond the zones of the heavens and the earth, pass you! Not without authority shall you be able to pass!

34. Then which of the favours of your Lord will you deny?

35. On you will be sent (O you evil ones twain!) a flame of fire (to burn) and a smoke (to choke): no defence will you have:

36. Then which of the favours of your Lord will you deny?

37. When the sky is rent asunder, and it becomes red like ointment:

38. Then which of the favours of your Lord will you deny?

39. On that day, no question will be asked of man or Jinn as to his sin,

40. Then which of the favours of your Lord will you deny?

41. (For) the sinners will be known by their marks: and they will be seized by their forelocks and their feet.

42. Then which of the favours of your Lord will you deny?

43. This is the hell which the sinners deny.

44. In its midst and in the midst of boiling hot water will they wander round!

45. Then which of the favours of your Lord will you deny?

46. But for such as fear the time when they will stand before (the judgement seat of) their Lord, there will be two gardens -

47. Then which of the favours of your Lord will you deny?

48. Containing all kinds (of trees and delights) -

49. Then which of the favours of your Lord will you deny?

50. In them (each) will be two springs flowing (free);

51. Then which of the favours of your Lord will you deny?

52. In them will be fruits of every kind, two and two.

53. Then which of the favours of your Lord will you deny?

54. They will recline on carpets, whose inner linings will be of rich brocade: the fruit of the gardens will be near (and easy of reach).

55. Then which of the favours of your Lord will you deny?

56. In them will be (maidens), chaste, restraining their glances, whom no man or Jinn before them has touched -

57. Then which of the favours of your Lord will you deny?

58. Like rubies and coral.

59. Then which of the favours of your lord will you deny?

60. Is there any reward for good - other than good?

61. Then which of the favours of your Lord will you deny?

62. And besides these two, there are two other gardens -

63. Then which of the favours of your Lord will you deny?

64. Dark green in colour (from plentiful watering).

65. Then which of the favours of your Lord will you deny?

66. In them (each) will be two springs pouring forth water in continuous abundance:

67. Then which of the favours of your Lord will you deny?

68. In them will be fruits, and dates and pomegranates:

69. Then which of the favours of your Lord will you deny?

70. In them will be fair (companions), good, beautiful -

71. Then which of the favours of your Lord will you deny?

72. companions restrained (as to their glances), in (goodly) pavilions -

73. Then which of the favour of your Lord will you deny?

74. Whom no man or Jinn before them has touched -

75. Then which of the favours of your Lord will you deny?

76. Reclining on green cushions and rich carpets of beauty.

77. Then which of the favours of your Lord will you deny?

78. Blessed be the name of your Lord, full of Majesty, bounty and Honour.

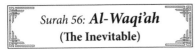

Surah 56: *Al-Waqi'ah*
(The Inevitable)

In the name of Allah,
Most Gracious, Most Merciful.

1. When the event inevitable comes to pass,

2. Then will no (soul) entertain falsehood concerning its coming.

3. (Many) will it bring low, (many) will it exalt;

4. When the earth shall be shaken to its depths,

5. And the mountains shall be crumbled to atoms,

6. Becoming dust scattered abroad,

7. And you shall be sorted out into three classes.

8. Then (there will be) the companions of the right hand - what will be the companions of the right hand?

9. And the companions of the left hand - what will be the companions of the left hand?

10. And those foremost (in faith) will be foremost (in the hereafter).

11. These will be those nearest to Allah:

12. In gardens of bliss:

13. A number of people from those of old,

14. And a few from those of later times.

15. (They will be) on thrones encrusted (with gold and precious stones),

16. Reclining on them facing each other.

17. Round about them will (serve) youths of perpetual (freshness),

18. With goblets, (shining) beakers, and cups (filled) out of clear-flowing fountains:

19. No after-ache will they receive from it, nor will they suffer intoxication:

20. And with fruits, any that they may select;

21. And the flesh of fowls, any that they may desire.

22. And (there will be) companions with beautiful, big, and lustrous eyes -

23. Like to pearls well-guarded.

24. A reward for the deeds of their past (life).

25. No frivolity will they hear in it nor any taint of ill -

26. Only the saying, "Peace! Peace."

27. The companions of the right hand - what will be the companions of the right hand?

28. (They will be) among lote trees without thorns,

29. Among Talh trees with flowers (or fruits) piled one above another -

30. In shade long-extended,

31. By water flowing constantly,

32. And fruit in abundance,

33. Whose season is not limited nor (supply) forbidden,

34. And on thrones (of dignity), raised high.

35. We have created (their companions) of special creation,

36. And made them virgin-pure (and undefiled) -

37. Beloved (by nature), equal in age -

38. For the companions of the right hand.

39. A (goodly) number from those of old,

40. And a (goodly) number from those of later times.

41. The companions of the left hand - what will be the companions of the left hand?

42. (They will be) in the midst of a fierce blast of fire and in boiling water,

43. And in the shades of black smoke:

44. Nothing (will there be) to refresh, nor to please:

45. For that they used to be indulged, before that, in wealth (and luxury),

46. And persisted obstinately in wickedness supreme!

47. And they used to say, "What! When we die and become dust and bones, shall we then indeed be raised up again? -

48. "(We) and our fathers of old?"

49. Say: "Yea, those of old and those of later times,

50. All will certainly be gathered together for the meeting appointed for a day well-known.

51. Then will you truly - O you that go wrong, and treat (truth) as falsehood!

52. You will surely taste of the tree of Zaqqum.

53. Then will you fill your insides therewith.

54. And drink boiling Water on top of it:

55. Indeed you shall drink like diseased camels raging with thirst!"

56. Such will be their entertainment on the day of requital!

57. It is We Who have created you: why will you not witness the truth?

58. Do you then see? - the (human seed) that you throw out, -

59. Is it you who create it, or are We the Creators?

60. We have decreed death to be your common lot, and We are not to be frustrated -

61. From changing your forms and creating you (again) in (forms) that you know not.

62. And you certainly know already the first form of creation: why then do you not celebrate His praises?

63. See you the seed that you sow in the ground?

64. Is it you that cause it to grow, or are We the cause?

65. Were it Our will, We could crumble it to dry powder, and you would be left in wonderment,

66. (Saying), "We are indeed left with debts (for nothing):

67. Indeed are we shut out (of the fruits of our labour)."

68. See you the water which you drink?

69. Do you bring it down (in rain) from the cloud or do We?

70. Were it Our will, We could make it salt (and unpalatable): then why do you not give thanks?

71. See you the fire which you kindle?

72. Is it you who grow the tree which feeds the fire, or do We grow it?

73. We have made it a memorial (of our handiwork), and an article of comfort and convenience for the denizens of deserts.

74. Then celebrate with praises the name of your Lord, the Supreme!

75. Furthermore, I call to witness the setting of the stars -

76. And that is indeed a mighty adjuration if you but knew -

77. That this is indeed a Qur'an most honourable,

78. In a book well-guarded,

79. Which none shall touch but those who are clean:

80. A revelation from the Lord of the Worlds.

81. Is it such a message that you would hold in light esteem?

82. And have you made it your livelihood that you should declare it false?

83. Then why do you not (intervene) when (the soul of the dying man) reaches the throat -

84. And you the while (sit) looking on-

85. But We are nearer to him than you, and yet see not -

86. Then why do you not - if you are exempt from (future) account -

87. Call back the soul, if you are true (in your claim of independence)?

88. Thus, then, if he be of those nearest to Allah,

89. (There is for him) rest and satisfaction, and a garden of delights.

90. And if he be of the companions of the right hand,

91. (For him is the salutation), "Peace be to you," from the companions of the right hand.

92. And if he be of those who treat (truth) as falsehood, who go wrong.

93. For him is entertainment with boiling water,

94. And burning in hellfire.

95. Verily, this is the very truth and certainty.

96. So celebrate with praises the name of your Lord, the Supreme.

Surah 57: **Al-Hadid**
(Iron)

In the name of Allah,
Most Gracious, Most Merciful.

1. Whatever is in the heavens and on earth - let it declare the praises and glory of Allah: for He is the Exalted in Might, the Wise.

2. To Him belongs the dominion of the heavens and the earth; it is He Who gives life and death; and He has power over all things.

3. He is the first and the last, the evident and the hidden: and He has full knowledge of all things.

4. He it is Who created the heavens and the earth in six days, and is moreover firmly established on the throne (of authority). He knows what enters within the earth and what comes out of it, what comes down from heaven and what mounts up to it. And He is with you wheresoever you may be. And Allah sees well all that you do.

5. To Him belongs the dominion of the heavens and the earth: and all affairs are referred back to Allah.

6. He merges night into day, and He merges day into night; and He has full knowledge of the secrets of (all) hearts.

7. Believe in Allah and His messenger, and spend (in charity) out of the (substance) of which He has made you heirs. For those of you who believe and spend (in charity) - for them is a great reward.

8. What cause have you why you should not believe in Allah? - And the messenger invites you to believe in your Lord, and has indeed taken your covenant, if you are men of faith.

9. He is the One Who sends to His servants manifest signs, that He may lead you from the depths of darkness into the light. And verily, Allah is to you Most Kind and Merciful.

10. And what cause have you why you should not spend in the cause of Allah? - For to Allah belongs the heritage of the heavens and the earth. Not equal among you are those who spent (freely) and fought, before the victory (with those who did so later). Those are higher in rank than those who spent (freely) and fought afterwards. But to all has Allah promised a goodly (reward) and Allah is well-acquainted with all that you do.

11. Who is he that will loan to Allah a beautiful loan? For (Allah) will increase it manifold to his credit, and he will have (besides) a liberal reward.

12. One day shall you see the believing men and the believing women - how their light runs forward before them and by their right hands: (their greeting will be): "Good news for you this day! Gardens beneath which flow rivers! To dwell in it for ever! This is indeed the highest achievement!"

13. One day will the hypocrites - men and women - say to the believers: "Wait for us! Let us borrow (a light) from your light!" It will be said: "Turn you back to your rear! Then seek a light (where you can)!" So a wall will be put up between them, with a gate in it. Within it will be mercy throughout, and without it, all alongside will be (wrath and) punishment!

14. (Those without) will call out, "Were we not with you?" (The others) will reply, "True! But you led yourselves into temptation; you looked forward (to our ruin); you doubted (Allah's promise); and (your false) desires deceived you; until there issued the command of Allah. And the deceiver deceived you in respect of Allah.

15. This day shall no ransom be accepted of you, nor of those who rejected Allah. Your abode is the fire: that is the proper place to claim you: and an evil refuge it is !"

16. Has not the time arrived for the believers that their hearts in all humility should engage in the remembrance of Allah and of the truth which has been revealed (to them), and that they should not become like those to whom was given revelation before, but long ages passed over them and their hearts grew hard? For many among them are rebellious transgressors.

17. Know you (all) that Allah gives life to the earth after its death! Already have We shown the signs plainly to you, that you may learn wisdom.

18. For those who give in charity, men and women, and loan to Allah a beautiful loan, it shall be increased manifold (to their credit), and they shall have (besides) a liberal reward.

19. And those who believe in Allah and His messengers - they are the sincere (lovers of truth), and the witnesses (who testify), in the eyes of their Lord: they shall have their reward and their light. But those who reject Allah and deny Our signs - they are the companions of hellfire.

20. Know you (all), that the life of this world is but play and amusement, pomp and mutual boasting and multiplying, (in rivalry) among yourselves, riches and children. Here is a similitude: how rain and the growth which it brings out delight (the hearts of) the tillers; soon it withers; you will see it grow yellow; then it becomes dry and crumbles away. But in the hereafter is a penalty severe (for the devotees of wrong). And forgiveness from Allah and (His) good pleasure (for the devotees of Allah). And what is the life of this world, but goods and chattels of deception?

21. Be you foremost (in seeking) forgiveness from your Lord, and a garden (of bliss), the width of which

is as the width of heaven and earth, prepared for those who believe in Allah and His messengers; that is the grace of Allah, which He bestows on whom He pleases: and Allah is the Lord of grace abounding.

22. No misfortune can happen on earth or in your souls but is recorded in a decree before We bring it into existence: that is truly easy for Allah:

23. In order that you may not despair over matters that pass you by, nor exult over favours bestowed upon you. For Allah loves not any vainglorious boaster -

24. Such persons as are covetous and commend covetousness to men, and if any turn back (from Allah's way), verily Allah is free of all needs, worthy of all praise.

25. We sent before our messengers with clear signs and sent down with them the book and the balance (of right and wrong), that men may stand forth in justice; and We sent down Iron, in which is (material for) mighty war, as well as many benefits for mankind, that Allah may test who it is that will help, unseen, Him and His messengers; for Allah is Full of Strength, Exalted in Might (and able to enforce His will).

26. And We sent Noah and Abraham, and established in their line prophethood and revelation: and some of them were on right guidance, but many of them became rebellious transgressors.

27. Then, in their wake, We followed them up with (others of) Our messengers: We sent after them Jesus

the son of Mary, and bestowed on him the gospel; and We ordained in the hearts of those who followed him compassion and mercy. But the monasticism which they invented for themselves, We did not prescribe for them: (We commanded) only the seeking for the good pleasure of Allah; but that they did not foster as they should have done. Yet We bestowed, on those among them who believed, their (due) reward, but many of them are rebellious transgressors.

28. O you that believe! Fear Allah and believe in His messenger, and He will bestow on you a double portion of His mercy: He will provide for you a light by which you shall walk (straight in your path), and He will forgive you (your past); for Allah is Oft-Forgiving, Most Merciful:

29. That the People of the Book may know that they have no power whatever over the grace of Allah, that (His) grace is (entirely) in His Hand, to bestow it on whomsoever He wills. For Allah is the Lord of grace abounding.

Surah 58: *Al-Mujadilah*
(The Woman Who Pleads)

In the name of Allah,
Most Gracious, Most Merciful.

1. Allah has indeed heard (and accepted) the statement of the woman who pleads with you concerning her husband and carries her complaint (in prayer) to Allah: and Allah (always) hears the arguments between both sides among you: for Allah hears and sees (all things).

2. If any men among you divorce their wives by *zihar* (calling them mothers), they cannot be their mothers: none can be their mothers except those who gave them birth. And in fact they use words (both) iniquitous and false: but truly Allah is One that blots out (sins), and forgives (again and again).

3. But those who divorce their wives by *zihar,* then wish to go back on the words they uttered - (it is ordained that such a one) should free a slave before they touch each other; this are you admonished to perform: and Allah is well-acquainted with (all) that you do.

4. And if any has not (the means), he should fast for two months consecutively before they touch each other. But if any is unable to do so, he should feed sixty needy ones. This, that you may show your faith in Allah and His messenger. Those are limits (set by) Allah. For those who reject (Him), there is a grievous penalty.

5. Those who resist Allah and His messenger will be humbled to dust, as were those before them: for We have already sent down clear signs. And the unbelievers (will have) a humiliating penalty.

6. On the day that Allah will raise them all up (again) and show them the truth (and meaning) of their conduct. Allah has reckoned its (value), though they may have forgotten it: for Allah is witness to all things.

7. Do you not see that Allah does know (all) that is in the heavens and on earth? There is not a secret consultation between three but He makes the fourth among them nor between five but He makes the sixth - nor between fewer nor more, but He is in their midst wheresoever they be: in the end will He tell them the truth of their conduct, on the day of judgement, for Allah has full knowledge of all things.

8. Do not turn your sight towards those who were forbidden secret counsels yet revert to that which they were forbidden (to do)? And they hold secret counsels among themselves for iniquity and hostility, and disobedience to the messenger. And when they come to you, they salute you, not as Allah salutes you, (but in crooked ways): and they say to themselves, "Why does not Allah punish us for our words?" Enough for them is hell: in it will they burn, and evil is that destination!

9. O you who believe! When you hold secret counsel, do it not for iniquity and hostility, and disobedience to the messenger; but do it for righteousness and self-restraint; and fear Allah, to Whom you shall be brought back.

10. Secret counsels are only (inspired) by the evil one, in order that he may cause grief to the believers; but he cannot harm them in the least, except as Allah permits; and on Allah let the believers put their trust.

11. O you who believe! When you are told to make room in the assemblies (spread out and) make room: (ample) room will Allah provide for you. And when you are told to rise up, rise up: Allah will raise up, to (suitable) ranks (and degrees), those of you who believe and who have been granted knowledge. And Allah is well-acquainted with all you do.

12. O you who believe! When you consult the messenger in private, spend something in charity before your private consultation. That will be best for you, and most conducive to purity (of conduct). But if you find not (the means), Allah is Oft-Forgiving, Most Merciful.

13. Is it that you are afraid of spending sums in charity before your private consultation (with him)? If, then, you do not so and Allah forgives you, then (at least) establish regular prayer; practice regular charity; and obey Allah and His messenger: and Allah is well-acquainted will all that you do.

14. Do you not turn your attention to those who turn (in friendship) to such as have the wrath of Allah upon them? They are neither of you nor of them, and they swear to falsehood knowingly.

15. Allah has prepared for them a severe penalty: evil indeed are their deeds.

16. They have made their oaths a screen (for their misdeeds): thus they obstruct (men) from the path of Allah: therefore shall they have a humiliating penalty.

17. Of no profit whatever to them, against Allah, will be their riches nor their sons: they will be companions of the fire to dwell in it (for ever)!

18. One day will Allah raise them all up (for judgement): then will they swear to Him as they swear to you: and they think that they have something (to stand upon). No, indeed! They are but liars!

19. The evil one has got the better of them: so he has made them lose the remembrance of Allah. They are the party of the evil one. Truly, it is the party of the evil one that will perish!

20. Those who resist Allah and His messenger will be among those most humiliated.

21. Allah has decreed: "It is I and My messengers who must prevail": for Allah is One full of strength, able to enforce His will.

22. You will not find any people who believe in Allah and the last day, loving those who resist Allah and His messenger, even though they were their fathers or their sons, or their brothers, or their relations. For such, He has written faith in their hearts, and strengthened them with a spirit from Himself. And He will admit them to gardens beneath which rivers flow, to dwell in it (forever). Allah will be well pleased with them, and they with Him. They are the party of Allah. Truly it is the party of Allah that will achieve felicity.

*Surah 59: **Al-Hashr***
(The Mustering)

In the name of Allah,
Most Gracious, Most Merciful.

1. Whatever is in the heavens and on earth, let it declare the praises and glory of Allah: for He is the Exalted in Might, the Wise.

2. It is He Who got out the unbelievers among the People of the Book from their homes at the first gathering (of the forces). Little did you think that they would get out: and they thought that their fortresses would defend them from Allah! But the (wrath of) Allah came to them from quarters from which they little expected (it), and cast terror into their hearts, so that they destroyed their dwellings by their own hands and the hands of the believers. Take warning, then O you with eyes (to see)!

3. And had it not been that Allah has decreed banishment for them, He would certainly have punished them in this world: and in the hereafter they shall (certainly) have the punishment of the fire.

4. That is because they resisted Allah and His messenger: and if anyone resists Allah, verily Allah is severe in punishment.

5. Whether you cut down (O you Muslims!) the tender palm-trees, or you left them standing on their roots, it was by leave of Allah, and in order that He might cover with shame the rebellious transgressors.

6. What Allah has bestowed on His messenger (and taken away) from them - for this you made no expedition with either cavalry or camelry: but Allah gives power to His messengers over any He pleases: and Allah has power over all things.

7. What Allah has bestowed on His messenger (and taken away) from the people of the townships - belongs to Allah - to His messenger and to relations and orphans, the needy and the wayfarer; in order that it may not (merely) make a circuit between the wealthy among you. So take what the messenger assigns to you, and deny yourselves that which he withholds from you. And fear Allah; for Allah is strict in punishment.

8. (Some part is due) to the needy *Muhajirs,* those who were expelled from their homes and their property, while seeking grace from Allah and (His) good pleasure, and aiding Allah and His messenger: such are indeed the sincere ones -

9. But those who before them, had homes (in Madinah) and had adopted the faith - show their affection to such as came to them for refuge, and entertain no desire in their hearts for things given to the (latter), but give them preference over themselves, even though poverty was their (own lot). And those saved from the covetousness of their own souls - they are the ones that achieve prosperity.

10. And those who came after them say: "Our Lord! Forgive us and our brothers who came before us into the faith, and leave not, in our hearts, rancour (or sense of injury) against those who have believed. Our Lord! You are indeed Full of Kindness, Most Merciful."

11. Have you not observed the hypocrites say to their misbelieving brothers among the People of the Book? - "If you are expelled, we too will go out with you, and we will never listen to anyone in your affair; and if you are attacked (in fight) we will help you." But Allah is witness that they are indeed liars.

12. If they are expelled, never will they go out with them; and if they are attacked (in fight), they will never help them; and if they do help them, they will turn their backs; so they will receive no help.

13. Of a truth you are stronger (than they) because of the terror in their hearts, (sent) by Allah. This is because they are men devoid of understanding.

14. They will not fight you (even) together, except in fortified townships or from behind walls. Strong is their fighting (spirit) amongst themselves; you would think they were united, but their hearts are divided: that is because they are a people devoid of wisdom.

15. Like those who lately preceded them, they have tasted the evil result of their conduct; and (in the hereafter there is) for them a grievous penalty -

16. (Their allies deceived them), like the evil one, when he says to man, "Deny Allah": but when (man) denies Allah, (the evil one) says, "I am free of you: I do fear Allah, the Lord of the Worlds!"

17. The end of both will be that they will go into the fire, dwelling in it forever. Such is the reward of wrongdoers.

18. O you who believe! Fear Allah, and let every soul look to what (provision) he has sent forth for the morrow. Yea, fear Allah: for Allah is well-acquainted with (all) they you do.

19. And be you not like those who forgot Allah; and He made them forget their own souls! Such are the rebellious transgressors!

20. Not equal are the companions of the fire and the companions of the garden: it is the companions of the garden, that will achieve felicity.

21. Had We sent down this Qur'an on a mountain, verily, you would have seen it humble itself and cleave asunder for fear of Allah. Such are the similitudes which We propound to men, that they may reflect.

22. Allah is He, than Whom there is no other god - Who knows (all things) both secret and open; He, Most Gracious, Most Merciful.

23. Allah is He, than Whom there is no other god - the Sovereign, the Holy One, the Source of Peace (and Perfection), the Guardian of faith, the Preserver of Safety, the Exalted in Might, the Irresistible, the Supreme: Glory to Allah! (High is He) above the partners they attribute to Him.

24. He is Allah, the Creator, the Evolver, the Bestower of forms (or colours). To Him belong the Most beautiful names: whatever is in the heavens and on earth, does declare His praises and glory: and He is the Exalted in Might, the Wise.

Surah 60: **Al-Mumtahanah**
(That Which Examines)

In the name of Allah,
Most Gracious, Most Merciful.

1. O you who believe! Take not My enemies and yours as friends (or protectors) - offering them (your) love, even though they have rejected the truth that has come to you, and have (on the contrary) driven out the messenger and yourselves (from your homes), (simply) because you believe in Allah your Lord! If you have come out to strive in My way and to seek

My good pleasure, (take them not as friends), holding secret converse of love (and friendship) with them: for I know full well all that you conceal and all that you reveal. And any of you that does this has strayed from the straight path.

2. If they were to get the better of you, they would behave to you as enemies, and stretch forth their hands and their tongues against you for evil; and they desire that you should reject the truth.

3. Of no profit to you will be your relatives and your children on the day of judgement: He will judge between you: for Allah sees well all that you do.

4. There is for you an excellent example (to follow) in Abraham and those with him, when they said to their people: "We are clear of you and of whatever you worship besides Allah: we have rejected you, and there has arisen between us and you, enmity and hatred forever - unless you believe in Allah and Him alone"; But not when Abraham said to his father: "I will pray for forgiveness for you, though I have no power (to get) anything on your behalf from Allah." (They prayed): "Our Lord! In You do we trust, and to You do we turn in repentance: to You is (our) final goal.

5. Our Lord! Make us not a (test and) trial for the unbelievers, but forgive us, our Lord! For You are the Exalted in Might, the Wise."

6. There was indeed in them an excellent example for you to follow - for those whose hope is in Allah and in the last day. But if any turn away, truly Allah is Free of all wants, Worthy of all praise.

7. It may be that Allah will grant love (and friendship) between you and those whom you (now) hold as enemies. For Allah has power (over all things); and Allah is Oft-Forgiving, Most Merciful.

8. Allah forbids you not, with regard to those who fight you not for (your) faith nor drive you out of your homes, from dealing kindly and justly with them: for Allah loves those who are just.

9. Allah only forbids you, with regard to those who fight you for (your) faith, and drive you out, of your homes, and support (others) in driving you out, from turning to them (for friendship and protection). It is such as turn to them (in these circumstances), that do wrong.

10. O you who believe! When there come to you believing women refugees, examine (and test) them: Allah knows best as to their faith: if you ascertain that they are believers, then send them not back to the unbelievers. They are not lawful (wives) for the unbelievers, nor are the (unbelievers) lawful (husbands) for them. But pay the unbelievers what they have spent (on their dower). And there will be no blame on you if you marry them on payment of their dower to them. But hold not to the guardianship of unbelieving women: ask for what you have spent on their dowers, and let the (unbelievers) ask for what they have spent (on the dowers of women who come over to you). Such is the command of Allah. He judges (with justice) between you. And Allah is Full of Knowledge and Wisdom.

11. And if any of your wives deserts you to the unbelievers, and you have an accession (by the coming over of a woman from the other side), then pay to those whose wives have deserted the equivalent of what they had spent (on their (dower). And fear Allah, in Whom you believe.

12. O prophet! When believing women come to you to take the oath of fealty to you, that they will not associate in worship any other thing whatever with Allah, that they will not steal, that they will not commit adultery (or fornication), that they will not kill their children, that they will not utter slander, intentionally forging falsehood, and that they will not disobey you in any just matter - then do you receive their fealty, and pray to Allah for the forgiveness (of their sins): for Allah is Oft-Forgiving, Most Merciful.

13. O you who believe! Turn not (for friendship) to people on whom is the wrath of Allah. Of the hereafter they are already in despair, just as the unbelievers are in despair about those (buried) in graves.

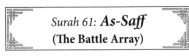

Surah 61: *As-Saff*
(The Battle Array)

In the name of Allah,
Most Gracious, Most Merciful.

1. Whatever is in the heavens and on earth, let it declare the praises and glory of Allah: for He is the Exalted in Might, the Wise.

2. O you who believe! Why do you say that which you do not?

3. Grievously odious is it in the sight of Allah that you say that which you do not.

4. Truly Allah loves those who fight in His cause in battle array, as if they were a solid cemented structure.

5. And remember, Moses said to his people: "O my people! Why do you vex and insult me, though you know that I am the messenger of Allah (sent) to you?" Then when they went wrong, Allah let their hearts go wrong. For Allah guides not those who are rebellious transgressors.

6. And remember, Jesus, the son of Mary, said: "O Children of Israel! I am the messenger of Allah (sent) to you, confirming the law (which came) before me, and giving glad tidings of a messenger to come after me, whose name shall be Ahmad." But when he came to them with clear signs, they said, "This is evident sorcery!"

7. Who does greater wrong than one who invents falsehood against Allah, even as he is being invited to Islam? And Allah guides not those who do wrong.

8. Their intention is to extinguish Allah's light (by blowing) with their mouths: but Allah will complete (the revelation of) His light even though the unbelievers may detest (it).

9. It is He Who has sent His messenger with guidance and the religion of truth, that he may proclaim it over all religion, even though the pagans may detest (it).

10. O you who believe! Shall I lead you to a bargain that will save you from a grievous penalty? -

11. That you believe in Allah and His messenger, and that you strive (your utmost) in the cause of Allah, with your property and your persons: that will be best for you, if you but knew!

12. He will forgive you your sins, and admit you to gardens beneath which rivers flow, and to beautiful mansions in gardens of eternity: that is indeed the supreme achievement.

13. And another (favour will He bestow), which you do love - help from Allah and a speedy victory. So give the glad tidings to the believers.

14. O you who believe! Be you helpers of Allah: as said Jesus, the son of Mary, to the disciples, "Who will be my helpers to (the work of) Allah?" Said the disciples, "We are Allah's helpers!" Then a portion of the Children of Israel believed, and a portion disbelieved: but We gave power to those who believed against their enemies and they became the ones that prevailed.

Surah 62: *Al-Jummu'ah*
(The Congregation)

In the name of Allah,
Most Gracious, Most Merciful.

1. Whatever is in the heavens and on earth, does declare the praises and glory of Allah - the Sovereign, the Holy One, the Exalted in Might, the Wise.

2. It is He Who has sent amongst the unlettered a messenger from among themselves, to rehearse to them His signs, to sanctify them, and to instruct them in scripture and wisdom -

although they had been, before, in manifest error -

3. As well as (to confer all these benefits upon) others of them, who have not already joined them: and He is Exalted in Might, Wise.

4. Such is the bounty of Allah, which He bestows on whom He will: and Allah is the Lord of the highest bounty.

5. The similitude of those who were charged with the (obligations of the) Mosaic law, but who subsequently failed in those (obligations), is that of a donkey which carries huge tomes (but understands them not). Evil is the similitude of people who falsify the signs of Allah: and Allah guides not people who do wrong.

6. Say: "O you that stand on Judaism! If you think that you are friends to Allah, to the exclusion of (other) men, then express your desire for death, if you are truthful!"

7. But never will they express their desire (for death), because of the (deeds) their hands have sent on before them! And Allah knows well those that do wrong!

8. Say: "The death from which you flee will truly overtake you: then will you be sent back to the Knower of things secret and open: and He will tell you (the truth of) the things that you did!"

9. O you who believe! When the call is proclaimed to prayer on Friday (the day of assembly), hasten earnestly to the remembrance of Allah, and leave off business (and traffic): that is best for you if you but knew!

10. And when the prayer is finished, then may you disperse through the land, and seek of the bounty of Allah: and celebrate the praises of Allah often (and without neglect): that you may prosper.

11. But when they see some bargain or some amusement, they disperse headlong to it, and leave you standing. Say: "The (blessing) from the presence of Allah is better than any amusement or bargain! And Allah is the Best to provide (for all needs)."

Surah 63: ***Al-Munafiqun***
(The Hypocrites)

In the name of Allah,
Most Gracious, Most Merciful.

1. When the hypocrites come to you, they say, "We bear witness that you are indeed the messenger of Allah." Yea, Allah knows that you are indeed His messenger, and Allah bears witness that the hypocrites are indeed liars.

2. They have made their oaths a screen (for their misdeeds): thus they obstruct (men) from the path of Allah: truly evil are their deeds.

3. That is because they believed, then they rejected faith: so a seal was set on their hearts: therefore they understand not.

4. When you look at them, their exteriors please you; and when they speak, you listen to their words. They are as (worthless as hollow) pieces of timber propped up, (unable to stand on their own). They think that every call is against them. They are the enemies; so beware of them. The curse of Allah be on them! How are they deluded (away from the truth)!

5. And when it is said to them, "Come, the messenger of Allah will pray for your forgiveness," they turn aside their heads, and you would see them turning away their faces in arrogance.

6. It is equal to them whether you pray for their forgiveness or not. Allah will not forgive them. Truly Allah guides not rebellious transgressors.

7. They are the ones who say, "Spend nothing on those who are with Allah's messenger, to the end that they may disperse (and quit Madinah). But to Allah belong the treasures of the heavens and the earth; but the hypocrites understand not.

8. They say, "If we return to Madinah surely the more honourable (element) will expel therefrom the meaner." But honour belongs to Allah and His messenger, and to the believers; but the hypocrites know not.

9. O you who believe! Let not your riches or your children divert you from the remembrance of Allah. If any act thus, the loss is their own.

10. And spend something (in charity) out of the substance which We have bestowed on you, before death should come to any of you and he should say, "O my Lord! Why did you not give me respite for a little while? I should then have given (largely) in charity, and I should have been one of the doers of good."

11. But to no soul will Allah grant respite when the time appointed (for it) has come: and Allah is well-acquainted with (all) that you do.

Surah 63: *At-Taghabun*
(The Mutual Loss and Gain)

In the name of Allah,
Most Gracious, Most Merciful.

1. Whatever is in the heavens and on earth, does declare the praises and glory of Allah: to Him belongs dominion and to Him belongs praise: and He has power over all things.

2. It is He Who has created you; and of you are some that are unbelievers and some that are believers: and Allah sees well all that you do.

3. He has created the heavens and the earth in just proportions and has given you shape, and made your shapes beautiful: and to Him is the final goal.

4. He knows what is in the heavens and on earth: and He knows what you conceal and what you reveal: yea, Allah knows well the (secrets) of (all) hearts.

5. Has not the story reached you of those who rejected faith before? So they tasted the evil result of their conduct; and they had a grievous penalty.

6. That was because there came to them messengers with clear signs, but they said: "Shall (mere) human beings direct us?" So they rejected (the message) and turned away. But Allah can do without (them): and Allah is free of all needs, worthy of all praise.

7. The unbelievers think that they will not be raised up (for judgement). Say: "Yea, by my Lord, you shall surely be raised up: then shall you be told (the truth) of all that you did. And that is easy for Allah."

8. Believe, therefore, in Allah and His messenger, and in the light which We have sent down. And Allah is well-acquainted with all that you do.

9. The day that He assembles you (all) for a day of assembly - that will be a day of mutual loss and gain (among you). And those who believe in Allah and work righteousness - He will remove from them their ills, and He will admit them to gardens beneath which rivers flow, to dwell in it forever: that will be the supreme achievement.

10. But those who reject faith and treat Our signs as falsehoods, they will be companions of the fire, to dwell in it for ever: and evil is that goal.

11. No kind of calamity can occur, except by the leave of Allah: and if anyone believes in Allah, (Allah) guides his heart (aright): for Allah knows all things.

12. So obey Allah, and obey His messenger; but if you turn back, the duty of Our messenger is but to proclaim (the message) clearly and openly.

13. Allah! There is no god but He: and on Allah therefore let the believers put their trust.

14. O you who believe! Truly, among your wives and your children are (some that are) enemies to yourselves: so beware of them! But if you forgive and overlook, and cover up (their faults), verily Allah is Oft- Forgiving, Most Merciful.

15. Your riches and your children may be but a trial: but in the presence of Allah is the highest reward.

16. So fear Allah as much as you can; listen and obey; and spend in charity for the benefit of your own souls. And those saved from the covetousness of their own souls - they are the ones that achieve prosperity.

17. If you loan to Allah a beautiful loan, He will double it to your (credit), and He will grant you forgiveness: for Allah is most Ready to appreciate (service), Most Forbearing -

18. Knower of what is hidden and what is open, Exalted in Might, Full of Wisdom.

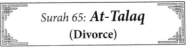

Surah 65: *At-Talaq*
(Divorce)

In the name of Allah,
Most Gracious, Most Merciful.

1. O prophet! When you do divorce women, divorce them at their prescribed periods, and count (accurately) their prescribed periods; and fear Allah your Lord; and turn them not out of their houses, nor shall they (themselves) leave, except in case they are guilty of some open lewdness. Those are limits set by Allah: and any who transgresses the limits of Allah, does verily wrong his (own) soul: you know not if perhaps Allah will bring about after that some new situation.

2. Thus when they fulfil their term appointed, either take them back on equitable terms or part with them on equitable terms; and take for witness two persons from among you, endued with justice, and establish the evidence (as) before Allah. Such is the admonition given to him who believes in Allah and the last day. And for those who fear Allah, He (ever) prepares a way out,

3. And He provides for him from (sources) he never could imagine. And if anyone puts his trust in Allah, sufficient is (Allah) for him. For Allah will surely accomplish His purpose: verily, for all things has Allah appointed a due proportion.

4. Such of your women as have passed the age of monthly courses, for them the prescribed period, if you have any doubts, is three months, and for those who have no courses (it is the same): for those who carry (life within their wombs), their period is until they deliver their burdens: and for those who fear Allah, He will make their path easy.

5. That is the command of Allah, which He has sent down to you: and if anyone fears Allah, He will remove his ills from him, and will enlarge his reward.

6. Let the women live (in Iddah) in the same style as you live, according to your means: annoy them not, so as to restrict them. And if they carry (life in their wombs), then spend (your substance) on them until they deliver their burden; and if they suckle your (offspring), give them their recompense; and take mutual counsel together, according to what is just and reasonable. And if you find yourselves in difficulties, let another woman suckle (the child) on the (father's) behalf.

7. Let the man of means spend according to his means; and the man whose resources are restricted, let him spend according to what Allah has given him. Allah puts no burden on any person beyond what He has given him. After a difficulty, Allah will soon grant relief.

8. How many populations that insolently opposed the command of their Lord and of His messengers, did We call to account - to severe account? - And We imposed on them an exemplary punishment.

9. Then did they taste the evil result of their conduct, and the end of their conduct was perdition.

10. Allah has prepared for them a severe punishment (in the hereafter). Therefore, fear Allah, O you men of understanding - who have believed! - For Allah has indeed sent down to you a message -

11. A messenger, who rehearses to you the signs of Allah containing clear explanations, that he may lead forth those who believe and do righteous deeds from the depths of darkness into light. And those who believe in Allah and work righteousness, He will admit to gardens beneath which rivers flow to dwell in it forever: Allah has indeed granted for them a most excellent provision.

12. Allah is He Who created seven firmaments and of the earth a similar number. Through the midst of them (all) descends His command: that you may know that Allah has power over all things, and that Allah comprehends all things in (His) knowledge.

Surah 66: **At-Tahrim**
(Prohibition)

In the name of Allah,
Most Gracious, Most Merciful.

1. O Prophet! Why do you hold to be forbidden that which Allah has made lawful to you? You seek to please your consorts. But Allah is Oft-Forgiving, Most Merciful.

2. Allah has already ordained for you, (O men), the dissolution of your oaths (in some cases): and Allah is your protector, and He is Full of Knowledge and Wisdom.

3. When the prophet disclosed a matter in confidence to one of his consorts, and she then divulged it (to another), and Allah made it known to him, he confirmed part of it and repudiated a part. Then when he told her of it, she said, "Who told you this?" He said, "He told me Who knows and is well-acquainted (with all things)."

4. If you two turn in repentance to Him, your hearts are indeed so inclined; but if you back up each other against him, truly Allah is his protector, and Gabriel, and (every) righteous one among those who believe - and furthermore, the angels - will back (him) up.

5. It may be, if he divorced you (all), that Allah will give him in exchange consorts better than you - who submit (their wills), who believe, who are devout, who turn to Allah in repentance, who worship (in humility), who travel (for faith) and fast - previously married or virgins.

6. O you who believe! Save yourselves and your families from a fire whose fuel is men and stones, over which are (appointed) angels stern (and) severe, who flinch not (from executing) the commands they receive from Allah, but do (precisely) what they are commanded.

7. (They will say), "O you unbelievers! Make no excuses this day! You are being but repaid for all that you did!"

8. O you who believe! Turn to Allah with sincere repentance: in the hope that your Lord will remove from you your ills and admit you to gardens beneath which rivers flow - the day that Allah will not permit to be humiliated the prophet and those who believe with him. Their light will run forward before them and by their right hands, while they say, "Our Lord! Perfect our light for us and grant us forgiveness; for You have power over all things."

9. O Prophet! Strive hard against the unbelievers and the hypocrites, and be firm against them. Their abode is hell - an evil refuge (indeed).

10. Allah sets out for an example to the unbelievers, the wife of Noah and the wife of Lot: they were (respectively) under two of Our righteous servants but they were false to their (husbands) and they profited nothing before Allah on their account, but were told: "Enter you the fire along with (others) that enter!"

11. And Allah sets out, as an example to those who believe, the wife of Pharaoh: See, she said: "O my Lord! Build for me, in nearness to You, a mansion in the garden, and save me from Pharaoh and his doings, and save me from those that do wrong";

12. And Mary the daughter of 'Imran, who guarded her chastity; and We breathed into her (body) of Our spirit; and she testified to the truth of the words of her Lord and of His revelations, and was one of the devout (servants).

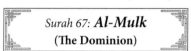

Surah 67: *Al-Mulk*
(The Dominion)

In the name of Allah,
Most Gracious, Most Merciful.

1. Blessed be He in Whose hands is dominion: and He over all things has power -

2. He Who created death and life, that He may try which of you is best in deed; and He is the Exalted in Might, Oft-Forgiving -

3. He Who created the seven heavens one above another: no want of proportion will you see in the creation of (Allah) Most Gracious. So turn your vision again: do you see any flaw?

4. Again turn your vision a second time: (your) vision will come back to you dull and discomfited, in a state worn out.

5. And We have, (from of old) adorned the lowest heaven with lamps, and We have made such lamps) (as) missiles to drive away the Evil Ones, and have prepared for them the penalty of the blazing fire.

6. For those who reject their Lord (and Cherisher) is the penalty of hell: and evil is (such) destination.

7. When they are cast in it, they will hear the (terrible) drawing in of its breath even as it blazes,

8. Almost bursting with fury: every time a group is cast in it, its keepers will ask, "Did no warner come to you?"

9. They will say: "Yes indeed; a warner did come to us, but we rejected him and said, 'Allah never sent down any (message): you are in nothing but an egregious delusion!'"

10. They will further say: "Had we but listened or used our intelligence, we should not (now) be among the companions of the blazing fire!"

11. They will then confess their sins: but far will be (forgiveness) from the companions of the blazing fire!

12. As for those who fear their Lord unseen, for them is forgiveness and a great reward.

13. And whether you hide your word or publish it, He certainly has (full) knowledge of the secrets of (all) hearts.

14. Should He not know - He that created? And He is the One that understands the finest mysteries (and) is well-acquainted (with them).

15. It is He Who has made the earth manageable for you, so traverse you through its tracts and enjoy of the sustenance which He furnishes: but to Him is the resurrection.

16. Do you feel secure that He Who is in heaven will not cause you to be swallowed up by the earth when it shakes (as in an earthquake)?

17. Or do you feel secure that He Who is in heaven will not send against you a violent tornado (with showers of stones) so that you shall know how (terrible) was My warning?

18. But indeed men before them rejected (My warning): then how (terrible) was My rejection (of them)?

19. Do they not observe the birds above them, spreading their wings and folding them in? None can uphold them except (Allah) Most Gracious: truly it is He that watches over all things.

20. Nay, who is there that can help you, (even as) an army, besides (Allah) Most Merciful? In nothing but delusion are the unbelievers.

21. Or who is there that can provide you with sustenance if He were to withhold His provision? Nay, they obstinately persist in insolent impiety and flight (from the truth).

22. Is then one who walks headlong, with his face grovelling, better guided - or one who walks evenly on a straight way?

23. Say: "It is He Who has created you (and made you grow), and made for you the faculties of hearing, seeing, feeling and understanding: little thanks it is you give."

24. Say: "It is He Who has multiplied you through the earth, and to Him shall you be gathered together."

25. They ask: when will this promise be (fulfilled)? If you are telling the truth.

26. Say: "As to the knowledge of the time, it is with Allah alone: I am (sent) only to warn plainly in public."

27. At length when they see it close at hand, grieved will be the faces of the unbelievers, and it will be said (to them): "This is (the promise fulfilled) which you were calling for!"

28. Say: "Do you see? - If Allah were to destroy me and those with me, or if He bestows His mercy on us - yet who can deliver the unbelievers from a grievous penalty?"

29. Say: "He is (Allah) Most Gracious: we have believed in Him, and on Him have we put our trust: so, soon will you know which (of us) it is that is in manifest error."

30. Say: "Do you see? - If your stream be some morning lost (in the underground earth), who then can supply you with clear-flowing water?"

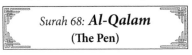

Surah 68: *Al-Qalam*
(The Pen)

In the name of Allah,
Most Gracious, Most Merciful.

1. Nun. By the pen and by the (record) which (men) write -

2. You are not by the grace of your Lord mad or possessed.

3. Nay, verily for you is a reward unfailing:

4. And you (stand) on an exalted standard of character.

5. Soon will you see, and they will see,

6. Which of you is afflicted with madness.

7. Verily it is your Lord that knows best, which (among men) has strayed from His path: and He knows best those who receive (true) guidance.

8. So listen not to those who deny (the truth).

9. Their desire is that you should be accommodating; so would they be accommodating.

10. Heed not the type of despicable man - ready with oaths,

11. A slanderer, going about with calumnies,

12. (Habitually) hindering (all) good, transgressing beyond bounds, deep in sin,

13. Violent (and cruel) with all that base-born -

14. Because he possesses wealth and (numerous) sons.

15. When to him are rehearsed Our signs, "Tales of the ancients," he cries!

16. Soon shall We brand (the beast) on the snout!

17. Verily We have tried them as We tried the people of the garden, when they resolved to gather the fruits of the (garden) in the morning.

18. But made no reservation, ("If it be Allah's will").

19. So there came on the (garden) a visitation from your Lord, (which swept away) all around, while they were asleep.

20. So the (garden) became, by the morning, like a dark and desolate spot, (whose fruit had been gathered).

21. As the morning broke, they called out, one to another -

22. "Go you to your tilth (early) in morning, if you would gather the fruits."

23. So they departed, conversing in secret low tones, (saying) -

24. "Let not a single needy person break in upon you into the (garden) this day."

25. And they opened the morning, strong in an (unjust) resolve.

26. But when they saw the (garden), they said: "We have surely lost our way:

27. Indeed we are shut out (of the fruits of our labour)!"

28. Said one of them, more just (than the rest): "Did I not say to you, 'Why not glorify (Allah)?'"

29. They said: "glory to our Lord! Verily we have been doing wrong!"

30. Then they turned, one against another, in reproach.

31. They said: "Alas for us! We have indeed transgressed!

32. It may be that our Lord will give us in exchange a better (garden) than this: for we do turn to Him (in repentance)!"

33. Such is the punishment (in this life); but greater is the punishment in the hereafter - if only they knew!

34. Verily, for the righteous are gardens of delight, in the presence of their Lord.

35. Shall We then treat the people of faith like the people of sin?

36. What is the matter with you? How do you judge?

37. Or do you have a book through which you learn -

38. That you shall have, through it whatever you choose?

39. Or do you have covenants with Us on oath, reaching to the day of judgement, (providing) that you shall have whatever you shall demand?

40. Do you ask of them which of them will stand surety for that!

41. Or do they have some "partners" (in Allah)? Then let them produce their "partners" if they are truthful!

42. The day that the shin shall be laid bare, and they shall be summoned to bow in adoration, but they shall not be able -

43. Their eyes will be cast down - disgrace will cover them; seeing that they had been summoned before to bow in adoration, while they were whole (and had refused).

44. Then leave Me alone with such as reject this message: by degrees shall We punish them from directions they perceive not.

45. A (long) respite will I grant them: truly powerful is My plan.

46. Or is it that you do ask them for a reward, so that they are burdened with a load of debt? -

47. Or that the unseen is in their hands, so that they can write it down?

48. So wait with patience for the command of your Lord, and be not like the companion of the fish - when he cried out in agony.

49. Had not grace from His Lord reached him, he would indeed have been cast off on the naked shore, in disgrace.

50. Thus did his Lord choose him and make him of the company of the righteous.

51. And the unbelievers would almost trip you up with their eyes when they hear the message; and they say: "Surely he is possessed!"

52. But it is nothing less than a message to all the worlds.

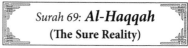

Surah 69: **Al-Haqqah**
(The Sure Reality)

In the name of Allah,
Most Gracious, Most Merciful.

1. The sure reality!

2. What is the sure reality?

3. And what will make you realise what the sure reality is?

4. The Thamud and the 'Ad people (branded) as false the stunning calamity!

5. But the Thamud - they were destroyed by a terrible storm of thunder and lightning!

6. And the 'Ad - they were destroyed by a furious wind, exceedingly violent;

7. He made it rage against them seven nights and eight days in succession: so that you could see the (whole) people lying prostrate in its (path), as if they had been roots of hollow palm-trees tumbled down!

8. Then do you see any of them left surviving?

9. And Pharaoh and those before him, and the cities overthrown, committed habitual sin,

10. And disobeyed (each) the messenger of their Lord; so He punished them with an abundant penalty.

11. We, when the water (of Noah's flood) overflowed beyond its limits, carried you (mankind) in the floating (ark).

12. That We might make it a message to you, and that ears (that should hear the tale and) retain its memory should bear its (lessons) in remembrance.

13. Then, when one blast is sounded on the trumpet,

14. And the earth is moved, and its mountains, and they are crushed to powder at one stroke -

15. On that day shall the (great) event come to pass,

16. And the sky will be rent asunder, for it will that day be flimsy,

17. And the angels will be on its sides, and eight will, that day bear the throne of your Lord above them.

18. That day shall you be brought to judgement: not an act of yours that you hide will be hidden.

19. Then he that will be given his record in his right hand will say: "Ah here! Read you my record!

20. I did really understand that my account would (one day) reach me!"

21. And he will be in a life of bliss,

22. In a garden on high,

23. The fruits of which (will hang in bunches) low and near.

24. "Eat you and drink you, with full satisfaction; because of the (good) that you sent before you, in the days that are gone!"

25. And he that will be given his record in his left hand, will say: "Ah! Would that my record had not been given to me!

26. And that I had never realised how my account (stood)!

27. Ah! Would that (death) had made an end of me!

28. Of no profit to me has been my wealth!

29. My power has perished from me!"

30. (The stern command will say): "Seize you him, and bind you him,

31. And burn you him in the blazing fire.

32. Further, make him march in a chain, of which the length is seventy cubits!

33. This was he that would not believe in Allah Most High,

34. And would not encourage the feeding of the needy!

35. So no friend has he here this day.

36. Nor has he any food except the corruption from the washing of wounds,

37. Which none do eat but those in sin."

38. So I do call to witness what you see,

39. And what you do not see,

40. That this is verily the word of an honoured messenger;

41. It is not the word of a poet: little it is you believe!

42. Nor is it the word of a soothsayer: little admonition it is you receive.

43. (This is) a message sent down from the Lord of the worlds.

44. And if (the messenger) were to invent any sayings in Our name,

45. We should certainly seize him by his right hand,

46. And We should certainly then cut off the artery of his heart:

47. Nor could any of you withhold him (from Our wrath).

48. But verily this is a message for the God-fearing.

49. And We certainly know that there are amongst you those that reject (it).

50. But truly (revelation) is a cause of sorrow for the unbelievers.

51. But verily it is truth of assured certainty.

52. So glorify the name of your Lord Most High.

Surah 70: *Al-Ma'arij*
(The Ways Of Ascent)

In the name of Allah,
Most Gracious, Most Merciful.

1. A questioner asked about a penalty to befall -

2. The unbelievers, the which there is none to ward off -

3. (A penalty) from Allah, Lord of the ways of ascent.

4. The angels and the spirit ascend to Him in a day the measure of which is (as) fifty thousand years:

5. Therefore, do you hold patience - a patience of beautiful (contentment).

6. They see the (day) indeed as a far-off (event):

7. But We see it (quite) near.

8. The day that the sky will be like molten brass,

9. And the mountains will be like wool,

10. And no friend will ask after a friend,

11. Though they will be put in sight of each other - the sinner's desire will be: would that he could redeem himself from the penalty of that day by (sacrificing) his children,

12. His wife and his brother,

13. His relations who sheltered him.

14. And all, all that is on earth - so it could deliver him:

15. By no means! For it would be the fire of hell! -

16. Plucking out (his being) right to the skull! -

17. Inviting (all) such as turn their backs and turn away their faces (from the right),

18. And collect (wealth) and hide it (from use)!

19. Truly man was created very impatient -

20. Fretful when evil touches him;

21. And niggardly when good reaches him -

22. Not so those devoted to prayer -

23. Those who remain steadfast to their prayer;

24. And those in whose wealth is a recognised right -

25. For the (needy) who asks and him who is prevented (for some reason from asking);

26. And those who hold to the truth of the day of judgement;

27. And those who fear the displeasure of their Lord -

28. For their Lord's displeasure is the opposite of peace and tranquillity -

29. And those who guard their chastity,

30. Except with their wives and the (captives) whom their right hands possess - for (then) they are not to be blamed,

31. But those who trespass beyond this are transgressors -

32. And those who respect their trusts and covenants;

33. And those who stand firm in their testimonies;

34. And those who guard (the sacredness) of their worship -

35. Such will be the honoured ones in the gardens (of bliss).

36. Now what is the matter with the unbelievers that they rush madly before you -

37. From the right and from the left, in crowds?

38. Does every man of them long to enter the garden of bliss?

39. By no means! For We have created them out of the (base matter) they know!

40. Now I do call to witness the Lord of all points in the east and the west that We can certainly -

41. Substitute for them better (men) than they; and We are not to be defeated (in Our plan).

42. So leave them to plunge in vain talk and play about, until they encounter that day of theirs which they have been promised! -

43. The day whereon they will issue from their sepulchres in sudden haste as if they were rushing to a goalpost (fixed for them) -

44. Their eyes lowered in dejection - disgrace covering them (all over)! Such is the day the which they are promised!

Surah 71: *Nuh*
(Noah)

In the name of Allah,
Most Gracious, Most Merciful.

1. We sent Noah to his people (with the command): "Do you warn your people before there comes to them a grievous penalty."

2. He said: "O my people! I am to you a warner, clear and open:

3. That you should worship Allah, fear Him and obey me:

4. So He may forgive you your sins and give you respite for a stated term: for when the term given by Allah is accomplished, it cannot be put forward: if you only knew."

5. He said: "O my Lord! I have called to my people night and day:

6. But my call only increases (their) flight (from the right)."

7. And every time I have called to them, that you might forgive them, they have (only) thrust their fingers into their ears, covered themselves up with their garments, grown obstinate, and given themselves up to arrogance.

8. So I have called to them aloud;

9. Further, I have spoken to them in public and secretly in private,

10. Saying: "Ask forgiveness from your Lord; for He is Oft-Forgiving;

11. He will send rain to you in abundance;"

12. Give you increase in wealth and sons; and bestow on you gardens and bestow on you rivers (of flowing water).

13. What is the matter with you, that you place not your hope for kindness and long-suffering in Allah -

14. Seeing that it is He that has created you in diverse stages?

15. Do you not see how Allah has created the seven heavens one above another,

16. And made the moon a light in their midst, and made the sun as a (glorious) lamp?

17. And Allah has produced you from the earth growing (gradually),

18. And in the end He will return you into the (earth), and raise you forth (again at the resurrection)?

19. And Allah has made the earth for you as a carpet (spread out),

20. That you may go about in it in spacious roads.'"

21. Noah said: "O my Lord! They have disobeyed me, but they follow (men) whose wealth and children give them no increase but only loss.

22. And they have devised a tremendous plot.

23. And they have said (to each other), 'abandon not your gods; abandon neither *Wadd* nor *Suwwa,* neither *Yaguth* nor *Ya'uq,* nor *Nasr'* -

24. They have already misled many; and grant You no increase to the wrongdoers but in straying (from their mark)."

25. Because of their sins they were drowned (in the flood), and were made to enter the fire (of punishment): and they found - in lieu of Allah - none to help them.

26. And Noah said: "O my Lord! Leave not of the unbelievers, a single one on earth!

27. For, if You do leave (any of) them, they will but mislead your devotees, and they will breed none but wicked ungrateful ones.

28. O my Lord! Forgive me, my parents, all who enter my house in faith and (all) believing men and believing women: and to the wrongdoers grant You no increase but in perdition!"

Surah 72: **Al-Jinn**
(The Spirits)

In the name of Allah,
Most Gracious, Most Merciful.

1. Say: It has been revealed to me that a company of Jinns listened (to the Qur'an). They said, "We have really heard a wonderful recital!

2. It gives guidance to the right, and we have believed in it: we shall not join (in worship) any (gods) with our Lord.

3. And exalted is the Majesty of our Lord: He has taken neither a wife nor a son.

4. There were some foolish ones among us, who used to utter extravagant lies against Allah;

5. But we do think that no man or spirit should say anything that is untrue against Allah.

6. True, there were persons among mankind who took shelter with persons among the Jinns, but they increased them in folly.

7. And they (came to) think as you thought, that Allah would not raise up anyone (to judgement).

8. And we pried into the secrets of heaven; but we found it filled with stern guards and flaming fires.

9. We used indeed, to sit there in (hidden) stations, to (steal) a hearing; but any who listens now will find a flaming fire watching him in ambush.

10. And we understand not whether ill is intended to those on earth, or whether their Lord (really) intends to guide them to right conduct.

11. There are among us some that are righteous, and some the contrary: we follow divergent paths.

12. But we think that we can by no means frustrate Allah throughout the earth, nor can we frustrate Him by flight.

13. And as for us, since we have listened to the guidance, we have accepted it: and any who believes in his Lord has no fear, either of a short (account) or of any injustice.

14. Amongst us are some that submit their wills (to Allah), and some that swerve from justice. Now those who submit their wills - they have sought out (the path) of right conduct:

15. But those who swerve - they are (but) fuel for hellfire" -

16. (And Allah's message is): "If they (the pagans) had (only) remained on the (right) way, We should certainly have bestowed on them rain in abundance.

17. That We might try them by that (means). But if any turns away from the remembrance of his Lord, He will cause him to undergo a severe penalty.

18. And the places of worship are for Allah (alone): so invoke not anyone along with Allah;

19. Yet when the devotee of Allah stands up to invoke Him, they just make round him a dense crowd."

20. Say: "I do no more than invoke my Lord, and I join not with Him any (false god)."

21. Say: "It is not in my power to cause you harm, or to bring you to right conduct."

22. Say: "No one can deliver me from Allah (if I were to disobey Him), nor should I find refuge except in Him.

23. Unless I proclaim what I receive from Allah and His messages: for any that disobey Allah and His messenger for them is hell: they shall dwell in it forever."

24. At length, when they see (with their own eyes) that which they are promised - then will they know who it is that is weakest in (his) helper and least important in point of numbers.

25. Say: "I know not whether the (punishment) which you are promised is near, or whether my Lord will appoint for it a distant term.

26. He (alone) knows the unseen, nor does He make any one acquainted with His mysteries -

27. Except a messenger whom He has chosen: and then He makes a band of watchers march before him and behind him,

28. That he may know that they have (truly) brought and delivered the messages of their Lord: and He surrounds (all the mysteries) that are with them, and takes account of every single thing."

Surah 73: **Al-Muzzammil**
(The Enfolded One)

In the name of Allah,
Most Gracious, Most Merciful.

1. O you (Muhammad) folded in garments!

2. Stand (to pray) by night, but not all night -

3. Half of it - or a little less,

4. Or a little more; and recite the Qur'an in slow, measured rhythmic tones.

5. Soon shall We send down to you a weighty message.

6. Truly the rising by night is most potent for governing (the soul), and most suitable for (framing) the word (of prayer and praise).

7. True, there is for you by day prolonged occupation with ordinary duties:

8. But keep in remembrance the name of the Lord and devote yourself to Him wholeheartedly.

9. (He is) Lord of the east and the west: there is no god but He: take Him therefore for (your) disposer of affairs.

10. And have patience with what they say, and leave them with noble (dignity).

11. And leave Me (alone to deal with) those in possession of the good things of life, who (yet) deny the truth; and bear with them for a little while.

12. With Us are fetters (to bind them), and a fire (to burn them),

13. And a food that chokes, and a penalty grievous.

14. One day the earth and the mountains will be in violent commotion. And the mountains will be as a heap of sand poured out and flowing down.

15. We have sent to you (O men!) a messenger, to be a witness concerning you, even as We sent a messenger to Pharaoh.

16. But Pharaoh disobeyed the messenger; so We seized him with a heavy punishment.

17. Then how shall you, if you deny (Allah) guard yourselves against a day that will make children hoary-headed? -

18. On which the sky will be cleft asunder? His promise needs must be accomplished.

19. Verily this is an admonition: therefore, whoso will let him take a (straight) path to his Lord!

20. Your Lord does know that you stand up (to prayer) near two-thirds of the night, or half the night, or a third of the night, and so does a party of those with you. But Allah does appoint night and day in due measure. He knows that you are unable to keep count of it. So He has turned to you (in mercy): read you, therefore, of the Qur'an as much as may be easy for you. He knows that there may be (some) among you in ill-health; others travelling through the land, seeking of Allah's bounty; yet others fighting in Allah's cause. Read you, therefore, as much of the Qur'an as may be easy (for you); and establish regular prayer and give regular charity; and loan to Allah a beautiful loan. And whatever good you send ahead for your souls, You shall find it in Allah's presence - Yea, better and greater in reward, and seek you the grace of Allah: for Allah is Oft-Forgiving, Most Merciful.

Surah 74: *Al-Muddaththir*
(The Wrapped Up One)

In the name of Allah,
Most Gracious, Most Merciful.

1. O you (Muhammad) wrapped up (in a mantle)!

2. Arise and deliver your warning!

3. And your Lord do you magnify!

4. And your garments keep free from stain!

5. And all abomination shun!

6. Nor expect, in giving, any increase (for yourself)!

7. But, for your Lord's (cause) be patient and constant!

8. Finally, when the trumpet is sounded,

9. That will be - that day - a day of distress -

10. Far from easy for those without faith.

11. Leave Me alone, (to deal) with the (creature) whom I created (bare and) alone! -

12. To whom I granted resources in abundance.

13. And sons to be by his side! -

14. To whom I made (life) smooth and comfortable!

15. Yet is he greedy - that I should add (yet more) -

16. By no means! For to Our signs he has been refractory!

17. Soon will I visit him with a mount of calamities!

18. For he thought and he plotted -

19. And woe to him! How he plotted! -

20. Yea, woe to him; how he plotted! -

21. Then he looked round;

22. Then he frowned and he scowled;

23. Then he turned back and was haughty;

24. Then said he: "This is nothing but magic, derived from of old";

25. "This is nothing but the word of a mortal!"

26. Soon will I cast him into hellfire!

27. And what will explain to you what hellfire is?

28. Nothing does it permit to endure, and nothing does it leave alone! -

29. Darkening and changing the colour of man!

30. Over it are nineteen.

31. And We have set none but angels as guardians of the fire; and We have fixed their number only as a trial for unbelievers - in order that the People of the Book may arrive at certainty, and the believers may increase in faith - and that no doubts may be left for the People of the Book and the believers, and that those in whose hearts is a disease and the unbelievers may say, "What symbol does Allah intend by this?" Thus does Allah leave to stray whom He pleases, and guide whom He pleases; and none can know the forces of the Lord, except He. And this is no other than a warning to mankind.

32. Nay, verily: by the moon,

33. And by the night as it retreats,

34. And by the dawn as it shines -

35. This is but one of the mighty (signs),

36. A warning to mankind -

37. To any of you that chooses to press forward, or to follow behind -

38. Every soul will be (held) in pledge for its deeds.

39. Except the companions of the right hand.

40. (They will be) in gardens (of delight); they will question each other,

41. And (ask) of the sinners:

42. "What led you into hellfire?"

43. They will say: "We were not of those who prayed;

44. Nor were we of those who fed the needy;

45. But we used to talk vanities with vain talkers;

46. And we used to deny the day of judgement,

47. Until there came to us (the hour) that is certain."

48. Then will no intercession of (any) intercessors profit them.

49. Then what is the matter with them that they turn away from admonition? -

50. As if they were affrighted asses,

51. Fleeing from a lion!

52. Each one of them wants to be given scrolls (of revelation) spread out!

53. By no means! But they fear not the hereafter.

54. Nay, this surely is an admonition:

55. Let any who will, keep it in remembrance!

56. But none will keep it in remembrance except as Allah wills: He is the Lord of Righteousness and the Lord of forgiveness.

Surah 75: *Al-Qiyamah*
(The Resurrection)

In the name of Allah,
Most Gracious, Most Merciful.

1. I do call to witness the resurrection day;

2. And I do call to witness the self-reproaching spirit; (eschew evil).

3. Does man think that We cannot assemble his bones?

4. Nay, We are able to put together in perfect order the very tips of his fingers.

5. But man wishes to do wrong (even) in the time in front of him.

6. He questions: "When is the day of resurrection?"

7. At length, when the sight is dazed,

8. And the moon is buried in darkness.

9. And the sun and moon are joined together -

10. That day will man say: "Where is the refuge?"

11. By no means! No place of safety!

12. Before your Lord (alone), that day will be the place of rest.

13. That day will man be told (all) that he put forward, and all that he put back.

14. Nay, man will be evidence against himself,

15. Even though he were to put up his excuses.

16. Move not your tongue concerning the (Qur'an) to make haste with it.

17. It is for Us to collect it and to promulgate it:

18. But when We have promulgated it, follow you its recital (as promulgated):

19. Nay more, it is for Us to explain it (and make it clear):

20. Nay, (you men!) but you love the fleeting life,

21. And leave alone the hereafter.

22. Some faces, that day, will beam (in brightness and beauty) -

23. Looking towards their Lord;

24. And some faces, that day, will be sad and dismal,

25. In the thought that some back-breaking calamity was about to be inflicted on them;

26. Yea, when (the soul) reaches to the collarbone (in its exit),

27. And there will be a call, "Who is a magician (to restore him)?"

28. And he will conclude that it was (the time) of parting;

29. And one leg will be joined with another:

30. That day the drive will be (all) to your Lord!

31. So he gave nothing in charity, nor did he pray! -

32. But on the contrary, He rejected truth and turned away!

33. Then did he stalk to his family in full conceit!

34. Woe to you, (O man!) yea, woe!

35. Again, woe to you (O man!) yea, woe!

36. Does man think that he will be left uncontrolled, (without purpose)?

37. Was he not a drop of sperm emitted (in lowly form)?

38. Then did he become a clinging clot; then did (Allah) make and fashion (him) in due proportion.

39. And of him He made two sexes, male and female.

40. Has not He, (the same), the power to give life to the dead?

Surah 76: **Ad-Dahr or Al-Insan** (The Time)

In the name of Allah, Most Gracious, Most Merciful.

1. Has there not been over man a long period of time, when he was nothing - (not even) mentioned?

2. Verily We created man from a drop of mingled sperm, in order to try him: so We gave him (the gifts) of hearing and sight.

3. We showed him the way: whether he be grateful or ungrateful (rests on his will).

4. For the rejecters We have prepared chains, yokes, and a blazing fire.

5. As to the righteous. They shall drink of a cup (of wine) mixed with Kafur -

6. A fountain where the devotees of Allah do drink, making it flow in unstinted abundance.

7. They perform (their) vows, and they fear a day whose evil flies far and wide.

8. And they feed, for the love of Allah, the needy, the orphan, and the captive -

9. (Saying) "We feed you for the sake of Allah alone: no reward do we desire from you, nor thanks.

10. We only fear a day of distressful wrath from the side of our Lord."

11. But Allah will deliver them from the evil of that day, and will shed over them a light of beauty and a (blissful) joy.

12. And because they were patient and constant, He will reward them with a garden and (garments of) silk.

13. Reclining in the (garden) on raised thrones, they will see there neither the sun's (excessive heat) nor (the moon's) excessive cold.

14. And the shades of the (garden) will come low over them, and the bunches (of fruit), there will hang low in humility.

15. And amongst them will be passed round vessels of silver and goblets of crystal -

16. Crystal-clear made of silver: they will determine the measure of it (according to their wishes).

17. And they will be given to drink there of a cup (of wine) mixed with Zanjabeel -

18. A fountain there, called Salsabeel.

19. And round about them will (serve) youths of perpetual (freshness): if you see them, you would think them scattered pearls.

20. And when you look, it is there you will see a bliss and a realm magnificent.

21. Upon them will be green garments of fine silk and heavy brocade, and they will be adorned with bracelets of silver; and their Lord will give to them to drink of a wine pure and holy.

22. "Verily this is a reward for you, and your endeavour is accepted and recognised."

23. It is We Who have sent down the Qur'an to you by stages.

24. Therefore, be patient, with constancy to the command of your Lord, and listen not to the sinner or the ungrateful among them.

25. And celebrate the name of your Lord morning and evening,

26. And part of the night, prostrate yourself to Him; and glorify Him a long night through.

27. As to these, they love the fleeting life, and put away behind them a day (that will be) hard.

28. It is We Who created them, and We have made their joints strong; but, when We will We can substitute the like of them by a complete change.

29. This is an admonition: whosoever will, let him take a (straight) path to his Lord.

30. But you will not, except as Allah wills; for Allah is full of Knowledge and Wisdom.

31. He will admit to His mercy Whom He will; but the wrongdoers - for them has He prepared a grievous penalty.

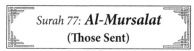

Surah 77: **Al-Mursalat**
(Those Sent)

In the name of Allah,
Most Gracious, Most Merciful.

1. By the (winds) sent one after another (to man's profit);

2. Which then blow violently in tempestuous gusts,

3. And scatter (things) far and wide;

4. Then separate them, one from another,

5. Then spread abroad a message,

6. Whether of justification or of warning -

7. Assuredly, what you are promised must come to pass.

8. Then when the stars become dim;

9. When the heaven is split apart;

10. When the mountains are scattered (to the winds) as dust;

11. And when the messengers are (all) appointed a time (to collect) -

12. For what day are these (signs) deferred?

13. For the day of sorting out.

14. And what will explain to you what is the day of sorting out?

15. Ah woe, that day, to the rejecters of truth!

16. Did We not destroy the men of old (for their evil)?

17. So shall We make later (generations) follow them.

18. Thus do We deal with men of sin.

19. Ah woe, that day to the rejecters of truth!

20. Have We not created you from a fluid (held) despicable? -

21. Then We placed it in a place of rest firmly fixed,

22. For a period (of gestation), determined (according to need)?

23. For We do determine (according to need); for We are the best to determine (things).

24. Ah woe, that day! To the rejecters of truth!

25. Have We not made the earth (as a place) to draw together

26. The living and the dead,

27. And made in it mountains standing firm, lofty (in stature); and provided for you water sweet (and wholesome)?

28. Ah woe, that day, to the rejecters of truth!

29. (It will be said:) "Depart you to that which you used to reject as false!

30. Depart you to a shadow (of smoke ascending) in three columns,

31. (Which yields) no shade of coolness, and is of no use against the fierce blaze.

32. Indeed it throws about sparks (huge) as forts,

33. As if there were (a string of) yellow camels (marching swiftly)."

34. Ah woe, that day, to the rejecters of truth!

35. That will be a day when they shall not be able to speak,

36. Nor will it be open to them to put forth pleas.

37. Ah woe, that day, to the rejecters of truth!

38. That will be a day of sorting out! We shall gather you together and those before (you)!

39. Now, if you have a trick (or plot) use it against Me!

40. Ah woe, that day, to the rejecters of truth!

41. As to the righteous, they shall be amidst (cool) shades and springs (of water).

42. And (they shall have) fruits - all they desire.

43. "Eat you and drink you to your heart's content: for that you worked (righteousness)."

44. Thus do We certainly reward the doers of good.

45. Ah woe, that day, to the rejecters of truth!

46. (O you Unjust!) Eat you and enjoy yourselves (but) a little while, for that you are sinners.

47. Ah woe, that day, to the rejecters of truth!

48. And when it is said to them, "Prostrate yourselves!" They do not so.

49. Ah woe, that day, to the rejecters of truth!

50. Then what message, after that, will they believe in?

Surah 78: **An-Naba**
(The Great News)

In the name of Allah,
Most Gracious, Most Merciful.

1. Concerning what are they disputing?

2. Concerning the great news,

3. About which they cannot agree.

4. Verily they shall soon (come to) know!

5. Verily, verily they shall soon (come to) know!

6. Have We not made the earth as a wide expanse,

7. And the mountains as pegs?

8. And (have We not) created you in pairs,

9. And made your sleep for rest,

10. And made the night as a covering,

11. And made the day as means of subsistence?

12. And (have We not) built over you the seven firmaments,

13. And placed (in it) a light of splendour?

14. And do We not send down from the clouds water in abundance,

15. That We may produce with it corn and vegetables,

16. And gardens of luxurious growth?

17. Verily the day of sorting out is a thing appointed -

18. The day that the trumpet shall be sounded and you shall come out in crowds;

19. And the heavens shall be opened as if there were doors,

20. And the mountains shall vanish, as if they were a mirage.

21. Truly hell is as a place of ambush -

22. For the transgressors a place of destination:

23. They will dwell in it for ages.

24. Nothing cool shall they taste in it, nor any drink,

25. Save a boiling fluid and a fluid, dark, murky, intensely cold -

26. A fitting recompense (for them).

27. For that they used not to fear any account (for their deeds),

28. But they (impudently) treated Our signs as false.

29. And all things have We preserved on record.

30. "So taste you (the fruits of your deeds); for no increase shall We grant you, except in punishment."

31. Verily for the righteous there will be a fulfilment of (the heart's) desires;

32. Gardens enclosed and grapevines;

33. Companions of equal age;

34. And a cup full (to the brim).

35. No vanity shall they hear in it, nor untruth -

36. Recompense from your Lord, a gift, (amply) sufficient -

37. (From) the Lord of the heavens and the earth, and all between - (Allah) Most Gracious: none shall have power to argue with Him.

38. The day that the spirit and the angels will stand forth in ranks, none shall speak except any who is permitted by (Allah) Most Gracious, and he will say what is right.

39. That day will be the sure reality: therefore, whoso will, let him take a (straight) return to his Lord!

40. Verily, We have warned you of a penalty near - the day when man will see (the deeds) which his hands have sent forth and the unbeliever will say, "Woe to me! Would that I were (mere) dust!"

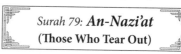

Surah 79: **An-Nazi'at**
(Those Who Tear Out)

In the name of Allah,
Most Gracious, Most Merciful.

1. By the (angels) who tear out (the souls of the wicked) with violence;

2. By those who gently draw out (the souls of the blessed);

3. And by those who glide along (on errands of mercy),

4. Then press forward as in a race,

5. Then arrange to do (the commands of their Lord) -

6. One day everything that can be in commotion will be in violent commotion,

7. Followed by oft-repeated (commotions):

8. Hearts that day will be in agitation;

9. Cast down will be (their owners') eyes.

10. They say (now): "What! Shall we indeed be returned to (our) former state?" -

11. "What! - When we shall have become rotten bones?"

12. They say: "It would in that case be a return with loss!"

13. But verily, it will be but a single (compelling) call,

14. When, behold, they will be in the (full) awakening (to judgement).

15. Has the story of Moses reached you?

16. See, your Lord did call to him in the sacred valley of Tuwa -

17. "Go you to Pharaoh, for he has indeed transgressed all bounds.

18. And say to him, 'Would you that you should be purified (from sin)? -

19. And that I guide you to your Lord, so you should fear Him?' "

20. Then did (Moses) show him the great sign.

21. But (Pharaoh) rejected it and disobeyed (guidance);

22. Further, he turned his back, striving hard (against Allah).

23. Then he collected (his men) and made a proclamation,

24. Saying "I am your Lord, Most High."

25. But Allah did punish him (and made an) example of him - in the hereafter as in this life.

26. Verily in this is an instructive warning for whosoever fears (Allah):

27. What! Are you the more difficult to create of the heaven (above)? (Allah) has constructed it:

28. On high has He raised its canopy, and He has given it order and perfection.

29. Its night does He endow with darkness, and its splendour does He bring out (with light).

30. And the earth, moreover, has He extended (to a wide expanse);

31. He draws out from it its moisture and its pasture;

32. And the mountains has He firmly fixed -

33. For use and convenience to you and your cattle.

34. Therefore, when there comes the great, overwhelming (event) -

35. The day when man shall remember (all) that he strove for,

36. And hellfire shall be placed in full view for (all) to see -

37. Then, for such as had transgressed all bounds,

38. And had preferred the life of this world,

39. The abode will be hellfire;

40. And for such as had entertained the fear of standing before their Lord's (tribunal) and had restrained (their) souls from lower desires,

41. Their abode will be the garden.

42. They ask you about the hour - 'When will be its appointed time?'

43. In which are you (concerned) with the declaration of it?

44. With your Lord is the limit fixed for it.

45. You are but a warner for such as fear it.

46. The day they see it, (it will be) as if they had tarried but a single evening, or (at most 'till) the following morn!

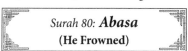

Surah 80: *Abasa*
(He Frowned)

In the name of Allah,
Most Gracious, Most Merciful.

1. (The prophet) frowned and turned away,

2. Because there came to him the blind man (interrupting).

3. But what could tell you but that perhaps he might grow (in spiritual understanding)?

4. Or that he might receive admonition, and the teaching might profit him?

5. As to one who regards himself as self-sufficient,

6. To him do you attend;

7. Though it is no blame on you if he grow not (in spiritual understanding).

8. But as to him who came to you striving earnestly,

9. And with fear (in his heart),

10. Of him were you unmindful.

11. By no means (should it be so)! For it is indeed a message of instruction:

12. Therefore, let whoso will, keep it in remembrance.

13. (It is) in books held (greatly) in honour,

14. Exalted (in dignity), kept pure and holy,

15. (Written) by the hands of scribes -

16. Honourable and pious and just.

17. Woe to man! What has made him reject Allah?

18. From what stuff Has He created him?

19. From a sperm-drop: He has created him, and then moulded him in due proportions;

20. Then does He make His path smooth for him;

21. Then He causes him to die, and puts him in his grave;

22. Then, when it is His will, He will raise him up (again).

23. By no means has he fulfilled what Allah Has commanded him.

24. Then let man look at his food, (and how We provide it):

25. For that We pour out water in abundance,

26. And We split the earth in fragments,

27. And produce in it corn,

28. And grapes and nutritious plants,

29. And olives and dates,

30. And enclosed gardens, dense with lofty trees,

31. And fruits and fodder -

32. For use and convenience to you and your cattle.

33. At length, when there comes the deafening noise -

34. That day shall a man flee from his own brother,

35. And from his mother and his father,

36. And from his wife and his children.

37. Each one of them, that day, will have enough concern (of his own) to make him indifferent to the others.

38. Some faces that day will be beaming,

39. Laughing, rejoicing.

40. And other faces that day will be dust-stained;

41. Blackness will cover them:

42. Such will be the rejecters (of Allah), the doers of iniquity.

Surah 81: *At-Takwir*
(The Folding Up)

In the name of Allah,
Most Gracious, Most Merciful.

1. When the sun (with its spacious light) is folded up;

2. When the stars fall, losing their lustre;

3. When the mountains vanish (like a mirage);

4. When the she-camels, ten months with young, are left untended;

5. When the wild beasts are herded together (in human habitations);

6. When the oceans boil over with a swell;

7. When the souls are sorted out, (being joined, like with like);

8. When the female (infant), buried alive, is questioned -

9. For what crime she was killed;

10. When the scrolls are laid open;

11. When the world on high is unveiled;

12. When the blazing fire is kindled to fierce heat;

13. And when the garden is brought near -

14. (Then) shall each soul know what it has put forward.

15. So verily I call to witness the planets - that recede,

16. Go straight, or hide;

17. And the night as it dissipates;

18. And the dawn as it breathes away the darkness -

19. Verily this is the word of a most honourable messenger,

20. Endued with power, with rank before the Lord of the throne,

21. With authority there, (and) faithful to his trust.

22. And (O people!) Your companion is not one possessed;

23. And without doubt he saw him in the clear horizon.

24. Neither does he withhold grudgingly a knowledge of the unseen.

25. Nor is it the word of an evil spirit accursed.

26. Then where do you go?

27. Verily this is no less than a message to (all) the worlds:

28. (With profit) to whoever among you wills to go straight:

29. But you shall not will except as Allah wills - the Cherisher of the Worlds.

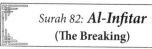

Surah 82: *Al-Infitar*
(The Breaking)

In the name of Allah,
Most Gracious, Most Merciful.

1. When the sky is broken;

2. When the stars are scattered;

3. When the oceans are suffered to burst;

4. And when the graves are turned upside down -

5. (Then) shall each soul know what it has sent forward and (what it has) kept back.

6. O man! What has seduced you from your Lord Most Beneficent? -

7. Him Who created you. Fashioned you in due proportion, and gave you a just bias;

8. In whatever form He wills, does He put you together.

9. Nay! But you do reject right and judgement!

10. But verily over you (are appointed angels) to protect you -

11. Kind and honourable - writing down (your deeds):

12. They know (and understand) all that you do.

13. As for the righteous, they will be in bliss;

14. And the wicked - they will be in the fire,

15. Which they will enter on the day of judgement,

16. And they will not be able to keep away from it.

17. And what will explain to you what the day of judgement is?

18. Again, what will explain to you what the day of judgement is?

19. (It will be) the day when no soul shall have power (to do) anything for another: for the command, that day, will be (wholly) with Allah.

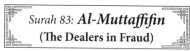

Surah 83: *Al-Muttaffifin*
(The Dealers in Fraud)

In the name of Allah,
Most Gracious, Most Merciful.

1. Woe to those that deal in fraud -

2. Those who, when they have to receive by measure from men, exact full measure,

3. But when they have to give by measure or weight to men, give less than due.

4. Do they not think that they will be called to account? -

5. On a mighty day,

6. A day when (all) mankind will stand before the Lord of the Worlds?

7. Nay! Surely the record of the wicked is (preserved) in Sijjin.

8. And what will explain to you what Sijjin is?

9. (There is) a register (fully) inscribed.

10. Woe, that day, to those that deny -

11. Those that deny the day of judgement.

12. And none can deny it but the transgressor beyond bounds, the sinner!

13. When Our signs are rehearsed to him, he says, "tales of the ancients!"

14. By no means! But on their hearts is the stain of the (ill) which they do!

15. Verily, from (the light of) their Lord, that day, will they be veiled.

16. Further, they will enter the fire of hell.

17. Further, it will be said to them: "This is the (reality) which you rejected as false!"

18. Nay, verily the record of the righteous is (preserved) in 'Illiyin.

19. And what will explain to you what 'Illiyin is?

20. (There is) a register (fully) inscribed,

21. To which bear witness those nearest (to Allah).

22. Truly the righteous will be in bliss:

23. On thrones (of dignity) will they command a sight (of all things):

24. You will recognise in their faces the beaming brightness of bliss.

25. Their thirst will be slaked with pure wine sealed:

26. The seal of it will be musk: and for this let those aspire, who have aspirations:

27. With it will be (given) a mixture of Tasnim:

28. A spring, from (the waters) of which drink those nearest to Allah.

29. Those in sin used to laugh at those who believed,

30. And whenever they passed by them, used to wink at each other (in mockery);

31. And when they returned to their own people, they would return jesting;

32. And whenever they saw them, they would say, "See! These are the people truly astray!"

33. But they had not been sent as keepers over them!

34. But on this day the believers will laugh at the unbelievers:

35. On thrones (of dignity) they will command (a sight) (of all things).

36. Will not the unbelievers have been paid back for what they did?

Surah 84: *Al-Inshiqaq*
(The Splitting)

In the name of Allah,
Most Gracious, Most Merciful.

1. When the sky is split apart,

2. And listens to (the command of) its Lord - and it must needs (do so) -

3. And when the earth is flattened out,

4. And casts out what is within it and becomes (clean) empty,

5. And listens to (the command of) its Lord - and it must needs (do so) - (then will come home the full reality).

6. O you man! Verily you are ever toiling on towards your Lord - painfully toiling - but you shall meet Him.

7. Then he who is given his record in his right hand,

8. Soon will his account be taken by an easy reckoning,

9. And he will turn to his people, rejoicing!

10. But he who is given his record behind his back -

11. Soon will he call for perdition,

12. And he will enter a blazing fire.

13. Truly, did he go about among his people, rejoicing!

14. Truly, did he think that he would not have to return (to Us)!

15. Nay, nay! For his Lord was (ever) watchful of him!

16. So I do call to witness the ruddy glow of sunset;

17. The night and its homing;

18. And the moon in her fullness:

19. You shall surely travel from stage to stage.

20. What then is the matter with them, that they believe not? -

21. And when the Qur'an is read to them, they fall not prostrate,

22. But on the contrary the unbelievers reject (it).

23. But Allah has full knowledge of what they secrete (in their breasts).

24. So announce to them a penalty grievous,

25. Except to those who believe and work righteous deeds: for them is a reward that will never fail.

Surah 85: *Al-Buruj*
(The Constellations)

***In the name of Allah,
Most Gracious, Most Merciful.***

1. By the sky, (displaying) the zodiacal signs;

2. By the promised day (of judgement);

3. By one that witnesses, and the subject of the witness -

4. Woe to the makers of the pit (of fire),

5. Fire supplied (abundantly) with fuel:

6. See! They sat over against the (fire),

7. And they witnessed (all) that they were doing against the believers.

8. And they ill-treated them for no other reason than that they believed in Allah, Exalted in power, worthy of all praise! -

9. Him to Whom belongs the dominion of the heavens and the earth! And Allah is Witness to all things.

10. Those who persecute (or draw into temptation) the believers, men and women, and do not turn in repentance, will have the penalty of hell: they will have the penalty of the burning fire.

11. For those who believe and do righteous deeds, will be gardens, beneath which rivers flow: that is the great salvation, (the fulfilment of all desires).

12. Truly strong is the grip (and power) of your Lord.

13. It is He Who creates from the very beginning, and He can restore (life).

14. And He is the Oft-Forgiving, Full of loving-kindness,

15. Lord of the throne of glory,

16. Doer (without let) of all that He intends.

17. Has the story reached you of the Forces -

18. Of Pharaoh and the Thamud?

19. And yet the unbelievers (persist) in rejecting (the truth)!

20. But Allah does encompass them from behind!

21. Nay, this is a Glorious Qur'an,

22. (Inscribed) in a tablet preserved!

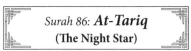

Surah 86: *At-Tariq*
(The Night Star)

In the name of Allah,
Most Gracious, Most Merciful.

1. By the sky and the night-visitant (in it) -

2. And what will explain to you what the night-visitant is? -

3. (It is) the star of piercing brightness -

4. There is no soul but has a protector over it.

5. Now let man but think from what he is created!

6. He is created from a drop emitted -

7. Proceeding from between the backbone and the ribs:

8. Surely (Allah) is able to bring him back (to life)!

9. The day that (all) things secret will be tested,

10. (Man) will have no power and no helper.

11. By the firmament which returns (in its round)

12. And by the earth which opens out (for the gushing of springs or the sprouting of vegetation) -

13. See this is the word that distinguishes (good from evil):

14. It is not a thing for amusement.

15. As for them, they are but plotting a scheme,

16. And I am planning a scheme.

17. Therefore, grant a delay to the unbelievers: give respite to them gently (for a while).

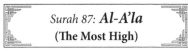

Surah 87: *Al-A'la*
(The Most High)

In the name of Allah,
Most Gracious, Most Merciful.

1. Glorify the name of your Guardian-Lord Most High,

2. Who has created, and further, given order and proportion;

3. Who has ordained laws. And granted guidance;

4. And Who brings out the (green and luscious) pasture,

5. And then does make it (but) swarthy stubble.

6. By degrees shall We teach you to declare (the message), so you shall not forget,

7. Except as Allah wills: for He knows what is manifest and what is hidden.

8. And We will make it easy for you (to follow) the simple (path).

9. Therefore, give admonition in case the admonition profits (the hearer).

10. The admonition will be received by those who fear (Allah):

11. But it will be avoided by those most unfortunate ones,

12. Who will enter the great fire,

13. In which they will then neither die nor live.

14. But those will prosper who purify themselves,

15. And glorify the name of their Guardian-Lord and (lift their hearts) in prayer.

16. Nay (see), you prefer the life of this world;

17. But the hereafter is better and more enduring.

18. And this is in the books of the earliest (revelations) -

19. The books of Abraham and Moses.

Surah 88: **Al-Ghashiyah**
(The Overwhelming Event)

In the name of Allah,
Most Gracious, Most Merciful.

1. Has the story reached you, of the overwhelming (event)?

2. Some faces, that day, will be humiliated,

3. Labouring (hard), weary -

4. The while they enter the blazing fire -

5. The while they are given to drink, of a boiling hot spring.

6. No food will there be for them but a bitter Dhari

7. Which will neither nourish nor satisfy hunger.

8. (Other) faces that day will be joyful,

9. Pleased with their striving -

10. In a garden on high,

11. Where they shall hear no (word) of vanity:

12. In it will be a bubbling spring:

13. In it will be thrones (of dignity), raised on high,

14. Goblets placed (ready),

15. And cushions set in rows,

16. And rich carpets (all) spread out.

17. Do they not look at the camels, how they are made? -

18. And at the sky, how it is raised high? -

19. And at the mountains, how they are fixed firm? -

20. And at the earth, how it is spread out?

21. Therefore, do you give admonition, for you are one to admonish.

22. You are not one to manage (men's) affairs.

23. But if any turn, away and reject Allah -

24. Allah will punish him with a mighty punishment.

25. For to Us will be their return;

26. Then it will be for Us to call them to account.

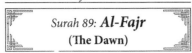

Surah 89: **Al-Fajr**
(The Dawn)

In the name of Allah,
Most Gracious, Most Merciful.

1. By the break of day;

2. By the ten nights;

3. By the even and odd (contrasted);

4. And by the night when it passes away -

5. Is there (not) in these an adjuration (or evidence) for those who understand?

6. Do you not see how your Lord dealt with the 'Ad (people) -

7. Of the (city of) Iram with lofty pillars,

8. The like of which were not produced in (all) the land?

9. And with the Thamud (people), who cut out (huge) rocks in the valley? -

10. And with Pharaoh, Lord of stakes?

11. 11.(All) these transgressed beyond bounds in the lands.

12. And heaped in it mischief (on mischief).

13. Therefore, did your Lord pour on them a scourge of diverse chastisements:

14. For your Lord is (as a Guardian) on a watchtower.

15. Now, as for man, when his Lord tries him giving him honour and gifts, then says he, (puffed up), "My Lord has honoured me."

16. But when He tries him, restricting his subsistence for him, then says he (in despair), "My Lord has humiliated me!"

17. Nay, nay! But you do not honour the orphans!

18. Nor do you encourage one another to feed the poor! -

19. And you devour inheritance - all with greed,

20. And you love wealth with inordinate love!

21. Nay! When the earth is pounded to powder,

22. And your Lord comes, and His angels, rank upon rank,

23. And hell, that day, is brought (face to face) - on that day will man remember, but how will that remembrance profit him?

24. He will say: "Ah! Would that I had sent forth (good deeds) for (this) my (future) life!"

25. For, that day, His chastisement will be such as none (else) can inflict,

26. And His bonds will be such as none (other) can bind.

27. (To the righteous soul will be said:) "O (you) soul, in (complete) rest and satisfaction!

28. Come back you to your Lord - well pleased (yourself) and well-pleasing to Him!

29. Enter you, then among my devotees!

30. Yea, enter you my heaven!"

Surah 90: *Al-Balad*
(The City)

In the name of Allah,
Most Gracious, Most Merciful.

1. I do call to witness this city -

2. And you are a freeman of this city -

3. And (the mystic ties of) parent and child -

4. Verily We have created man into toil and struggle.

5. Does he think, that none has power over him?

6. He may say (boastfully): "Wealth have I squandered in abundance!"

7. Does he think that none beholds him?

8. Have We not made for him a pair of eyes? -

9. And a tongue, and a pair of lips? -

10. And shown him the two highways?

11. But he has made no haste on the path that is steep.

12. And what will explain to you the path that is steep? -

13. (It is:) freeing the bondman;

14. Or the giving of food in a day of privation,

15. To the orphan with claims of relationship,

16. Or to the needy (down) in the dust.

17. Then will he be of those who believe, and enjoin patience, (constancy and self-restraint), and enjoin deeds of kindness and compassion.

18. Such are the companions of the right hand.

19. But those who reject Our signs, they are the (unhappy) companions of the left hand.

20. On them will be fire vaulted over (all round).

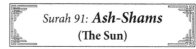

Surah 91: *Ash-Shams*
(The Sun)

In the name of Allah,
Most Gracious, Most Merciful.

1. By the sun and his (glorious) splendour;

2. By the moon as it follows (the sun);

3. By the day as it shows up (the sun's) glory;

4. By the night as it conceals it;

5. By the firmament and its (wonderful) structure;

6. By the earth and its (wide) expanse;

7. By the soul, and the proportion and order given to it;

8. And its enlightenment as to its wrong and its right -

9. Truly he succeeds that purifies it,

10. And he fails that corrupts it!

11. The Thamud (people) rejected (their prophet) through their inordinate wrongdoing.

12. See, the most wicked man among them was deputed (for impiety).

13. But the messenger of Allah said to them: "It is a she-camel of Allah! And (bar her not from) having her drink!"

14. Then they rejected him (as a false prophet), and they hamstrung her. So their Lord, on account of their crime, obliterated their traces and made them equal (in destruction high and low)!

15. And for Him is no fear of its consequences.

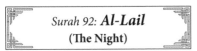

Surah 92: **Al-Lail**
(The Night)

In the name of Allah, Most Gracious, Most Merciful.

1. By the night as it conceals (the light);

2. By the day as it appears in glory;

3. By (the mystery of) the creation of male and female -

4. Verily, (the ends) you strive for are diverse.

5. So he who gives (in charity) and fears (Allah)

6. And (in all sincerity) testifies to the Best -

7. We will indeed make smooth for him the path to bliss.

8. But he who is a greedy miser and thinks himself self-sufficient,

9. And gives the lie to the best -

10. We will indeed make smooth for him the path to misery;

11. Nor will his wealth profit him when he falls headlong (into the pit).

12. Verily We take upon Ourselves to guide,

13. And verily to Us (belong) the end and the beginning.

14. Therefore, do I warn you of a fire blazing fiercely;

15. None shall reach it but those most unfortunate ones,

16. Who give the lie to truth and turn their backs.

17. But those most devoted to Allah shall be removed far from it -

18. Those who spend their wealth for increase in self-purification,

19. And have in their minds no favour from anyone for which a reward is expected in return,

20. But only the desire to seek for the countenance of their Lord Most High;

21. And soon will they attain (complete) satisfaction.

Surah 93: **Ad-Duha**
(The Glorious Morning Light)

In the name of Allah, Most Gracious, Most Merciful.

1. By the glorious morning light,

2. And by the night when it is still -

3. The Guardian-Lord has not forsaken you, nor is He displeased.

4. And verily the hereafter will be better for you than the present.

5. And soon will your Guardian-Lord give you (that with which) you shall be well-pleased.

6. Did He not find you an orphan and give you shelter (and care)?

7. And He found you wandering, and He gave you guidance.

8. And He found you in need, and made you independent.

9. Therefore, treat not the orphan with harshness,

10. Nor repulse the petitioner (unheard);

11. But the bounty of your Lord - rehearse and proclaim!

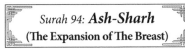

Surah 94: *Ash-Sharh*
(The Expansion of The Breast)

***In the name of Allah,
Most Gracious, Most Merciful.***

1. Have We not expanded you your breast?

2. And removed from you your burden,

3. Which did break your back? -

4. And raised high the esteem (in which) you (are held)?

5. So, verily, with every difficulty, there is relief:

6. Verily, with every difficulty there is relief.

7. Therefore, when you are free (from your immediate task), still labour hard,

8. And to your Lord turn (all) your attention.

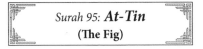

Surah 95: *At-Tin*
(The Fig)

***In the name of Allah,
Most Gracious, Most Merciful.***

1. By the fig and the olive,

2. And the mount of Sinai,

3. And this city of security -

4. We have indeed created man in the best of moulds,

5. Then do We abase him (to be) the lowest of the low -

6. Except such as believe and do righteous deeds: for they shall have a reward unfailing.

7. Then what can, after this contradict you, as to the judgement (to come)?

8. Is not Allah the Wisest of judges?

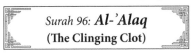

Surah 96: *Al-'Alaq*
(The Clinging Clot)

***In the name of Allah,
Most Gracious, Most Merciful.***

1. Proclaim! (or read!) In the name of your Lord and Cherisher, who created

2. Created man, out of a (mere) clot of congealed blood:

3. Proclaim! And your Lord is Most Bountiful -

4. He Who taught (the use of) the pen -

5. Taught man that which he knew not.

6. Nay, but man does transgress all bounds,

7. In that he looks upon himself as self-sufficient.

8. Verily, to your Lord is the return (of all).

9. See you one who forbids -

10. A votary when he (turns) to pray?

11. See you if he is on (the road of) guidance? -

12. Or enjoins righteousness?

13. See you if he denies (truth) and turns away?

14. Knows he not that Allah does see?

15. Let him beware! If he desist not, We will drag him by the forelock -

16. A lying, sinful forelock!

17. Then, let him call (for help) to his council (of comrades):

18. We will call on the angels of punishment (to deal with him)!

19. Nay, heed him not: but bow down in adoration and bring yourself the closer (to Allah)!

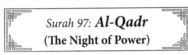

Surah 97: **Al-Qadr**
(The Night of Power)

In the name of Allah,
Most Gracious, Most Merciful.

1. We have indeed revealed this (message) in the night of power:

2. And what will explain to you what the night of power is?

3. The night of power is better than a thousand months.

4. In it come down the angels and the spirit by Allah's permission, on every errand:

5. Peace! This until the rise of morning!

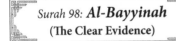

Surah 98: **Al-Bayyinah**
(The Clear Evidence)

In the name of Allah,
Most Gracious, Most Merciful.

1. Those who reject (truth) among the People of the Book and among the polytheists, were not going to depart (from their ways) until there should come to them clear evidence -

2. A messenger from Allah rehearsing scriptures kept pure and holy:

3. In which are laws (or decrees) right and straight.

4. Nor did the People of the Book make schisms, until after there came to them clear evidence.

5. And they have been commanded no more than this: to worship Allah, offering Him sincere devotion, being True (in faith); to establish regular prayer; and to practice regular charity; and that is the religion right and straight.

6. Those who reject (truth), among the People of the Book and among the polytheists, will be in hellfire, to dwell in it (for ever). They are the worst of creatures.

7. Those who have faith and do righteous deeds - they are the best of creatures.

8. Their reward is with Allah: gardens of eternity, beneath which rivers flow; they will dwell in it for ever; Allah well pleased with them, and they with Him: all this for such as fear their Lord and Cherisher.

Surah 99: **Al-Zalzalah**
(The Earthquake)

In the name of Allah,
Most Gracious, Most Merciful.

1. When the earth is shaken to her (utmost) convulsion,

2. And the earth throws up its burdens (from within),

3. And man cries (distressed): 'What is the matter with it?' -

4. On that day will it declare its tidings:

5. For that your Lord will have given it inspiration.

6. On that day will men proceed in companies sorted out, to be shown the deeds that they (had done).

7. Then shall anyone who has done an atom's weight of good, see it!

8. And anyone who has done an atom's weight of evil, shall see it.

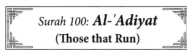

Surah 100: *Al-'Adiyat*
(Those that Run)

In the name of Allah,
Most Gracious, Most Merciful.

1. By the (steeds) that run, with panting (breath),

2. And strike sparks of fire,

3. And push home the charge in the morning,

4. And raise the dust in clouds the while,

5. And penetrate forthwith into the midst (of the foe) en masse -

6. Truly man is, to his Lord, ungrateful;

7. And to that (fact) he bears witness (by his deeds);

8. And violent is he in his love of wealth.

9. Does he not know - when that which is in the graves is scattered abroad,

10. And that which is (locked up) in (human) breasts is made manifest -

11. That their Lord had been well-acquainted with them, (even to) that day?

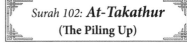

Surah 101: *Al-Qari'ah*
(Day of Noise and Clamour)

In the name of Allah,
Most Gracious, Most Merciful.

1. The (day) of noise and clamour:

2. What is the (day) of noise and clamour?

3. And what will explain to you what the (day) of noise and clamour is?

4. (It is) a day on which men will be like moths scattered about,

5. And the mountains will be like carded wool.

6. Then, he whose balance (of good deeds) will be (found) heavy,

7. Will be in a life of good pleasure and satisfaction.

8. But he whose balance (of good deeds) will be (found) light -

9. Will have his home in a (bottomless) pit.

10. And what will explain to you what this is?

11. (It is) a fire blazing fiercely!

Surah 102: *At-Takathur*
(The Piling Up)

In the name of Allah,
Most Gracious, Most Merciful.

1. The mutual rivalry for piling up (the good things of this world) diverts you (from the more serious things),

2. Until you visit the graves.

3. But nay, you soon shall know (the reality).

359

4. Again, you soon shall know!

5. Nay, were you to know with certainty of mind (You would beware!)

6. You shall certainly see hellfire!

7. Again, you shall see it with certainty of sight!

8. Then, shall you be questioned that day about the joy (you indulged in!)

Surah 103: *Al-ʿAsr*
(Time Through the Ages)

In the name of Allah,
Most Gracious, Most Merciful.

1. By (the token of) time (through the ages),

2. Verily man is in loss,

3. Except such as have faith, and do righteous deeds, and (join together) in the mutual teaching of truth, and of patience and constancy.

Surah 104: *Al-Humazah*
(The Scandal Mongerer)

In the name of Allah,
Most Gracious, Most Merciful.

1. Woe to every (kind of) scandalmonger and backbiter,

2. Who piles up wealth and lays it by,

3. Thinking that his wealth would make him last for ever!

4. By no means! He will be sure to be thrown into that which breaks to pieces.

5. And what will explain to you that which breaks to pieces?

6. (It is) the fire of (the wrath of) Allah kindled (to a blaze),

7. The which does mount (right) to the hearts:

8. It shall be made into a vault over them,

9. In columns outstretched.

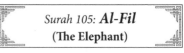

Surah 105: *Al-Fil*
(The Elephant)

In the name of Allah,
Most Gracious, Most Merciful.

1. Do you not see how your Lord dealt with the companions of the elephant?

2. Did He not make their treacherous plan go astray?

3. And He sent against them flights of birds,

4. Striking them with stones of baked clay.

5. Then did He make them like an empty field of stalks and straw, (of which the corn) has been eaten up.

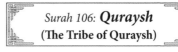

Surah 106: *Quraysh*
(The Tribe of Quraysh)

In the name of Allah,
Most Gracious, Most Merciful.

1. For the covenants (of security and safeguard enjoyed) by the Quraysh,

2. Their covenants (covering) journeys by winter and summer-

3. Let them adore the Lord of this house,

4. Who provides them with food against hunger, and with security against fear (of danger).

Surah 107: *Al-Maun*
(The Neighbourly Assistance)

In the name of Allah,
Most Gracious, Most Merciful.

1. Do you see who denies the judgement (to come)?

2. Then such is the (man) who repulses the orphan (with harshness),

3. And encourages not the feeding of the needy.

4. So woe to the worshippers,

5. Who are neglectful of their prayers,

6. Those who (want but) to be seen (of men),

7. But refuse (to supply) (even) neighbourly needs.

Surah 108: *Al-Kauthar*
(The Abundance)

In the name of Allah,
Most Gracious, Most Merciful.

1. To you have We granted the fount (of abundance).

2. Therefore, to your Lord turn in prayer and sacrifice.

3. For he who hates you - he will be cut off (from future hope).

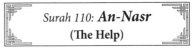

Surah 109: *Al-Kafirun*
(Those Who Reject Faith)

In the name of Allah,
Most Gracious, Most Merciful.

1. Say: O you that reject faith!

2. I worship not that which you worship,

3. Nor will you worship that which I worship.

4. And I will not worship that which you used to worship,

5. Nor will you worship that which I worship.

6. To you be your way, and to me mine.

Surah 110: *An-Nasr*
(The Help)

In the name of Allah,
Most Gracious, Most Merciful.

1. When comes the help of Allah, and victory,

2. And you do see the people enter Allah's religion in crowds,

3. Celebrate the praises of your Lord, and pray for His forgiveness: for He is Oft-Returning (in grace and mercy).

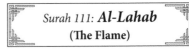

Surah 111: *Al-Lahab*
(The Flame)

In the name of Allah,
Most Gracious, Most Merciful.

1. Perish the hands of the father of flame! Perish he!

2. No profit to him from all his wealth and all his gains!

3. Burnt soon will he be in a fire of blazing flame!

4. His wife shall carry the (crackling) wood - as fuel! -

5. A twisted rope of palm-leaf fibre round her (own) neck!

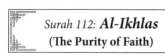

Surah 112: *Al-Ikhlas*
(The Purity of Faith)

In the name of Allah,
Most Gracious, Most Merciful.

1. Say: He is Allah, the One and Only;

2. Allah, the Eternal, Absolute;

3. He begets not, nor is He begotten;

4. And there is none like unto Him.

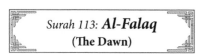

Surah 113: *Al-Falaq*
(The Dawn)

In the name of Allah,
Most Gracious, Most Merciful.

1. Say: I seek refuge with the Lord of the dawn,

2. From the mischief of created things;

3. From the mischief of darkness as it overspreads;

4. From the mischief of those who practice secret arts;

5. And from the mischief of the envious one as he practises envy.

Surah 114: *An-Nas*
(Mankind)

In the name of Allah,
Most Gracious, Most Merciful.

1. Say: I seek refuge with the Lord and Cherisher of mankind,

2. The King (or Ruler) of mankind,

3. The God (or Judge) of mankind,

4. From the mischief of the whisperer (of evil) who withdraws (after his whisper) -

5. (The same) who whispers into the hearts of mankind -

6. Among Jinns and among men.

Brief Index of Subjects

A

A'ad, people of 7:65-74; 9:70; 11:50; 11:59; 11:60; 14:9; 22:42; 25:38; 26:123; 29:38; 38:12; 40:31; 41:13; 41:15; 46:21; 50:13; 51:41; 53:50; 54:18; 69:4-6; 89:6

Aaron *[Harun]*, 2:248; 4:163; 6:84; 7:122; 7:142; 10:75; 19:53; 20:30; 20:70; 20:90; 20:92; 21:48; 23:45; 25:35; 26:13; 26:48; 28:34; 37:114; 37:120

Ablution, 4:43; 5:6

Abraham *[Ibrahim]*, S. 14; 2:124-127; 2:130; 2:132-133; 2:135-136; 2:140; 2:258; 2:260; 3:33; 3:65; 3:67; 3:68; 3:84; 3:95; 3:97; 4:54; 4:125; 4:163; 6:74-75; 6:83; 6:161; 9:70; 9:114; 11:69; 11:74-76; 12:6; 12:38; 14:35; 15:51; 16:120; 16:123; 19:41; 19:58; 21:51; 21:60; 21:62; 21:69; 22:26; 22:43; 22:78; 26:69; 29:16; 33:7; 37:83; 37:104; 37:109; 38:45; 42:13; 43:26; 51:24; 53:37; 57:26; 60:4; 87:19

Abu Lahab (Father of Flame), 111:1-5

Adam, 2:31; 2:33-35, 2:37, 3:33, 3:59, 5:27, 7:11, 7:19, 7:26-27, 7:31, 7:35, 7:172, 17:61, 17:70, 18:50, 19:58, 20:115-117, 20:120-121, 36:60

Ahmad (Praised One), 61:6

Adultery, *see Zina*

Allah*,

accepts repentance, 40:3; 42:25

all beings in the Heavens and Earth declare His glory, 17:44; 21:19-20; 24:41; 57:1; 59:1; 59:24; 61:1; 62:1; 64:1

all faces shall be humbled before Him, 20:111

all good is from Him, 4:79; 16:30; 16:53

all things are from Him, 4:78; 15:21

listens to the soul distressed, 27:62

ascribe no partners to Him, 3:64; 4:36; 4;48; 4:116; 5:72; 6:14; 6:81; 6:88; 6:136; 6:148; 6:151; 9:31; 10:28-29; 13:16; 13:33; 13:36; 16:51-57; 16:73; 16:86; 17:22; 17:39-40; 17:56-57; 18:110; 22:31; 23:59; 23:117; 24:55; 25:68; 28:87-88; 29:8; 30:31; 31:13; 35:13-14; 39:64-65; 40:41-43; 40:66; 41:6; 43:45; 46:4-6; 50:26; 51:51; 60:12; 72:2; 72:18

begets not, nor is He begotten, 112:3

belief in, 2:62; 2:177; 2:256; 3:179; 3:193; 4:38-

39; 4:59; 4:136; 4:152; 4:162; 4:171; 4:175; 7:158; 9:18-19; 9:44-45; 24:2; 24:62; 36:25; 40:84; 48:13; 49:15; 57:7-8; 57:19; 58:22; 60:4; 60:11; 61:11; 64:8; 64:11; 65:2; 67:29; 72:13; 85:8

Blessed be He, 7:54; 23:14; 25:1; 25:10; 25:61; 43:85; 55:78;

bounties in His hand, 3:73

call upon Him, 6:52; 6:63; 7:29; 7:55-56; 7:180; 13:36; 18:28; 40:14; 40:60; 40:65

creates what He will, 3:47; 5:17; 24:45; 28:68; 30:54; 35:1; 42:49; 82:8

does what He will, 2:253; 3:40; 11:107; 14:27; 22:14-18; 85:16

created you in the wombs, 3:6; 39:6

enlarges provision and tightens it, 13:26; 17:30; 28:82; 29:62; 30:37; 34:36; 34:39; 39:52; 42:12; 42:27; 89:15-16

feeds but is not fed, 6:14; 51:57-58

forgives sins, 2:284; 3:31; 3:195; 4:116; 5:18; 5:39-40; 7:161; 8:29; 8:70; 12:92; 13:6; 14:10; 26:82; 28:16; 33:71; 36:27; 39:53; 40:3; 42:25; 42:30; 42:34; 46:31; 48:14; 67:28; 61:12; 64:17; 71:4

gives life to the dead, 2:28; 2:243; 2:259-260; 3:27; 6:36; 7:57; 10:31; 22:6; 30:19; 30:40; 30:50; 36:12; 36:79; 41:39; 42:9; 46:33; 50:11; 75:40; 80:22; 86:8

gives sustenance, 2:57; 2:126; 2:172; 3:27; 3:37; 3:169; 5:114; 6:151; 7:50; 7:160; 8:26; 10:31; 10:93; 11:88; 14:37; 16:72; 16:75; 17:31; 17:70; 20:81; 20:132; 27:64; 29:60; 30:40; 34:24; 35:3; 40:13; 40:40; 40:64; 42:19; 45:5; 45:16; 50:11; 65:3; 67:15; 67:21; 106:4

glory be to Him, 2:32; 2:116; 3:191; 4:171; 5:116; 6:100; 7:143; 9:31; 10:10; 10:18; 10:68; 12:108; 16:1; 17:43-44; 17:108; 21:22; 21:26; 21:87; 24:16; 24:36; 25:18; 27:8; 28:68; 30:17; 30:40; 33:42; 34:41; 36:83; 37:159; 37:180; 39:4; 39:67; 40:64; 43:13; 43:82; 59:23; 68:28-29; 69:52; 76:26; 87:1

guides whom He will, 2:213; 2:272; 10:25; 13:27; 13:31; 14:4; 16:93; 22:16; 24:35; 24:46; 28:56; 35:8; 39:23; 42:52; 74:31

has no partner, 6:163; 7:191-198; 9:31; 10:66; 17:111; 23:91; 25:2; 35:40; 42:21; 68:41; 72:3

---

* Due to the recurrence of the mention of the name of Allah throughout the Qur'an, only verses containing specific information on the given subjects have been included for reference

Allah *(cont'd.)*

has no son, 2:116; 4:171; 6:101; 9:30; 10:68; 17:111; 18:4; 19:35; 19: 88-92; 21:26; 23:91; 25:2; 37:152; 39:4; 43:81-82; 72:3

hears the arguments from both husband and wife, 58:1

is not unmindful of what you do, 2:74; 2:85; 2:140; 2:144; 2:149; 3:99; 6:132; 11:123; 14:42; 22:68; 23:17; 27:93

is sufficient, 2:137; 3:173; 4:6; 4:45; 4:70; 4:79; 4:81; 4:132; 4:166; 4:171; 8:62; 8:64; 9:59; 9:129; 10:29; 13:43; 17:17; 17:65; 17:96; 25:31; 25:58; 29:52; 33:3; 33:48; 39:38; 46:8; 48:28; 65:3

is the best of planners, 3:54; 8:30; 13:42

knows all you conceal and reveal, 2:33; 2:77; 2:284; 3:29; 5:99; 6:3; 11:5; 14:38; 16:19; 16:23; 21:110; 27:25; 27:74; 28:69; 33:54; 36:76; 60:1; 64:4; 87:7

knows best who is guided, 6:117; 16:125; 17:84; 28:56; 53:30; 68:7

knows what is hidden (the Unseen), 2:33; 5:109; 5:116; 6:59; 6:73; 9:78; 9:94; 9:105; 10:20; 11:123; 13:9; 16:77; 18:26; 20:7; 23:92; 25:6; 27:65; 32:6; 34:3; 34:48; 49:18; 72:26; 84:23

love for Him, 2:165; 2:177; 3:31; 5:54; 76:8

made all things good which He created, 32:7

meeting with Him, 2:46; 2:223; 2:249; 6:154; 10:11; 10:15; 10:45; 13:2; 18:110; 25:21; 29:5; 29:23; 30:8; 32:10; 33:44; 41:54; 84:6

nearness to Him, 2:186; 7:206; 11:61; 34:37; 34:50; 39:3; 50:16; 83:21; 83:28; 96:19

never breaks His promise, 3:9; 3:194; 13:31; 14:47; 30:6

no God but He (One God), 2:133; 2:163; 2:255; 3:2; 3:6; 3:18; 3:62; 4:87; 5:73; 6:102; 6:106; 7:59; 7:65; 7:85; 7:158; 9:31; 9:129; 11:14; 11:50; 11:61; 11:84; 16:2; 20:8; 20:14; 20:98; 20:14; 20:98; 21:22; 21:25; 21:87; 23:23; 23:32; 23:116-117; 27:26; 27:60-64; 28:70; 28:88; 35:3; 38:65; 39:6; 40:3; 40:62; 40:65; 44:8; 47:19; 52:43; 59:22-23; 64:13

no calamity occurs except by His permission, 64:11

no strength except in Him, 18:39

no refuge from Him except towards Him, 9:118; 72:22

obey Him, 3:132; 4:59; 4:69; 8:1; 8:20-21; 8:46; 9:71; 24:51-54; 33:33; 33:71; 47:33; 48:16-17; 49:14; 58:13; 64:12; 64:16

Praise be to Him, 1:2; 6:1; 6:45; 10:10;14:39; 15:98; 16:75; 17:111; 18:1; 23:28; 25:58; 27:15; 27:59; 27:93; 28:70; 29:63; 30:18; 31:25; 34:1; 35:1; 35:34; 37:182; 39:29; 39:74-75; 40:55; 40:65; 50:39-40; 52:48-49; 64:1; 110:3

prostration to Him, 15:98; 16:49; 19:58; 20:70; 22:77; 25:64; 32:15; 39:9; 48:29; 50:40; 53:62; 76:26; 96:19

regulates affairs, 10:3; 10:31; 13:2; 32:5

the return to Him, 2:46; 2:156; 6:36; 6:60; 6:108; 10:23; 10:46; 10:70; 11:4; 11:34; 13:36; 19:40; 19:80; 21:93; 23:60; 26:50; 29:8; 29:17; 31:23; 39:7; 40:43; 40:77; 89:28; 96:8

says "Be" and it is, 2:117; 3:47; 3:59; 6:73; 16:40; 19:35; 36:82

seek His forgiveness, 2:285-286; 3:16; 3:135; 3:147; 3:193; 4:64; 5:74; 7:155; 11:3; 11:52; 11:61; 11:90; 12:29; 12:98; 14:41; 19:47; 23:109; 23:118; 24:62; 28:16; 40:55; 41:6; 47:19; 51;18; 60:5; 71:10; 71:28; 73:20: 110:3

seek His help, 1:5; 2:45; 2:153;

seek refuge in Him, 7:200-201; 16:98; 19:18; 23:97-98; 40:56; 41:36; 113:1; 114:1

there is none like Him, 42:11; 112:4;

to Him belong the forces of the Heavens and the earth, 48:4; 48:7

to Him belong the keys of the Heavens and the Earth, 39:63; 42:12

to Him belong the Most Beautiful Names, 7:180; 17:110; 20:8; 59:24

to Him you shall be brought (returned) back, 2:28; 2:46; 2:156; 2:281; 3:158; 5:96; 6:12; 6:36; 6:38; 6:60; 8:24; 10:4; 10:23; 10:45; 10:56; 11:4; 19:40; 21:35; 23:115; 24:64; 28:70; 28:88; 29:8; 29:57; 30:11; 31:15; 32:11; 36:22; 36:32; 36:83; 39:44; 43:85; 45:15; 67:24; 96:8

trust in Him, 3:159-160; 3:173; 4:81; 5:11; 5:23; 7:89; 8:2; 9:51; 9:129; 10:71; 10:84-85; 11:56; 11:88; 11:123; 12:67; 13:30; 14:11-12; 16:42; 16:99; 17:65; 25:58; 26:217; 27:79; 29:59; 33:3; 33:48; 39:38; 42:10; 42:36; 58:10; 60:4; 64:13; 65:3

will not change the condition of a people until they change, 13:11

Allah *(cont'd.)*

will not suffer the reward to be lost, 3:195; 9:120; 12:56; 12:90; 18:30; 21:94; 52:21

worship Him (alone), 1:5; 3:64; 6:56; 6:102; 7:59; 7:65; 7:85; 7:206; 11:2; 11:26; 11:50; 11:61; 11:84; 11:123; 12:40; 13:36; 17:23; 19:65; 21:25; 22:77; 23:23; 24:55; 25:60; 39:66; 41:37; 46:21; 53:62; 71:3; 98:5; 106:3

Allah's attributes, 7:180; 17:110; 20:8, 59:24

All-Embracing (cares for all) *[Al-Wasi']*, 2:115; 2:247; 2:261; 2:268; 3:73; 4:130; 5:54; 24:32; 53:32;

answers petitions *[Al-Mujib]*, 11:61; 37:75

Aware (Well-aquainted) *[Al-Khabir]*, 2:234; 2:271; 3:153; 3:180; 4:35; 4:94; 4:128; 4:135; 5:8; 6:18; 6:73; 6:103; 9:16; 11:1; 11:111; 17:17; 17:30; 17:96; 22:63; 24:30; 24:53; 25:58; 25:59; 27:88; 31:16; 31:29; 31:34; 33:2; 33:34; 34:1; 35:14; 35:31; 42:27; 48:11; 49:13; 57:10; 58:3; 58:11; 58:13; 59:18; 63:11; 64:8; 66:3; 67:14; 100:11

Beneficent *[Al-Barr]*, 52:28

Best of judges *[Khayr al-Fasilin]*, 6:57

Best of those who show mercy,

[Arham al Rahimin], 7:151; 12:64; 12:92; 21:83

[Khayr al-Rahimin], 23:109; 23:118

Bestower of Forms and Colours *[Al-Musawwir]*, 59:24

Best to decide (command) *[Khayr al-Hakimin]*, 7:87; 10:109; 11:45; 12:80

Blots out sins *[Al-'Afu]*, 4:43; 4:99; 4:149; 22:60; 58:2

Calls to account *[Al-Hasib]*, 4:6; 4:86; 6:62; 17:14; 21:47; 33:39

Cherisher and Sustainer *[Al-Rabb]*, 1:2 2:131; 5:28; 6:45; 6:71; 6:162; 7:54; 7:61; 7:67; 7:104; 7:121; 10:10; 10:37; 26:16; 26:23; 26:47; 26:77; 26:98; 26:109; 26:127; 26:145; 26:164; 26:180; 26:192; 27:8; 27:44; 28:30; 32:2; 37:87; 37:182; 39:75; 40:64-66; 41:9; 43:46; 45:36; 56:80; 59:16; 69:43; 81:29; 83:6; 96:1; 98:8

Creator *[Al-Khaliq; Al-Khallaq]*, 6:102; 13:16; 15:28; 15:86; 35:3; 36:81; 37:125; 38:71; 39:62; 40:62; 59:24

Disposer of affairs *[Al-Wakil]*, 4:171; 6:102; 17:65; 28:28; 33:3; 33:48; 39:62; 73:9

Eternal, Absolute *[Al-Samad]*, 112:2

Evident *[Al-Zahir]*, 57:3

Evolver *[Al Bari']*, 59:24

Exalted in Power and Might *[Al-'Aziz]*, 2:209; 2:220; 2:228; 2:240; 3:6; 3:18; 3:62; 3:126; 4:56; 4:158; 4:165; 5:38; 5:118; 6:96; 8:10; 8:63; 9:40; 9:71; 11:66; 14:4; 14:47; 16:60; 22:40; 22:74; 26:9; 26:104; 26:122; 26:140; 26:159; 26:175; 26:191; 26:217; 27:9; 27:78; 29:26; 29:42; 30:27; 31:9; 31:27; 32:6; 33:25; 34:6; 34:27; 35:2; 35:28; 36:5; 38:9; 38:66; 39:1; 39:5; 39:37; 40:2; 40:42; 41:12; 42:3; 42:19; 43:9; 44:42; 45:2; 45:37; 46:2; 48:7; 48:19; 54:42; 57:1; 57:25; 58:21; 59:1; 59:23-24; 60:5; 61:1; 62:1; 62:3; 64:18; 67:2; 85:8

First *[Al-Awwal]*, 57:3

Forbearing *[Al-Halim]*, 2:225; 2:263; 3:155; 4:12; 5:101; 17:44; 22:59; 33:51; 35:41; 64:17

Forgives again and again *[Al-Ghaffar]*, 20:82; 38:66; 39:5; 40:42; 71:10

Free of all wants *[Al-Ghani]*, 2:263; 2:267; 4:131; 6:133; 10:68; 14:8; 22:64; 27:40; 29:6; 31:12; 31:26; 35:15; 39:7; 47:38; 57:24; 60:6; 64:6

Full of all glory *[Al-Majid]*, 11:73; 85:15

Full of bounty *[Dhu al Fadl]*, 2:105; 2:243; 2:251; 3:74; 8:29; 10:58; 10:60; 27:73; 40:61; 57:21; 62:4

Full of Kindness *[Al-Ra'uf]*, 2:143; 2:207; 3:30; 9:117; 9:128; 16:7; 16:47; 22:65; 24:20; 57:9; 59:10

Full of loving-kindness *[Al-Wadud]*, 11:90; 85:14

Full of Majesty, Bounty and Honour *[Dhu al-Jalal wa al-Ikram]*, 55:27; 55:78

Full of mercy *[Dhu al-Rahmah]*, 6:133; 6:147; 18:58

Hears all things *[Al-Sami']*, 2:127; 2:224; 2:256; 3:34; 4:58; 4:134; 4:148; 5:76; 6:13; 6:115; 8:17; 8:42; 8:53; 8:61; 9:103; 10:65; 14:39; 17:1; 21:4; 22:61; 22:75; 24:21; 26:220; 29:5; 29:60; 31:28; 34:50; 40:20; 40:56; 41:36; 42:11; 44:6; 49:1; 58:1

Helper *[Al-Nasir]*, 3:150; 4:45; 8:40; 9:116; 22:78; 25:31

Hidden *[Al-Batin]*, 57:3

Holy One *[Al-Quddus]*, 59:23; 62:1

Inheritor *[Al-Warith]*, 15:23

Allah's attributes, *(cont'd.)*

Irresistable *[Al-Jabbar]*, 59:23

Irresistable *[Al-Qahir, Al-Qahhar]*, 6:18; 6:61; 12:39; 14:48; 38:65; 39:4; 40:16

King (Master, Sovereign) *[Al-Malik; Al-Maalik]*, 1:4; 20:114; 23:116; 54:55; 59:23; 62:1; 114:2

Knower of the hidden and open *['Alim al-Ghayb wa al-Shahadah]*, 2:33; 6:59; 9:94; 9:105; 10:20; 11:123; 13:9; 16:77; 18:26; 23:92; 27:65; 32:6; 34:3; 35:38; 39:46; 49:18; 59:22; 62:8; 64:18; 72:26

Knows all things *[Al-'Alim]*, 2:224; 2:227; 2:256; 3:34; 3:73; 4:12; 4:17; 4:24; 4:26; 4:32; 4:39; 4:70; 4:147-148; 4:170; 4:176; 5:76; 5:97; 6:13; 6:83; 6:96; 6:101; 6:115; 6:128; 8:17; 8:42; 8:53; 8:61; 8:71; 8:75; 9:15; 9:28; 9:98; 9:103; 9:106; 9:115; 10:36; 10:65; 12:76; 12:83; 12:100; 15:25; 15:86; 21:4; 22:52; 22:59; 24:18; 24:21; 24:28; 24:35; 24:41; 24:58-60; 24:64; 26:220; 27:6; 27:78; 29:5; 29:60; 29:62; 30:54; 31:23; 31:34; 33:34; 33:40; 33:51; 34:26; 35:8; 35:38; 35:44; 36:81; 40:2; 41:12; 41:36; 42:12; 42:50; 43:9; 43:84; 44:6; 48:4; 48:26; 49:1; 49:16; 51:30; 57:3; 58:7; 60:10; 62:7; 64:11; 66:2-3; 67:13; 76:30

Last *[Al-Akhir]*, 57:3

Light of the heavens and the earth *[Al-Nur]*, 24:35

Living *[Al-Hayy]*, 2:255; 3:2; 20:111; 25:58; 40:65

Lord of grace abounding *[Dhu al-Fadl al-'Azim]*, 2:105; 3:174; 57:21; 57:29; 62:4

Lord of Honour and Power *[Rabb al-'Izzah]*, 37:180

Lord of Power *[Dhu al- Quwwah]*, 51:58

Lord of Power and Rule *[Malik al-Mulk]*, 3:26

Lord of Retribution *[Dhu Intiqam]*, 3:4; 14:47; 39:37

Lord of the Dawn *[Rabb al-Falaq]*, 113:1

Lord of the East and the West *[Rabb al-Mashriq wa al-Maghirb; Rabb al- Mashriqayn wa al-Maghirbayn; Rabb al- Mashariq wa al-Magharib]*, 26:28; 37:5; 55:17; 70:40; 73:9

Lord of the heavens and the earth *[Rab al-Samawat wa al-Ard]*, 17:102; 18:14; 19:65; 21:56; 26:24; 37:5; 38:66; 43:82; 44:7; 45:36; 51:23; 78:37

Lord of the Throne *[Rabb al- 'Arsh]*, 9:129; 17:42; 21:22; 23:86-87; 23:116; 27:26; 40:15; 43:82; 85:15

Lord of the Ways of Ascent, *[Dhu al- Ma'arij]*, 70:3

Lord of the Worlds *[Rabb al 'Alamin]*, 1:2; 2:131; 5:28; 6:45; 6:71; 6:162; 7:54; 7:61; 7:67; 7:104; 7:121; 10:10; 10:37; 26:16; 26:23; 26:47; 26:77; 26:98; 26:109; 26:127; 26:145; 26:164; 26:180; 26:192; 27:8; 27:44; 28:30; 32:2; 37:87; 37:182; 39:75; 40:64-66; 41:9; 43:46; 45:36; 56:80; 59:16; 69:43; 81:29; 83:6

Maker of the heavens and the earth *[Al-Fatir]*, 6:14; 12:101; 14:10; 35:1; 39:46; 42:11

Master of the Day of Judgment *[Malik Yawm al-Din]*, 1:4

Most Bountiful *[Al-Akram]*, 96:3

Most Gracious *[Al-Rahman]*, 1:1; 1:3; 2:163; 13:30; 17:110; 19:18; 19:26; 19:44-45; 19:58; 19:61; 19:69; 19:75; 19:78; 19:85; 19:88; 19:91-93; 19:96; 20:5; 20:90; 20:108-109; 21:26; 21:36; 21:42; 21:112; 25:26; 25:59-60; 25:63; 26:5; 27:30; 36:15; 36:23; 36:52; 41:2; 43:17; 43:20; 43:33; 43:36; 43:45; 43:81; 50:33; 55:1; 59:22; 67:3; 67:19-20; 67:29; 78:37-38

Most Great *[Al-Kabir]*, 4:34; 13:9; 22:62; 31:30; 34:23; 40:12

Most High *[Al-'Ali; Al-A'la; Al-Muta'ali]*, 2:255; 4:34; 13:9; 22:62; 31:30; 34:23; 40:12; 42:4; 42:51; 87:1

Most Merciful *[Al-Rahim]*, 1:1; 1:3; 2:160; 2:163; 2:192; 2:218; 2:226; 3:31; 3:89; 4:16; 4:23; 4:25; 4:29; 4:96; 4:100; 4:106; 4:110; 4:129; 4:152; 5:3; 5:34; 5:39; 5:74; 5:98; 6:145; 6:165; 7:153; 7:167; 9:91; 9:99; 9:102; 9:104; 9:117-118; 10:107; 11:90; 12:98; 15:49; 16:7; 16:18; 16:47; 16:110; 16:115; 16:119; 17:66; 22:65; 24:5; 24:20; 24:22; 24:33; 24:62; 25:6; 25:70; 26:9; 26:104; 26:122; 26:140; 26:159; 26:175; 26:191; 26:217; 27:11; 27:30; 28:16; 32:6; 33:5; 33:24; 33:43; 33:50; 33:73; 34:2; 36:5; 36:58; 39:53; 41:2; 41:32; 42:5; 44:42; 46:8;

Most Merciful *[Al-Rahim]*, (cont'd), 48:14; 49:5; 49:12; 52:28; 57:9; 57:28; 58:12; 59:10; 59:22; 60:7; 60:12; 66:1; 73:20

Most Merciful of all (those) who show mercy *[Arham al-Rahimin]*, 7:151; 12:64; 12:92; 21:83

Allah's attributes, *(cont'd.)*

Most Ready to appreciate *[Al-Shakur]*, 35:30; 35:34; 42:23; 64:17

Near *[Al-Qarib]*, 2:186; 11:61; 34:50

Oft-Forgiving *[Al-Ghafur]*, 2:173; 2:182; 2:192; 2:199; 2:218; 2:225-226; 2:235; 3:31; 3:89; 3:129; 3:155; 4:23; 4:25; 4:43; 4:96; 4:99-100; 4:106; 4:110; 4:129; 4:152; 5:3; 5:34; 5:39; 5:74; 5:98; 5:101; 6:145; 6:165; 7:153; 7:167; 8:69; 8:70; 9:5; 9:27; 9:91; 9:99; 9:102; 10:107; 11:41; 12:53; 12:98; 14:36; 15:49; 16:18; 16:110; 16:115; 16:119; 17:25; 17:44; 18:58; 22:60; 24:22; 24:33; 24:62; 25:6; 25:70; 27:11; 28:16; 33:5; 33:24; 33:50; 33:59; 33:73; 34:2; 35:28; 35:30; 35:34; 35:41; 39:53; 41:32; 42:5; 42:23; 46:8; 48:14; 49:5; 49:14; 57:28; 58:2; 58:12; 60:7; 60:12; 64:14; 66:1; 67:2; 71:10; 73:20; 85:14

Oft-Returning *[Al-Tawwab]*, 2:37; 2:54; 2:160; 4:16; 4:64; 9:104; 9:118; 24:10; 49:12

One God *[Al-Wahid; Al-Ahad]*, 2:133; 2:163; 4:171; 5:73; 6:19; 9:31; 12:39; 13:16; 14:48; 14:52; 16:22; 16:51; 18:110; 21:108; 29:46; 37:4; 38:65; 39:4; 40:16; 41:6; 112:1

Originator of the heavens and the earth *[Al-Badi']*, 2:117; 6:101

Praiseworthy *[Al-Hamid]*, 4:131, 11:73; 14:1; 14:8; 22:24; 22:64; 31:12; 31:26; 34:6; 35:15; 41:42; 42:28; 57:24; 60:6; 64:6; 85:8

Preserver of safety *[Al-Muhaymin]*, 59:23

prevails over all things *[Al-Muqtadir]*, 18:45; 43:42; 54:42

Protector *[Al-Wali; Al-Mawlaa]*, 2:107; 2:120; 2:257; 2:286; 3:68; 3:150; 4:45; 4:75; 6:14; 6:62; 7:155; 7:196; 8:40; 9:51; 9:116; 12:101; 22:78; 34:41; 42:9; 42:28; 45:19; 47:11; 66:2; 66:4

Provider of sustenance *[Al-Razzaq; Al-Raziq]*, 5:22; 5:58; 5:114; 23:72; 34:39; 51:58; 62:11

Quick in Punishment *[Sari 'al-'Iqab]*, 6:165; 7:167

Sees all things *[Al-Basir]*, 4:58; 4:134; 8:72; 17:1; 17:96; 22:61; 22:75; 25:20; 31:28; 33:9; 34:11; 35:31; 35:45; 40:20; 40:44; 40:56; 41:40; 42:11; 42:27; 49:18; 57:4; 58:1; 60:3; 64:2; 67:19; 84:15

Self-Subsisting Eternal *[Al-Qayyum]*, 2:255; 3:2; 20:111

Source of peace *[Al-Salam]*, 59:23

Steadfast *[Al-Matin]*, 51:58

Strict in punishment *[Shadid al-Iqab]*, 2:165; 2:196; 2:211; 3:11; 5:2; 5:98; 8:13; 8:25; 8:48; 8:52; 13:6; 40:3; 40:22; 59:4; 59:7

Strong *[Al-Qawi]*, 8:52; 11:66; 22:40; 22:74; 33:25; 57:25; 58:21

Supreme (Most Great) *[Al-'Azim]*, 2:255; 42:4; 56:74; 56:96; 69:52

Supreme *[Al-Mutakabbir]*, 59:23

Supreme in Honour (Beneficent) *[Al-Karim]*, 27:40; 82:6

Swift in taking account *[Sari 'al-Hisab]*, 2:202; 3:19; 3:199; 5:4; 6:62; 13:41; 14:51; 24:39; 40:17

The One to Decide *[Al-Fattah]*, 34:26

Truth *[Al-Haqq]*, 18:44; 22:6; 22:62; 23:116; 24:25; 31:30

Understands the finest mysteries *[Al-Latif]*, 6:103; 12:100; 22:63; 33:34; 42:19; 67:14

Watcher *[Al-Raqib]*, 5:117

Wise *[Al-Hakim]*, 2:32; 2:209; 2:129; 2:220; 2:228; 2:240; 2:260; 3:6; 3:18; 3:62; 3:126; 4:11; 4:17; 4:24; 4:26; 4:56; 4:92; 4:104; 4:111; 4:158; 4:165; 4:170; 5:118; 6:18; 6:73; 6:83; 6:128; 6:139; 8:10; 8:49; 8:63; 8:67; 8:71; 9:15; 9:28; 9:40; 9:60; 9:71; 9:97; 9:106; 9:110; 11:1; 12:6; 12:83; 12:100; 15:25; 16:60; 22:52; 24:10; 24:18; 24:58-59; 27:6; 27:9; 29:26; 29:42; 30:27; 31:9; 31:27; 33:1; 34:1; 34:27; 35:2; 39:1; 41:42; 42:3; 42:51; 43:84; 45:2; 45:37; 46:2; 48:4; 48:7; 48:19; 49:8; 51:30; 57:1; 59:1; 59:24; 60:5; 60:10; 61:1; 62:1; 62:3; 64:18; 66:2; 76:30

Wisest of Judges *[Ahkam al-Hakimin]*, 95:8

Witness to all things *[Al-Shahid]*, 4:33; 4:79; 4:166; 5:117; 10:46; 13:43; 17:96; 29:52; 33:55; 34:47; 46:8; 48:28; 58:6; 85:9

Allah's blessings on the Prophet, 33:56

Allah's Bounty, 2:105; 2:251; 3:174; 4:130; 4:173; 8:29; 9:28; 9:59; 9:74-76; 10:58; 17:20-21; 30:45; 31:20; 35:30; 35:35; 38:54; 42:22-23; 42:26; 44:57; 57:21; 57:29; 62:4; 93:11;

seek of it, 4:32; 16:14; 17:12; 17:66; 28:73; 30:23; 30:46; 35:12; 45:12; 62:10; 73:20

Allah's Commands, 7:54; 11:76; 16:1-2; 16:33; 21:73; 22:65; 28:70; 28:88; 30:25; 30:46; 33:38-39: 40:15; 40:78; 51:44; 52:48; 57:14; 65:8; 68:48

His Command descends down, 65:12

His Command is like the twinkling of an eye, 54:50

Allah's Covenant, 2:27; 3:77; 6:152; 9:75-77; 9:111; 13:20; 13:25; 16:91; 16:95; 33:23; 57:8;

with the Children of Israel, 2:40; 2:83-84; 2:93

Allah's curse, 2:89; 2:161; 3:61; 3:87; 7:44; 9:68; 11:18; 24:7; 28:42; 38:78; 47:23; 48:6; 63:4

Allah's Face [*Wajh*], 2:115; 6:52; 13:22; 18:28; 28:88; 30:38; 30:39; 55:27

Allah's help, 8:62; 8:64; 12:110; 22:40; 40:51; 61:13, 110:1

Allah's promise, 3:152; 4:122; 6:134; 10:4; 10:55; 14:22; 17:108; 18:21; 18:98; 20:86; 21:9; 21:104; 22:47; 25:15-16; 28:13; 28:61; 30:6; 30:60; 31:9; 31:33; 35:5; 36:52; 39:20; 39:74; 40:8; 40:55; 40:77; 45:32; 46:16-17; 48:20; 48:29; 51:5; 73:18

Allah's signs (revelations), 2:73; 2:242; 2:252; 3:103; 3:108; 4:155; 5:75; 5:89; 6:33; 6:35; 6:37; 6:157-158; 7:26; 7:40; 7:175-177; 8:2; 10:71; 16:104-105; 17:1; 18:9; 18:17; 18:57; 18:105; 19:58; 19:73; 19:77; 20:22-23; 20:42; 20:126-128; 21:37; 22:52; 23:30; 23:58; 24:1; 25:73; 27:13-14; 27:93; 29:47; 29:49-50; 32:22; 32:24; 33:34; 36:46; 39:52; 40:4; 40:13; 40:34-35; 40:63; 40:81; 41:15; 42:35; 43:69; 45:6-9; 45:31; 46:27; 57:9; 62:2; 68:15; 74:16

explained, 2:187; 2:221; 6:46; 6:55; 6:65; 6:97-98; 6:105; 7:32; 7:58; 7:174; 9:11; 10:5; 10:24; 11:1; 13:2; 24:58-59; 24:61; 30:28; 41:3; 57:17

not for a miserable price, 3:199; 5:44; 9:9

not to be treated as a jest or falsehood, 2:231; 4:140; 6:150; 7:37; 17:59; 18:56; 18:106; 23:105; 37:14; 45:9; 45:35; 46:26; 62:5; 64:10; 78:28;

shown in the furthest regions and in souls, 41:53

the greatest, 53:18

see also Signs in creation

Allah's Throne, 2:255; 7:54; 10:3; 11:7; 13:2; 20:5; 25:59; 39:75; 40:7; 57:4; 69:17

Alms, [*Sadaqah*], 9:58; 9:60; 9:103-104

Angels, 2:161; 2:210; 2:248; 3:18; 3:39; 3:42; 3:45; 3:80; 3:87; 4:166; 6:8-9; 6:111; 6:158; 11:12; 13:23; 15:7-8; 16:32-33; 17:40; 17:92; 17:95; 21:103; 22:75; 23:24; 25:7; 25:21-22; 41:14; 43:60; 53:26-27; 66:4; 79:1-5

and Adam, 2:31; 2:34; 7:11; 15:28-30; 17:61; 18:50; 38:71-73

appointed over the fire, 39:71; 66:6-7; 67:8; 74:30-31; 96:18

ascent of, 70:4

Pray for forgiveness for all beings on Earth, 42:5

implore forgiveness for those who believe, 40:7-9

belief in, 2:177; 2:285; 4:136

creation, of 35:1; 37:150; 43:19

descent of, 16:2; 19:64-65; 25:25; 41:30-32; 97:4

fighting, 3:124-125; 8:9; 8:12; 9:26

given female names by those who disbelieve in the Hereafter, 53:27-28

guardians, 6:61; 13:11; 82:10

on the Day of Judgment, 34:40-41; 39:75; 50:21; 69:17; 78:38; 89:22

recording, 50:17-18

send blessings, 33:43

send blessings on the Prophet, 33:56

serve and worship Allah, 2:30; 4:172; 13:13; 16:49-50; 21:19-20; 37:164-166; 39:75; 40:7; 42:5

take the souls of the dying, 4:97; 6:61; 6:93; 7:37; 8:50; 16:28; 16:32; 32:11; 47:27; 79:1-2

see also Gabriel and Michael

Apostates, 47:25,

B

Babylon, 2:102

Backbiting, 49:12; 104:1

Badr (battle of), 3:13

lessons from, 8:5-19, 8:42-48

Balance,

in Creation, 15:19; 55:7-9

in weighing, 17:35; 26:182

on the Day of Judgment, 7:8-9; 21:47; 23:102-103; 101:6-8

Barrier *[Barzakh]*

a barrier between (the two seas), 25:53; 55:19-20

see also, 18:94-97; 34:54; 36:9

Beast (of the last days), 27:82

Bedouins, 9:90; 9:97-99; 9:101; 9:120; 33:20; 48:11; 48:16; 49:14

Bee, 16:68-69

Believers,

Allah listens to them, 42:26

Allah has put affection between their hearts, 8:63

Allah has purchased from them, 9:111

Allah is with them, 8:19; 47:35

Allah forgives them, 33:73

Allah will remove their ills and improve their condition, 3:195; 47:2; 48:5; 64:9

among Egyptians, 7:120-126; 10:83; 20:70-73; 26:46-51; 40:28-45; 66:11

are but a single Brotherhood, 49:10

best of creatures, 98:7

covenant with Allah, 33:23

delivered, 41:18

descriptions of, 2:285; 8:2-4; 8:74; 9:112; 13:19-22; 13:27; 23:1-11; 24:51; 24:62; 27:2-3; 32:15-19; 47:3; 48:29; 49:15; 58:22; 66:5; 66:11-12; 70:22-35; 90:17; 103:3

do not disrespect one another, 49:11-12

loved by Allah, 19:96

make peace between your brothers, 49:9-10

men and women, 9:71-72; 33:35

on them is no fear, nor shall they grieve, 2:38; 2:62; 2:112; 2:262; 2:274; 2:277; 3:170; 5:69; 6:48; 7:35; 10:62; 39:61; 46:13

overflowing in their love for Allah, 2:165

protectors of one another, 8:72; 9:71; 42:39

rewarded, 2:62; 2:277; 17:9; 18:2-3; 23:10-11; 32:17; 33:35; 33:44; 33:47; 34:4; 34:37; 41:8; 45:30; 48:29; 57:7; 57:19; 84:25; 95:6

rewarded with Gardens, 2:25; 9:72; 13:22-24; 14:23; 19:60-63; 20:75-76; 22:23; 32:19; 42:22; 43:68-73; 47:12; 48:5; 57:12; 58:22; 61:12; 64:9; 65:11; 66:8; 70:35; 85:11; 98:8

saved, 10:103; 26:118-119; 27:53

why say you that which you do not do?, 61:2

Betray (treason), 4:107; 8:27; 8:58; 8:71; 12:52; 66:10

Birds, 2:260; 3:49; 5:110; 6:38; 12:36-41; 16:79; 21:79; 22:31; 24:41; 27:16-20; 34:10; 38:19; 56:21; 67:19; 105:3

Blood-Money, 2:178-179; 4:92; 17:33

Bribery, 2:188

Burden,

Allah burdens not a soul beyond its scope, 2:286; 6:152; 7:42; 23:62; 65:7

borne on the Day of Judgment, 16:25; 20:100; 29:12-13

no bearer of burdens can bear the burden of another, 6:164; 17:15; 35:18; 39:7; 53:38

released by Muhammad, 7:157

removed from Muhammad, 94:1-6

C

Camel, 6:144; 7:40; 77:33; 88:17

Captives, 8:67; 8:70-71; 76:8

see also Prisoners of War

Cattle, 3:14; 4:119; 5:1; 6:136; 6:138-139; 6:142; 7:179; 16:5-8; 16:66; 20:54; 22:28; 22:30; 23:21; 25:44; 26:133; 32:27; 35:28; 36:71-73; 39:6; 40:79; 42:11; 43:12-13; 47:12; 79:33; 80:32

Cave, people of the, 9:40; 18:9-22; 18:25; 18:26

Cave of Thawr, 9:40

Charity *[Zakah]*, 2:43; 2:83; 2:110; 2:177; 2:270-274; 2:276-277; 4:77; 4:162; 5:12; 5:55; 7:156; 9:71; 9:79; 19:31; 19:55; 21:73; 22:41; 22:78; 23:4; 23:60; 24:37; 24:56; 27:3; 28:54; 30:39; 31:4; 32:16; 33:33; 33:35; 35:29; 41:7; 57:7; 58:12-13; 63:10; 64:16; 75:31; 98:5

Children, 7:189-190; 8:28; 13:38; 16:72; 17:64; 24:31; 42:49-50; 46:15; 60:3; 63:9; 64:14-15; 71:12; 90:3

after divorce, 2:233; 65:6

and inheritance, 4:11

do not kill, 6:137; 6:140; 6:151; 17:31; 60:12

Children of Israel, 2:211; 2:246-252; 3:49; 3:93; 5:12; 5:32; 7:159-171; 10:93; 17:2; 17:101; 20:80; 26:17; 26:22; 32:23-24; 40:53

and Jesus, 3:49-51; 5:46; 5:72; 5:110; 61:14

and the calf, 2:51-54; 2:93; 4:153; 7:148; 7:152; 20:87-97

Children of Israel, (cont'd.)

and the Qur'an, 26:197; 27:76; 46:10

deliverance from Pharoah, 2:48-49; 7:136-141; 10:90; 14:6; 20:77-80; 26:60-67; 44:30-33

distort the book, 3:78; 5:14; 7:162

dwellings in Egypt, 10:87

forty years in the wilderness, 5:26

granted Prophethood, 45:16

like a donkey which carries huge tomes, 62:5

told to remember Allah's favours, 2:40; 2:47; 2:122; 5:20

warning given to them, 17:4-8; 17:104

Christians, 2:111; 2:113; 2:120; 2:135; 5:14; 5:18; 22:17

believers rewarded, 2:62; 5:69; 5:82-85; 57:27-29

Compassion and Mercy in their hearts, 57:27

in love to the believers, 5:82

recognise the Truth, 5:83-84

Confederates, 33:22

Creation, 2:164; 3:190-191; 6:1-2; 6:73; 9:36; 10:6; 14:19; 14:32-33; 15:85; 16:3; 17:70; 18:51; 20:50; 21:30-33; 21:56; 25:2; 27:64; 29:61; 30:8; 30:22; 31:10-11; 35:1; 36:81; 39:5-6; 39:38; 40:57; 42:29; 43:9-13; 45:4; 45:22; 46:3; 46:33; 51:47-49; 52:36; 56:59; 64:3; 65:12; 77:20; 78:6-16; 79:27-33; 88:17-20

a new, 13:5; 14:19; 17:49; 17:98; 34:7; 35:16; 53:47; 56:60-61

in pairs 13:3; 35:11; 36:36; 42:11; 43:12; 51:49; 53:45; 78:8

in six days, 7:54; 10:3; 11:7; 25:59; 32:4; 50:38; 57:4

not for sport, 21:16; 38:27; 44:38-39

purpose of, 51:56

of which you have no knowledge, 16:8; 36:36

D

David [Dawud], 4:163; 5:78; 6:84; 17:55; 21:78-80; 27:15; 27:16; 34:10; 34:13; 38:17-30

fights Goliath, 2:251

Day of Judgment, 1:4; 2:281; 3:9; 3:25; 3:106; 3:161; 3:185; 3:194; 4:87; 4:109; 5:14; 6:12; 6:16; 6:22-23; 7:53; 7:59; 7:167; 10:45; 10:93; 11:3; 11:84; 11:103-108; 14:31; 14:41-42; 14:48-51; 16:25; 16:27-34; 16:92; 16:124; 17:13-14; 17:97;

18:98-101; 18:105; 19:37-40; 20:100-109; 22:7; 22:56; 23:16; 23:100; 25:17-30; 26:82; 26:87-102; 30:12-16; 30:43-44; 30:55-57; 39:15; 39:31; 39:47-48; 39:67-75; 40:15-20; 42:45-47; 43:65-77; 45:26-35; 50:42; 55:39-41; 56:1-56; 58:6-7; 58:18; 60:3; 60:6; 66:7-8; 67:27; 68:42-43; 69:13-37; 70:1-4; 75:1; 75:6; 75:7-15; 77:29-49; 78:17-40; 79:34-46; 80:33-42; 81:1-14; 84:1-15; 85:2; 86:9-10; 89:21-30; 99:1-8; 100:9-11; 102:8

the Caller will call out from a place quite near, 50:41

a Day of dire difficulty, 25:26;

a Day of distress 74:9-10

a Day of mutual loss and gain, 64:9

a Day well-known, 56:50

all mankind will stand before the Lord of the Worlds, 83:4-6

appointed time of the Hour, 7:187; 10:48-51; 11:104; 16:61; 16:77; 18:21; 18:36; 20:15; 21:38-40; 27:71-72; 31:34; 32:28-30; 33:63; 34:3; 34:29-30; 36:48-50; 40:59; 41:47; 42:17-18; 43:61: 43:66; 43:85; 45:32; 47:18; 51:12-14; 54:1; 56:1; 67:25-26; 70:6-7; 72:25; 78:17; 79:42-46

dreadul, horror, and terror, 21:97; 22:1-2; 27:87; 34:23; 34:51; 73:17; 75:7; 79:6-9; 101:4

belief in, 2:177; 3:114; 4:38-39; 4:59; 4:136; 4:162; 5:69; 9:18-19; 9:44-45; 24:2; 40:27; 42:18; 58:22; 65:2; 70:26

Compelling Cry 79:13-14

covering is removed from your sight, 50:22

Day of Account, 38:16; 38:26; 38:53; 40:27

Day of Assembly, 42:7; 64:9

Day of Eternal Life, 50:34

Day of Gathering, 50:44

Day of Noise and Clamour, 101: 1-11

Day of Decision, 37:19-74

Day of Sorting out, 44:40-42; 77:13-15; 77:38; 78:17

Deafening Noise 80:33

draws near, 21:1; 40:18; 53:57-58; 54:1; 70:7

no excuses, 66:7; 75:13-15

no one can avail another, 31:33; 44:41; 80:34-37; 82:19

not able to speak, 11:105; 77:35-36: 78:37-38

single Blast, 36:49; 36:53; 38:15; 50:42; 69:13

Day of Judgment, *(cont'd.)*

people will not be unjustly dealt with, 17:71; 18:49; 19:60; 21:47; 36:54; 39:69-70; 40:17; 43:76; 45:22

Overwhelming event, 88:1-16

the Sure reality, 69:1-3; 78:39

will surely come to pass, 51:5-6; 52:7-8; 74:47; 77:7

Death, 2:180; 2:243; 3:143-145; 3:154; 3:156-158; 4:78; 4:97; 4:100; 5:106; 6:61; 6:162; 7:25; 7:37; 8:50; 16:28; 16:32; 16:70; 23:15; 23:99; 31:34; 39:30; 45:21; 50:19; 56:60; 56:83-87; 62:6-8; 63:10; 67:2; 75:22-30; 80:21; 102:2

every soul shall have a taste of, 3:185; 21:35; 29:57

only happens once, 37:58-60; 44:56

Debts, 2:280-282; 4:12; 56:66

Decree,

when He decrees a matter, he says to it, "Be," - and it is, 2:117

Deeds,

evil conduct seems pleasing, 47:14

fastened to his own kneck, 17:13

right and wrong, are for and against his own soul, 41:46; 45:15

to us our, to you yours, 28:55; 42:15

Desire,

one who takes for his god his own passion, 25:43

those who follow their own lusts, 47:14; 47:16

Dhu'l-Kifl, 21:85

Dhu al-Qarnayn, 18:83-98

Distress, 3:154; 16:127

distraction and anguish, 12:86

suffering changed into prosperity, 7:95

Ditch (pit), people of the, 85:4-10

Divorce, 2:227-232; 2:236-237; 2:241; 33:49; 58:2-3; 65:1-7

Drink,

alcoholic, 2:219

a cup from a clear-flowing fountain, 37:45; 76:21

pure wine, sealed, 83:25

pure and holy, 37:46

E

Earth,

becomes clothed with green, 22:63

bestowed blessings on it, 41:10

created seven, 65:12

creation in four days, 41:9-10

for a resting place, 40:64

for the living and dead, 77:25-26

is Allah's, 7:128

made manageable to humans, 67:15

mischief (corruption; evil) in, 2:251; 7:56; 7:74; 8:73; 11:116; 12:73; 13:25; 26:152; 26:183; 27:48; 30:41; 47:22

on the Day of Judgment. 14:48; 18:47; 20:105-107; 39:67; 39:69; 50:44; 52:10; 56:4-6; 69:14; 70:9; 73:14; 77:10; 78:20; 81:3-6; 82:3-4; 84:3-5; 89:21: 99:1-5

revive it after its death, 2:164; 7:57; 16:65; 22:5; 25:49; 29:63; 30:19; 30:24; 30:50; 35:9; 36:33-36; 41:39; 43:11; 45:5; 50:11; 57:17

split, 80:26; 86:12

spread out, 13:3; 15:19; 51:48; 71:19-20; 88:20; 91:6

things of all kinds produced in it , 26:7; 31:10; 50:7

wide and spacious, 4:97; 4:100; 29:56; 39:10; 78:6; 79:30

Elephant army, 105:1-5

Elias *[Elijah; Ilyasin; Ilyas]*, 6:85; 37:123-132

Elisha, 6:86

Emigration, 2:218; 3:195; 4:97; 4:100; 8:72; 8:74; 9:20; 16:41; 16:110; 22:58; 24:22

Evil, 4:123; 10:27-30; 19:83; 59:15

appeared on land and sea, 30:41

changed into prosperity, 7:95

consequence for those who do, 30:10

cover, with pardon 4:149

from yourselves, 4:79

devise, plots, 16:45-47

recompensed, 6:160

turn off, with good, 13:22;

repel, 23:96; 41:34

those who follow their own lusts, 47:14; 47:16

Evil One, *see Satan*

Excess forbidden,

in food, 5:87; 20:81

in religion, 4:171; 5:77-81

Eyes, ears and skins will testify against sinners, 41:20-23

Ezekiel, see Dhu'l Kifl

Ezra *[Uzair]*, 9:30

F

Faith (belief), 2:108; 3:167; 3:177; 3:193; 5:5; 9:23; 16:106; 30:56; 40:10; 42:52; 49:14; 52:21; 58:22; 59:9; 59:10

assured, 44:7; 45:4; 45:20; 51:20

He has guided you as a favour, 49:17

increased, 3:173

False Gods, 7:194-198; 16:20-21; 16:73; 16:86; 21:22; 21:24; 34:22; 34:27; 41:47; 41:48; 46:5-6; 53:19-24; 71:23-24

revile not those whom they worship besides Allah, 6:108

Falsehood *[Batil]*, 2:42; 3:71; 8:8; 13:17; 17:81; 22:62; 29:52; 29:67; 31:30; 34:49; 40:5; 41:42; 42:24; 47:3

perishes, 21:18

Fasting,

in expiation, 2:196; 4:92; 5:89; 5:95; 58:4

in Ramadan, 2:183-185; 2:187

men and women, 33:35

Fear of Allah, 2:223; 3:175; 4:77; 7:56; 9:13; 9:18; 22:1; 23:57; 32:16; 33:37; 35:28; 39:23; 59:21; 64:16; 70:27; 79:26; 79:40; 87:10; 98:8

in secret, 35:18; 36:11; 50:33; 67:12

Fear no evil, 3:175

Fear, none for the Righteous, 2:38;

or for Allah's devotees, 43:68

or for Believers, 2:62

or for friends of Allah, 10:62

or for those who remain firm in Allah, 46:13

or those who believe and do righteousness, 2:277

or those who believe and mend their lives, 6:48; 7:35

or those who believe in Allah and the Last Day, 5:69

or those who submit to Allah, 2:112

or whoever spends for Allah, 2:262-274

Female infanticide, 16:58; 81:8-9

Fig, 95:1

Fighting (strive),

against those who believe not in Allah, 9:29

by Children of Israel, 2:246-251

in the Cause of Allah, 4:74-77

in the way of Allah against disbelievers (who fight against you), 2:190-193; 2:244; 4:84; 4:95; 8:72; 8:74-75; 9:12-16; 9:20; 9:36; 9:123; 47:4; 61:11

in sacred months, 2:217; 9:5

no blame for the blind, lame and sick, 48:16-17

prescribed, 2:216

permission given to those who are wronged, 22:39-41

until there is no more tumult or oppression, 8:39

twenty overcoming two hundred, 8:65

in whose hearts is a disease (hypocrites), 47:20

Food,

in paradise, 2:25; 19:62; 37:41-42; 38:51; 43:73; 44:55; 47:15; 52:22; 55:52-54; 55:68; 56:20-21; 56:32-33; 69:23-24; 76:14; 77:42-43

lawful and unlawful (Halal and Haram), 2:168; 2:172-173; 5:1; 5:3-5; 5:88; 6:118-119; 6:121; 6:136-146; 10:59; 16:114-115; 22:30

make not unlawful which Allah has made lawful, 5:87; 7:32

no sin for what they ate in the past, 5:93

Forbidden conduct, 6:151-152; 7:33

Forgiveness, 7:199; 39:53; 45:14; 53:32; 57:20-21

a duty of Believers, 45:14

Allah forgives all sins, 39:53

Allah forgives to whom he pleases, 4:48; 4:116

Allah forgives not joining other partners with Him, 4:116

Angels pray for, for for all beings on Earth, 42:5

forgive, when they are angry, 42:37

forgive and make reconciliation, 42:40-43

not to pray for forgiveness for Pagans, 9:113

people of the book wish to take you to infidelity, 2:109

be foremost in seeking, 57:21

seek Allah's, 4:110

Fornication, *see Zina*

Fraud, 83:1-6

Free will,

    take a straight path to his Lord, 76:29

    limited by Allah's will (plan), 6:107; 10:99; 74:56; 76:31; 81:28-29

    to go straight, 81:28

    whosoever, let him: believe and disbelieve, 18:29

Friday prayers, 62:9-11

Fruit, 16:11

    all they desire, 77:42

    all kinds, of 47:15

    in abundance in Paradise, 43:73

G

Gabriel, 2:97-98; 66:4

    spirit of faith and truth, 26:193

Gambling, 2:219; 5:90; 5:91

Gardens, 6:141; 13:4; 23:19; 26:57; 26:134; 26:147; 34:15-16; 44:25; 50:9; 71:12; 78:16; 80:30

Gardens of Paradise, 3:15; 3:133; 3:136; 3:195; 3:198; 4:57; 4:122; 5:85; 5:119; 7:19; 7:42-43; 7:49; 9:21-22; 13:35; 15:45-48; 18:31; 18:107-108; 20:76; 22:14; 22:23; 25:10; 25:15-16; 25:24; 31:8-9; 35:33-35; 36:26; 36:55-58; 38:49-54; 39:73-74; 40:40; 43:70-73; 44:51-57; 51:15; 52:17-28; 54:54; 56:11-40; 59:20; 76:5-22; 78:31-36; 79:41

    home of Peace, 6:127; 10:25

    Bliss and a Realm Magnificent, 76:20

    as the width of the heaven and earth, 57:21

    brought near. 50:31-35; 81:13

    carpets, 55:54; 55:76; 88:16

    drink in, 37:45-47; 38:51; 52:23; 56:18-19; 76:5-6; 76:15-18; 76:21; 77:43; 78:34; 83:25-28

    Garden of Abode, 53:15

    Gardens of Eternity, 25:15; 1631; 18:31; 19:61; 20:76; 35:33; 38:50; 40:8; 61:12;

    Gardens of Delight, 68:34: 22:56; 56:89

    Gardens of Bliss, 5:65; 10:9; 26:85; 31:8; 56:12; 76:20

    Gardens of Felicity, 37:43-49

    Gardens of Eden, 9:72: 13:23; 38:50; 98:8

    sorrow removed, 35:34

    in a high garden, 69:22-24; 88:10-16

    lofty mansions, 39:20

    eternal homes, 35:35

    no toil nor sense of weariness, 35:35

    reclining on thrones and couches, 18:31; 36:56; 52:20; 56:15-16; 56:34; 76:13: 83:23; 83:35; 88:13

    place of peace and security, 44:51; 44:55

    parable of, 47:15

    two Gardens, 55:46-47

    in the presence of Allah, 50:35; 68:34; 73:20

    youths to serve them, 52:24; 56:17; 76:19

Gog and Magog, *[Ya'juj and Ma'juj]*, 18:94-99; 21:96

Goliath, 2:249-251

Good,

    Allah revealed all, 16:30

    Allah rewards those who do, 53:31

    an increase of, 42:23

    do, as Allah has been, to you, 28:77

    for those who do, in this world, 39:10

    repel evil, 28:54; 41:34

    reward, 55:60

    rewarded double, 28:54

    rewarded ten times, 6:160

    you dislike a thing which is, for you, 2:216

Good and Evil,

    every soul will be confronted with all the, it has done, 3:30

Good deed,

    openly or conceal it, 4:149

    strive as in a race with each other, 5:48

Gospel, 3:3; 3:48; 3:65; 5:46; 5:47; 5:66; 5:68; 5:110; 7:157; 9:111; 48:29; 57:27

Greeting (Salutation), 4:86; 10:10; 14:23; 24:61; 25:75; 33:44

H

Hands and Feet will bear witness, 36:65

Hardship (difficulty), 94:5-6

Hearts,

    a disease, 2:10; 5:52; 8:49; 9:125; 22:53; 24:50; 33:12; 33:32; 33:60; 47:20; 47:29; 74:31

    covered, 17:46; 41:5

    divided, 59:14

    hardened, 2:74; 22:53; 39:22; 57:16

    locked up, 47:24

    sealed, 7:100; 7:101; 40:35; 47:16; 63:3

    when Allah is mentioned, 22:35

Heavens,

as a canopy (roof), 2:22; 21:32; 40:64; 52:5; 79:28

as smoke (primeval matter), 41:11

built with power and skill, 51:47

completed them in two days, 41:12

ladder to (hypothetical), 6:35; 52:38

no flaws in it, 50:6; 67:3-4

numerous Paths, 51:7

on the Day of Judgment, 14:48; 21:104; 25:25; 39:67; 52:9; 55:37; 69:16; 70:8; 73:18; 77:8-9; 78:19; 81:1-2; 82:1-2; 84:1-2

raised by Allah, 13:2; 55:7; 79:27-28

rent asunder, 42:5

seven in number, 2:29; 17:44; 23:17; 23:86; 41:12; 65:12; 67:3; 71:15; 78:12

Hell, 2:206; 3:12; 3:103; 3:131; 3:151; 3:191-192; 3:197; 4:56; 4:121; 7:18; 7:38; 9:35; 9:81; 14:16; 14:28-30; 15:43-44; 16:29; 17:97; 18:29; 21:98-100; 22:19-22; 23:103-108; 25:65-66; 29:54-55; 32:20; 36:63-64; 38:55-64; 39:16; 39:60; 40:71-76; 43:74-77; 44:43-50; 45:10; 50:24-26; 52:13-16; 54:48; 55:43-44; 56:41-56; 56:94; 57:14-15; 58:8; 59:3; 69:30-37; 70:15-18; 72:23; 73:12-13; 74:26-31; 74:42-48; 76:4; 77:29-33; 82:14-16; 83:16-17; 88:4-7; 90:20; 102:6-7

place of ambush, 78:21-30

blazing fire, 25:11-12; 67:7-8; 77:31-33; 81:12; 92:14-16; 101:11; 111:3

filled with Jinn and men, 7:18; 7:179; 11:119; 32:13; 38:85

fuel is men and stones, 2:24; 66:6

insatiable, 50:30

neither dying nor living there, 14:16-17; 20:74; 35:36; 87:13

punishment of Eternity, 10:52; 32:14; 41:28

placed in full view, 79:36-39; 89:23

Hereafter, 2:94; 2:200-201; 2:220; 3:22; 3:85; 3:145; 3:148; 4:77; 4:134; 9:69; 10:64; 12:57; 12:101; 13:34; 16:107; 16:122; 17:72; 20:127; 22:11; 22:15; 24:14; 24:19; 24:23; 27:66; 29:27; 38:46; 39:9; 39:26; 40:43; 41:16; 41:31; 59:3; 60:13; 68:33; 75:21

belief in, 6:92; 6:113; 6:150; 11:19; 16:22; 17:19; 27:3; 31:4; 34:21; 39:45; 41:7

better than worldly life, 2:86; 3:77; 3:152; 4:74; 6:32; 7:169; 9:38; 13:26; 14:27; 16:30; 20:131; 28:80; 29:64; 40:39; 42:20; 43:35; 57:20; 87:14-17

Hour,

all of a sudden it is on them, 6:31; 12:107; 43:66

comes upon you, 6:40; 20:15; 34:3

convulsion (earthquake) of the, 22:1

is as the twinkling of the eye, 16:77

is near, 54:1-5

the guilty will be struck, 30:12

the knowledge of it is with Allah only, 7:187; 33:63; 41:47

there is no doubt about its coming, 45:32

will certainly come, 40:59

Houses, manners about entering, 24:27-29

Hunayn (battle), 9:25

Hur (females in Paradise), 44:54; 52:20; 56:22

Hypocrites,

afraid of being found out, 9:64-65

Allah punishes, 33:73

beware of them, 63:4

they do not understand, 63:7; 63:8

deceive themselves, 2:9

deaf, dumb and blind, 2:17-18

disbelievers success, 4:141

disease in their hearts, 2:10; 8:49; 22:53; 33:12; 47:29

go for judgment to Satan, 4:60-62

in fear of death and darkness, 2:19-20

in the lowest depths of the Fire, 4:145

Curse of Allah is on them, 9:67-69

truly evil are their deeds, 63:2

mischief makers, 2:11-12

mockers, 2:13-15

most contentious enemies, 2:204-206

not to be taken as friends, 4:89

not to pray for, 9:84

seek to deceive Allah, 4:142-143

strive against, 66:9

their hearts are sealed, 63:3

they say a thing which is not in their hearts, 3:167

they are liars, 59:11-14

they do not believe, 2:8

I

Imran,
  daughter of, 66:12
  wife of, 3:35

Inheritance, 2:180; 2:240; 4:7-9; 4:11; 4:12; 4:33; 4:176; 5:106-108

Injustice, 4:30; 4:148

Intercession, 6:51; 6:70; 6:94; 10:3; 19:87; 20:109; 30:13; 34:23; 39:44; 40:18; 43:86; 53:26; 74:48

Interest, *see Usury*

Intoxicants, 5:90; 5:91
  wine, 2:219

Isaac *[Ishaq]*, 2:133; 4:163; 6:84; 19:49; 21:72; 29:27; 37:112; 37:113

Ishmael *[Isma'il]*, 2:125-129; 2:133; 4:163; 6:86; 19:54-55; 21:85; 38:48

Islam, 3:19; 3:85; 5:3; 6:125; 39:22; 61:7
  as a favour, 49:17
  first of those who submit as Muslims, 6:14; 6:163; 39:12
  whose heart Allah has opened, 39:22

J

Jacob *[Yaqub]*, 2:132; 2:133; 4:163; 6:84; 19:49; 21:72; 29:27

Jesus, son of Mary
  and the Holy Spirit, 2:87; 2:253; 5:110
  annunciation of, 3:45-51; 19:16-21
  a sign, 21:91; 23:50; 43:57-61
  belief in, 4:159
  covenant with Allah, 33:7
  cursed the Children of Israel, 5:78
  disciples of, 3:52-54; 5:111-113; 61:14
  given the revelation, 2:87; 2:136; 3:48; 3:84; 4:163; 5:46; 19:30; 57:27
  gives good tidings of the Praised One (Ahmad), 61:6
  he is not Allah (God), 5:17; 5:72; 9:30-31
  like Adam, 3:59
  messenger to Children of Israel, 3:49-51; 5:46; 5:72; 43:59; 61:6; 61:14
  miracles of, 5:110; 5:113-115
  no more than a Messenger, 4:171; 5:75; 43:59
  raised up to Allah, 3:55; 4:158
  religion of, 42:13
  serves and worships Allah, 4:172; 19:30; 43:64
  spoke in childhood, 3:46; 5:110; 19:30-33
  testifies before Allah, 5:116-118
  was of the righteous, 6:85
  was not killed, 4:157, 5:110
  came with wisdom, 43:63

Jews; 2:111; 2:113; 2:120; 2:135; 4:160; 5:18; 16:118
  among them some believe; 2:62; 4:162; 5:69
  became apes and swine; 2:65; 5:60; 7:166
  claim that they are favoured by Allah, 62:6-8
  cursed; 4:46-47; 5:78; 9:30
  enmity; of 5:64; 5:82
  greediest of people, 2:96
  judged; by the Torah 5:44
  slew prophets; 2:87; 2:91; 3:21; 3:181; 4:155; 5:70
  took usury; 4:161
  unbelief and blasphemy of; 5:41; 5:64; 59:2; 59:11
  work iniquity; 5:41-42; 5:78-81; 59:2-4; 59:11-17
  write the Book with their own hands; 2:79

Jinn, 6:100; 6:112; 15:27; 34:41; 46:18; 46:29; 55:15; 55:33; 55:39; 72:1-15

Job *[Ayyub]*, 4:163; 6:84; 21:83
  he suffered, 21:84; 38:41-44

John, the Baptist *[Yahya]*, 19:7
  glad tidings of, 3:39; 21:90
  righteous, 6:85
  wise; kind; devout, 19:12-15

Jonah *[Jonas or Yunus]*, 4:163; 6:86; 10:98; 37:139-148

Joseph *[Yusuf]*, 6:84; 12:4-101; 40:34
  false blood on his shirt, 12:18

Judgment Day, *see Day of Reserruction*

Judi, Mount, 11:44

Justice, 4:58; 4:135; 7:29; 16:90

K

Ka'bah, 2:144, 2:149-150; 2:158; 3:96-97; 5:2; 5:95-97; 9:19; 17:1; 22:29; 22:33; 48:27
  and the disbelievers, 8:34-35; 9:7; 9:28; 22:25; 48:25
  built by Abraham and Ishmael, 2:125-127; fighting at, 2:191; 2:217;

Keys,
  of the Heavens and the Earth, 39:63; 42:12
  of the invisible, 6:59

Killing,
  not to kill anyone, 17:33
  if anyone slew a person, 5:32

Kind words 2:263

Kindred, rights of, 4:7-9; 4:36; 8:41; 16:90; 17:26; 30:38; 42:23

Knowledge,
  not a leaf falls, but with his knowledge, 6:59
  of five things, with Allah alone, 31:34
  slain their children without, 6:140

Korah [Qarun], 28:76-82; 29:39; 40:24

L

Lamp, 25:61; 67:5; 71:16

Languages,
  variations in, 30:22

Law, prescribed, 5:48

Liars, 26:221-223

Life, if anyone saves a, 5:32

Life of this World,
  bought the, at the price of the Hereafter, 2:86
  desires the, 11:15-16; 17:18; 42:20
  good tidings in the, 10:64
  is deception, 3:185
  little is the comfort of this, 9:38; 13:26; 28:60
  love for, 75:20-21; 76:27
  mutual boasting, 57:20
  play and amusement, 6:32; 29:64; 47:36
  sell the, for the Hereafter, 4:74
  similitude of the, 10:24
  deceived Jinns and humans, 6:130
  Hereafter is better, 87:16-17

Light,
  from Allah, 5:15-16; 64:8
  of Allah, 9:32; 24:35-36; 61:8
  of the Believers, 57:12-13; 57:19; 57:28; 66:8

Lighting, 24:43; 69:5
  fear and hope, 13:12-13; 30:24
  similitude of, 2:19-20

Lion, 74:51

Loan,
  lend to Allah a beautiful loan, 2:245; 73:20
  doubled for them, 64:17
  increased manifold, 57:11; 57:18

Loss, 39:15

Lot [Lut], 6:86; 7:80; 11:70; 11:74; 11:77; 11:81; 11:89; 21:71; 21:74; 22:43; 26:160; 26:161; 26:167; 27:54-56; 29:26; 29:28; 29:32; 29:33; 37:133; 38:13; 50:13; 54:33; 54:34
  his disobedient wife, 11:81; 15:60; 66:10

Lote-tree, 34:16; 53:14-16; 56:28

Luqman, 31:12-14

M

Madinah [Yathrib], 9:120; 33:13; 63:8

Midian, [Madyan], 7:85-93; 11:84-95; 20:40; 22:44; 28:22; 28:23; 29:36-37

Mahr (bridal-money), 2:229; 2:236; 2:237; 4:4; 4:19-21; 4:24; 4:25; 5:5; 33:50; 60:10; 60:11

Makkah [Bakkah], 3:96; 48:24
  City, 90:1; 90:2
  Ciy of security, 95:3

Man,
  Allah is nearer to him than his jugular vein, 50:16
  created according to the will of Allah, 30:30; 82:8
  created in the best of moulds, 95:4
  created into toil and struggle, 90:4
  created to serve (worship) Allah, 51:56
  created very impatient, 70:19-21
  created weak, 4:28; 30:54
  creation of, 2:30; 4:1; 6:2; 6:98; 7:11; 7:189; 15:26; 15:28-29; 15:33; 16:4; 18:37; 19:67; 22:5; 23:12-14; 25:54; 30:20; 30:54; 32:7-9; 35:11; 36:36; 36:77-78; 37:11; 38:71-72; 39:6; 40:57; 40:64; 40:67; 45:4; 49:13; 50:16; 53:45-46; 55:3-4; 55:14; 56:57-59; 67:23; 71:14; 74:11; 75:36-39; 76:2; 76:28; 77:20-23; 78:8; 79:27; 80:18-19: 82:7-8; 86:5-7; 90:4-9; 96:2
  disputatious, 16:4; 18:54; 22:3; 22:8; 36:49; 36:77
  is hasty, 17:11; 21:37
  not assigned with two hearts, 33:4
  stages of growth, 46:15
  toiling towards Allah, 84:6
  travel from stage to stage, 84:19
  undertook the Trust, 33:72
  was nothing mentioned, 76:1

Mankind,

be careful of your duty to your Lord, 4:1

insolence is only against your own souls, 10:23

made you into nations and tribes, 49:13

makes you in the wombs of your mothers, 39:6

witnesses, 2:143

Manna and the Quails, 2:57; 7:160; 20:80-81

Manners,

about entering houses, 24:27-29

in assemblies, 58:11

in the home, 24:58-61

in the Prophet's house, 33:53

in the Prophet's presence, 2:104; 24:62; 49:1-5

not to mock another, 49:11

send blessings on the Prophet, 33:56

Marriage, 2:221; 4:3-4; 4:20-21; 4:24-25; 4:34-35; 4:128-130; 23:6; 24:3; 24:26; 24:32-33; 25:54; 30:21; 60:10

of the Prophet, 33:50-52; 66:5

prohibited degrees in, 4:22-24

with women among the People of the Book, 5:5

Martyrs,

bounty provided by Allah, 3:170-171

not dead, 2:154; 3:169

receive a goodly provision, 22:58; 22:59

receive forgiveness and mercy, 3:157

Mary (mother of Jesus),

a sign for all people, 21:91; 23:50

birth, 3:35-77

brought Jesus to her own people, 19:27-33

false charge, 4:156

glad tidings of Jesus, 3:42-51; 19:16-21

guarded her chastity, 21:91; 66:12

in childbirth, 19:23-26

Meeting,

with Allah, 6:31

of an Momentous Day, 19:37

of the Hereafter, 30:16

Messengers, 2:253; 4:164; 4:165; 57:27

an angel as a, 17:95; 25:7

and their wives and children, 13:38

as a witness from every nation, 16:89

belief in, 2:177; 2:285; 3:179; 4:171; 5:12;

57:19; 57:21

believing in some and rejecting others, 4:150-152

for every people (nation), was sent a, 10:47; 16:36

gathering of the, 5:109

mocked, 6:10; 13:32; 15:11; 21:41

rehearsing Allah's signs, 7:35-36

no more than human beings, 14:10-12; 17:94; 21:8; 25:7; 25:8; 25:20

rejected by their people, 3:184; 4:150; 5:70; 6:34; 7:101; 10:13; 10:74; 14:9-13; 16:113; 22:42-44; 23:44; 23:69; 26:105-191; 30:9; 34:34-35; 34:45; 35:4; 35:25; 36:13-19; 38:12-14; 40:22; 40:83; 41:14; 43:24; 50:12-15; 51:52; 54:9; 54:23; 54:33; 54:42; 64:6; 67:9; 69:9-10

slain, 3:183

sent as givers of good news and warners, 6:48;

sent to make things clear14:4-8

succession of, 2:87; 23:44

threatened, 14:13

testify before Allah, 5:109; 7:6; 39:69; 40:51; 43:45; 77:11

Messiah, *see Jesus*

Michael *[Mikail]*, 2:98

Months, number of, 9:36; 9:37

Moon, 7:54; 10:5; 16:12; 22:18; 25:61; 36:39; 36:40; 71:16; 91:2;

split in two (cleft asunder), 54:1

Moses *[Musa]*,

and calf-worship of his people, 7:148-156; 20:86-98

and his people, 2:51-61; 5:20-29; 7:138-141; 7:159-162; 14:5-8; 61:5

Books (Scripture) of, 53:36; 87:19

called and given messengership, 19:51-53; 20:9-56; 28:29-35

came with clear signs, 29:39

given the Book, 17:2

granted the Criterion, 21:48

guided by Allah, 6:84

guided to the Straight way, 37:114-122

his book, differences arose in it, 11:110

his childhood, mother and sister, 20:38-40; 28:7-13

his mishap in the city, 28:15-21

in Madyan, 20:40; 28:22-28

Moses, *(cont'd.)*

   junction of the two seas, 18:60-82

   magicians converted, 20:70-73; 26:46-52

   mountain and Lord's appearance, 7:142-145

   mystic fire, 27:7-12; 28:29-35

   nine Clear signs, 7:133; 17:101

   Pharaoh, and his people (chiefs), 2:49; 2:50; 7:103-137; 10:75-92; 11:96-99; 17:101-103; 20:17-53; 20:56-79; 23:45-49; 26:10-69; 28:4-21; 28:31-42; 40:23-46; 43:46-56; 51:38-40; 73:16; 79:15-26

Mosque (of Jerusalem),

   temple, 17:7

Mosque (of Quba), 9:107; 9:108

Mosques, 2:187; 9:17-19; 22:40

   maintained by, 9:18

Mountains (hills), 15:19; 16:15; 20:105-107; 21:31; 22:18; 31:10; 59:21; 77:10; 77:27; 81:3; 101:5

Muhammad,

   a mercy to the believers, 9:61

   a warner, 7:184; 7:188; 11:2; 15:89; 33:45; 34:28; 48:8; 53:56

   a witness over believers, 2:143

   Allah is Witness between me and you, 13:43; 29:52; 46:8

   and the blind man, 80:1-12

   as a mercy from Allah, 28:46-47

   ask no reward, 25:57; 38:86; 42:23

   close to the believers, 33:6

   covenant to believe in, 3:81

   devoted to prayer, 73:1-8; 73:20

   foretold by Jesus, 61:6

   from darkness to light, 65:11

   good example to follow, 33:21

   has been commanded to, 27:91-93; 66:9

   his sayings, 11:2-4; 12:108; 34:46-50

   his work, 3:164; 7:157; 36:6; 52:29

   lenient with them, 3:159

   men who molest the, 9:61

   mocked, 25:41-42; 34:7; 34:8

   no more than a Messenger, 3:144

   not a madman or possessed, 68:2; 81:22

   not a poet or a soothsayer, 69:41-42

   not to be distressed, 16:127

   nothing new among the Messengers, 46:9

   only a man, 41:6

   only follow that which is inspired, 10:15; 10:16; 46:9

   rehearsing scriptures, 98:2

   respect the Messenger, 2:104; 49:1-5

   reward is from Allah only, 34:47

   saw Gabriel, 53:4-18; 81:22-25

   seal of the Prophets, 33:40

   send blessings on, 33:56

   sent as a great favour to the believers, 3:164

   sent in truth, 4:170

   sent to all mankind, 34:28

   sent to be a witness, 16:89; 22:78; 33:45; 48:8; 73:15

   sent to mankind as the Messenger of Allah, 7:158; 48:9; 48:29

   swore allegiance under the tree, 48:18

   to bow down and draw near to Allah, 96:19

   to make Religion of truth victorious over all religions, 61:9

   to strive hard against the unbelievers and hypocrites, 66:9

   unlettered, 7:157; 62:2

   verses regarding family, of 33:28-34; 33:50-53; 33:59; 66:1; 66:3-6

   who slanders you, 9:58

   witness from among the Children of Israel, 46:10

   you are of an exalted standard of character, 68:4

Mules, Horses, 16:8

Murder, 2:178-179

Muslims,

   first of those, 6:14; 6:163; 9:100; 39:12

   prepared for them forgiveness and a great reward, 33:35

   He has named you, 22:78

N

Necessity, if one is forced by, 2:173; 6:145

Neighbour, 4:36

New moons, 2:189

Niggards condemned, 17:29; 47:38

Night, 92:1; 93:2

as a covering, 78:10

as a veil, 13:3

for rest, 10:67

Night of Power *[Al-Qadr]*, 44:3-4; 97:1-5

Noah *[Nuh]*, 3:33; 4:163; 6:84; 7:59-69; 9:70; 10:71; 11:25; 11:32; 11:36; 11:42; 11:43; 11:46; 11:48; 17:3; 21:76; 23:23; 25:37; 26:105; 29:14; 37:75; 51:46; 54:9; 71:1- 28

unrighteous son not saved, 11:45-47

unrighteous wife, 66:10

with them for a thousand years, 29:14

O

Oaths, 2:224-227; 5:89; 6:109; 16:38; 16:91; 16:92; 16:94; 24:22; 24:53; 66:2; 68:10; 68:39

Obedience, 3:132; 4:34; 4:59; 4:64; 4:66; 4:80; 4:81; 24:51-52; 24:53; 24:54; 47:33; 64:12

Offspring,

He bestows male and female, according to His will, 42:49-50

Olive, 6:99; 6:141; 16:11; 23:20; 24:35; 80:29; 95:1

Orphans, 2:83; 2:177; 2:215; 2:220; 4:2; 4:3; 4:8; 4:10; 4:36; 4:127; 6:152; 8:41; 17:34; 18:82; 59:7; 76:8; 89:17; 90:15; 93:6; 107:2

guardians of, 4:6

P

Pairs, in all creatures, 13:3; 36:36; 42:11; 43:12; 51:49; 53:45

Palm tree, 13:4; 19:23; 19:25; 20:71; 59:5

Parables (likeness, example, similitudes),

a fly, 22:73

a man belonging to many partners, 39:29

ashes which the wind blows furiously, 14:18

blind and deaf, 11:24

city, secure and well content, 16:112-113

companions of the city, 36:13-32

darkness in a vast deep ocean, 24:40

dog who lolls out his tongue, 7:176

donkey, 62:5

dumb man who is a burden to his master (owner), 16:76

evil tree, 14:26

fallen from the heaven and snatched by birds, 22:31

garden, 2:265-266

goodly tree, 14:24-25

grain of corn, 2:261

hard, barren rock, 2:264

icy wind, 3:117

light is a niche, 24:35-36

mirage, 24:39

mountain humbled, 59:21

partners, 30:28

people of the garden, 68:17-33

rain, 10:24; 18:45

rainstorm from the sky, 2:19-20

rope, 3:103

seed growing, 48:29

slave and a man, 16:75

spider, 29:41

two men with gardens of grapes, 18:32-44

vegetation after rain, 57:20

water were to disappear, 67:30

who kindles fire, 2:17-18

who shout, 2:171

Paradise, *see Gardens of Paradise*

Parents, kindness to 2:83; 2:215; 4:36; 6:151; 17:23; 29:8; 31:14; 46:15-17

Path,

even way 5:77

straight way 42:52-53; 43:43

Patience, 3:186; 3:200; 8:46; 10:109; 11:115; 16:126-127;20:130; 39:10; 40:55; 40:77; **42:43**; 46:35; 70:5; 73:10

seek help in, and prayer 2:45; 2:153

Peace,

after war, 8:61; 9:11

greeting in Paradise, 10:10; 13:24; 14:23; 15:46; 16:32; 19:62; 25:75; 33:44; 36:58; 39:73 56:26; 56:91

sent down by Allah, 9:40: 48:4; 48:26

upon Allah's servants and Messengers, 27:59; 37:79-81; 37:108-111; 37:119-122; 37:129-132; 37:181

Pen 68:1; 96:4

People of the Book (Scripture), 2:146; 3:20; 3:98; 3:110-115; 3:187; 4:51; 4:123; 4:131; 4:153; 4:159; 4:171; 5:65-66; 5:68; 6:20; 74:31

People of the Book (Scripture), *(cont'd.)*

among them are those who believe, 2:62; 3:113-115; 3:199; 4:162; 5:66; 5:83; 28:53; 29:47; 57:27-29

among them are unbelievers, 59:2; 59:11; 98:1; 98:6

differed among themselves, 2:213; 3:19; 3:66; 27:76; 32:25; 41:45; 42:14; 43:65; 45:17; 59:14; 98:4

do not exceed the bounds, 5:77

relationship to Muslims, 3:64-80; 3:99-101; 4:44; 5:5; 5:57-59; 5:82; 29:46

treachery of, 33:26-27; 59:2-4

warner has come to them, 5:15-16; 5:19

Pharaoh,

a believing man from among the people of Pharaoh 40:28-44

building of a lofty palace, 40:36-37

claims to be god 28:38; 79:24

dead body out from sea 10:90-92

dealings with Moses 7:103-137; 10:75-92

destroyed 29:39

drowned 2:50

people of 2:49; 3:11; 7:141; 44:17-33

righteous wife of 28:9

transgressed all bounds; committed sins and disobeyed 20:24; 20:43; 69:9; 73:16; 89:10-14

Plead

not on behalf of such who betray their own souls, 4:107

who will, on the Day of Judgement, 4:109

Poetry, 36:69

Poets, 26:224-227; 69:41

Pomegranates, 6:99; 6:141; 55:68

Poor, 2:177; 2:215; 2:273; 2:277; 4:8; 4:36; 8:41; 9:60; 17:26; 24:22; 24:32; 30:38; 47:38; 51:19; 59:7; 69:34; 74:44; 76:8; 89:18; 90:16; 93:8-9; 107:2-3

Prayer, 1:1-7; 3:8; 3:26; 3:27; 3:147; 3:191-194; 4:103; 17:80; 23:118

do not be loud voiced nor yet silent, 17:110

approach not, with a mind beffogged (drunken), 4:43

facing towards Qiblah, 2:144; 2:149; 2:150

guard your prayers, 2:238

in travel and attack, 2:239; 4:101; 4:102

not to pray for pagans, 9:113; 9:114

of disbelievers, 13:14

purifying for, 5:6

times of, 11:114; 17:78; 17:79; 20:130; 30:17; 30:18; 50:39; 50:40; 52:48-49; 73:1-6; 73:20

when you have performed the, 4:103

Precautions in danger, 4:71

Prisoners of war, 8:67-71; 33:26

Promise of Truth, 46:16

Property, wealth, 2:188; 3:186; 4:5; 4:7; 4:29; 51:19; 59:7-9

Prophets, 3:33; 3:146; 4:163; 6:84-90; 23:23-50; 57:26

an enemy to every, 6:112

covenant of, 3:81; 33:7-8

not for any, to be false to his trust, 3:161

Provision (sustenance), 10:59; 13:26; 14:32; 16:73; 34:36; 34:39; 42:12; 51:57-58; 67:21;

Psalms, 4:163

Punishment, 3:178

cutting of hands or feet, 5:33

in this life and in the Hereafter, 24:19; 68:33

Q

Qur'an,, 4:82; 9:111; 10:15-16; 11:1; 12:1-3; 13:1; 13:31; 14:1 ;15:1; 15:91; 17:41; 17:89; 18:54; 21:106; 25:30; 26:2; 27:1; 28:2; 30:58; 36:69-70; 39:27; 43:44; 47:20; 47:24; 50:45; 55:2; 69:43-51; 86:13-14;

a Light, 42:52

a Message for the heart, 50:37

a Message to all the Worlds, 38:87; 68:52; 81:26-28

Arabic, 12:2; 13:37; 16:103; 20:113; 26:195; 39:28; 41:3; 41:44; 42:7; 43:3

belief in, 2:177; 17:107; 42:15; 72:2; 77:50

Book of Wisdom, 10:1; 31:2; 36:2;

confirms earlier Scripture, 5:48; 6:92; 10:37; 46:12

full of admonition, 38:1

full of blessings, 38:29

glorious, 50:1; 85:21

guarded by Allah, 15:9;

guidance, 2:2; 2:159; 12:111; 16:64; 16:89; 16:102; 17:9; 27:2; 27:76-77; 31:3; 41:44; 42:52; 45:20; 72:2

Qur'an, *(cont'd.)*

heard by Jinn, 46:29-32; 72:1-2

honourable, 56:75-82; 80:11-16

inimitability of, 17:88

made easy, 44:58; 54:17; 54:22; 54:32; 54:40

makes things clear, 43:2; 44;2

meditate on its signs, 38:29

no falsehood can approach it, 41:41-42

no one touches except the clean, 56:79

power of, 13:31; 59:21

preserved, 85:22

pure and holy, 98:2-3

recitation of, 10:61; 16:98; 17:45-46; 17:106; 18;27; 27:92; 29:45; 35:29; 73:4; 73:20; 75:18; 84:21; 96:1; 96:3

revelation of, 2:176; 2:185; 2:213; 2:231; 3:3; 3;7; 4:105; 4:113; 5:48; 5;101; 6:19; 6:114; 6:155-157; 7:2-3; 14:1; 15:87; 16:64; 17:82; 17:105-106; 18:1; 20:2-4; 20:114; 21:10; 24:1; 25:6; 26:192-199; 29:51; 32:2 36:5; 38:29; 39:1-2; 39:23; 40:2; 41:2-4; 42:17; 44:3-6; 45:2; 46:2; 69:43; 75:16-19; 87:6-7

the truth, 17:105; 32:3; 34:6; 35:31; 39:2; 39:41; 46:30; 47:2-3; 56:95; 57:16; 69:51

when read, listen to it with attention, 7:204; 46:29

Quraysh, 106:1-4

R

Rain, sent down by Allah, 2:22; 2:164; 6:6; 6:99; 7:57; 8:11; 11:52; 13:17; 14:32; 15:22; 16:10; 16:65; 18:45; 20:53; 22:5; 22:63; 23:18; 24:43; 25:48-49; 27:60; 29:63; 30:24; 30:48-49; 31:10; 31:34; 32:27; 39:21; 41:39; 42:28; 43:11; 45:5; 50:9; 56:68-69; 57:20; 71:11; 78:14

Ramadan, 2:185

Ransom,

no, shall be accepted, 57:15

offered as, by disbelievers, 10:54; 13:18

of fasting or almsgiving, 2:196

Reconciliation,

if a person forgives, 42:40

between man and wife 4:35

between believers, 49:9; 49:10

Record,

a register fully inscribed, 83:7-9; 83:18-21

every sect will be called to its, 45:28; 45:29

scrolls are laid open, 81:10

which speaks the truth, 23:62

Recording angels, 50:17; 50:18; 50:23

Religion,

before Allah is Islam, 3:19

excesses in, 4:171;

fathers following a certain, 43:22-24

no compulsion in, 2:256

imposed no difficulties in, 22:78

of Allah, 3:83-84

other than Islam, 3:85

perfected, 5:3

same, for other Prophets, 42:13-15

exceed not in your, 5:77

who divide their, into sects, 6:159; 23:53; 30:32

who take their, to be play and amusement, 6:70

Remembrance of Allah, 63:9

hearts find satisfaction in, 13:28

Repentance, 2:54; 2:160; 3:89-90; 4:17-18; 5:34; 5:74; 6:54; 7:153; 9:3; 9:112; 9:118; 9:126; 11:3; 11:52; 11:61; 11:90; 16:119; 17:25; 19:60; 24:5; 25:70-71; 28:67;   30:33; 39:8; 39:17; 39:54; 40:7; 60:4

accepted by Allah, 40:3; 42:25

of Adam and Eve, 2:37; 7:23

of Moses, 7:143

Respite for evil, 3:178; 10:11; 12:110; 14:42; 14:44; 29:53-55; 86:15-17

Restraint from evil, 7:26

Resurrection, 16:38-40; 17:49-52; 19:66-72; 22:5; 23:15-16; 46:33-34; 50:3; 50:20-29; 50:41-44; 75:1-15; 79:10-12; 86:5-8

Revelation, 6:93; 10:2; 10:109; 12:102; 17:86; 40:15; 42:3; 42:7; 42:51; 42:52; 53:4; 53:10

a guidance and a mercy, 7:203; 16:64; 31:3

do not abrogate or cause to be forgotten, 2:106

explained, 41:2-4

for people who understand, 6:98

if you are in doubt, 2:23-24

in truth, 6:114

is from Allah, 46:2

sent to someone else, 3:73

the Holy Spirit, 16:102-103; 26:192-193

Righteous,

in the midst of gardens and springs, 51:15-19

shall drink from a cup of wine, mixed with Kafur 76:5-12

shall inherit the Earth, 21:105

the best of company, 4:69

Righteousness, 2:112; 2:177; 2:207; 2:208; 3:16; 3:17; 3:92; 3:133-135; 3:191-195; 4:36; 4:125; 5:93; 7:42-43

Rivalry in worldly increase, 102:1-4

Roads, way, 43:10

Romans, 30:2-5

S

Sabbath,

appointed only for, 16:124

transgress not the, 2:65; 4:154; 7:163-166

Sabians, 5:69; 22:17

Safa and Marwah, 2:158

Salih, 7:73-79; 11:61-68; 26:141-159; 27:45-53

Samiri, 20:85

Satan, 2:36; 2:168; 2:208; 2:268; 2:275; 3:36; 3:155; 3:175; 4:38; 4:60; 4:76; 4:83; 4:119; 4:120; 5:91; 6:43; 6:68; 6:142; 7:20; 7:22; 7:27; 7:175; 7:200; 7:201; 8:48; 16:63; 16:98; 20:120; 24:21; 25:29; 27:24; 41:36; 58:10; 58:19

an enemy 12:5; 35:6; 36:60

excites enmity and hatred, 5:91

has no authority over those who believe, 16:99-100

made their sinful acts seem alluring to them, 8:48

promised you, then failed you, 14:22

proposes a temptation, 22:52-53

seek refuge with Allah, 7:200-201

Scripture,

belief in 2:285; 4:136; 6:92

Seas,

are suffered to burst, 82:3

the two, 25:53; 35:12; 55:19-20

Secret, 4:114

consultation between three, 58:7

private consultation with the Messenger, 58:12-13

Sects and division in religion, 23:53; 30:32; 42:13-14; 45:17

Senses (ears, eyes), 23:78

Shadow,

turn around from the right and the left 16:48

prolonged 25:45

prostrating to Allah 13:15

She-camel as a clear sign to the people of Thamud, 7:73; 17:59; 26:155-158

Ships,

are of His signs, 42:32-33

for the profit of mankind, 2:164

made for you, 43:12

ploughing the waves, 16:14; 35:12

sail by His command, 22:65; 45:12

sail by the grace of Allah, 31:31

sailing smoothly, 17:66; 55:24

subject to you, 14:32

Siege of Al-Madinah, 33:9-27

Signs in creation, 2:164; 3:190; 6:99; 10:6; 10:67; 16:69; 17:12; 20:53-54; 24:44-46; 26:7-8; 27:86; 29:44; 30:20-25; 30:46; 31:31; 32:26-27; 34:15; 36:33-34; 41:37; 41:39; 42:29; 42:32; 45:3-6; 45:12-13; 50:7-11; 51:20-21; 71:14-20; 78:6-16; 79:27-33; 88:17-20

Sin, 7:100; 74:43-56

Allah, who forgives all, 39:53

blaming the innocent, 4:112

cannot hide their crimes from Allah, 4:108

earned against his own soul, 4:111

if you avoid the most heinous things, 4:31

illegal sexual intercourse, 4:15; 4:16; 24:2

joining other gods with Allah, 4:116

those who avoid the greater crimes, 42:37

those who, will never prosper, 10:17

will get due recompense for their earnings, 6:120

Sinai, Mount, 19:52; 23:20; 95:2

Slanderer, 68:11-12; 104:1

Slaves, 2:177; 2:178; 4:25; 4:36; 4:92; 5:89; 24:33; 58:3; 90:13

Sodomy, 7:80-82; 11:77-83; 29:28-29

Solomon [Sulaiman], 2:102; 4:163; 6:84; 21:78-82; 27:15-44; 34:12-14; 38:30-40

and the ants, 27:18-19

and the Queen of Sheba [Saba], 27:22-44; 34:15

Soul,

Allah does not place a burden greater than it can bear, 2:286; 7:42; 23:62

will be held in pledge for its deeds , 74:38

will be confronted with all the good it has done, 3:30

will be recompensed for all its actions, 16:111

Spending in the cause of Allah, 2:177; 2:195; 2:215; 2:261-274; 3:134; 4:39; 8:60; 9:34; 9:53-54; 9:60; 25:67; 47:38; 92:18-20

Spirit, the 15:29; 17:85; 21:91; 26:193; 38:72; 40:15; 58:22; 70:4; 78:38; 97:4

Spoils of war, 3:152-153; 8:1; 8:41; 8:69; 48:15

Spying, 49:12

Star, 16:16; 53:1; 86:1-4

Stars, 7:54; 16:12; 22:18; 37:6-10: 56:75; 77:8; 81:2

Straight Path, 1:6; 6:153

Striving, 4:95; 9:20; 9:24; 9:81; 22:78; 25:52; 29:69; 60:1; 61:11

Suckling, the term of, 2:233

Sun, 7:54; 10:5; 14:33; 16:12; 22:18; 36:38; 36:40; 71:16; 81:1; 91:1

Suspicion, 49:12

T

Tabuk, battle of, 9:40-59; 9:81-89

Talut (Saul), 2:247-249

Term, every nation has its, 7:34; 10:49; 15:4-5; 16:61; 20:129

Test, by Allah, 3:154

Thamud, 7:73-79; 11:61-68; 17:59; 25:38; 26:141-159; 27:45-53; 29:38; 41:17; 51:43-45; 54:23-31; 69:4-8; 85:17-20; 89:9-14; 91:11-15

Thief, punishment of, 5:38-39

Throne, 7:54; 9:129; 10:3; 13:2; 20:5; 23:86; 23:116; 32:4; 40:15; 57:4; 85:15

angels surrounding the, 39:75

eight will uphold the, 69:17

those who sustain the, 40:7

over the water, 11:7

Thunder, 13:13; 69:5

Time, 9:36; 10:5; 17:12; 22:47; 32:5; 76:1; 103:1-2

destroys disbelievers, 45:24

Torah, *[Tawrah]*, 3:3; 3:48; 3:50; 3:65; 3:93; 5:43-44; 5:66; 5:68; 5:110; 6:91; 7:157; 9:111; 11:17; 48:29; 61:6; 62:5

confirmed by the Gospel, 5:46

confirmed by Jesus, 61:6

confirmed by the Qur'an, 46:12

mention of Muhammad in, 7:157

revelation of, 7:144-145

Trade and wealth, 4:29

Travel, in the land, 6:11; 10:22; 12:109; 22:46; 27:69; 29:20; 30:9; 30:42; 34:18; 35:44; 40:21; 40:82; 47:10

Treachery, 8:58; 22:38

Treasures of Allah, 6:50

Tree of eternity, 20:120

Trees, 22:18

Trials and tests, 2:49; 2:124; 2:155; 2:214; 2:249; 3:142; 3:154; 3:186; 5:48; 5:94; 6:53; 6:165; 7:141; 7:155; 7:163; 7:168; 8:17; 8:28; 9:49; 9:126; 11:9-10; 14:6; 16:92; 16:110; 17:60; 18:7; 21:111; 22:11; 23:30; 25:20; 27:47; 33:11; 34:21; 37:106; 39:49; 44:17; 47:4; 47:31; 49:3; 64:15; 67:2; 68:17; 72:17; 89:15-16

Trumpet, on the Day of Resurrection, 6:73; 18:99; 20:102; 23:101; 27:87; 36:51; 39:68; 50:20; 69:13; 74:8; 78:18; 79:6-7

Trusts (pledges), 2:283; 8:27; 33:72; 70:32

Truth, 5:48; 23:70-71; 23:90; 25:33; 69:51

cover not, with falsehood, 2:42

has arrived and falsehood has perished, 17:81

the promise of Allah, 46:16-17

U

Uhud, battle of, 3:121-128; 3:140-180

Unbelievers, 3:156; 3:176-178; 3:196; 4:42; 4:76; 4:84; 4:151; 6:1; 8:30-40; 8:55; 9:73; 16:107; 22:72; 29:68; 40:4; 61:8; 66:9-10; 74:43-53; 75:31-35; 78:40; 80:42; 88:23-24; 109:1-6

astray, 1:7; 4:136-137; 6:110; 14:2-3; 14:18; 17:48; 17:72; 23:106; 25:9; 25:34; 25:44; 27:4-5; 42:18; 42:44; 43:40; 45:23; 46:32

companions of Hell Fire, 5:10; 5:86; 22:19; 40:6; 57:19; 67:10-11; 72:15

covered with shame and disgrace, 3:112; 3:192; 16:27; 68:42-43; 70:44

cursed, 2:89; 2:161: 4:52

deaf, dumb and blind, 2:18; 2:171; 6:39; 17:72; 17:97; 20:124-126; 21:45; 27:66; 27:80-81; 30:52-53; 31:7; 41:44; 47:23

deny the Day of Judgment, 34:3; 41:50; 42:18; 45:32; 64:7; 83:10-13

Unbelievers, *(cont'd.)*

despair of Mercy, 15:56

despair of the Hereafter, 60:13

do not obey them, 33:48; 96:19

do not take for friends or helpers, 3:28; 4:139; 4:144; 5:57; 9:23; 60:1-2; 60:9; 60:13

doubt Revelation, 6:7-8; 6:25; 16:101; 25:4-8; 30:58; 34:31; 37:12-17; 37:35-36; 37:170; 38:4-8; 40:70; 43:31; 45:11; 50:2; 52:30-44; 67:9; 68:15; 74:24-25; 84:20-22

forbidden Paradise, 7:50; 70:38-39

fuel for the Fire, 3:10-12; 3:151; 21:98; 72:15

hearts are sealed, 2:7; 7:101; 10:74; 16:108; 30:59; 40:35; 45:23; 47:24; 63:3

in delusion, 67:20-21

ordered to prostrate, but do not, 68:42-43; 77:48

persecuting the Believers, 85:4-8; 85:10

plotting and planning, 8:30; 13:42; 14:46; 52:42; 71:22; 74:18-20; 86:15-17; 105:2

protectors of one another, 8:73; 45:19

ransom not accepted, 3:91; 5:36; 13:18

render their deeds asray, 47:1; 47:8-9

takes as his god, his own vain desires, 45:23

their deeds are as a mirage, 24:39

their own deeds seem pleasing to them, 6:122; 8:48; 9:37; 27:4; 35:8

will blame each other on the Day of Judgement, 34:31-33; 37:24-32; 38:59-64; 40:47; 41:29

will not be successful, 23:117

wish to be muslims, 15:2

Unseen, the

belief in, 2:3; 52:41

keys of, 6:59

Usury *[Riba],* 2:275; 2:276; 2:278-280; 3:130; 4:161; 30:39

V

Veiling, 24:31; 33:59

Verses, seven often repeated, 15:87

Victory, 48:1; 61:13

W

Wait, 7:71; 9:52; 10:102; 11:122; 20:135; 44:59; 52:31

Waste not, 6:141; 7:31; 17:26

Water, 13:4; 13:14; 13:17; 15:22; 18:41; 24:39; 25:48-50; 25:53; 35:12; 38:42; 47:15; 54:11-12; 54:28; 55:19-20; 56:31; 56:68-70; 67:30; 77:27; 79:31; 80:25

Allah's Throne upon the, 11:7

every living thing made of 21:30; 24:45; 25:54

Way, right (straight) path, 1-6; 42:52-53

Wayfarer, 2:177; 2:215; 8:41; 17:26; 30:38; 59:7

Wealth, 104:2-4

allurement of the life of this world, 18:46

Widows, 2:234; 2:240

Will of Allah, 10:99-100; 30:5; 81:29; 82:8

Winds, 7:57; 30:46; 77:1-3

fertilising (fecundating), 15:22

who sends the, and they raise the clouds, 30:48

Wine, 2:219; 5:90-91; 12:36; 12:41; 47:15; 76:21; 83:25-27

Witnesses, 3:81

against mankind, 2:143; 22:78

hands and legs will bear, 36:65

illegal sexual intercourse, 4:15; 24:4

man is a telling, against himself, 75:14

when you contract, 2:282

Wives,

are a tilth for you, 2:223

garment for you, 2:187

of your own nature, 16:72

Women, 2:222; 2:223; 3:14; 4:15; 4:19-25; 4:34; 4:127; 9:71; 24:26; 24:31; 24:60; 33:32; 33:35; 33:73; 47:19; 48:5; 48:25; 65:1-2; 65:6; 66:5; 71:28

in pregnancy, 7:189; 31:14; 39:6; 41:47; 46;15; 65:4; 65:6

modesty of, 24:30-31; 33:53

Wood, dwellers of the, 15:78; 26:176-191; 38:13; 50:14

Wrongdoers, 11:18-22; 11:101-104; 11:116; 11:117; 39:47

X

No references

Y

Yathrib *[Al-Madina],* people of, 33:13

Z

Zachariah *[Zakariya],* 3:37-41; 6:85; 19:2-11; 21:89; 21:90

Zakat, *see Charity*

Zeyd bin Haritha, 33:37

Zina, 4:15-56; 17:32; 24:2-4; 25:68; 60:12

accusations of, 24:4-9; 24:11-19; 24:23